Introduction to
Gifted
Education

Introduction to
Gifted
Education

Edited by

Julia Link Roberts, Ed.D.,
Tracy Ford Inman, Ed.D.,
and Jennifer H. Robins, Ph.D.

PRUFROCK
PRESS INC.™

PRUFROCK
ACADEMIC
PRESS

A line of materials supporting scholarship and research-based practices in education

Library of Congress Cataloging-in-Publication Data

Names: Roberts, Julia L. (Julia Link), editor. | Inman, Tracy F. (Tracy
  Ford), 1963- editor. | Robins, Jennifer H., editor.
Title: Introduction to gifted education / edited by Julia Link Roberts,
  Ed.D., Tracy Ford Inman, Ed.D., & Jennifer H. Robins, Ph.D.
Description: Waco, Texas : Prufrock Press Inc., [2018]
Identifiers: LCCN 2017030535 (print) | LCCN 2017033055 (ebook) | ISBN
  9781618216625 (pdf) | ISBN 9781618216618 (pbk.)
Subjects: LCSH: Gifted children--Education.
Classification: LCC LC3993 (ebook) | LCC LC3993 .I68 2018 (print) | DDC
  371.95--dc23
LC record available at https://lccn.loc.gov/2017030535

Edited by Lacy Compton

Cover design by Raquel Trevino and layout design by Allegra Denbo
Illustrations by Judy Kay Bellemere

ISBN-13: 978-1-61821-661-8

At the time of this book's publication, all facts and figures cited are the most current available. All telephone
numbers, addresses, and websites URLs are accurate and active. All publications, organizations, websites,
and other resources exist as described in the book, and all have been verified. The authors and Prufrock Press
Inc. make no warranty or guarantee concerning the information and materials given out by organizations or
content found at websites, and we are not responsible for any changes that occur after this book's publication. If you find an error, please contact Prufrock Press Inc.

Prufrock Press Inc.
P.O. Box 8813
Waco, TX 76714-8813
Phone: (800) 998-2208
Fax: (800) 240-0333
http://www.prufrock.com

Table of Contents

Introduction

This book presents a practical, friendly introduction to gifted education. This text is inclusive, objective, and eclectic, filled with varied perspectives and approaches to topics and issues that educators need to know about gifted education. Chapters are research based and appropriate for a target audience of experienced educators or for those who are taking their first course in gifted education.

Chapters are authored by individuals with expertise on the topic. Because these authors have written and presented extensively on the focus of the chapter, readers may notice distinct voices and unique approaches to the material. Readers also may notice various synonyms for gifted children—advanced learners, children with gifts and talents, gifted and talented students, high-potential learners, and so forth. It is important to note that *children* is meant to include young people, as the content of the book describes what is appropriate in gifted education in K–12 settings.

The format of chapters is the same from one chapter to the next. Each begins with a quote followed by Essential Questions to Guide the Reader that focus the reader's attention. Each chapter also presents a brief history or overview of the topic. This is followed by a thorough discussion of the topic, highlighting varied perspectives and approaches, using best practice, current literature, and examples. A list of Big Ideas summarizes the chapter, with Discussion Questions included to extend the learning.

Chapters are organized into six major sections: Getting Started, The Gifted Learner, The Basics for Advanced Learning, Programming for Advanced Learning and Talent Development, Diversity of Learners, and Improving Services for Gifted Learners: Moving Forward. Each section introduction includes common myths and information to discredit the myths.

A metaphor of building a house is used to tie the sections of the book together. Getting Started mirrors the *blueprint*, an intentional plan; likewise, gifted education must have a design or plan in place before implementing next steps. The Gifted Learner himself provides the solid base on which to anchor gifted programming, much as the *foundation* of the house anchors the building. The Basics for Advanced Learning (such as identification, curriculum, assessment, and the learning environments) frame gifted education just as wood and metal *frame* the house. Programming for Advanced Learning and Talent Development serves in the capacity as the *roof* for the house, overarching the basic components. The Diversity of Learners resembles the interior and exterior *finishing* of the house as so many details must be attended to in order to reach the intended outcome (i.e., continuous progress for learners). Finally, there is a *punch list* in which final tasks are listed. There are details that need additional attention, whether that be in building a house or educating the gifted and talented (as delineated in Improving Services for Gifted Learners: Moving Forward). In the chapters, that list includes other responsibilities that are ongoing: professional learning, policy, and advocacy.

Getting Started

The homeowner has envisioned the ideal home. Now it is time to add reality to the plans. This means figuring how much storage space is needed and where it will be located. It means discussing with the homeowner how much morning sun should come in through the breakfast windows. The grandiose ideas must be translated into a plan that others can follow. That plan is the blueprint. The homeowner will rely on experts to render the blueprint. The architects will depend on principles for constructing buildings and on experiences they have had with what works well for specific types of buildings. They will rely on other experts if they have questions. And, of course, they will follow all building codes and get the appropriate permits.

This section, Getting Started, provides the blueprint in gifted education. Just as an architect provides the plan before building begins, so effective gifted education depends on understanding the conceptual framework, the history of the field, and gifted education standards. So many decisions will depend on understanding the field. For example, how can a school possibly consider a professional learning plan or the best way to serve children who are gifted in creativity without a conceptual framework and knowledge of gifted education standards?

There are three chapters in this section: "Conceptual Frameworks in Gifted Education as the Foundation for Services," "History of Gifted Education," and "Standards in Gifted Education."

Myths

» **All children are gifted.** Although all children are special, gifted children are exceptional learners, often learning at a pace and level of complexity that exceeds other children of the same age.

» **You must be gifted in everything if you are truly gifted.** Children vary greatly in how their giftedness is demonstrated. Some are gifted in one area and at grade level (or below) in other areas, while some may show their exceptionalities in multiple areas.

CHAPTER 1

Conceptual Frameworks in Gifted Education as the Foundation for Services

Ann Robinson

We must have perseverance and above all confidence in ourselves. We must believe that we are gifted for something and that this thing must be attained.—Marie Curie

Essential Questions to Guide the Reader

1. What is a conceptual framework, and why does it matter in gifted education?

2. In what ways are conceptual, operational, and policy definitions of giftedness and talent alike and different?

3. What are the relationships among the components of a conceptual framework (beliefs, philosophies, definitions, student needs, community and cultural contexts, identification and talent spotting, services, and outcomes)?

4. How do we encourage multiple perspectives in conceptual frameworks, but a unified voice for advocacy?

This chapter on conceptual frameworks begins with strong words about commitment from one of the world's greatest scientists for a reason. Marie Curie is a poster child for gifted education: a precocious youngster whose life and whose accomplishments were powered by passion, a belief in her work, and a talent for overcoming barriers from the time she was small through her adulthood, Marie is an apt metaphor for what can be done with a clear vision and a desire to discover what makes things tick. As educators, we can take a page out of Marie's book. She was a builder of ideas and institutions. Marie's approach to life was comprehensive. She was the consummate theoretician, but she applied herself to practical problems like developing and funding a scheme to equip ambulances with portable X-ray machines.

Delivering services to advanced learners is a comprehensive undertaking that requires both foundational knowledge of the field and the ability to take action. Beneath even the most elegant or the most skeletal infrastructures lies a collection of beliefs and concepts about what gifted education should do. In the real world, no educational enterprise can do everything, so how do thoughtful educators make choices about what gifted education can and should do in their particular context?

One avenue for stepping up to the challenge of serving advanced learners in school is to make explicit the conceptual framework that serves as the foundation. Miles and Huberman (1994) defined a conceptual framework as a visual or written product that "lays out key factors, constructs, or variables and presumes relationships among them" (p. 18). The power of a conceptual framework is that it not only informs research, but also informs practice—where the rubber meets the road. By guiding our thinking about what we do and why we do it, a conceptual framework makes explicit our beliefs and knowledge so that we can take informed action on behalf of children and adolescents whose talents demand our attention and support.

The purposes of this chapter are to:

- define a conceptual framework;
- provide a graphic representation of a conceptual framework for the beginning educator in gifted education;
- summarize example conceptualizations of giftedness and talent development;
- differentiate among conceptual, operational, and policy definitions of giftedness and talent development; and
- provide examples of the alignment of definitions, target students, identification and talent spotting, services, and desired outcomes that can be derived from a conceptual framework.

This chapter proposes a model for a comprehensive conceptual framework for gifted education that lays out the key components and the relationships among them that educators may use for guidance as they plan services for talented learners. The focus of the conceptual framework is to summarize comprehensive components that beginning professionals can use as they explore these concepts in depth in subsequent chapters in this book. Although there is a range of theoretical frameworks

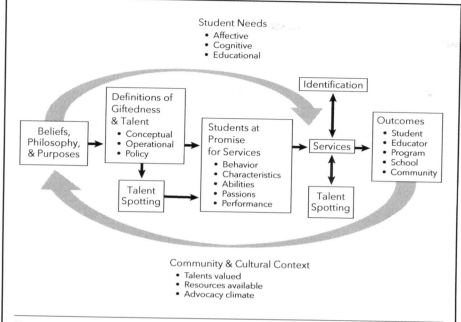

Figure 1.1. *Note.* From *Conceptual framework for gifted education services* by A. Robinson (2016), retrieved from http://ualr.edu/gifted/research. Copyright 2016 by Ann Robinson. Reprinted with permission.

for giftedness (Feldhusen, 1996; Gagné, 2003, 2005; Gardner, 2000; Kaufman & Sternberg, 2007; Moon, 2003; Renzulli, 1978; Tannenbaum, 1986), philosophies of gifted education (Ward, 1961), policy architecture (Gallagher, 2002, 2013), best practices (Plucker & Callahan, 2014; Robinson & Dailey, 2014; Robinson, Shore, & Enersen, 2007), and systems and models for services (Renzulli, Gubbins, McMillen, Eckert, & Little, 2009), this conceptual framework is designed to make explicit the components in a practical way useful to educators who must make decisions about the actions taken for their advanced students. A graphic rather than a written conceptual framework is offered to provide the practicing professional with an image that presents the big picture succinctly (see Figure 1.1).

The conceptual framework highlights students' affective and cognitive needs, as well as community and cultural contexts. How we conceptualize educational services to advanced learners cannot be separated from this foundation. Needs and context are both critical and foundational and provide the frame for the external boundary of the graphic. Within the frame of student needs and community and cultural context, the components include beliefs about giftedness, talent development, and the purposes of gifted education that subsequently translate into a philosophy. Beliefs, purposes, and philosophy lead to the adoption or development of definitions of giftedness and talent reflected in a range of conceptual, operational, and policy definitions. The definitions in turn drive schools to determine who will be served through their programs, how the learners and their needs will be identified, and what outcomes are important for the students, their educators, programs, schools, and community. It is a truism that the most coherent services are driven by an explicit philosophy with which a definition, identification processes, service delivery models, and a set of outcomes can be aligned. Figure 1.1 illustrates this alignment, but it also captures the interactive nature of this conceptual framework. When educators see that the talent-spotting strategies and services they provide to advanced students result in positive outcomes, their beliefs about the phenomena of giftedness and talent development can change and inform subsequent actions.

Definitions of Giftedness and Talent

According to Moon (2006), definitions of giftedness and talent can be conceptual or operational. The beginning gifted education professional needs to become familiar with both kinds of definitions. In addition, a third kind of definition also is useful in developing a conceptual framework: Policy definitions provide the basis for resource allocation. All three kinds of definitions can work in concert to inform a conceptual framework.

Conceptual Definitions

Conceptual definitions carve out territory, usually in psychology and/or education. They tend to be based on existing theory and research. Early definitions of giftedness often equated it with a score on an IQ measure (Terman, 1922), but more recent definitions are broader and more nuanced. For example, one American definition of giftedness was offered by Witty (1959) who wrote, "Perhaps it is desirable to broaden our definition of the gifted and to consider as 'gifted' any child whose performance, in a valuable line of human activity, is consistently or repeatedly remarkable" (p. 10). Witty's conceptual definition includes at least three notable ideas. First, it focuses on high-level performance. Second, it is domain-specific. Third, it includes an ethical component: The domain must be judged to be valuable by a community.

Another conceptual definition was proposed by Renzulli (1978, 1986) and is popularly known as the Three-Ring Conception of Giftedness. In a recent exploration, Renzulli and Delcourt (2013) summarized the key features of the definition in the following way: "Persons who have achieved recognition because of their unique accomplishments and creative contributions possess a relatively well-defined set of three interlocking clusters of traits. These clusters consist of above-average, though not necessarily superior, ability, task commitment, and creativity" (p. 42). They emphasized that Renzulli's conceptualization defines gifted behaviors rather than gifted persons. Renzulli's definition includes notable ideas that affect a conceptual framework. First, the focus is on behavior, not on a person, which implies that giftedness is situation-specific rather than static. Second, the inclusion of creativity in the definition implies that giftedness involves more than high achievement in school subjects. In fact, Renzulli is explicit about the difference between "schoolhouse" giftedness and giftedness that results in creative productivity. Third, Renzulli conceptualizes giftedness as the interaction among the three clusters of traits, not as the result of any one of them in isolation.

Gagné (2003, 2005) proposed another widely adopted conceptualization. His theory of giftedness emphasizes the talent development process. He focused on critiquing and clarifying the differences between the use of the term *gifted* and the use of the term *talented*. In other words, Gagné applied precision to terminology in order to construct his definition. His Differentiated Model of Giftedness and Talent (DMGT) proposed that gifts in intellectual, creative, social, and sensorimotor domains are transformed into specific talents in fields such as academics, technical areas (i.e., transport, construction, crafts, manufacturing, and agriculture), science and technology, the arts, social service, administration, business, gaming, and sports through a combination of environmental and intrapersonal catalysts and development processes. For Gagné, gifts are natural abilities whereas talents are the product of many factors including ability, environmental influences, and personal commitment to a field.

A final example of a conceptual definition is one developed by Tannenbaum (1983, 1986) through his Star or Sea Star Model of Giftedness. The emphasis in Tannenbaum's conceptualization is psychosocial and links potential in children to fulfillment in later life. In fact, Tannenbaum eschewed the application of the term *gifted* to children whom he viewed as promising and instead applied giftedness to adults and their accomplishments. His conceptualization focuses on five psychosocial components that form the points of a star. These components are (a) general ability, (b) special aptitudes, (c) nonintellective factors such as motivation and perseverance, (d) environmental influences ranging from the immediate family to the broad social milieu, and (e) chance, such as a child or adolescent encountering the right opportunity at the right time.

The selected conceptual definitions from Witty (1959), Renzulli (1978, 1986), Gagné (2003, 2005), and Tannenbaum (1983, 1986) are but a few of the conceptualizations from the history of gifted education to its present state. There are a range of other conceptual definitions of giftedness, each with implications for the kinds of identification processes and services that flow logically from them. A comprehensive review is beyond the scope of this chapter, but two resources provide the beginning educator with extensive background: a survey of multiple conceptions of giftedness (Sternberg & Davidson, 2005) and a survey of conceptualizations of giftedness in world cultures (Phillipson & McCann, 2007).

Policy Definitions

Conceptual definitions of giftedness and talent are based on theory and research; they represent the field grappling with big, important, and sometimes abstract ideas. In contrast, *policy* definitions are about resource allocation—a very practical matter. They help to answer the question of which students will be the recipients of attention and services. In some, but certainly not all, cases, policy definitions may actually identify funding sources. Policy definitions are often found in legal statutes or the rules and regulations that flow from them. In the United States, the most enduring example of a policy definition appeared in the Marland Report (Marland, 1972). It has appeared in various forms with some modifications. For example, the No Child Left Behind Act (2001) included the following language:

> The term "gifted and talented," when used with respect to students, children, or youth, means students, children, or youth who give evidence of high performance capability in areas such as intellectual, creative, artistic, or leadership capacity, or in specific academic fields, and who need services or activities not ordinarily provided by the school in order to fully develop those capabilities. (Section 9101{22})

What a policy definition like the one above does is to offer a statement that a State Education Authority (SEA) and a Local Education Authority (LEA) can use to understand the scope of who needs to be served. There are at least three important ideas embedded in the language of this policy definition. First, the use of the words *high performance capability* implies that the students could be currently high performing, but also that there are students who are capable of high performance but may not be exhibiting it. Second, the policy definition provides a broadened set of areas in which talent might be displayed. Third, these students need something not generally available in schools.

Operational Definitions

If conceptual definitions carve out psychological or educational theoretical territory and policy definitions focus on resource allocation, *operational* definitions as conceived by Moon (2006) are practical and precise enough that schools can act on them in terms of determining which students are to receive services and how they might do so. One way to think about an operational definition as opposed to a policy definition is that an operational definition will be sufficiently precise in that it communicates to other educators and to parents which children and adolescents will receive what services. Even in conceptualizations that eschew formal labeling, some students will be receiving services at a point in time from teachers. Operational definitions provide the answers to the following questions: Which students? What services? When and where are the services delivered? Who delivers the services?

Students at Promise for Gifted Education Services

Depending on the definition of giftedness and talent selected or developed as part of the conceptual framework, different kinds of students become the intended target for services. For example, if the definition focuses on academic precocity in school subjects, the target students will be high-performing learners in mathematics, science, or the humanities disciplines. These students are performing well above grade-level expectations, are likely to score high on traditional achievement measures or aptitude tests, and are good candidates for some form of educational acceleration. If the definition includes creativity, above-average ability, and motivation, as does the Renzulli (1986) conceptualization, then the target students are those most likely to demonstrate behaviors indicative of the interaction among those three clusters of traits with an emphasis on creative productivity. Psychosocial definitions of giftedness such as Tannenbaum's (1983, 1986) explicitly include the societal context as part of the definition and introduce factors such as chance. Target students under this conceptualization might include academic achievers, but would also include students with potential yet to be discovered in a variety of domains. Tannenbaum's distinction between fragmentary provisions for students and comprehensive programs implies that any school-based area of programming is desirable.

Identification and Talent Spotting

Formal identification procedures and more informal talent-spotting perspectives for locating who is to be served should also be aligned with the definition of giftedness and talent in a conceptual framework. For example, formal identification procedures can take the traditional form of nomination, screening, and placement in services. Some definitions of giftedness, for example Renzulli's (1986) Three-Ring Conception, encourage the use of multiple criteria. If the definition of giftedness includes ability, creativity, and task commitment, then the processes used to identify the behaviors that exemplify each of these constructs provide multiple pathways. If the definition focuses on domain-specific academic talent, then the identification protocol is likely to be the use of above-level testing related to achievement in that academic domain—an elegant linkage of identification and service.

In addition to formal identification procedures, students may be located by more informal talent spotting. For example, creative instructional activities or high-level curriculum designed for advanced learners may be implemented in classrooms, and teachers have an opportunity to observe and document student performance.

In this case, curriculum and instruction serve as a platform to encourage the development of talent. In fact, some conceptualizations of giftedness that eschew formal identification procedures and labeling are likely to engage in talent spotting in order to serve target students embedded in grade-level classrooms or to incorporate talent-spotting opportunities as a precursor to more intensive services.

Services and Outcomes

Conceptual frameworks are ultimately operationalized through the kinds of services offered to advanced students and are on a continuum from modest adaptations to more intensive and comprehensive delivery models. For example, differentiating instruction through tiered activities delivered in the grade-level classroom is one form of service for advanced learning (see Chapter 14). Providing creative enrichment (see Chapter 12) within the grade-level classroom or in flexibly grouped pull-out programs in elementary schools or interdisciplinary seminars in secondary schools is another. Multiple types of acceleration also meet the needs of advanced learners (see Chapter 13). Comprehensive K–12 programs may involve guidance components to develop talents. This text includes chapters exploring several forms of services and either implicitly or explicitly identifies the student outcomes associated with them (see Chapters 15 and 16).

Conclusion

To summarize, the field of gifted education provides a smorgasbord of conceptualizations about giftedness and talent. The beginning gifted educator should first review several conceptualizations while keeping an eye on the educational needs of the students he or she encounters every day and the values held by the communities in which he or she lives. Student needs and community context inform what definition of giftedness and talent is likely to drive thriving services in the schools enrolling those students and embedded in those communities.

Second, whatever conceptualization of giftedness and talent is selected, a coherent conceptual framework aligns the constituent components identified in Figure 1.1. The conceptualization should be operationalized by the formal identification or talent-spotting procedures best aligned with the adopted definition to determine the target students. The services and outcomes should also be aligned with this conceptualization and the students.

Third, the beginning gifted educator may find the differences in beliefs, purposes, philosophies, and definitions in the field initially frustrating. In fact, the variety of current conceptualizations and the failure of the field to agree upon a unitary conceptual framework are criticisms leveled from within and from outside gifted education. An alternative perspective is that in a world characterized by diversity, there is a richness to differing conceptualizations. The key is to allow for a diversity of conceptualizations that define, talent spot, identify, and serve students in ways that best meet their needs. The field need not always agree on its conceptual frameworks, but it does need to agree on their necessity.

Big Ideas

1. Conceptual frameworks provide coherence for school-based services.

2. Conceptual definitions, policy definitions, and operational definitions are related but are not the same and do not necessarily serve the same purpose.

3. Conceptual frameworks should be informed by both student needs and community and cultural contexts.

4. Effective conceptual frameworks align definitions, identification or talent-spotting procedures, services, and desired outcomes.

5. A variety of conceptual frameworks is defensible, but advocacy for effective services is a nonnegotiable.

Discussion Questions

1. Compare and contrast at least two definitions of giftedness and/or talent found in this chapter. In what ways do they differ? In what ways are they alike? Do you have a preference? Why?

2. Why might conceptual, operational, and policy definitions of giftedness and/or talent be useful to the gifted education professional?

3. What elements are necessary for a conceptual framework in gifted education?

4. What are the implications for holding a domain-specific or a domain-general conceptualization of giftedness and/or talent?

5. Some experts specifically suggest a percentage of the student population in their definition of giftedness and/or talent who should be considered for identification or for services. What are the advantages and disadvantages of definitions that specify percentages of the population? What are the advantages and disadvantages of definitions that do not specify percentages?

References

Feldhusen, J. F. (1996). Talent as an alternative conception of giftedness. *Gifted Education International, 11,* 124–127.

Gagné, F. (2003). Transforming gifts into talents: The DMGT as a developmental theory. In N. Colangelo & G. A. Davis (Eds.), *Handbook of gifted education* (3rd ed., pp. 60–74). Boston, MA: Allyn & Bacon.

Gagné, F. (2005). Transforming gifts into talents: The DMGT as a developmental theory. In R. J. Sternberg & J. E. Davidson (Eds.), *Conceptions of giftedness* (2nd ed., pp. 98–119). Cambridge, England: Cambridge University Press.

Gallagher, J. J. (2002). *Society's role in education gifted students: The role of public policy* (RM02162). Storrs: University of Connecticut, The National Research Center on the Gifted and Talented.

Gallagher, J. J. (2013). Political issues in gifted education. In C. M. Callahan & H. L. Hertberg-Davis (Eds.), *Fundamentals of gifted education: Considering multiple perspectives* (pp. 458–469). New York, NY: Routledge.

Gardner, H. (2000). The giftedness matrix: A developmental perspective. In R. Friedman & B. Shore (Eds.), *Talents unfolding: Cognition and development* (pp. 77–88). Washington, DC: American Psychological Association.

Kaufman, S. B., & Sternberg, R. J. (2007). Giftedness in the Euro-American culture. In S. N. Phillipson & M. McCann (Eds.), *Conceptions of giftedness: Sociocultural perspectives* (pp. 377–413). Mahwah, NJ: Lawrence Erlbaum.

Marland, S. P., Jr. (1972). *Education of the gifted and talented: Report to the Congress of the United States by the U. S. Commissioner of Education: Vol. 1.* Washington, DC: U.S. Government Printing Office.

Miles, M. B., & Huberman, A. M. (1994). *Qualitative data analysis: An expanded source book* (2nd ed.). Thousand Oaks, CA: Sage.

Moon, S. M. (2003). Personal talent. *High Ability Studies, 14,* 5–21.

Moon, S. M. (2006). Developing a definition of giftedness. In J. H. Purcell & R. D. Eckert (Eds.), *Designing services and programs for high-ability learners: A guidebook for gifted education* (pp. 23–31). Thousand Oaks, CA: Corwin Press.

No Child Left Behind Act, 20 U.S.C. §6301 (2001).

Phillipson, S. N., & McCann, M. (2007). *Conceptions of giftedness: Sociocultural perspectives.* Mahwah, NJ: Lawrence Erlbaum.

Plucker, J. A., & Callahan, C. M. (2014). *Critical issues and practices in gifted education: What the research says* (2nd ed.). Waco, TX: Prufrock Press.

Renzulli, J. S. (1978). What makes giftedness? Reexamining a definition. *Phi Delta Kappan, 60,* 180–184, 261.

Renzulli, J. S. (1986). The three-ring conception of giftedness. In R. J. Sternberg & J. E. Davidson (Eds.), *Conceptions of giftedness* (pp. 53–92). New York, NY: Cambridge University Press.

Renzulli, J. S., & Delcourt, M. A. B. (2013). Gifted behaviors versus gifted individuals. In C. M. Callahan & H. L. Hertberg-Davis (Eds.), *Fundamentals of gifted education: Considering multiple perspectives* (pp. 36–48). New York, NY: Routledge.

Renzulli, J. S., Gubbins, E. J., McMillen, K. S., Eckert, R. D., & Little, C. A. (2009). *Systems and models for developing programs for the gifted and talented* (2nd ed.). Mansfield Center, CT: Creative Learning Press.

Robinson, A. (2016). *Conceptual framework for gifted education services.* Retrieved from http://ualr.edu/gifted/research

Robinson, A., & Dailey D. (2014). Effective practices and the development of talent in schools and classrooms. In J. P. Bakken, F. E. Obiakor, & A. F. Rotatori (Eds.), *Gifted education: Current perspectives and issues* (Advances in Special Education, Vol. 26, pp. 167–190). Bingley, UK: Emerald.

Robinson, A., Shore, B. M., & Enersen, D. A. (2007). *Best practices in gifted education: An evidence-based guide.* Waco, TX: Prufrock Press.

Sternberg, R. J., & Davidson, J. E. (Eds.). (2005). *Conceptions of giftedness* (2nd ed.). Cambridge, England: Cambridge University Press.

Tannenbaum, A. J. (1983). *Gifted children: Psychological and educational perspectives.* New York, NY: Macmillan.

Tannenbaum, A. J. (1986). Giftedness: A psychosocial approach. In R. J. Sternberg & J. E. Davidson (Eds.), *Conceptions of giftedness* (pp. 21–52). New York, NY: Cambridge University Press.

Terman, L. M. (1922). A new approach to the study of genius. *Psychological Review, 29,* 310–318.

Ward, V. S. (1961). *Educating the gifted: An axiomatic approach.* Columbus, OH: Charles Merrill.

Witty, P. (1959). Identifying and educating gifted and talented pupils. In P. Witt, J. B. Conant, & R. Strang (Eds.), *Creativity of gifted and talented children* (pp. 1–15). New York, NY: Teachers College Bureau of Publications, Columbia University.

CHAPTER 2

History of Gifted Education

Jennifer L. Jolly and Jennifer H. Robins

With civilization rapidly growing more complex, a greater need exists than ever before for original thinkers and wise leaders. . . . Thoughtful educators . . . are sponsoring a rapidly growing movement for the better training of gifted children.—Stedman (1924, p. 5)

Essential Questions to Guide the Reader

1. What does the history of gifted education offer contemporary researchers and practitioners?

2. How have legislative trends impacted gifted education?

3. What is the legacy of the pioneers of the field on current issues in gifted education?

4. What are the inhibitors and accelerators to progress in gifted education?

Why is a chapter on the history of gifted education necessary or important? The history of a field provides context to examine the current research and practices in terms of contributions of moving the field forward. Paradigm shifts or great leaps are rare, and more often changes in a field are meted out over time with incremental advances occurring over decades with converging and diverging theory, research, and practice. This chapter seeks to outline the great leaps and incremental changes that have occurred in gifted education over the past 100 years.

Gifted education as a formal field of study has a rather abbreviated history in comparison to other fields of study. In her seminal text, Hollingworth (1926) remarked, "Nearly all we know about gifted children has been learned through investigations of the past ten years. A decade ago it would have been impossible to write the book which these pages introduce" (p. vii). The field's trajectory was influenced by individuals, the impact of other fields of study, and the context of the times in which these people lived.

Every society throughout history has identified its best and brightest members, and many societies have also sought to encourage the potential of these members of society. The Ancient Greeks identified young men who would make talented soldiers and leaders. Plato's Academy catered to "advanced students with exceptional intellectual acumen" (Power, 1964, p. 163). Although benefactors during the Renaissance afforded exceptional talented artists and writers the ability to practice their crafts, many of these artists rose to great fame, which allowed them to acquire immense wealth of their own. The Chinese Tang Dynasty (A.D. 46) identified and valued talents in young children by providing support for the development of these talents to serve the court (Colangelo & Davis, 2003).

As a newly established nation, the United States had a vested interest in identifying its most capable members of society in order to prevent the fledging nation from falling into tyranny and safeguarding the freedoms that were hard won from the British. The country was largely agrarian, and most children did not receive formal schooling. Formal schooling usually took place as private tutoring in the family home by those who had the financial resources to pay for the services. Thomas Jefferson, in his Bill for the More General Diffusion of Knowledge, argued for a democratic way to produce citizens to contribute to the new republic. The bill was not only a blueprint for public education, but it was also the opportunity to identify "boys of best geniuses" whose parents were too poor to further their education, with the final goal of the young men attending the College of William and Mary (Jefferson, 1784, p. 673). Ultimately, the bill did not pass, but the implications for advancing those of high ability are clear. Systematic programming for advanced and gifted programming would be nearly another 150 years away, and the scientific study of this particular group of students would not begin in earnest for 100 years.

Precocious Curiosities

Children of high intellectual ability have long attracted the public's curiosity: "many . . . burned brightly and then faded into obscurity, succumbed to a mental illness, or an early death, or entered into a career deemed below their mental capacity"

(Jolly & Bruno, 2010, p. 61). These displays of precocious talent formed a mythology and long-standing misunderstanding about the nature and needs of those of high intellectual ability. Lombroso's (1891) *The Man of Genius* only exacerbated the mythologizing when he suggested through "empirical evidence" that genius was indeed linked to madness.

German toddler Christian Heinrich Heineken appeared as one of the first documented child prodigies in the early 1700s. His ability to memorize and recite large volumes of vocabulary in French and Latin and general mathematical knowledge was exploited in the press, and he was even presented before the Danish court. He became a minor celebrity throughout Europe. However, young Christian would meet an untimely death before his fifth birthday due to unknown causes (Whipple, 1924), linking the coincidence of early death and sickness to mental prowess.

William James Siddis enrolled at Harvard University at the age of 11 in 1909. His father, Boris, had previously homeschooled William, noting his advanced abilities and knowledge across domains, especially in mathematics and anatomy. At Harvard, William continued to flex his intellectual prowess, and Boris was ever present to capitalize on his son's extraordinary abilities, alerting various media outlets to the boy's accomplishments. The American press documented William's rise and was ever present to record his missteps. Despite his "genius," William struggled with adolescence, and this was captured in the media, including his indecisiveness as to what career path to eventually pursue and an arrest in 1919 at the age of 21 (Jolly & Bruno, 2010). Despite such early promise, he eventually faded into obscurity, cutting himself off from his family and dying at the relatively young age of 46.

Christian and William are but two examples of sensational and interesting stories that fueled the general public's initial (mis)understanding of prodigious children. However, the collective narratives of these and similar children helped to inspire some of the earliest studies of gifted children. In 1924, the *Twenty-Third Yearbook of the National Society for the Study of Education* set forth some of the most pressing questions that were under inquiry by leading researchers of the time:

> (1) By what methods can the real degree of intellectual capacity of this youngster be determined? (2) How early in life can we correctly diagnose intrinsic capacity? (3) Is the child's ability all-around or restricted to some specific trait or group of traits, like memory or linguistic fluency? (4) How early ought systematic training to be begun? (5) Is there danger of "forcing" his mental development at the expense of his physical or social development? (6) What ought to be the subject matter and what the methods of instruction in the early years of his life? (7) Is his exceptional accomplishment due primarily to his endowment, exceptionally

skillful training, or to some happy combination of nature and nurture? (Whipple, 1924, p. 3)

Early School Accommodations

Initial school interventions for gifted children typically focused on ability grouped classes, grade skipping, and/or university laboratory or experimental schools. However, the implementation of these arrangements was without an empirical understanding of the impact on ability, achievement, or the social-emotional needs of students. These practices were not systematically implemented and were the exception rather than the rule (Jolly, 2004). The earliest evidence of continuous efforts toward making special allowances for children of high ability occurred in St. Louis Public Schools. At the commencement of his tenure as superintendent of schools in 1868, William Torrey Harris originated a number of innovative practices that would be adopted across the American public schooling system; unfortunately, the provisions he had designed for the academically able were not one of them. In the later part of his life, Harris remarked that one of his 12 accomplishments was the "plan for promotion according to ability in school work" (Kohlbrenner, 1950, p. 21) in which he had established a protocol for students to be promoted according to their ability at regular intervals.

Still, sporadic attempts were made by isolated school districts across the United States to address the learning needs of those with high ability. These included ability grouping, grade promotion, or a combination of both. Other arrangements allowed students to truncate 3 or 4 years of schoolwork into 2 (Tannenbaum, 1983). Opportunity or enrichment classes for the gifted were evidenced in cities such as Los Angeles and Cincinnati (Davis & Rimm, 1994). Overall, there appears to be little evidence of systematic changes to the curricula, except in the case of experimental classes, which would become synonymous with the early research studies as part of the burgeoning field of gifted education.

Formalized Field of Gifted Education

The late 1800s and early 1900s in the United States experienced massive migration from Europe, and compulsory schooling laws witnessed millions of children entering schools across the United States. At the same time, a new scientific rigor was being applied to the social sciences, psychology in particular. The study of gifted children rose out of the convergence of these forces and eventually formed the field of gifted education.

The foundations of the field lie with the work of several individuals, two of the most influential being Francis Galton and Alfred Binet. Galton's (1869) *Heredity*

Genius was one of the first empirical studies of intelligence that attempted to measure individual differences. Retrospectively, Galton gathered family histories of notable scientists, artists, politicians, and academics. He used these data to illustrate the extent to which eminence was achieved, the frequency with which degrees were obtained, and why some individuals managed to achieve prominence in comparison to others (Hollingworth, 1926). Nearly 50 years later, French psychologist Alfred Binet developed a measure of intelligence for French schoolchildren who had been classified as "feebleminded" and proposed a mental age (Jolly, 2005; Stanley, 1976). Stern furthered this idea by introducing a numerical value, the IQ score, to Binet's work and illustrated Galton's differing degrees of intelligence distributed across populations (Jolly, 2005).

The early 20th century witnessed American researchers Lewis Terman and Leta Hollingworth applying the concepts and instruments developed by Galton and Binet to precocious children in the American context. Widely acknowledged as the founders of the field of gifted education in the United States, Terman and Hollingworth, both psychologists, set in motion a body of work that continues to influence and impact contemporary gifted researchers and practitioners (Jolly, 2004; Robins, 2010).

Lewis Terman completed his Ph.D. in psychology at Clark University in 1906. His dissertation, "Genius and Stupidity: A Study of Some of the Intellectual Processes of Seven 'Bright' and Seven 'Stupid' Boys," would be the impetus for his lifelong work on the psychometric development of intelligence measures and the study of those children at the bright end of the spectrum (Winkler & Jolly, 2014). Terman secured a faculty position at Stanford University in 1910, which provided him access to a student sample and resources to earnestly begin work to further validate Binet's measure and develop the Stanford-Binet. In 1921, he embarked on the longitudinal study of nearly 1,500 gifted children, employing "scientifically verifiable facts" (Jolly, 2008, p. 32) to disrupt the mythology that surrounded this group of children by collecting information on nearly every conceivable data point, including IQ and achievement scores, home and school environments, family hereditary, social interests, and personality measures. Terman (and later his colleagues) would continue to collect data over the course of these children's lifetimes, which would extend beyond his own. These data and findings are recorded in the volumes of *Genetic Studies of Genius* (Burks, Jensen, & Terman, 1930; Cox, 1926; Terman, 1925; Terman & Oden, 1947, 1959). Terman's legacy does not come without its own controversies. Few of the children in his study developed into geniuses during their lifetimes or became eminent in their chosen fields or professions as Terman had hypothesized. Terman also rejected the idea of environmental influence and steadfastly believed in heredibility. The sample of approximately 1,500 students was criticized for its narrow and biased sample, which was overwhelmingly identified through teacher nominations. It consisted predominantly of White Jewish students from middle to upper middle class backgrounds and from one geographic region of the United States (Jolly, 2008).

Beginning her own inquiry almost concurrently to Terman's, Leta Hollingworth, working in New York City at Teachers College, began a longitudinal study with students from schools specially designed for gifted children. Hollingworth was actively involved in the collection of a wealth of data points at P.S. 165, an authentic environment where the academic needs of gifted children were served (Jolly, 2006). Her experiences at P.S. 165 would become the basis for *Gifted Children: Their Nature and Nurture* (Hollingworth, 1926), the first textbook on gifted children. In 1939, during her work at P.S. 500, the Speyer School, Hollingworth would continue to consider the qualitatively different curricular needs of gifted students, indicating that even students in the upper ranges of high IQ needed different types of challenge in their schoolwork and that social-emotional needs of gifted children were as important as the academic work (Jolly, 2006). Hollingworth also highlighted the particular academic and affective needs that profoundly gifted children (with IQs over 180) encountered (Hollingworth, 1942).

As a burgeoning field, a group of researchers and practitioners began to emerge, including Paul Witty, Martin Jenkins, Florence Goodenough, Ruth Strang, A. Harry Passow, Robert Havighurst, and Robert DeHaan (Stanley, 1976). Some of these individuals would play an instrumental role in moving the field from emerging to fully functioning.

The Eras of the Cold War and Civil Rights Movement

As the country exited World War II (WWII) and found itself mired in a new type of war, the Cold War, gifted education began to solidify its position as a bona fide field of study with the establishment of several professional organizations and founding of a journal (Guilford, 1950; Robins, 2010). WWII had also revealed gaps in American scientific talent, which left the country vulnerable during the war and dependent on scientists from other countries. These weaknesses in part helped to reinvigorate an interest in gifted education and gifted children given its rather fallow state following the war (Jolly, 2009).

In 1950, J. P. Guilford's American Psychological Association Presidential Speech "Creativity" asked psychologists and educational researchers to consider the nature of creativity and how it factored into intelligence; this challenged the unitary view of intelligence that most psychologists held at the time and introduced the multidimensional views of intelligence that contemporary theorists and practitioners hold today (Comrey, 1993; Guilford, 1950). Researchers such as J. W. Getzel, Phillip Jackson, Calvin Taylor, and E. Paul Torrance would take up Guilford's challenge.

Each worked to understand creativity's interaction with intelligence and eventually impacted the definition of giftedness (Jolly, 2009). An expanded definition of giftedness would be reflected in the subsequent Marland Report (Marland, 1972).

National advocacy organizations also were established during this time period, which provided a unified and consistent message regarding the needs of gifted children. The American Association for Gifted Children (AAGC) was established in 1946 and the National Association for Gifted Children (NAGC) in 1954. The AAGC was formed in New York City with a membership of university faculty and educators (Robins, 2010). Their publication, *The Gifted Child,* edited by Paul Witty, was one of the most important publications of the period distributing an overview of the important issues and research (Robins & Jolly, 2013). NAGC was founded by Ann Fabe Issacs, director of a preschool in Cincinnati, OH. In 1957, NAGC would begin publishing *Gifted Child Quarterly,* the first journal devoted to gifted education (Rogers, 2014). The Association for the Gifted (CEC-TAG), a division of the Council for Exceptional Children, was established in 1958. The organization established its own journal, *The Journal for the Education of the Gifted,* in 1978 (Council for Exceptional Children, The Association for the Gifted, n.d.).

The Soviet launch of Sputnik on October 4, 1957, provoked an alarm among the American public and U.S. policymakers. A swift reaction came with the U.S. Congress passing the National Defense Education Act (NDEA) in 1958 to fund public education reform, train young scientists, and prepare a select group of young people for work in STEM fields (Passow, 1957). Representative Carl Elliott, cosponsor of NDEA, recognized gifted children as one of America's most underdeveloped and underresourced student groups. Language included in two of the Act's titles would directly impact those of high ability and the gifted. Title III of NDEA sought the fortification of instruction in STEM subjects and foreign languages while Title V targeted funding for counseling and guidance, testing and identification, and encouragement of gifted students. Title V's ramification on gifted education has had lasting implications for contemporary gifted education research and practices. The definition of giftedness promoted by Terman and Hollingworth was based solely on measures of IQ. As part of the identification of gifted students under NDEA, a wider net was cast, and both aptitude and ability measures were used to distinguish students with exceptional talents in STEM areas rather than relying on IQ measures alone. Sputnik's launch and NDEA provided gifted education one of its most vibrant periods of renewed research and expanded programming in schools, due in large part to a combination of public goodwill toward this group of students and legislation and funding to support highly able students, particularly those in STEM fields (Jolly, 2009).

As the 1960s progressed, the Civil Rights Movement changed the focus of educational resolves. Legislative priorities and funding were now dedicated to underserved populations, including special education, low-income, and minority students.

The educational opportunities gained for marginalized students due to the work of the Civil Rights Movement would eventually transition to later Javits legislation and the "recognition and cultivation of outstanding potential" (Coleman, 1999, p. 18).

The Marland Report and National/ State Leadership Training Institute on the Gifted and Talented

As the 1960s drew to a close, attention turned back toward the needs of the gifted and talented. Senator Jacob Javits and Representative John Erlenborn sponsored P.L. 91–230, which provided funding and tasked the Commissioner of Education with determining the types of services available to meet the needs of gifted and talented students and what new types of services and programs were needed. Sidney Marland, Jr. had just moved into the position as Commissioner and began the data gathering in earnest. Between the resources available to Marland's office and the experts whom he consulted, the Marland Report was produced and distributed in 1972 (Jolly & Matthews, 2014). Apart from the report's findings, it also provided the first federal definition of giftedness, which read:

> Children capable of high performance include those with demonstrated achievement and/or potential ability in any of the following areas, singly or in combination:
> a. General specific ability
> b. Specific academic aptitude
> c. Creative or productive thinking
> d. Leadership ability
> e. Visual and performing arts
> f. Psychomotor ability [removed from the definition in 1978] (Marland, 1972, p. 10)

This definition reflected a move away from the unitary description of giftedness toward one of multidimensionality, which also necessitated a multiple criteria process of identification (Johnsen, 2011).

The Marland Report had also revealed a muddled arrangement of state provisions across the United States. Twenty-one states provided incentives to local and regional education agencies to offer special programming for gifted students, while 19 states had no provisions whatsoever. To correct this lopsidedness, a systematic structure was suggested throughout the states "to initiate and/or improve programs for the gifted" (Plantec & Hospodar, 1973, p. 6). In August of 1972, grant monies through the Education Professions Development Act allowed for the establishment of the National/State Leadership Training Institute on the Gifted and Talented (N/S-LTI-G/T). The N/S-LTI-G/T ran from 1973 to 1976, training more than 1,000 stakeholders that included an array of participants such as university researchers, teachers, parents, school board members, and representatives from private companies. Provisions were developed to address state, regional, and local needs. These included but were not limited to Advanced Placement (AP) courses, early college admission, cluster grouping, improved identification procedures, and revisions to curriculum design. There were also a number of publications and documents published to strengthen the knowledge and awareness of the needs of gifted students. The hallmarks of the work undertaken during this time period can still be found throughout the United States today (Jolly, 2014).

At a national level, the report recognized that inadequate services and programming were being provided for the gifted and talented. The report, however, failed to insist on federally mandated services or funding. This missed opportunity left gifted education and gifted students vulnerable to the often-volatile nature of interest and apathy toward this particular group of students. This period also witnessed an exponential growth in researchers and research programs throughout the United States, establishing a research network in gifted education that continues to function (Jolly, 2014).

Both the Beleaguered and Championed

Established in 1972, the Office of Gifted and Talented (OGT) housed within the U.S. Office of Education (USOE) was responsible for raising the profile and priority of gifted and talented students. However, the OGT was not provided any programmatic funding to support its mission until 1974. The OGT worked with other groups within the USOE in order to build partnerships and further the needs of gifted students. The N/S-LTI-G/T and the OGT, which held such promise of expanding gifted education programs and services throughout the United States, soon fell victim once again to a shifting political landscape and the ephemerality that exists without the protection of a federal legal mandate (Harrington, Harrington, & Karns, 1991). The only constant in gifted education is the inconsistent and unpredictable nature that involves support and funding at all levels of government, the general public, and educators.

Gifted education's champions have taken several forms since the Marland Report was issued. The Jacob K. Javits Gifted and Talented Students Education Act (1988) has provided a level of funding at the federal level to identify evidence-based practices and fund the National Research Center on the Gifted and Talented (NRCGT). However, this funding has fluctuated with the budgetary health of the nation and goodwill of legislators (Winkler & Jolly, 2011). Two reports were issued approximately a decade apart, *A Nation at Risk* (National Commission on Excellence in

Education, 1983) and *National Excellence: A Case for Developing America's Talent* (U.S. Department of Education, 1993), indicating the neglect shown toward gifted children's needs, which resulted in their poor educational outcomes. The reports also provided recommendations for services and programming to support gifted learner needs and recommendations for research.

No Child Left Behind (NCLB), the reauthorization of the Elementary and Secondary Education Act (ESEA) in 2001, resulted in one of the most fallow periods in gifted education and for gifted children in schools. With the focus of the legislation on children reaching levels of minimum proficiency, teachers and schools concentrated their efforts on students who were struggling to attain these goals of mastery. This accountability system created under NCLB jeopardized the educational progress of high-ability students, especially for students from low-income backgrounds, groups who lacked English language proficiency, and other underserved gifted students (Loveless, 2008; Plucker, Burroughs, & Song, 2010). The most recent reauthorization of the Elementary and Secondary Education Act, the Every Student Succeeds Act (ESSA, 2015), holds the most promise for gifted students since the Marland Report in that it includes language that relates to the specific needs of gifted and talented learners. Targeted professional development for educators must address the needs of gifted learners, and achievement data are now disaggregated to include achievement level rather than just reporting out students who attained proficiency or below (NAGC, 2015).

Conclusion

Once dominated by a few key personalities with limited influence in K–12 public education, gifted education has now grown to populate several dozen graduate programs across the United States, and individuals responsible for gifted education are present in many state departments of education (NAGC, 2014). However, the level of service remains variable, and research visibility and funding remain uneven in comparison to similar special education programs. The possibilities of ESSA have yet to be fully realized, but their provisions for gifted education acknowledge a forward trajectory in history that has been mired in a cycle where "No other special group of children has been alternately embraced and repelled with so much vigor by educators and laymen alike" (Tannenbaum, 1979, p. 5).

Big Ideas

1. The interest and support in gifted education has ebbed and flowed over time.

2. Gifted education remains largely a state department of education or local education agency responsibility.

3. Lewis Terman and Leta Hollingworth's IQ-centric view of giftedness remains an underlying issue for the field.

4. Federal education initiatives have impacted gifted education both positively and negatively.

5. An account of the field can help contemporary researchers and practitioners understand current themes and trends.

Discussion Questions

1. How did/does federal educational policy impact gifted education?

2. What are the challenges for gifted education in the next 10 to 20 years, and how do they relate to the past challenges the field has experienced?

3. What is the most pivotal event in the history of gifted education in the past 100 years? Why?

4. What can current gifted educators learn from the past?

References

Burks, B. S., Jensen, D. W., & Terman, L. S. (1930). *Genetic studies of genius, Vol. III: The promise of youth.* Palo Alto, CA: Stanford University Press.

Colangelo, N., & Davis, G. A. (2003). Introduction and overview. In N. Colangelo & G. A. Davis (Eds.), *Handbook of gifted education* (3rd ed., pp. 3–11). Boston, MA: Allyn & Bacon.

Coleman, M. R. (1999). Back to the future: The top 10 events that have shaped gifted education in the last century. *Gifted Child Today, 22*(6), 16–18.

Comrey, A. L. (1993). Joy Paul Guilford 1897–1987. In National Academy of Sciences (Ed.), *Biographical memoirs* (Vol. 62, pp. 199–210). Washington, DC: National Academy Press.

Council for Exceptional Children, The Association for the Gifted. (n.d.). *About.* Retrieved from http://cectag.com

Cox, C. M. (1926). *Early mental traits of three hundred geniuses: Genetic studies of genius, Vol. 2.* Stanford, CA: Stanford University Press.

Davis, G. A., & Rimm, S. B. (1994). *Education of the gifted and talented.* Boston, MA: Allyn & Bacon.

Elementary and Secondary Education Act of 1965, 20 U.S.C. 6301 et seq.

Every Student Succeeds Act, 20 U.S.C. 6301 (2015).

Galton, F. (1869). *Hereditary genius: An inquiry into its laws and consequences.* London, England: Macmillan.

Guilford, J. P. (1950). Creativity. *American Psychologist, 5,* 444–454.

Harrington, J., Harrington, C., & Karns, E. (1991). The Marland Report: Twenty years later. *Journal for the Education of the Gifted, 15,* 31–43.

Hollingworth, L. S. (1926). *Gifted children: Their nature and nurture.* New York, NY: Macmillan.

Hollingworth, L. S. (1942). *Children above 180 IQ.* Yonkers, NY: World Book.

Jefferson, T. (1784). *Notes on the State of Virginia.* Retrieved from http://press-pubs.uchicago.edu/founders/print_documents/v1ch18s16.html

Johnsen, S. K. (Ed.). (2011). *Identifying gifted students: A practical guide* (2nd ed.). Waco, TX: Prufrock Press.

Jolly, J. L. (2004). *A conceptual history of gifted education: 1910–1940* (Unpublished doctoral dissertation). Waco, TX: Baylor University.

Jolly, J. L. (2005). Foundations of the field of gifted education. *Gifted Child Today, 28*(2), 14–18, 65.

Jolly, J. L. (2006). Leta S. Hollingworth: P.S. 165 & 500: Lessons learned. *Gifted Child Today, 29*(3), 28–34.

Jolly, J. L. (2008). Lewis Terman: Genetic Study of Genius–elementary school students. *Gifted Child Today, 31*(1), 27–33.

Jolly, J. L. (2009). The National Defense Education Act, current STEM initiative, and the gifted. *Gifted Child Today, 32*(2), 50–53.

Jolly, J. L. (2014). Building gifted education: One state at a time. *Gifted Child Today, 37,* 258–260.

Jolly, J. L., & Bruno, J. (2010). The public's fascination with prodigious youth. *Gifted Child Today, 33*(2), 61–65.

Jolly, J. L., & Matthews, M. S. (2014). Sidney Marland. In A. Robinson & J. L. Jolly (Eds.), *A century of contributions to gifted education: Illuminating lives* (pp. 289–301). New York, NY: Routledge.

Kohlbrenner, R. J. (1950). William Torrey Harris, Superintendent of Schools, St. Louis, 1868–1880, *History of Education Journal, 2,* 18–24.

Lombroso, C. (1891). *The man of genius.* London, England: W. Scott.

Loveless, T. (2008). *High-achieving students in the era of NCLB: Part I—An analysis of NAEP data.* Washington, DC: Thomas Fordham Institute.

Marland, S. P., Jr. (1972). *Education of the gifted and talented: Report to the Congress of the United States by the U. S. Commissioner of Education: Vol. 1.* Washington, DC: U.S. Government Printing Office.

National Association for Gifted Children. (2014). *2014–2015 state of the states in gifted education: National policy and practice data.* Washington, DC: Author.

National Association for Gifted Children. (2015). *Gifted education provisions in final version of ESEA—The Every Student Succeeds Act.* Retrieved from http://www.nagc.org/sites/default/files/Advocacy/ESSA%20-%20GT%20provisions.pdf

National Commission on Excellence in Education. (1983). *A nation at risk: The imperative for educational reform.* Washington, DC: U.S. Government Printing Office.

National Defense Education Act of 1958, Pub. L. No 85-864, § 72 Stat. 1580 (1958).

No Child Left Behind Act, 20 U.S.C. §6301 (2001).

Passow, A. H. (1957). Developing a science program for rapid learners. *Science Education, 41,* 104–112.

Plantec, P., & Hospodar, J. (1973). *Evaluation of the National/State Leadership Training Institute on the Gifted and Talented: Final report.* Silver Spring, MD: Operations Research.

Plucker, J. A., Burroughs, N., & Song, R. (2010). *Mind the (other) gap! The growing excellence gap in K–12 education.* Bloomington: Indiana University, School of Education, Center for Evaluation and Education Policy.

Power, E. J. (1964). Plato's Academy: A halting step toward high education. *History of Education Quarterly, 4,* 155–166.

Robins, J. H. (2010). *An explanatory history of gifted education: 1940–1960* (Unpublished doctoral dissertation). Waco, TX: Baylor University.

Robins, J. H., & Jolly, J. L. (2013). The establishment of advocacy organizations. *Gifted Child Today, 36,* 139–141.

Rogers, K. B. (2014). Ann Fabe Isaacs: She made our garden grow. In A. Robinson & J. L. Jolly (Eds.), *A century of contributions to gifted education: Illuminating lives* (pp. 256–276). New York, NY: Routledge.

Stanley, J. C. (1976). Concern for intellectually talented youths: How it originated and fluctuated. *Journal of Clinical Child Psychology, 5,* 38–42.

Stedman, L. (1924). *Education of gifted children.* Yonkers-on-Hudson, NY: World Book.

Tannenbaum, A. (1979). Pre-Sputnik to Post-Watergate concern about the gifted. In A. Passow (Ed.), *The gifted and the talented: Their education and development: The seventy-eighth yearbook of the National Society for the Study of Education* (pp. 5–27). Chicago, IL: University of Chicago Press.

Tannenbaum, A. (1983). *Gifted children.* New York, NY: Macmillan.

Terman, L. M. (1925). *Genetic studies of genius: Volume I.* Palo Alto, CA: Stanford University Press.

Terman, L. M., & Oden, M. (1947). *The gifted child grows up: Twenty-five years' follow-up of a superior group: Genetic studies of genius, Vol. 4.* Stanford, CA: Stanford University Press.

Terman, L. M., & Oden, M. (1959). *The gifted group at mid-life: Thirty-five years' follow-up of the superior child: Genetic studies of genius, Vol. 5.* Stanford, CA: Stanford University Press.

Title V, Part D. [Jacob K. Javits Gifted and Talented Students Education Act of 1988], Elementary and Secondary Education Act of 1988 (2002), 20 U.S.C. sec. 7253 et seq.

U.S. Department of Education. (1993). *National excellence: A case for developing America's talent.* Washington, DC: Author.

Whipple, G. (1924). Historical and introductory. In G. Whipple (Ed.), *The twenty-third yearbook of the National Society for the Study of Education, Part I: Report of the society's committee on the education of gifted children* (pp. 1–24). Bloomington, IN: Public School Publishing.

Winkler, D. L., & Jolly, J. L. (2011). The Javits Act: 1988–2011. *Gifted Child Today, 34*(4), 61–63.

CHAPTER 3

Standards in Gifted Education

Susan K. Johnsen

Our goals can only be reached through a vehicle of a plan, in which we must fervently believe, and upon which we must vigorously act. There is no other route to success.—Pablo Picasso

Essential Questions to Guide the Reader

1. Why do we need standards?
2. What are the standards in gifted education?
3. How are standards used in practice?

In 1983, the National Commission on Excellence in Education published *A Nation at Risk: The Imperative for Educational Reform.* The Commission recommended that schools, colleges, and universities adopt more rigorous and measurable standards and be held accountable for the level of educational excellence they provided to students. Because the report was written in a language that appealed to the general public (Jolly, 2015), it had profound effects on policymakers, educator preparation agencies, professional organizations, the community, and other stakeholders who began to question the validity of K–12 education and the preparation of teachers. Since that time, all states have adopted some form of standards-based education system, professional associations have approved content standards in most subject areas, and the No Child Left Behind Act of 2001 has required that states report results on standards-related accountability measures (U.S. Department of Education, 2008). More recently, the Council of Chief State School Officers (CCSSO), along with the National Governors Association Center for Best Practices (NGA), developed the Common Core State Standards (CCSS) in the subject areas of English language arts and mathematics (NGA & CCSSO, 2010a, 2010b), which have been adopted by 42 states and five territories (see http://www. corestandards.org). Similarly, the National Research Council (NRC), the National Science Teachers Association, the American Association for the Advancement of Science, and Achieve (n.d.) together developed national science standards: the Next Generation Science Standards (see http://www.nextgenscience.org). Following the development of the CCSS, the Interstate Teacher Assessment and Support Consortium (InTASC), which comprises state education agencies and national educational organizations, developed common standards in teacher preparation (CCSSO, 2011). All of these standards are intended to improve the quality of education in K–12 schools and in educator preparation programs.

Responding to the need for standards in gifted education, the National Association for Gifted Children (NAGC), in partnership with The Association for the Gifted, a division of the Council for Exceptional Children (CEC-TAG), developed a set of standards to address teacher preparation. These teacher preparation standards (NAGC & CEC-TAG, 2013) are used as part of the process of accrediting schools of education (see http://www.caepnet.org) and for developing guidelines for professional development. The teacher preparation standards are part of a wider network of professional standards that influence the education of all teachers and students, which include the INTASC Model Core Teaching Standards, the National Board for Professional Teaching Standards (see http://boardcertifiedteachers.org/ certificate-areas), other professional association standards (e.g., National Council of Teachers of Mathematics, National Council of Teachers of English), and specific state standards. Following the development of the initial teacher preparation standards, NAGC updated its previous Gifted Program Standards and aligned them to these new standards. The 2010 *Pre-K–Grade 12 Gifted Programming Standards* focus on the characteristics of quality programs in schools serving gifted and talented students.

This chapter will discuss the reasons for standards, both sets of standards in gifted education, how they relate to one another, and applications at the national, state, and local levels.

Rationale for Standards in Gifted Education

In the most recent State of the States Report (NAGC & Council of State Directors of Programs for the Gifted [CSDPG], 2015), only 32 states have a mandate related to identification and/or services for gifted students, only 17 states have one full-time staff person at the state level dedicated to gifted education, and states primarily allow local education agencies to determine program components and services. Given the lack of a federal mandate to identify and serve students with gifts and talents and the great variations in services across states, standards are particularly critical to the field of gifted education.

First and foremost, educators can identify research-based practices of effective programming in gifted education that improve student outcomes and increase the likelihood that all students receive a quality education (Johnsen, VanTassel-Baska, & Robinson, 2008). Common standards provide consistency, ensuring that each gifted learner receives a challenging curriculum and the pedagogical supports needed to master it effectively.

Second, the standards stress the importance that the field of gifted education places on serving underrepresented populations. They reinforce the idea that (a) diversity exists in society, (b) students with identified talents represent diverse backgrounds, (c) curriculum needs to be culturally responsive, and (d) all students need to learn how to be productive in a multicultural, diverse, and global society.

Third, universities and schools can use the standards in identifying the important content and pedagogical skills needed for teaching gifted and talented students. At the university level, they can help faculty in teacher preparation institutions identify relevant theory, research, and pedagogy in designing courses, developing assessments, and meeting requirements for national recognition. At the state level, they can be used to establish policies, rules, and regulations regarding certification and licensure. At the school district level, they can be used as a guide for professional development, selecting teachers for specialized positions in supporting gifted and talented learners, and identifying general education teachers serving clusters of gifted and talented students in their classrooms.

Fourth, they provide a structure for developing national, state, and local policies, rules, and procedures. In this way, policymakers, boards, and other stakeholders can focus on what is important in gifted education and use them for accountability. Schools are able to set short- and long-term goals to assess their programs and set benchmarks for improvement.

Fifth, they can provide points for discussion and collaboration among educators, families, and other community stakeholders (Johnsen, 2011, 2012). Through informing families and educators about the specialized knowledge and skills needed by teachers of gifted students, they can advocate for local-, state-, and national-level policies supporting certification of general and gifted education teachers. They may then direct educators' efforts toward adequately recognizing gifted and talented students, developing and implementing programming, and ultimately raising the quality of services provided to gifted and talented students and their families.

Validation

Finally, standards define gifted education and build consensus and respect toward the field. With standards, educators in gifted education can point to evidence-based practices that are important to implement. Standards also offer a focus and a direction for new research efforts that link seminal ideas about teaching with ways of studying their effects on gifted and talented students' learning (Johnsen, 2011).

Teacher Preparation Standards in Gifted Education

The first set of teacher preparation standards in the field of gifted education were developed for teachers in the early 1980s when the NAGC Professional Training Institutes involved university faculty and practitioners in discussions of professional development issues and training guidelines (Kitano, Montgomery, VanTassel-Baska, & Johnsen, 2008). Concurrently, CEC-TAG established standards in 1989 to address professional development of teachers, including coursework for initial teacher preparation programs. The NAGC Professional Development Division continued this early work by conducting a series of symposia, which eventually resulted in the NAGC Standards for Graduate Programs in Gifted Education (Parker, 1996). CEC-TAG then collaborated with NAGC to develop initial and advanced standards (NAGC & CEC-TAG, 2013). Initial standards are for those programs that are directed toward educators who are seeking their first certificate in gifted education, whether it is at the undergraduate or graduate level. Advanced standards are for those educators who already have an initial certificate.

To be included, each of the initial and advanced standards needed to be supported by a strong research base, which was organized into three categories:

- *Literature/Theory-Based.* The knowledge and/or skills are based on theories or philosophical reasoning that include sources such as position papers, policy analyses, and descriptive reviews of the literature (CEC, 2010).
- *Research-Based.* The knowledge and/or skills are based on peer-reviewed studies that use appropriate research methodologies to address questions of cause and effect, and that researchers have independently replicated and found to be effective (CEC, 2010).
- *Practice-Based.* The knowledge and/or skills are derived from a number of sources. Practices based on a small number of studies or nomination procedures, such as promising practices, are usually practice-based. Practice-based knowledge or skills include those derived primarily from model and lighthouse programs and professional wisdom. These practices have been used so widely with practical evidence of effectiveness that there is an implicit professional assumption that the practice is effective. Practice-based knowledge and skills also include "emerging practice," practices that

arise from teachers' classroom experiences validated through some degree of action research (CEC, 2010).

(Visit The Association for the Gifted to examine the research for the initial and advanced standards: http://cectag.com/standards-2.)

The initial teacher preparation standards were approved and adopted by the National Council for Accreditation of Teacher Education in 2006; the advanced standards, in 2011. Both sets of teacher preparation standards were revised in 2013 to meet new Council for the Accreditation of Educator Preparation (CAEP) requirements, which required reducing the total number of standards to seven and the elements to 28. In addition, the teacher preparation standards were aligned to the INTASC Model Core Teaching Standards, which were published in 2011. The resulting NAGC-CEC Teacher Preparation Standards define the content knowledge about gifted and talented students, which includes "critical concepts, theories, skills, processes, principles, and structures and organizes ideas within a field" (CAEP, 2013, p. 4). They also identify pedagogical knowledge, which includes the "core activities of teaching such as figuring out what students know; choosing and managing representations of ideas; appraising, selecting, and modifying [instructional materials]" (CAEP, 2013, p. 5). Moreover, they describe collaboration and professional and ethical principles for teachers of gifted and talented students.

Initial Teacher Preparation Standards

Because both content and pedagogical knowledge are based on a thorough understanding of learners, Standard 1 (Learning Development and Individual Learning Differences) focuses on gifted and talented students' development and how they are similar to and different from other gifted and talented learners and the general population. Learning differences address how language, culture, economic status, family background, and/or disability impact the learning of individuals with gifts and talents. Based on these understandings, gifted education professionals respond to learners' individual needs.

Standards 2 through 5 focus on curriculum, instruction, and overall services for gifted and talented students. Standard 2 (Learning Environments) emphasizes the nature of multiple learning environments for gifted learners, which includes creating safe, inclusive, and culturally responsive environments for all learners. These environments provide the framework for a continuum of services that respond to an individual's gifts, talents, motivations, and cultural and linguistic differences.

Standards 3, 4, and 5 focus on gifted education professionals' knowledge and implementation of the learning process. Standard 3 (Curricular Content Knowledge) emphasizes educators' knowledge and use of core and specialized curricula to advance learning for individuals with gifts and talents. Standard 4

Introduction to Gifted Education

(Assessment) concentrates on assessment, both for identifying individuals with gifts and talents and also the types of assessment used to differentiate and accelerate instruction. Standard 5 (Instructional Planning and Strategies) addresses the selection, adaption, and planned use of a variety of evidence-based instructional strategies to advance learning of gifted and talented individuals.

The final two standards emphasize the importance of ethical practices and the collaboration with families and other professionals. Standard 6 (Professional Learning and Ethical Practice) emphasizes the use of foundational knowledge of the field and professional ethical principles as well as national Pre-K–Grade 12 Gifted Education Programming Standards to inform gifted education practice, to engage in lifelong learning, and to advance the profession. Finally, Standard 7 (Collaboration) focuses on gifted education professionals' collaboration with families, other educators, related service providers, individuals with gifts and talents, and personnel from community agencies in culturally responsive ways to address the needs of individuals with gifts and talents across a range of learning experiences (for a complete listing of the initial teacher preparation standards, visit http://cectag.com/standards-2).

Advanced Teacher Preparation Standards

The Advanced Standards in Gifted Education address the knowledge and skills needed by those educators who already have an initial certificate or license in gifted education. Standards 1 and 2 address the important role that gifted educators assume in developing and organizing programs. Standard 1 concentrates on Leadership and Policy. Gifted educators in advanced roles promote high expectations, help others understand the field of gifted education, advocate for policies that impact quality education for students with gifts and talents, mentor new educators, and conduct leadership activities. In Standard 2 (Program Development and Organization), gifted educators in advanced roles develop programs for students with gifts and talents based on principles of development and learning theory and the current literature on evidence-based practices. They design and develop program and curriculum models for enhancing talent development in multiple settings.

Standards 3 and 4 focus on ways that gifted educators may improve the overall program through research and evaluation. To meet Standard 3 (Research and Inquiry), gifted educators in advanced roles evaluate and modify instructional practices based on assessment data; use educational research to improve instruction, intervention strategies, and curricular materials; and disseminate this research to others. Standard 4 (Evaluation) focuses on evaluating gifted education programs using psychometrically sound assessments to monitor the progress of gifted and talented students and designing and implementing culturally responsive evaluation procedures.

Similar to initial standards in teacher preparation, Standard 5 (Professional Development and Ethical Practice) encourages gifted educators in advanced roles to not only improve their own professional practice, but also to plan, present, and evaluate professional development based on models that apply adult learning theories. Standard 6 (Collaboration), which is also emphasized in the initial standards, requires gifted educators to collaborate and consult across different stakeholder groups, build consensus, and create networks and coalitions to improve the education of individuals with gifts and talents.

[handwritten margin note: Most important and hardest to meet!]

Pre-K–Grade 12 Programming Standards in Gifted Education

The 2010 NAGC Pre-K–Grade 12 Gifted Programming Standards are the result of many years of effort on the part of the NAGC members in collaboration with the CEC-TAG members and others who have sought to improve the education of gifted and talented students. The effort began more than 15 years ago with the development of the 1998 Pre-K–Grade 12 Gifted Program Standards, which were designed to assist school districts in developing and implementing programs (Landrum, Callahan, & Shaklee, 2001; NAGC, 2000).

When the teacher preparation standards were published in 2006, NAGC wanted to revise the 1998 program standards and created a Professional Standards Committee (PSC) to oversee the work. Initially the PSC aligned each of the 1998 program standards to the teacher preparation standards and identified research support for each standard. Next, the PSC surveyed NAGC and CEC-TAG members to identify their use of the standards and other areas for revision. From the alignment results and the surveys, the PSC developed these principles in revising the standards (Johnsen, 2012; NAGC, 2010):

- *Giftedness is dynamic and is constantly developing.* Within the Gifted Programming Standards, students are defined as those having gifts and talents rather than those with stable traits. This definition is in line with current understandings of giftedness. Instead of a static definition of giftedness (i.e., a student is either gifted or not), more researchers have acknowledged the developmental nature of giftedness, which includes a set of interacting components such as general intelligence, domain-related skills, creativity, and nonintellective factors (Cattell, 1971; Gagné, 1999; Renzulli, 1978; Tannenbaum, 1991). This developmental perspective strongly influences identification and programming practices because educators are aware that a point-in-time test or a once-a-week program may not recognize or develop giftedness that takes time and supports.

- *Giftedness is found among students from a variety of backgrounds.* Diversity was defined as differences among groups of people and individuals based on ethnicity, race, socioeconomic status, gender, exceptionalities, language, religion, sexual orientation, and geographical area. Because the underrepresentation of diverse students in gifted education programs is well documented (Ford & Harris, 1994; Morris, 2002), specific evidence-based practices needed to be incorporated to ensure that identification procedures were equitable (Ford & Harmon, 2001; Harris, Plucker, Rapp, & Martinez, 2009), curriculum was culturally responsive (Ford, Tyson, Howard, & Harris, 2000; Kitano & Pedersen, 2002a, 2002b), and learning environments fostered cultural understanding for success in a diverse society (Harper & Antonio, 2008; Zirkel, 2008).

  What does giftedness look like in different backgrounds cultures

- *Standards should focus on student outcomes rather than practices.* Rather than counting the number of practices used, it is more important to examine the effect of the practices on the gifted and talented students' social, emotional, and cognitive development. This emphasis on student outcomes is in agreement with the national movement toward accountability.

- *All educators are responsible for the education of students with gifts and talents.* Educators were defined as administrators, teachers, counselors, and other instructional support staff from a variety of professional backgrounds (e.g., general education, special education, and gifted education). Research suggests that collaboration enhances talent development (Gentry & Ferriss, 1999; Landrum, 2002; Purcell & Leppien, 1998) and improves the likelihood that gifted students with disabilities receive services in gifted education programs (Coleman & Johnsen, 2011).

- *Students with gifts and talents should receive services throughout the day and in all environments that are based on their abilities, needs, and interests.* The word *programming* was used rather than the word *program*, which might connote a unidimensional approach (e.g., a once-a-week type of program option). The emphasis is critical given the patchwork of programs and services that are currently provided to gifted and talented students, which vary from state to state and from school to school (NAGC & CSDPG, 2013).

Using the principles, the research base, and the initial teacher preparation standards, 36 student outcomes were organized within six programming standards. Each of the six standards represents an important emphasis in developing and implementing effective programming for students with gifts and talents. Practices that are based on research evidence are also included and aligned with each student outcome (see an example in Table 3.1). These evidence-based practices provide guidance to educators in specific strategies that might be implemented to achieve the student outcomes.

Table 3.1

Organization of the Pre-K–Grade 12 Programming Standards in Gifted Education

Standard 4. Learning environments foster personal and social responsibility, multicultural competence, and interpersonal and technical communication skills for leadership in the 21st century to ensure specific student outcomes.	
Student Outcome	**Evidence-Based Practices**
4.3 Leadership. Students with gifts and talents demonstrate personal and social responsibility and leadership skills.	4.3.1 Educators establish a safe and welcoming climate for addressing social issues and developing personal responsibility.
	4.3.2. Educators provide environments for developing many forms of leadership and leadership skills.
	4.3.3. Educators promote opportunities for leadership in community settings to effect positive change.

Standard 1 (Learning and Development) encourages educators to recognize the learning and developmental differences of students with gifts and talents and promote ongoing self-understanding, awareness of their needs, and cognitive and affective growth of these students in school, home, and community settings to ensure specific student outcomes (NAGC, 2010, p. 8). The student outcomes within this standard recognize the learning and developmental differences of students with gifts and talents, and encourage the students' ongoing self-understanding, awareness of their needs, and cognitive and affective growth in the school, home, and community.

Standard 2 (Assessment) focuses on multiple types of assessment information: identification, learning progress and outcomes, and evaluation of programming for students with gifts and talents in all domains (NAGC, 2010, p. 9). This standard incorporates knowledge of all forms of assessments, including identification, the assessment of learning progress and outcomes, and evaluation of programming because they are inextricably linked to one another. The student outcomes within this standard relate to equal access, representation of students from diverse backgrounds, and the expression of individual differences in talents and gifts during the identification process. Students with gifts and talents also demonstrate advanced and complex learning and progress as a result of ongoing assessments and evaluation.

To meet Standard 3 (Curriculum Planning and Instruction), educators apply the theory and research-based models of curriculum and instruction related to students with gifts and talents and respond to their needs by planning, selecting, adapting, and creating culturally relevant curriculum and by using a repertoire of evidence-based instructional strategies to ensure specific student outcomes (NAGC, 2010, p. 10). This standard not only addresses curricular planning, but also talent development, instructional strategies, culturally relevant curriculum, and accessing appropriate resources to engage a variety of learners. Desired outcomes include students' demonstrating growth commensurate with their aptitude, becoming competent in talent areas and as independent investigators, and developing knowledge and skills for being productive in a multicultural, diverse, and global society.

Standard 4, Learning Environments, fosters personal and social responsibility, multicultural competence, and interpersonal and technical communication skills for leadership in the 21st century to ensure specific student outcomes (NAGC, 2010, p. 11). This standard focuses on the creation of safe learning environments where students are able to develop personal, social, cultural, communication, and leadership competencies. Specific student outcomes include the development of self-awareness, self-advocacy, self-efficacy, confidence, motivation, resilience, independence, and curiosity. Students also learn how to develop positive peer relationships, social interactions, and interpersonal and technical communication skills with diverse individuals and across diverse groups. In their development of leadership skills, they also demonstrate personal and social responsibility.

For Standard 5 (Programming), educators are aware of empirical evidence regarding the cognitive, creative, and affective development of learners with gifts and talents and programming that meets their concomitant needs. Educators use this expertise systematically and collaboratively to develop, implement, and effectively manage comprehensive services for students with a variety of gifts and talents to ensure specific student outcomes (NAGC, 2010, p. 12). This standard includes an array of programming options that are coordinated and implemented by teams of educators who have adequate resources and policies and procedures to implement comprehensive services, which include talent development and career planning. Outcomes include students demonstrating growth and enhanced performance in cognitive and affective areas and identifying future career pathways and talent development pathways to reach their goals.

To meet Standard 6 (Professional Development), all educators (administrators, teachers, counselors, and other instructional support staff) need to build their knowledge and skills using the NAGC/CEC-TAG Teacher Standards for Gifted and Talented Education and the National Staff Development Standards. They formally assess professional development needs related to the standards, develop and monitor plans, systematically engage in training to meet the identified needs, and demonstrate mastery of standards. They access resources to provide for release time, funding for continuing education, and substitute support. These practices are judged through the assessment of relevant student outcomes (NAGC, 2010, p. 13). This standard examines the preparation of educators and the knowledge and skills needed to develop their students' talents and socioemotional development. It also emphasizes high-quality educator development that creates lifelong learners who are ethical in their practices. Student outcomes include the development of their talents in academic and social and emotional areas.

Similarities and Differences Across the Two Sets of Standards

In comparing the Pre-K–Grade 12 Gifted Programming Standards with the NAGC-CEC Teacher Preparation Standards, the two clearly relate to one another in important ways:

- *Learning and Development*. The gifted and talented student's learning and development are the focus of the first standard in both sets. The learning needs of gifted and talented students are foundational to gifted education and must be placed at the center of curriculum and instruction. Educators should understand how characteristics vary between and among individuals with and without gifts and talents and how various factors contribute to the development of each gifted individual's self-understanding, awareness of needs, and cognitive and affective growth.

- *Assessment*. Assessment is viewed as important in decisions made regarding identification, placement, learning progress, and evaluating the effectiveness of programming. Both sets emphasize how assessments should be differentiated or modified to provide equal access to programming and to minimize bias. For the successful implementation of short- and long-range goals, colleagues and families need to be involved in the decision-making process. Moreover, engaging gifted individuals in assessing their own progress is emphasized in the teacher preparation standards.

- *Curriculum Planning and Instruction*. Within the programming standards, Standard 3 addresses curriculum planning and instruction, whereas in the teacher preparation standards, two standards address this area, with Standard 5 focusing on instructional strategies and Standard 3 on curricular content knowledge of general and specialized curricula. Across all three standards, a repertoire of evidence-based instructional strategies in all domains (e.g., cognitive, affective, aesthetic, social, and leadership) is emphasized. These strategies include acceleration, critical and creative thinking, problem solving, and research. The general education curriculum needs to be modified or differentiated and specialized curriculum developed to advance the learning of students in their areas of talent or interest. Both standards also emphasize the importance of culturally relevant curriculum so that individuals with gifts and talents might have productive careers in a multicultural, global society.

- *Learning Environments*. Although both sets of standards address the importance of safe, inclusive, and culturally responsive environments where gifted individuals learn how to adapt to different settings, the programming standards identify specific competency areas for student growth: personal, social, leadership, cultural, and communication.

- *Professional Learning and Development.* The standards emphasize the importance of educators' awareness of the foundational knowledge of the field and their engagement in lifelong learning that is based on the awareness of their strengths and needs. They are also aware of their own cultural and personal frames of reference and comply with ethical principles. The teacher preparation standards cite the programming standards, and the programming standards cite the teacher preparation standards in terms of important benchmarks to evaluate.

Although addressed in other standards, each of the sets does have a standard that is different from the other set. In the teacher preparation standards, there is a separate standard on Collaboration. The programming standards do integrate collaboration within Standard 1 (i.e., collaboration with families), Standard 4 (i.e., cultural competence), and Standard 5 (i.e., collaborative planning, developing, and implementing services), and the teacher preparation standards not only emphasize the use of collaboration in developing services, but also in serving as a resource to colleagues across a wide range of settings. In the programming standards, there is a separate standard on Programming. Again the teacher preparation standards include program services within Standard 2 (i.e., continuum of services) and Standard 5 (i.e., transfer of advanced knowledge and skills across environments), but the programming standards not only include these topics, but also address grouping arrangements, individualized learning options, distance learning, and resource support.

Clearly, the two sets of standards are closely aligned to one another with some differences in emphasis and elaboration. The standards may be used separately or together to develop policies, state and local standards, self-assessment of current and desired practices in identification and services offered to gifted and talented students, the identification of teacher and student outcomes, professional development, assessments of teacher performances and their relationship to student outcomes, the design of an action plan, and the implementation of the plan. All of these areas will be discussed in the next set of cases.

Application of the Standards

How might educators in gifted education use the national gifted education teacher preparation and programming standards? Both sets of standards may be used in a variety of ways: assessing whether or not a teacher, school, school district, or a state is implementing best practices; identifying and assessing gifted and talented student outcomes; selecting teachers and administrators of gifted education programs; designing professional development related to the school and teacher self-assessments; evaluating programs to monitor progress toward specific evidence-based practices; and advocating for gifted education programs (Johnsen, 2011). The case studies that follow discuss some of these uses at the state and local levels.

Case 1: Revising and Updating Standards at the State Level

In 1989, the state decided to pass a bill that would require comprehensive services for gifted and talented students in grades K–12. Students were to be identified beginning in the spring of their kindergarten year and provided comprehensive services through high school. The state education agency (SEA) developed accountability standards for school districts to follow in implementing assessments, curriculum and instruction, program delivery, professional development, and community involvement (i.e., the State Plan for Gifted and Talented Students). The SEA monitored individual districts' implementation of the State Plan.

With the development of national teacher preparation standards and programming standards in gifted education, this SEA decided to revise the State Plan and align the accountability standards with the new standards. One of its major targets was in the area of professional development, which addressed only a few of the teacher preparation standards. They knew that if teachers had greater knowledge and skills regarding gifted and talented students, then services would improve. An appointed state-level committee comprising gifted education teachers, coordinators, administrators, university faculty, state gifted association board members, regional service center representatives, and state agency personnel began the revision process by aligning the state standards with the national standards (see Table 3.2).

Although there was some degree of alignment between the state plan and the national standards, the Committee noticed that no comparable accountability standard had been developed for the first national standard related to Learning and Development. Moreover, at first glance, it didn't appear that many of the state's professional development accountability standards were aligned to the national teacher preparation standards. The second table that aligned specific accountability standards with specific elements from the national standards revealed the gaps between the national programming standards and state accountability standards (see Table 3.3).

The committee was now able to accomplish its task of identifying new accountability standards that would address all of the evidence-based practices. The new state plan was eventually posted online for public comment and approved by the state agency.

Table 3.2

Alignment of State Standards to National Standards

State Plan for the Education of Gifted and Talented Students	NAGC/CEC Teacher Preparation Standards	NAGC Programming Standards
1. Assessments	2. Learner Development and Individual Differences	1. Learning and Development
2. Curriculum and Instruction	4. Assessment	2. Assessment
3. Program Delivery	4. Curricular Content Knowledge 5. Instructional Planning and Strategies	3. Curriculum Planning and Instruction
4. Professional Development	2. Learning Environments	4. Learning Environments 5. Programming
5. Community Involvement	8. Professional Learning and Ethical Practice	6. Professional Development
	7. Collaboration	5. Programming

Case 2: Ensuring Quality Programming at the School District and Classroom Level

Supported by its Board of Trustees, the High Country School District had decided to change its delivery of services to its elementary gifted and talented students, moving from a resource room model where gifted students were served once a week to a cluster model where gifted students were grouped together in a general education classroom and served every day. They believed that the cluster group model would provide more comprehensive and continuous services than a resource model. To monitor the change and ensure that the quality of services was maintained and improved, the School Board allocated funds for an external evaluation. The superintendent wanted the evaluation team to initially focus on evaluating specific elements of Standards 3, 4, and 5 of the NAGC-CEC Teacher Preparation Standards and Standards 2 and 3 of the NAGC Programming Standards (see Table 3.4). The evaluation team observed in cluster group classrooms, using several instruments that were aligned to the standards (Johnsen, 1992; Johnsen, Haensly, Ryser, & Ford, 2002; VanTassel-Baska et al., 2003), and collected interviews with teachers, students, and principals to triangulate their data to address the standards' elements (see Table 3.4).

The evaluation team recommended several areas for professional development as an outcome of their observations and interviews. Although variations were appar-

Table 3.3

Specific Relationships Between the NAGC Pre-K–Grade 12 Gifted Programming Standards Student Outcomes and the State Accountability Standards

NAGC Pre-K–Grade 12 Student Outcomes (Number of Aligned Standards)	1. Assessments												2. Curriculum and Instruction						3. Program Delivery				4. Professional Development					5. Community Involvement		
	a	b	c	d	e	f	g	h	i	j	k	l	a	b	c	d	e	f	a	b	c	d	a	b	c	d	e	a	b	c
1.1																														
1.2																														
1.3 (1)														*																
1.4 (1)																													*	
1.5																														
1.6																														
1.7																														
1.8																														
2.1																														
2.2 (11)	*	*	*	*	*	*	*	*	*	*		*																		
2.3 (4)	*	*					*				*																			
2.4 (2)																				*		*								
2.5 (2)																		*												*
2.6 (4)																		*				*					*			*
3.1 (4)																			*	*	*	*								
3.2 (1)															*															
3.3 (2)																						*							*	
3.4																														
3.5																														
3.6 (1)																													*	

Table 3.3, Continued.

NAGC Pre-K-Grade 12 Student Outcomes (Number of Aligned Standards)	1. Assessments												2. Curriculum and Instruction						3. Program Delivery				4. Professional Development					5. Community Involvement		
	a	b	c	d	e	f	g	h	i	j	k	l	a	b	c	d	e	f	a	b	c	d	a	b	c	d	e	a	b	c
4.1																														
4.2																														
4.3 (1)																			*											
4.4																														
4.5																														
5.1 (6)													*	*	*	*					*								*	
5.2																														
5.3 (2)																						*							*	
5.4 (3)																	*					*							*	
5.5 (1)													*																	
5.6 (7)	*	*	*													*		*			*									
5.7 (1)																			*											
6.1 (5)																							*	*	*	*		*		
6.2																														
6.3 (4)																								*	*	*	*			
6.4																														

Table 3.4

Baseline Evaluation of Cluster Teacher Classrooms

Standard Element	COS-R (VanTassel-Baska et al., 2003)	CIPS (Johnsen, 1992: Johnsen et al., 2002)	Interviews
NAGC Program Standard 2.4.1. Use pre- and postassessments		*	*
NAGC Program Standard 2.4.2. Use product-based assessments		*	*
NAGC Program Standard 2.4.3. Use of off-level assessments		*	*
NAGC Program Standard 2.4.4. Interpret quality of assessments		*	*
NAGC Program Standard 3.13. Modify curriculum	*	*	*
NAGC Program Standard 3.14. Use complex, challenging, in-depth curriculum	*	*	*
NAGC Program Standard 3.16. Pace instruction	*	*	*
NAGC Program Standard 3.3.1, 3.3.3, 3.4. Use repertoire of strategies—research, critical thinking, creative thinking, problem solving	*	*	*
NAGC Teacher Prep Standard 3.1. Organize knowledge—cross-disciplinary, learning progressions	*	*	*
NAGC Teacher Prep Standard 3.2. Modify curriculum—creativity, acceleration, depth, complexity	*	*	*
NAGC Teacher Prep Standard 3.3, 3.4, 4.4. Use assessments to differentiate	*	*	*
NAGC Teacher Prep Standard 5.1. Use repertoire of strategies—critical thinking, creative thinking, problem solving	*	*	*

ent across classrooms, teachers needed individualized assistance in these areas: using pre- and postassessments to differentiate the curriculum (see NAGC Program standard 2.4.4 and NAGC Teacher Preparation 3.3) and incorporating more critical thinking, problem solving, and independent research into their learning activities (see NAGC Program standards 3.3.1, 3.3.3, 3.4 and NAGC Teacher Preparation standard 5.1). Based on these recommendations, the school district developed an action plan that included a timeline for incorporating these standards into their professional development; identifying, developing, and disseminating needed material resources; and identifying and training individuals to provide classroom follow up to ensure that the cluster-group gifted education program incorporated these evidence-based practices. They then planned to monitor progress and examine the relationships between these practices to the student outcomes listed in the programming standards.

Conclusion

Over the past 30 years, standards have assumed a major role in influencing K–12 education and teacher preparation. Responding to the need for standards in gifted education, NAGC and CEC-TAG have collaborated in developing standards to address teacher preparation and program quality. These standards are particularly important in gifted education because of the lack of a federal mandate to identify and serve students with gifts and talents. They identify research-based practices that can be implemented consistently across states and local education agencies to effect positive student outcomes. Quality standards in gifted education are now readily available to all stakeholders in gifted education for improving the overall quality of programming.

Big Ideas

1. Standards in gifted education are part of a broader landscape of professional preparation and program standards that influence the education of all students.

2. Standards provide a structure for developing policies, rules, and procedures.

3. Because standards are research-based, they can be used in developing quality programs that are consistent across schools and states.

4. Standards define the field of gifted education and build respect toward programming for gifted students.

5. Standards can be used to advocate for gifted and talented students.

Discussion Questions

1. How do standards help the overall quality of gifted education?

2. How have standards been implemented in my school or my state?

3. How do the standards in gifted education relate to other standards in my school district?

4. What are the challenges in implementing gifted education standards?

5. In what ways might I advocate for gifted education using the standards?

References

Cattell, R. B. (1971). *Abilities: Their structure, growth, and action.* Boston, MA: Houghton Mifflin.

Coleman, M. R., & Johnsen, S. K. (Eds.). (2011). *RtI for gifted students.* Waco, TX: Prufrock Press.

Council for the Accreditation of Educator Preparation. (2013). *CAEP accreditation standards and evidence: Aspirations for educator preparation.* Retrieved from http://caepnet.org/~/media/Files/caep/standards/commrpt.pdf?la=en

Council for Exceptional Children. (2010). *Validation study resource manual.* Arlington, VA: Author.

Council of Chief State School Officers. (2011, April). *InTASC model core teaching standards: A resource for state dialogue.* Retrieved from http://www.ccsso.org/Documents/2011/InTASC_Model_Core_Teaching_Standards_2011.pdf

Ford, D. Y., & Harmon, D. A. (2001). Equity and excellence: Providing access to gifted education for culturally diverse students. *Journal of Secondary Gifted Education, 12,* 141–148.

Ford, D. Y., & Harris, J. J., III. (1994). *Multicultural gifted education.* New York, NY: Teachers College Press.

Ford, D., Tyson, C., Howard, T., & Harris, J. J., III. (2000). Multicultural literature and gifted Black students: Promoting self-understanding, awareness, and pride. *Roeper Review, 22,* 235–240.

Gagné, F. (1999). My convictions about the nature of abilities, gifts, and talents. *Journal for the Education of the Gifted, 22,* 109–136.

Gentry, M., & Ferriss, S. (1999). StATS: A model of collaboration to develop science talent among rural students. *Roeper Review, 21,* 316–320.

Harper, S. R., & Antonio, A. (2008). Not by accident: Intentionality in diversity, learning and engagement. In S. R. Harper (Ed.), *Creating inclusive campus environments for cross-cultural learning and student engagement* (pp. 1–18). Washington, DC: National Association of Student Personnel Administrators.

Harris, B., Plucker, J. A., Rapp, K. E., & Martinez, R. S. (2009). Identifying gifted and talented English language learners: A case study. *Journal for the Education of the Gifted, 32,* 368–393.

Johnsen, S. K. (1992). *Classroom Instructional Practices Scale.* Unpublished manuscript, Baylor University, Waco, TX.

Johnsen, S. K. (2011). A comparison of the Texas State Plan for the Education of Gifted/Talented Students and the 2010 NAGC Pre-K–Grade 12 Gifted Programming Standards. *Tempo, 31*(1), *10–28.*

Johnsen, S. K. (Ed.). (2012). *Using the NAGC Pre-K–Grade 12 Gifted Programming Standards.* Waco, TX: Prufrock Press.

Johnsen, S. K., Haensly, P. A., Ryser, G. R., & Ford, R. F. (2002). Changing general education classroom practices to adapt for gifted students. *Gifted Child Quarterly, 46,* 45–63.

Johnsen, S., VanTassel-Baska, J., & Robinson, A. (2008). *Using the national gifted education standards for university teacher preparation programs.* Thousand Oaks, CA: Corwin Press.

Jolly, J. L. (2015). The gifted at risk. *Gifted Child Today, 38,* 124–127.

Kitano, M., Montgomery, D., VanTassel-Baska, J., & Johnsen, S. (2008). *Using the national gifted education standards for PreK–12 professional development.* Thousand Oaks, CA: Corwin Press.

Kitano, M. K., & Pedersen, K. S. (2002a). Action research and practical inquiry: Multicultural-content integration in gifted education: Lessons from the field. *Journal for the Education of the Gifted, 26,* 269–289.

Kitano, M. K., & Pedersen, K. S. (2002b). Action research and practical inquiry: Teaching gifted English learners. *Journal for the Education of the Gifted, 26,* 132–147.

Landrum, M. S. (2002). *Resource consultation and collaboration in gifted education.* Mansfield Center, CT: Creative Learning Press.

Landrum, M. S., Callahan, C. M., & Shaklee, B. D. (2001). *Aiming for excellence: Gifted program standards.* Waco, TX: Prufrock Press.

Morris, J. E. (2002). African American students and gifted education. *Roeper Review, 24,* 59–53.

National Association for Gifted Children. (2000). *Pre-K–Grade 12 Gifted Program Standards.* Washington, DC: Author.

National Association for Gifted Children. (2010). *NAGC Pre-K–Grade 12 Gifted Programming Standards: A blueprint for quality gifted education programs.* Washington, DC: Author.

National Association for Gifted Children, & Council for Exceptional Children, The Association for the Gifted. (2013). *NAGC-CEC teacher knowledge and skill standards for gifted and talented education.* Retrieved from http://www.ncate.org/Standards/ProgramStandardsandReportForms/tabid/676/Default.aspx

National Association for Gifted Children, & Council of State Directors of Programs for the Gifted. (2013). *2012–2013 State of the states in gifted education: National policy and practice data.* Washington, DC: Author.

National Association for Gifted Children, & Council of State Directors of Programs for the Gifted. (2015). *2014–2015 State of the states in gifted education: Policy and practice data.* Washington, DC: Author.

National Commission on Excellence in Education. (1983). *A nation at risk: The imperative for educational reform.* Washington, DC: U.S. Department of Education.

National Governors Association Center for Best Practices, & Council of Chief State School Officers. (2010a). *Common Core State Standards for English language arts.* Washington, DC: Author.

National Governors Association Center for Best Practices, & Council of Chief State School Officers. (2010b). *Common Core State Standards for mathematics.* Washington, DC: Author.

National Research Council, National Science Teachers Association, the American Association for the Advancement of Science, & Achieve. (n.d.). *Next Generation Science Standards.* Retrieved from http://www.nextgenscience.org

No Child Left Behind Act, 20 U.S.C. §6301 (2001).

Parker, J. (1996). NAGC standards for personnel preparation in gifted education: A brief history. *Gifted Child Quarterly, 40,* 158–164.

Purcell, J. H., & Leppien, J. H. (1998). Building bridges between general practitioners and educators of the gifted: A study of collaboration. *Gifted Child Quarterly, 42,* 172–181.

Renzulli, J. (1978). What makes giftedness? Reexamining a definition. *Phi Delta Kappan, 60,* 180–184.

Tannenbaum, A. (1991). The social psychology of giftedness. In N. Colangelo & G. A. Davis (Eds.), *Handbook of gifted education* (pp. 27–44). Boston, MA: Allyn & Bacon.

U.S. Department of Education. (2008). *A nation accountable: Twenty-five years after a nation at risk.* Washington, DC: U. S. Department of Education. Retrieved from http://www2.ed.gov/rschstat/research/pubs/accountable/accountable.pdf

VanTassel-Baska, J., Avery, L., Struck, J., Feng, A., Bracken, B., Drummond, D., & Stambaugh, T. (2003). *The William and Mary Classroom Observation Scales Revised.* Williamsburg, VA: The College of William and Mary, School of Education, Center for Gifted Education.

Zirkel, S. (2008). The influence of multicultural educational practices on student outcomes and intergroup relations. *Teachers College Record, 110,* 1147–1181.

SECTION II

The Gifted Learner

With the blueprint ready, it is time to lay the foundation of the building. With footers in place, more is needed to support the structure. A critical component in building, the foundation must be made of strong materials because it provides the base for all subsequent parts of the building.

Just as the foundation anchors the building, knowledge of gifted learners themselves must provide the basis for decision making in gifted education. Educators of gifted children must understand the social, emotional, and cognitive needs of gifted learners. Addressing these needs forms the foundation for gifted education.

There are three chapters in this section: "Characteristics of Gifted Learners," "Social and Emotional Development of Students With Gifts and Talents," and "Cognitive Development of Giftedness and Talents: From Theory to Practice."

Myths

» **Gifted children will make it on their own.** Just as athletes need coaches to be their best selves, so gifted children need effective teachers to develop their potential.

» **It is most important for teachers to work with struggling students.** It is important for all students to learn on an ongoing basis. Educators need a repertoire of strategies in order to appropriately challenge all students.

» **Gifted learners make straight A's.** Because a child has the potential to do well in a class does not mean that he has the motivation or work ethic to perform at the A level.

CHAPTER 4

Characteristics of Gifted Learners

Lynette Breedlove

Persons of genius, it is true, are, and are always likely to be, a small minority; but in order to have them, it is necessary to preserve the soil in which they grow. Genius can only breathe freely in an atmosphere of freedom.—John Stuart Mill (1869)

Essential Questions to Guide the Reader

1. How does asynchronous development affect a learner's interactions with others? How does it affect a learner's educational needs?

2. How do gifted students vary by degree of giftedness? Why does this matter?

3. What core attributes do gifted learners share, and how are they manifested differently in individual students?

4. How do Dabrowski's overexcitabilities impact a learner's experiences in and out of the classroom?

Gifted and talented learners fall within the category of exceptional learners, learners who need some support or adjustment made to the typical school environment, instructional strategies, or curriculum in order to have their educational needs met—their academic soil. When you first enter the field of gifted education, you are likely to encounter someone who suggests that all children are gifted. Yet when you enter the field of special education, you rarely encounter someone who suggests that all children have special needs. It is interesting that our society continues to be uncomfortable with the range of human intelligence and academic ability when we are clearly comfortable with the range of human physical abilities. Professional sports is a multibillion dollar industry. There are athletic development programs for a variety of sports starting at very young ages. If the talent development efforts devoted to developing physical abilities were applied to the development of intellectual abilities, our gifted and talented programs would be spectacular and meet the needs of gifted children from all populations. Until our society gets to that place, it is likely you will need to help others understand how gifted and talented learners are different from other learners.

In a 1998 speech at the Indiana Association for the Gifted's conference, Michael Clay Thompson spoke passionately about the difference between having gifts and being gifted and talented. As a specialist in language arts, particularly grammar, he provided a clear perspective and response to those who suggest "everyone is gifted in some way." He recommended we not confuse gifts with gifted: "*Gift* is a colloquial term that we use to describe people's best qualities, whereas *giftedness* is a technical, professional term that educators use to describe really smart kids who require differentiated educations." This is somewhat like the difference between being special and having special needs. Thompson went on to say:

> Giftedness is not ordinary; giftedness is extraordinary; this is the very pith and marrow of the term. Mozart, Shakespeare, Catherine the Great, Martin Luther King, and Sylvia Plath were gifted. Like gifted children in our schools, these people had special abilities and special needs, and as a society we must be able to say so, to admire ability, to support ability, to celebrate ability, and to nurture ability. It must be as socially acceptable to support genius that is intellectual as it is to support genius that is athletic.

In our society, we recognize that everyone does not have the same capacity to dunk a basketball, throw a baseball, or perform skateboard tricks. It is important to recognize learners' capacities for intellectual pursuits as well.

This chapter examines the ways in which gifted and talented learners differ from other learners. Understanding these differences is essential to understanding who gifted learners are and how to meet their educational needs.

Keys to Understanding Giftedness

As discussed in Chapter 1, theorists use various frameworks and models to describe the concept of giftedness. Additionally, there is no single accepted definition of giftedness. These varying and sometimes competing efforts have made advocacy for and understanding of gifted and talented learners a bit more complicated. Thankfully, there is far more agreement regarding the characteristics and core attributes of gifted learners.

Traits of Giftedness

An Internet search for "characteristics of gifted children" will result in more than a million hits. Numerous websites list characteristics. Some are for specific age groups, while others are for specific areas of giftedness. Although there is not a single definition of giftedness agreed upon by experts in the field, the various definitions do have several things in common. One of the commonalities is a reference to various types of giftedness. The Marland Report (Marland, 1972) included six areas of giftedness in the first federal definition of giftedness. These areas were general intellectual ability, specific academic aptitude, creative or productive thinking, leadership ability, visual and performing arts, and psychomotor ability. The 1988 Jacob K. Javits Act, which updated the federal definition, included the areas of intellectual, creative, artistic, and leadership abilities, along with higher performance capability in specific academic fields. The 2010 definition from the National Association for Gifted Children referred to giftedness in domains or structured areas of activity. This common feature of the definitions helps us to understand that giftedness in each area may look slightly different.

It is important to keep in mind that characteristics checklists are guides. No gifted person will possess all of the characteristics on a list. Gifted learners often display many of the characteristics in their areas of giftedness or interests, but the lists should not be considered definitive or be used in an exclusionary manner when identifying giftedness.

Core Attributes

When thinking about the characteristics of gifted learners, it is helpful to start with central traits that gifted learners share and then consider how these are manifested differently by area of giftedness or learner background. Mary Frasier and others at the University of Georgia conducted an extensive study to identify the "Core Attributes of Giftedness" (Frasier, Hunsaker, et al., 1995). They wanted to identify the characteristics that fit the construct of giftedness regardless of the gifted person's background, ethnicity, income level, or interest. Their goal was to address the underrepresentation of learners from specific minority groups and economically dis-advantaged learners in gifted and talented programs. They found 10 categories that represent the core attributes of gifted learners. They called these Traits, Aptitudes, and Behaviors (TABs), which included:

- motivation,
- communication skills,
- interest,
- problem-solving ability,
- imagination/creativity,
- memory,
- inquiry,
- insight,
- reasoning, and
- humor.

To help teachers understand each core attribute, Frasier, Martin, et al. (1995) added descriptions and examples of how each attribute, trait, or behavior might look in action. They built this into an identification system to help teachers identify more learners from underrepresented populations as gifted and talented. They called the system "Panning for Gold." The traits, aptitudes, and behaviors, along with their descriptions and how they might look, are in Table 4.1.

While Frasier, Hunsaker, et al.'s (1995) study was based on research and descriptions of gifted learners published in 1995 or earlier, the core attributes still fit characteristics lists published today. In 2004, Johnsen included "asks intelligent questions" as a characteristic of gifted learners in her book, *Identifying Gifted Students: A Practical Guide*. This characteristic fits within the core attribute of Inquiry. Johnsen also included "is able to identify the important characteristics of new concepts, problems," which fits Insight. The National Association for Gifted Children (n.d.) lists Traits of Giftedness on its website (https://www.nagc.org/resources-publications/resources/my-child-gifted/common-characteristics-gifted-individuals/traits). It includes the cognitive trait of the "power of critical thinking, skepticism, self-criticism." This characteristic fits the Reasoning core attribute. These examples are characteristics of general intellectual ability, but that is only one type of giftedness.

Areas of Giftedness

Although the core attributes remain constant, they may appear different according to a learner's area of giftedness. Renzulli, Siegle, Reis, Gavin, and Reed (2009) investigated the addition of domain-specific items to the Scales for Rating the Behavioral Characteristics of Superior Students (SRBCSS). The SRBCSS is a

Table 4.1
Panning for Gold TABs Descriptors

TAB	Description	How it may look
Motivation: Evidence of desire to learn	Forces that initiate, direct and sustain individual or group behavior in order to satisfy a need or attained goal	• Aspires to be somebody, to do something. • Is an enthusiastic learner. • Demonstrates persistence in pursuing or completing self-selected tasks (may be culturally influenced; evident in school or non-school activities).
Interest: Intense (sometimes unusual) interests	Activities, avocations, objects, etc. that have special worth or significance and are given special attention	• Demonstrates unusual or advanced interest in a topic or activity. • Is a self-starter. • Is beyond age-group. • Pursues activity unceasingly.
Communication skills: Highly expressive and effective use of words, numbers, symbols, etc.	Transmission and reception of signals or meanings through a system of symbols (codes, gestures, language, numbers)	• Demonstrates unusual ability to communicate (verbally, physically, artistically, or symbolically). • Uses particularly apt examples, illustrations or elaborations.
Problem-solving ability: Effective (often inventive) strategies for recognizing and solving problems	Process of determining a correct sequence of alternatives leading to a desired goal or to successful completion or performance of a task	• Demonstrates unusual ability to devise or adapt a systematic strategy for solving problems and to change the strategy if it is not working. • Creates new designs, invents.
Memory: Large storehouse of information on school or non-school topics	Exceptional ability to retain and retrieve information	• Already knows information. • Needs only 1–2 repetitions for mastery. • Has a wealth of information about school or non-school topics. • Pays attention to details. • Manipulates information. • Is highly curious.

TAB	Description	How it may look
Inquiry: Questions, experiments, explores	Method or process of seeking knowledge, understanding, or information	• Asks unusual questions for age. • Plays around with ideas. • Demonstrates extensive exploratory behaviors directed toward eliciting information about materials, devices or situations.
Insight: Quickly grasps new concepts and makes connections; senses deeper meanings	Sudden discovery of the correct solution following incorrect attempts based primarily on trial and error	• Demonstrates exceptional ability to draw inferences. • Appears to be a good guesser. • Keenly observant. • Possesses heightened capacity for seeing unusual and diverse relationships. • Integrates ideas and disciplines.
Reasoning: Logical approaches to figuring out solutions	Highly conscious, directed, controlled, active, intentional, forward-looking, goal oriented thought	• Makes generalizations. • Uses metaphors and analogies . . . thinks things through in a logical manner. • Thinks crucially . . . comes up with plausible answers.
Imagination/Creativity: Produces many ideas; Highly original	Process of forming mental images of objects, qualities, situations, or relationships, which are not immediately apparent to the sense; solve problems by pursuing nontraditional patterns of thinking	• Shows exceptional ingenuity using everyday materials. • Creates wild, seemingly silly ideas; often fluently/flexibly.
Humor: Conveys and picks up on humor well	Ability to synthesize key ideas or problems in complex situation in a humorous way; exceptional sense of timing in words and gestures	• Has a keen sense of humor, may be gentle/hostile. • See unusual relationships. • Demonstrates unusual emotional depth. • Demonstrates sensory awareness.

Note. From *A New Window for Looking at Gifted Children* (Rep. No. RM95222, p. 47), by M. M. Frasier, D. Martin, J. Garcia, V. S. Finley, E. Frank, S. Krisel, and L. L. King, 1995, Storrs: University of Connecticut, The National Research Center on the Gifted and Talented. Copyright ©2007 by The National Research Center on the Gifted and Talented. Research for the report was supported under the Javits Act Program (Grant No. R206R00001) as administered by the Office of Educational Research and Improvement, U. S. Department of Education. Grantees understanding such projects are encouraged to express freely their professional judgment. This report, therefore, does not necessarily represent positions or policies of the Government, and no official endorsement should be inferred. This has been reproduced with the permission of The National Research Center on the Gifted and Talented.

widely used screening instrument to help teachers identify learners as gifted and talented. One of the new items they tested was "organizes data and information to discover mathematical patterns" (Renzulli et al., 2009, p. 95). Although this characteristic specifically describes a learner gifted in the area of mathematics, it falls within the core attribute of Reasoning. A characteristic specific to giftedness in reading was "demonstrates tenacity when posted with challenging reading," which falls within the Interest core attribute. Johnsen (2004) included "uses content that is interesting, tells a story, or expresses feelings" as one of the characteristics of learners gifted in art. This is an example of Communication Skills. The core attributes serve as the foundation on which the layer of area of giftedness builds. According to Song and Porath (2006), domain-specific characteristics may come from common cognitive abilities acting in response to domain-specific stimuli. In other words, the foundation of giftedness may be the same, but how giftedness appears may be different due to learners' interests and exposure to different topics and subject areas.

Dual Nature of Strengths

Regardless of the type of giftedness, characteristics of these learners tend to be intense, so they can sometimes be problematic in the classroom or at home. Table 4.2 shows how strengths can potentially be interpreted as or even create problems. Educators and parents should remember that these learners are hardwired this way—it is a part of who they are. Choice comes in how gifted and talented young people handle themselves.

Asynchronous Development

Through the work of numerous researchers and theorists, a great deal has been discovered about the development of children, including what to expect physically, cognitively, socially, and emotionally of a child of a specific age. These four areas of development are interwoven and proceed at a similar rate. Although every child with typical development does not reach the same developmental benchmark at the same time, there are fairly narrow windows and stages through which children develop. For a gifted child, her development is often out of sync with other children her age. Her physical, cognitive, social, and emotional development progress at different rates. This asynchronous development is the basis of the 1991 Columbus Group definition of giftedness:

> Giftedness is asynchronous development in which advanced cognitive abilities and heightened intensity combine to create inner experiences and awareness that are qualitatively different from the norm. This asynchrony increases with higher intellectual capacity. The uniqueness of the gifted renders them particularly vulnerable

Table 4.2
Potential Problems

Strengths	Possible Problems
Acquires and retains information quickly	Impatient with slowness of others; dislikes routine and drill; may resist mastering foundation skills; may make concepts unduly complex
Inquisitive attitude; intellectual curiosity; intrinsic motivation; searches for significance	Asks embarrassing questions; strong willed; excessive in interests; expects same of others
Ability to conceptualize, abstract, synthesize; enjoys problem-solving and intellectual activity	Rejects or omits details; resists practice or drill; questions teaching practices
Can see cause-effect relations	Difficulty accepting the illogical, such as feelings, traditions, matters to be taken on faith
Love of truth, equity, and fair play	Difficulty in being practical; worries about humanitarian concerns
Enjoys organizing things and people into structure and order; seeks to systemize	Constructs complicated rules or systems; may be seen as bossy, rude, or domineering
Large vocabulary and facile verbal proficiency; broad information in advanced areas	May use words to escape or avoid situations; becomes bored with school and age peers; seen by others as a "know-it-all"
Thinks critically; has high expectations; is self-critical and evaluates others	Critical or intolerant toward others; may become discouraged or depressed; perfectionistic
Keen observer; willing to consider the unusual; seeks new experiences	Overly intense focus; may be gullible
Creative and inventive; likes new ways of doing things	May disrupt plans or reject what is already known; seen by others as different and out-of-step
Intense concentration; long attention span in areas of interest; goal-directed behavior; persistent	Resists interruption; neglects duties or people during periods of focused interest; seen as stubborn
Sensitivity, empathy for others; desire to be accepted by others	Sensitivity to criticism or peer rejection; expects others to have similar values; need for success and recognition; may feel different and alienated
High energy, alertness, eagerness; periods of intense efforts	Frustration with inactivity; eagerness may disrupt others' schedules; needs continual stimulation; may be seen as hyperactive
Independent; prefers individualized work; reliant on self	May reject parent or peer input; nonconformist; may be unconventional
Diverse interests and abilities; versatile	May appear scattered and disorganized; becomes frustrated over lack of time; others may expect continual competence
Strong sense of humor	Sees absurdities of situations; humor may not be understood by peers; may become "class clown" to gain attention

Note. From *A Parent's Guide to Gifted Children* (pp. 26–27), by J. T. Webb, J. L. Gore, E. R. Amend, and A. R. DeVries, 2007, Tucson, AZ: Great Potential Press. Copyright 2007 by Great Potential Press. Reprinted with permission.

and requires modifications in parenting, teaching and counseling in order for them to develop optimally.

The concept of asynchronous development of gifted and talented learners is derived from the work of Dabrowski, Hollingworth, Terrassier, and Vygotsky (Silverman, 1997). Essentially, their combined work describes the experiences of learners whose cognitive development is far more advanced than their physical, social, or emotional development, and more advanced than their chronological experience.

Consider the 6-year-old with an IQ of 135 in Table 4.3. This 6-year-old has the mental age of an 8-year-old. He may have the emotional maturity of a 7-year-old, and the social and physical development of his chronological peers. These developmental differences are likely to cause some difficulty for the child. He thinks like an 8-year-old but has the manual dexterity to write like a 6-year-old. It would be very frustrating not to be able to make hands build or write what the mind imagines. As most children's development is even across these areas, society often expects children to behave in ways congruent to how to they talk and think. Children with asynchronous development do not fit this expectation. This 6-year-old talks like an 8-year-old, so those around him will expect him to act like an 8-year-old—even though he only has the life experience and social development of a 6-year-old. Due to his asynchrony and their expectations of synchronous development, adults may be surprised and even disappointed by his behavior when he acts in ways consistent with his chronological age.

Each gifted learner will have a unique pattern of asynchrony. The higher the learner's IQ, the more out of sync she will be: "The greater the degree to which cognitive development outstrips physical development, the more out of sync the child feels internally, in social relations, and in relation to the school curriculum" (Silverman, 2013, p. 32). Imagine a 12-year-old with an IQ of 142 as outlined in Table 4.4. She has a mental age of 17, the life experience and physical ability of a 12-year-old, the social development of a 14-year-old, and the emotional development of a 15-year-old. Consider how difficult it would be to thrive in the milieu of middle school when a person has the analytical skills and awareness of a high school learner, without the benefits of the lived experiences.

If looking at the developmental profile of the gifted athlete, an observer would see a spike in his physical development; his physical ability would be more advanced than his chronological age. He would still have asynchronous development, as his physical development is not occurring at the same rate as his cognitive, social, and emotional development. Figure 4.1 contrasts the synchronous development of average and above-average learners to the asynchronous development of the gifted learner.

Table 4.3
Sample Student

IQ	135
Chronological Age	6
Cognitive Age	8
Physical Age	6
Social Age	6
Emotional Age	7

Table 4.4
Sample Student

IQ	142
Chronological Age	12
Cognitive Age	17
Physical Age	12
Social Age	14
Emotional Age	15

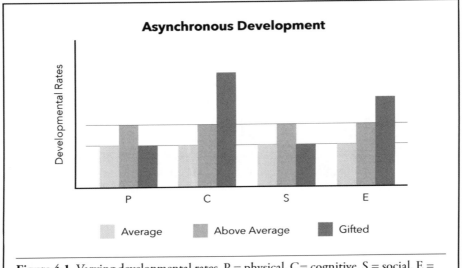

Figure 4.1. Varying developmental rates. P = physical, C= cognitive, S = social, E = emotional development.

Being asynchronous is really difficult in a world where everything is designed around even development. Society constantly groups learners by age in school, in church and community center groups, at camps, and, at least initially, in sports. The learner who doesn't follow this developmental pattern never quite fits with those around her. Children rarely move out of their age groups, other than in sports. In athletics, children are allowed to "play up." It may take an evaluation by several coaches or the athletic governing board, but child athletes are placed at the appropriate instructional and performance level much more readily than in educational settings and with much less controversy.

Asynchronous development can make finding friends difficult. Gifted learners need a variety of friends to match their varied areas of development. This is not unlike the friends adults have. As an adult, it is unlikely the majority of a person's friends are within one year of his age. Adults have friends from work, their neighborhoods, their churches and community centers, and their children's activities and schools. The friends who are the same age are likely to be from the adults' own school experiences. Children, however, are often limited to friends of the same age. Parents must be very mindful of creating opportunities for their gifted children to develop a variety of friendships to meet their children's various levels of development. Gifted children need cognitive friends, friends at the same physical level, at the same social and emotional levels, and friends who have similar interests.

Degrees of Giftedness

Gifted children are often treated like one homogeneous group, but there is as much variability within the group of gifted learners as there is between gifted learners and the general population. For example, "gifted learners may vary among themselves by as much as three standard deviations in respect to mental functioning in one or more areas" (VanTassel-Baska, 2000). The educational needs of the intellectually gifted vary with their degrees of giftedness or how advanced their cognitive development may be. Figure 4.2 shows the statistical distribution of index scores or scores similar to those on an IQ test.

The mean of most ability and IQ tests is considered to be 100. This indicates grade-level mastery, the target point for textbooks, educational standards, and typical classroom instruction. One step away from the mean, or one standard deviation, on most cognitive abilities tests or IQ tests is 15 or 16 points. In Figure 4.2, a standard deviation is 15 points. One step from the mean in each direction is the range from 85 to 115, which includes 68% of the population. Two steps from the mean, the range from 70 to 130, includes 95% of the population. At two steps from average, or two standard deviations from the mean, special educational services typically begin in a very systematic way. Two steps from average is a big enough difference that the system no longer meets a learner's educational needs. Learners who have an IQ of 70 or below are typically eligible for special education services for those with intellectual disabilities. Depending on the researcher and the school district, an IQ of 130 is likely to be one of the requirements to be identified as gifted and talented and eligible for services. (Ideally multiple measures will be used to identify general intellectual giftedness so that a child who scores a 125 may still be identified through additional means even though he missed the cut-off. However, if a child scores above a 140, that is sufficient evidence that the child will need some type of services.) The farther from the mean, the greater is his need. A gifted child's needs comes from his strengths, not his deficiencies (Roberts & Inman, 2015).

A learner who has an IQ of 70 and a learner who has an IQ of 55 have very different educational needs. It is the same for a learner with an IQ of 130 and one with an IQ of 145; they, too, have different educational needs. Degree of giftedness is determined by the level of the learner's ability, how far he or she is from aver-

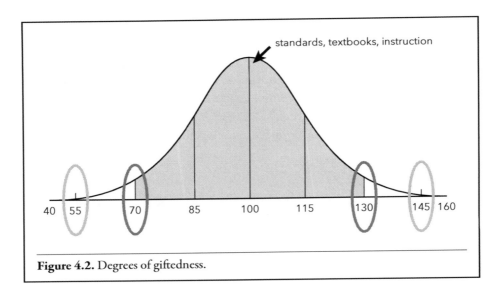

standards, textbooks, instruction

40 55   70   85   100   115   130   145 160

Figure 4.2. Degrees of giftedness.

age. Knowing a gifted learner's degree of giftedness is important because it provides direction as to the level of services the learner may need. A gifted learner's level of advanced cognitive ability affects how quickly he learns. The higher the ability of the child, the faster the pace of the learning and the more readily the child can learn complex content. Degree of giftedness also helps provide perspective on how different the learner is from her same-age peers. These differences make it very important for children to have time grouped with those of like ability and interest.

Gross (2000) defined a range of levels of giftedness as seen in Table 4.5. As IQ increases, the prevalence decreases. The Moderately Gifted are far more likely at the ratio of 44 out of 1,000 people than the Profoundly Gifted, who are fewer than one in a million. Learners who fall into the categories of highly, exceptionally, and profoundly gifted typically reach reading and speech milestones far earlier than their age peers. Unless these students find appropriate peers with whom to relate, it is likely they will appear to not be social (Gross, 2000).

Understanding these differences is essential to providing the appropriate educational setting and pace for gifted learners. The higher the degree of giftedness, the more out of sync a learner's cognitive development will be with his other areas of development. This makes challenging the learner cognitively and academically very difficult in the same classroom and grade level as same-age peers. Gifted learners' advanced cognitive development leads them to learn more rapidly than others. Gifted students learn in fewer presentations of material. Sousa (2003) suggested this may be due to their brains transitioning the new information from one hemisphere to the other "in less time and fewer exposures" (p. 42). This difference makes challenging gifted learners in a heterogeneous classroom very difficult.

Table 4.5
Levels of Giftedness

Mildly Gifted	115–129
Moderately Gifted	130–144
Highly Gifted	145–159
Exceptionally Gifted	160–179
Profoundly Gifted	180+

Note. From Gross (2000).

Culturally, Linguistically, and Economically Diverse Learners

Learners who are linguistically or culturally different from the majority and learners who are economically disadvantaged may exhibit different manifestations of the core attributes than other gifted learners (Olszewski-Kubilius & Clarenbach, 2012). Frasier, Martin, et al. (1995) based their identification system on the assumption that the way learners demonstrate their giftedness is affected by their culture and social context. Learners may demonstrate characteristics of giftedness in areas that are valued by their cultures and may do so largely outside of school. Many learners experience a conflict between the desire to belong and to achieve. (Read more about this in the Stigma of Gifted Paradigm section in Chapter 5.) It can be difficult to balance the varying values and demands within the cultures of school, community, and home. For example, Whiting (2009) stated, "peer pressures effectively place much strain and stress on the motivations and academic identities of gifted Black males" (p. 226). This conflict may lead them to hide their giftedness and avoid gifted programs or refuse services.

Baldwin (2004) suggested that observing everyday performances and considering context are important to identifying traits of gifted learners from underrepresented populations. For example, "the ability to recall and accurately report detailed information on events which occurred in the community can be a sign of high levels of memory skill" (Baldwin, 2004, p. 6). Learners who demonstrate the core attribute of Communication may do so differently depending upon their culture and environment. It may be demonstrated by a learner's remarkable facility with his native language or by the learner's rapid progress in learning English as a second language. It may be demonstrated through a learner's passionate composition and performance of spoken word poetry. Sometimes a learner's core attributes may be manifested in ways that are at odds with the culture of the school or authority. He may use his advanced humor to target an administrator or teacher with whom there is a disagreement or to get the class off track and challenge the teacher's authority. Other learners may display characteristics of giftedness outside of school where they have the freedom to pursue their individual interests. A learner building a computer from scratch or rebuilding a car may not share these projects with school personnel, yet they may still be displaying the core attributes of Motivation and Interest. It is important to think broadly when considering how the core attributes may look in learners. (See the section on Diverse Gifted Learners in this book for more information.)

Dabrowski's Overexcitabilities

The work of Kazimierz Dabrowski adds to our understanding of gifted learners' inherent characteristics and how gifted learners are different from other learners. Dabrowski, a Polish psychiatrist and psychologist, was particularly interested in why some people's personalities developed to the level they would sacrifice everything to help others, while other people never developed beyond being self-serving. His interest developed as a result of his experiences in both World Wars, including being twice imprisoned during World War II. He is the creator of the Theory of Positive Disintegration (also described in Chapter 5), which indicates that to reach very high levels of personality development, one must break down the self and then build it back up. The theory has multiple components and provides an explanation of personality development among the gifted. One of the components is called the overexcitabilities. Overexcitabilities help explain how gifted people experience things more intensely than others; their experience of the world is different. As Piechowski (2013) put it, "Intensities and sensitivities need to be accepted as the child's natural way of experiencing" (p. 112). Dabrowski identified five areas in which gifted people may express this intensity: psychomotor, sensual, intellectual, imaginational, and emotional.

Psychomotor

Many gifted learners have an abundance of physical energy. Their bodies have the need to move as fast as they think. Learners with intensity in this area tend to prefer fast games, move frequently, speak rapidly when excited about an idea, act impulsively, and have trouble quieting their bodies and mind for sleep (Piechowski, 2013). Teachers and parents can accommodate these learners by planning opportunities to move and allowing learners items such as stress balls or special furniture. Students can learn to wiggle and release the energy through small movements that do not distract others (Lind, 2011). It is important not to confuse this trait of gifted learners with Attention Deficit/Hyperactivity Disorder (ADHD). This trait may be characterized by an "extremely high energy level directed toward goals, but not a disorganized, ill-directed flow of energy as would be the case for ADD/ADHD" (Webb et al., 2005, p. 41). Learners demonstrating psychomotor overexcitability can sustain attention for long periods of time when interested in a project or subject.

Sensual

Sensual overexcitability indicates a heightened awareness of any of the five senses: hearing, seeing, touching, smelling, and tasting. Learners with this overexcitability notice things others do not; they may have an intense positive or negative reaction to any or all of these senses. Artists, composers, and chefs benefit from sensitivity in these areas, yet it can be overwhelming to have intense reactions to so many small stimuli in the environment. Teachers and parents can support learners by being aware of the sensitivity and removing offensive or intense smells, tastes, or sounds when possible. Removing tags in clothing or using alternative lighting to fluorescent flickering bulbs can decrease distraction. It is also helpful to teach these learners appropriate stress management strategies (Lind, 2011; Piechowski, 2013; Webb et al., 2005).

Intellectual

This heightened area of energy describes the more stereotypical characteristics of gifted learners: the ever-questioning learner who is not satisfied with "I don't know." Intellectual overexcitability overlaps with several core attributes identified by Frasier, Hunsaker, et al. (1995). Piechowski (2013) described this area of heightened response as "intensified activity of the mind," "passion for probing questions and solving problems," and "reflective thought" (p. 105). The first corresponds to Frasier's core attributes of Motivation, Interest, and Memory. These attributes highlight the deep interest and pursuit of knowledge through sustained efforts, which lead to the large storehouse of knowledge characteristic of gifted learners. Piechowski's description of the drive to problem solve is similar to Frasier's attribute of the same name. In addition, Piechowski lists metacognition, a focus on logic and theory, and "independence of thought" as pieces of "reflective thought" (p. 105). These directly relate to Frasier's Reasoning attribute. Learners high in this area are often concerned with ethical and moral world issues and express a need to help resolve them. Educators and parents can support learners by facilitating the pursuit of answers to questions and encouraging the creation of probing questions. They can also help learners create question journals where questions can be stored to address in time and not be forgotten (Lind, 2011).

Imaginational

This overexcitability corresponds to Frasier's Imagination/Creativity core attribute. Many gifted learners with imaginational excitability have a rich dream life. Their dream worlds can be much more compelling than everyday life. They can imagine extraordinary places, people, and scenarios, and they have vivid dreams, use strong imagery and metaphors, and occasionally mix truth and fiction. Webb et al. (2005) stated that "about three-fourths of gifted children during their pre-school years have one or more imaginary playmates who often have imaginary pets and who live on imaginary planets in imaginary universes" (p. 12). They seek novelty and may daydream in class. Learners need an outlet for their creative thoughts. They need the opportunity to write stories and draw what they see in their internal worlds. Teachers and parents can support learners by honoring the elaborate stories and embellishments added to otherwise routine retellings. Lind (2011) suggested it might "help individuals to differentiate between their imagination and the real world by having them place a stop sign in their mental videotape, or write down or draw the factual account before they embellish it" (para. 10). In addition, it is important to screen news reports, television shows, and movies before learners with this heightened sensitivity are exposed to them, as it can be difficult for them to let go of the images. Establishing positive pre-sleep routines to load learners' imaginations with positive images can be helpful along with relaxation techniques to quiet their minds (Piechowski, 2013).

Emotional

Gifted students are often very sensitive emotionally. They have more intense reactions than others and seem to overreact on a regular basis. The emotional over-excitability is characterized by intense empathy and strong attachment to people, places, and things. These learners empathize with others at a very young age, taking on the feelings and pain of others, sometimes without being aware of it. Change can be very difficult due to the emotional attachments the learners develop. Part of the sensitivity includes physical reactions to emotions, such as blushing or upset stomachs. Teachers and parents can help learners by assisting them in developing a feeling vocabulary. Helping learners identify the range of emotions they experience as well as the complexity of them can be soothing. It is important to accept and acknowledge learners' feelings without criticism, as what seems to be an overreaction is their real experience. It is useful to help students learn to anticipate when they may have a strong emotional response to something or to connect a physical symptom to the related emotion (Lind, 2011; Piechowski, 2013).

As with other traits or characteristics, all gifted learners do not exhibit all of Dabrowski's overexcitabilities; granted, these characteristics are more prevalent in gifted learners than in others. Understanding and recognizing these traits as part of giftedness is essential to providing a supportive and appropriate learning environment for gifted learners. These traits bring many learners heightened experiences that are positive and rewarding, particularly when they are recognized and valued. Teaching learners about their heightened sensitivities helps them cope with their experiences and see the positive aspects of experiencing the world in such an intense way.

Conclusion

Gifted and talented learners are a population that requires special services within their educational settings. Understanding their characteristics and needs is essential to understanding how to support them in the classroom and at home. Gifted and talented learners have a different developmental pattern than their same-age peers. Their physical, cognitive, social, and emotional development are often out of sync with one another. This asynchrony affects all aspects of their lives, from their readiness to learn in specific subject areas to their interactions with peers and adults. Gifted and talented students are not a homogeneous group. Each learner has an individual pattern of asynchronous development, and gifted learners vary in their degrees of giftedness. Gifted learners' educational needs vary by how gifted they are or, in other words, how advanced their cognitive development is compared to age-peers. They need instruction that matches their levels of giftedness. Although each gifted learner is an individual, there are core attributes that present across the group. These core attributes may be manifested differently due to differences in learners' backgrounds, experiences, and cultural norms. Understanding the core attributes helps teachers identify potentially gifted and talented learners and better meet their needs in the classroom. In addition to the core attributes, gifted and talented learners tend to respond to small stimuli in intense ways. These intensities, or overexcitabilities (in the areas of psychomotor, sensual, intellectual, imaginational, and emotional), impact how gifted learners experience and react to the world. Teachers and parents must understand these intensities to avoid misinterpreting learners' behaviors and to provide environments that build on the positive aspects of these sensitivities. Understanding who gifted and talented learners are and their needs provides teachers the foundation on which to build the expertise needed to provide the services and learning environments needed for gifted and talented learners to flourish.

Big Ideas

1. Gifted learners differ from others in ways that affect how they experience the world, how they learn, and what their needs are in the classroom.

2. Understanding traits, aptitudes, behaviors, and intensities can help educators and parents support gifted learners as they learn and grow. These characteristics address false claims that everyone is gifted, as the majority of learners do not share these traits or experience the world in the same way.

Big Ideas, *Continued.*

3. The word *gift* refers to people's strengths, while *gifted and talented* is a professional term describing learners with traits and intensities that result in their learning and experiencing the world differently from others.

4. Gifted and talented learners have asynchronous development in which their physical, cognitive, social, and emotional development are not in sync. This asynchronous development leads to challenges in several parts of gifted learners' lives, as our schools and communities are designed to meet the needs of learners who have more even development in these areas.

5. Within the population of gifted and talented learners, there is great variation. Understanding a learner's degree of giftedness is important to providing appropriate educational experiences and social/emotional support.

6. Students' needs for special educational services vary by how much their cognitive ability varies from that of the typical student. The more advanced or impaired a student's cognitive ability is, the greater the student's need for the modification to the regularly provided educational content, setting, and strategies.

7. Gifted and talented learners share core traits, aptitudes, and behaviors that are characteristic of gifted learners. The manifestation of the traits, or how they may be demonstrated, varies greatly based on learners' areas of giftedness, interest, cultural background, language, and economic opportunities.

8. Gifted and talented learners tend to be more intense and sensitive than others. Dabrowski's overexcitabilities help to explain how gifted learners experience the world more intensely than others.

9. Gifted students need a range of friends that meet their various developmental levels and interests.

Discussion Questions

1. Consider a student from an affluent neighborhood who regularly attends summer camps and travels on family vacations and a student who lives in an inner-city apartment complex whose parents work two jobs. How might these students display the core attributes of motivation, memory, and problem solving differently?

Discussion Questions, *Continued*

2. How might a school accommodate the asynchronous development of a student whose birthday indicates he should be in third grade, who is ready for fifth-grade math and fourth-grade science, yet is on grade level for reading and social studies?

3. In what ways can teachers and parents help gifted learners develop friendships that are based on interests, not age?

4. Describe someone you know who displays characteristics described by Dabrowski's overexcitabilities. How does that person cope with her sensitivities? How do others view those intensities?

References

Baldwin, A. Y. (2004). I'm Black but look at me, I am also gifted. In A. Y. Baldwin & S. M. Reis (Eds.), *Culturally diverse and underserved populations of gifted students* (pp. 1–9). Thousand Oaks, CA: Corwin Press.

Columbus Group. (1991, July). *Unpublished transcript of the meeting of the Columbus Group.* Columbus, OH: Author. Retrieved from http://www.gifteddevelopment.com/isad/columbus-group

Frasier, M. M., Hunsaker, S. L., Lee, J., Mitchell, S., Cramond, B., Krisel, S., . . . Finley, V. S. (1995). *Core attributes of giftedness: A foundation for recognizing the gifted potential of minority and economically disadvantaged students* (RM95210). Storrs: University of Connecticut, The National Research Center on the Gifted and Talented.

Frasier, M. M., Martin, D., Garcia, J., Finley, V. S., Frank, E., Krisel, S., & King, L. L. (1995). *A new window for looking at gifted children* (RM95222). Storrs: University of Connecticut, The National Research Center on the Gifted and Talented.

Gross, M. U. M. (2000). Exceptionally and profoundly gifted students: An underserved population. *Understanding Our Gifted, 12,* 3–9.

Johnsen, S. K. (Ed.). (2004). *Identifying gifted students: A practical guide.* Waco, TX: Prufrock Press.

Lind, S. (2011). *Overexcitability and the gifted.* Retrieved from http://sengifted.org/archives/articles/overexcitability-and-the-gifted

Marland, S. P., Jr. (1972). *Education of the gifted and talented: Report to the Congress of the United States by the U. S. Commissioner of Education: Vol. 1.* Washington DC: U.S. Government Printing Office.

Mill, J. S. (1869). *On liberty.* London, England: Longman, Roberts and Green.

National Association for Gifted Children. (2010). *Redefining giftedness for a new century: Shifting the paradigm.* Retrieved from http://www.nagc.org/sites/default/files/Position%20Statement/Redefining%20Giftedness%20for%20a%20New%20Century.pdf

National Association for Gifted Children. (n.d.) *Traits of giftedness.* Retrieved from https://www.nagc.org/resources-publications/resources/my-child-gifted/common-characteristics-gifted-individuals/traits

Olszewski-Kubilius, P., & Clarenbach, J. (2012). *Unlocking emerging talent: Supporting high achievement of low-income, high-ability students.* Washington DC: National Association for Gifted Children.

Piechowski, M. M. (2013). "A bird who can soar": Overexcitabilities in the gifted. In C. S. Neville, M. M. Piechowski, & S. S. Tolan (Eds.), *Off the charts: Asynchrony and the gifted child* (pp. 99–122). Unionville, NY: Royal Fireworks Press.

Renzulli, J. S., Siegle, D., Reis, S. M., Gavin, M. K., & Reed, R. E. (2009). An investigation of the reliability and factor structure of four new scales for Rating the Behavioral Characteristics of Superior Students. *Journal of Advanced Academics, 21,* 84–108.

Roberts, J. L., & Inman, T. F. (2015). *Assessing differentiated student products: A protocol for development and evaluation* (2nd ed.). Waco, TX: Prufrock Press.

Silverman, L. K. (1997). The construct of asynchronous development. *Peabody Journal of Education, 72*(3–4), 36–58. Retrieved from http://www.positivedisintegration.com/Silverman1997.pdf

Silverman, L. K. (2013). Asynchronous development: Theoretical bases and current applications. In C. S. Neville, M. M. Piechowski, & S. S. Tolan (Eds.), *Off the charts: Asynchrony and the gifted child* (pp. 18–47). Unionville, NY: Royal Fireworks Press.

Song, K., & Porath, M. (2006). Common and domain-specific cognitive characteristics of gifted students: An integrated model of human abilities. *High Ability Studies, 16,* 229–246.

Sousa, D. A. (2003). *How the gifted brain learns.* Thousand Oaks, CA: Corwin Press.

Thompson, M. C. (1998). *"Is everyone gifted?"* Retrieved from https://www.rfwp.com/pages/is-everyone-gifted-in-their-own-way

Title V, Part D. [Jacob K. Javits Gifted and Talented Students Education Act of 1988], Elementary and Secondary Education Act of 1988 (2002), 20 U.S.C. sec. 7253 et seq.

VanTassel-Baska, J. (2000). The on-going dilemma of effective identification practices in gifted education. *The Communicator, 31.* Williamsburg, VA: William & Mary, Center for Gifted Education. Retrieved from http://education.wm.edu/centers/cfge/_documents/resources/articles/ongoingdilemma.pdf

Webb, J. T., Amend, E. R., Webb, N. E., Goerss, J., Beljan, P., & Olenchak, F. R. (2005). *Misdiagnosis and dual diagnoses of gifted children and adults: ADHD, bipolar, OCD, Asperger's, depression, and other disorders.* Scottsdale, AZ: Great Potential Press.

Webb, J. T., Gore, J. L., Amend, E. R., & DeVries, A. R. (2007). *A parent's guide to gifted children.* Tucson, AZ: Great Potential Press.

Whiting, G. (2009). Gifted Black males: Understanding and decreasing barriers to achievement and identity. *Roeper Review, 31,* 224–233. doi:10.1080/02783190903177598

CHAPTER 5

Social and Emotional Development of Students With Gifts and Talents

Tracy L. Cross, Lori Andersen,
Sakhavat Mammadov, and Jennifer Riedl Cross

Understanding that children have an inner life means acknowledging "a person's experience is what the world is to that person."
—Coleman & Cross (2000, p. 211)

Essential Questions to Guide the Reader

1. What common characteristics of children with gifts and talents affect their social and emotional development?

2. How do the interactions of these students with their environment affect their social and emotional development?

3. How does the lived experience of students with gifts and talents affect their social and emotional development?

This chapter focuses on the social and emotional development of students with gifts and talents by illustrating the relationship between characteristics and their interaction in different contexts. From the lived experiences of this combination of relationships, a gifted student's life becomes idiosyncratic, so to depict his social and emotional development requires information about three things: characteristics (endogenous), interaction of the characteristics with the environment (exogenous), and the lived experience.

Cohen, Onunaku, Clothier, and Poppe (2005) described healthy social and emotional development as "a child's developing capacity to experience, manage and express the full range of positive and negative emotions; develop close, satisfying relationships with other children and adults; and actively explore their environment and learn" (p. 2). Social and emotional development represents the changes over time of two separate but related constructs that reflect characteristics, interactions, interpretations, and related behaviors in the lives of people that lead them to becoming adults. It includes the awareness, interpretations, and regulations of stimuli and events. As people develop, they become increasingly sophisticated and versatile when dealing with social and/or emotional experiences. In some cases, gifted children have unique characteristics and interactions with others, both of which may lead to unexpected interpretations and behaviors. In this chapter, we will describe theories and research that can help put the social and emotional development of gifted children into perspective.

Psychosocial Development

No person develops in a vacuum. Each one is the product of biology (nature) and experiences (nurture). Erikson (1963) proposed that psychological development progresses stage-like through a person's interactions with others. Erikson's theory of psychosocial development describes the challenges or *crises* people living in Western societies face across the lifespan. The lifespan emphasis of his theory was quite unique for its time. At each stage of life, people experience similar crises (see Table 5.1). If satisfactorily resolved, a person incorporates the lessons learned into her personal repertoire and successfully moves to the next level. If not, the issue can create challenges for the individual across his life. As humans, gifted individuals face these crises just as their peers do. From them, they internalize who they are in the social world.

All students must grapple with these psychosocial crises as described by Erikson (1963). As gifted young people experience each stage, they will face situations similar to those of their peers. However, their exceptional abilities may make some issues more difficult. For example, the verbally precocious 2-year-old may be ready to take more initiative than adults may expect, creating strife and possibly guilt in the child who progresses through the stages earlier than her peers. Likewise, the gifted young person with multipotentiality may experience more role confusion than his average peers. It may be more difficult for gifted young people to find intimacy among their nongifted peers, leading to a greater sense of isolation. It can be useful to consider each of Erikson's stages when planning instruction or engaging in formal or informal counseling with gifted young people or their caregivers.

Erikson's (1963) theory of psychosocial development offers an explanation for how circumstances (crises) individuals face can affect their social and emotional

Table 5.1

Erikson's Stages of Psychosocial Development (Erikson, 1963)

Approximate Age	Crisis to Be Resolved
0–1 ½	Trust vs. Mistrust
1 ½–3	Autonomy vs. Shame and Doubt
3–5	Initiative vs. Guilt
6–11	Industry vs. Inferiority
Adolescent	Identity vs. Role Confusion
Early Adult	Intimacy vs. Isolation
Middle Adult	Generativity vs. Stagnation
Late Adult	Ego-integrity vs. Despair

development. The malleable minds of gifted young people are being shaped by the experiences they have at each stage of development.

Dabrowski's Theory of Positive Disintegration

Another theory, Kazimierz Dabrowski's (1964) Theory of Positive Disintegration (TPD), has been widely regarded as having particular value in understanding the social and emotional development of gifted individuals. This theory explains differences in *personality*—a characteristic found within the person (endogenous)—that affect how people behave. Dabrowski created his TPD to explain differences in the behaviors of highly gifted and creative people, as well as the behaviors of ruthless leaders. Although most theories of advanced development primarily rely on intelligence, TPD relies on his definition of personality. He described personality as a psychological state that includes a personal value system and specific forces that drive behavior. He offered this as the explanation of why some people are more likely to achieve advanced personality development than others (development potential).

In the TPD, personality has five levels, as noted in Table 5.2. Primary integration is the lowest level, which is the starting point for everyone. Individuals at this level do not have their own value system and make decisions based on instinct or impulse. The development of a personal value system is a primary task of personality development and is called *multilevelness*. As individuals transition through Levels III and IV, they begin to consider other reasons for choices, such as how choices affect others. They are able to be more autonomous, act in accordance with personal ideals, and put these personal ideals above a need for societal approval or impulse. At the highest level, secondary integration, individuals live according to personal ideals.

Table 5.2
Personality Levels in TPD

Classification	Level	Descriptions
Unilevel	I–Primary Integration	Decisions are driven by impulse and instinct.
	II–Unilevel Disintegration	Decisions are driven by societal expectations.
Multilevel	III–Spontaneous Multilevel Disintegration	Decisions are driven by inner conflict about bringing behavior up to an ideal.
	IV–Organized Multilevel Disintegration	Through high levels of responsibility, authenticity, reflective judgment, empathy, autonomy, and self-awareness, decisions are driven by inner forces and values.
	V–Secondary Integration	By living according to the highest, most universal principles, self-actualization is achieved.

Note. Adapted from *The Theory of Positive Disintegration by Kazimierz Dabrowski* by B. Tillier, 1995, http://www.positivedisintegration.com/10concepts.html#ml.

The most important distinction between personality levels in TPD is multilevelness. For a *unilevel* personality, all personal choices seem to have equal value. A *multilevel* personality has an internal, hierarchical system of values that gives certain options higher values than others. Different forces, or dynamisms, dominate decisions at low and high personality levels. For low-level personality, decisions are driven by impulse and instinct, while for high-level personality, decisions are driven by inner voices and internal values. Dabrowski believed that only 35% of people achieved multilevelness and that multilevelness was more often present in highly gifted and creative people.

The Theory of Positive Disintegration explains how and why this development occurs. One difference between TPD and other developmental theories is that personality development is not universal; most people will not reach multilevelness. Dabrowski (1964) explained that personality development was a breakdown, or disintegration, of previously existing psychological structures that allowed the individual to examine his or her own values, emotions, and behavior. The phrase *positive disintegration* is used because the outcome of the disintegration process is a positive one—an advanced personality. Disintegration describes inner conflict and discontent with one's life compared to personal ideals. During disintegration, individuals experience distress and anxiety. A time period of disintegration is a natural part of the process of development.

Developmental potential explains why some people reach multilevelness and others do not. High developmental potential has three characteristics: (a) special abilities and talents, (b) certain overexcitabilities, and (c) a strong drive to be autonomous. *Overexcitabilities*, or responses to stimuli that are higher than average, occur in different sensory channels: emotional, imaginational, intellectual, psychomotor, and sensual. Table 5.3 provides a description of each type of overexcitability. (See Chapter 4 for additional information on overexcitabilities.)

Research findings regarding advanced developmental potential and gifted students are somewhat mixed (Mendaglio, 2012). Students with gifts and talents possess special abilities and talents, characteristic of developmental potential. However, comparisons of overexcitabilities in these learners with other students have had inconsistent findings. High intellectual ability does not generally coincide with high levels of intellectual overexcitability. This is probably not surprising to most teachers. Every teacher has likely observed students who have high cognitive abilities, but who are not passionate about intellectual pursuits. A student who has an intellectual overexcitability is one who derives pleasure from learning. Therefore, a student with high intellectual overexcitability is likely to be intellectually gifted, but not all intellectually gifted students will have high intellectual overexcitability.

Research on highly creative adults revealed stronger associations between creative and artistic talents and levels of emotional and imaginational overexcitabilities (Mendaglio & Tillier, 2006). Fewer studies have investigated the developmental potential or personality levels of gifted children or adults. Most research in this area has focused on measuring the overexcitabilities and comparing gifted and nongifted groups (Tillier, 2009). However, the overexcitabilities are not the only indicator of developmental potential. The third characteristic of developmental potential, the drive to be autonomous, has yet to be studied.

Although the research base is weak, those who subscribe to the theory find explanations for the intensities they observe among gifted children and for the development of personal values and decision making. Gifted students may see similarities in their experience and Dabrowski's proposed overexcitabilities, the positive disintegration process, and personality development. Discussing the lives of highly gifted and creative individuals who exemplify multilevelness and exploring their overexcitabilities can help gifted students to accept and appreciate their own experiences and development. Knowledge of the positive disintegration process can help students make sense of their inner conflicts and feel less different from other people.

Endogenous Characteristics

The combination of Erikson's (1963) Theory of Psychosocial Development and Dabrowski's (1964) Theory of Positive Disintegration lead to understanding how a gifted child is developing an inner life, a sense of personal agency, locus of control, perspectives, and values that guide one's behavior. One must also consider a number

Table 5.3
Overexcitabilities and Developmental Potential

	Overexcitability	**Description**
Increases developmental potential	Emotional	Intensity of feeling, strong affective memory, anxiety, fear
	Imaginational	Vivid imagery, invention, animated visualization, metaphor, fantasy
	Intellectual	Questioning, problem solving, theoretical thinking, sustained intellectual effort, derives pleasure from intellectual pursuits
Lowers developmental potential	Psychomotor	High degrees of energy, pursuits of intense physical activity
	Sensual	Intensity and craving for pleasure via sights, smells, tastes, textures, and sounds

Note. Adapted from Mendaglio (2012).

of characteristics gifted children bring to the development process. In some cases, all students who are gifted and talented are affected, but in others, only some are.

Asynchronous Development

All gifted children will experience some level of asynchronous development (see Chapter 4 for details), when their cognitive abilities develop out of sync with other dimensions of their development, such as their physical, social, and emotional abilities (Silverman, 2012). The asynchronies may be only minor, as in the child who begins to read at an early age, or dramatic, as in the child with verbal abilities at the college level while still an elementary student. The greater the asynchrony, the more difficulty the gifted child will have in negotiating Erikson's crises or determining what is an appropriate level of responsibility in the process of positive disintegration. Advanced cognitive abilities can lead adults interacting with gifted children to believe that they should have similarly advanced emotion regulation. When gifted children "act their age" emotionally, it may be seen as inappropriate behavior from someone who is cognitively advanced. Experiences that bring asynchronous development to the fore can influence the social and emotional development of gifted children.

Personality

Dabrowski was not alone in his interest in personality. In his early studies, Terman (1925) had a keen interest in the personality characteristics of gifted children. In his study of 1,528 geniuses (primarily Caucasian from professional class families), Terman found that they were well adjusted socially and possessed above-average physical health, eagerness, and curiosity. Olszewski-Kubilius and Kulieke (1989) studied personality constellations in gifted youth and compared this group to a same-aged norming group. The gifted group had higher emotional stability, dominance, cheerfulness, conformity, warmth, and self-sufficiency, and lower apprehension and tension. The contemporary five-factor model—comprising neuroticism, extraversion, openness to experience, agreeableness, and conscientiousness—provides the most comprehensive theoretical framework for understanding the basic personality dimensions (McCrae & Costa, 1996). Within the Big Five framework, intelligence has been documented to have the most consistent links to openness to experience and neuroticism. Higher intelligence and giftedness have been associated with a greater openness to new experiences (e.g., Goff & Ackerman, 1992; Zeidner & Shani-Zinovich, 2011) and, to some degree, with greater emotional stability (e.g., Ackerman & Heggestad, 1997; DeYoung, 2011), and a preference for introversion (i.e., 47.7% gifted versus 35% nongifted; Sak, 2004).

Personality is an enduring, relatively stable endogenous characteristic. Educators of gifted children may expect a greater likelihood of introversion among their students. This tendency may best be served by allowing quiet spaces and times and reducing the overall level of stimulation for students who struggle with crowds, loud noises, and other stimuli. One can expect that introverted gifted individuals will not thrive in environments that are geared toward the majority of extroverts in modern U.S. society. However, there will be gifted young people who would be considered extroverts. Such personality differences should be not be ignored in education settings.

Perfectionism

Perfectionism is another endogenous characteristic, one that may interfere with the positive social and emotional development of gifted children. The construct of perfectionism has received considerable attention over the past 25 years. Conceptions of perfectionism have moved from a single-faceted, always-detrimental phenomenon to a multifaceted phenomenon (see Fletcher & Speirs Neumeister, 2012, for a review). Based on the substantial research base, it is clear that not all forms of perfectionism are negative. Speirs Neumeister (2015) emphasized the distinction between the two core factors of *positive striving* and *evaluative concerns*. Students with high levels of positive striving (self-oriented or adaptive or healthy perfectionists) often have similarly high levels of self-esteem and an internal locus of control (Speirs Neumeister, 2015). When paired with high levels of evaluative concern, however, the positive outcomes of self-oriented perfectionism turn negative.

Perceived pressure from parents, teachers, and even peers to always be correct, to always be the best, can foster a belief that one must be perfect because others demand it. This *socially prescribed perfectionism* (Hewitt & Flett, 1991) has been associated with multiple negative outcomes, including suicidal behaviors (Cross & Cross, in press; Hewitt, Flett, & Turnbull-Donovan, 1992). The perception that others expect perfection may not be accurate, but beliefs are an important driver of behaviors. When gifted young people come to believe that they are only valued to the extent that they perform, their academic goals may be based on a fear of failure. Not enjoying the learning process can cause students to underachieve, drop out of school, or pursue an easier path in school. All of these issues can make life as a gifted child in school very difficult.

Excessive Self-Criticism

Excessive self-criticism is a learned phenomenon wherein a person becomes too critical of him- or herself (Cross, 1997), typically related to a dissatisfaction with actual performance compared to an idealized performance. For example, it is not uncommon to witness a 7-year-old gifted child wad up a picture she is coloring and begin again because it is not as ideal as she envisioned. These experiences can create anger and frustration. An outcome of being excessively self-critical is depression (Genshaft, Greenbaum, & Borovsky, 1995; Webb, 1993). Because excessive self-criticism is learned, it can be unlearned. Professional counselors can be helpful in cognitive retraining, much as they might in the case of phobias.

Multipotentiality

Multipotentiality, having the potential to become exceptional at more than one thing, is a positive characteristic made problematic by its interactions within contexts. It has been seen as both a negative, when it becomes problematic for educational and social development (e.g., Delisle & Squires, 1989; Kerr, 1991), and a positive, when it produces confidence and options (e.g., Sajjadi, Rejskind, & Shore, 2001; Sosniak, 1985). The majority of the research has focused on the negative impact of multipotentiality and the difficulties caused by delay or inability to commit to a career path (Rysiew, Shore, & Leeb, 1999).

When multiple talents become evident, the gifted child's family is often the first influence determining what talent the child values. One area of exceptional ability may be favored over another, or none of their potentials—or all—may be encouraged or discouraged. The financial and time costs of developing differing talents vary widely, so early decisions affect the family immensely. If the talent area is something that the local school develops, costs may be far less and more convenient relative to transportation and family commitment. Decisions to support the potential may need to be made early (e.g., violin) and may require considerable expertise on the part of the parent to nurture the student. Many of the same issues affect gifted children while they attend school. For example, becoming a basketball player may include early training in school, with more serious training out of school in the off-season. Training can often take place locally, whereas another domain, such as gymnastics, is typically taught outside of school and requires relatively expensive training and access to specific facilities often not located in the local community where the family lives. Thus, a person's talent domain may or may not be an issue based on access to facilities, experts, coaches and teachers, and practice time.

The more serious issues emerge when decisions favoring one area over the other are made. Societal prejudices may emerge, such as gender bias, racial bias, socioeconomic limitations, access issues, and so forth. In some cases, choices to develop a talent area are affected by society's prejudices. For example, boys becoming dancers or girls playing football are areas in which society's gender expectations limit opportunities. Students with multipotentiality may need more assistance to learn about career choices, with opportunities to shadow or intern as they explore their many options. Linking talent development opportunities to personal values, particularly as they relate to lifestyle preferences, can help multipotential gifted young people recognize priorities in choosing which talents to develop (Rysiew et al., 1999).

On Being Gifted in School

The previous descriptions of Erikson's (1963) Theory of Psychosocial Development and Dabrowski's (1964) Theory of Positive Disintegration and the endogenous characteristics of asynchronous development, personality, perfectionism, excessive self-criticism, and multipotentiality contribute to understanding of the social and emotional development of gifted young people. The picture is not complete, however, unless we consider exogenous (external) influences on their development. Schools, in particular, have great potential to affect students' social and emotional development.

Complexities of Schools

Because schools are inherently social enterprises that attempt to accommodate a very wide range of ages, many developmental stages, and a multitude of cultures, attending school as a gifted young person is inherently complicated. From teachers, principals, and counselors, to parents and even fellow students—nearly everyone holds deep-seated beliefs of giftedness that affect their interactions with gifted young people. Complicating matters even more is the fact that few educators are likely to have had training in gifted education. Consequently, being gifted in school settings tends to be replete with issues that may affect students' social and emotional development.

Lived Experience of Giftedness

Schools are representative of the societies in which they exist. They serve as a society's primary institution for transmitting its culture. Intellectuals are often seen as challenging the dominant culture and social mores. The United States has been described as anti-intellectual, with schools reflecting that value (Howley, Howley, & Pendarvis, 2017). With the mistrust of intellectuals generally and the anti-intellectual nature of U.S. schools more specifically, being a gifted child can be complicated and confusing. Given the wide-ranging academic conceptions and implicit theories of giftedness, most gifted young people receive mixed messages about giftedness (Coleman & Cross, 1988, 2000). As a result, a central component to the experience of being a gifted child is the need to determine the degree of acceptance and support one feels in the school environment, at home, at church, and so forth, and act in accordance. At times, the community's lack of support will conflict with a student's positive social and emotional development.

As gifted children mature into late elementary or middle school, social matters emerge as a central aspect of their development. Typically, the adults in their lives have taught them that differing environments require different comportment. For example, riding in elevators, attending church, or going to sports events requires/tolerates differing manifestations of behavior. When young gifted children become more socially aware, they deal with typical psychosocial issues common to virtually all children in Western societies. The need to feel special while also needing to feel accepted as the same and the need to stand out while at the same time desiring to blend in are common issues of development. Being identified as gifted can limit the perceived acceptance and, therefore, social latitude these learners feel. This phenomenon has been titled the stigma of giftedness (Coleman, 1985; Coleman & Cross, 1988, 2000), and the Stigma of Giftedness Paradigm (SGP) was created to study the phenomenon.

Stigma of Giftedness Paradigm

According to Coleman (1985, 2012), the Stigma of Giftedness Paradigm has three parts:

- Gifted students want to have normal social interactions.
- They learn that when others find out about their giftedness, they will be treated differently.
- They learn that they can manage information about themselves that will enable them to maintain a greater amount of social latitude.

As noted, gifted young people want normal social interactions. In this paradigm, there is not a generic expectation of normal. Introverted gifted students often prefer interactions with a single friend over large gatherings, whereas more extroverted gifted young people usually prefer the large gathering. Both situations would be normal. At home, gifted young people have been taught that it is appropriate to behave differently in differing situations. Gifted individuals do not want to lose social latitude, so they become aware of that possibility when others know about their exceptional abilities. Therefore, they determine that they can maintain the greatest degree of social latitude by managing the information they share with others.

Considerable research has been conducted on the lived experience of giftedness in school (Coleman, Micko, & Cross, 2015). For example, the Information Management Model (IMM; Coleman & Cross, 1988), shown in Figure 5.1, illustrates the social awareness of gifted children and how they attempt to develop the social latitude they desire. Children are acculturated to recognize that different environments have varied social expectations. The IMM describes the point at which a child enters these different environments and must make sense of them. At point "A" the child feels different ("Yes") or does not feel different from peers ("No") in the environment. If he feels different, a choice is made at point "B" to manage information about the self to cope with the differentness ("Yes") or not ("No"). At point "C" we see a child engaging in various strategies such as those described below.

When asked if they feel different from or the same as their nongifted peers, more than 85% of gifted and talented students in Cross, Coleman, and Terhaar-Yonkers' (1991) study indicated feeling different. The same percentage of students reported that they manage information about themselves through social coping mechanisms. Among the few students who reported feeling the same as their nongifted peers, most also gave examples of how they were, in fact, different. The same pattern emerged when they were asked if they managed information about themselves. After saying that they did not, virtually all gave examples of social coping behavior (Coleman & Cross, 1988). Denial of differences is inherently a coping behavior. These interviews with the gifted students led to the creation of the IMM.

From gifted young people's responses to questions, the researchers learned that the social goals they create for themselves fell into one of three categories: Standing Out, Invisibility, or Disidentifying. These categories of social goals were established as a continuum of visibility (Coleman & Cross, 1988; see Figure 5.2). Among the gifted young people who felt different and had managed information, all desired to reach one of these three social goal categories.

Cross and colleagues (1991) estimated that fewer than 5% of gifted students attempt to bring attention to themselves as gifted—"Standing Out." The second goal is to be Invisible among the school population, to blend in with others. This is done by wearing popular clothes, listening to popular music, talking like others, and so forth. Cross et al. estimated that approximately 70% of gifted individuals desire to blend in. Common strategies for becoming invisible include not admitting that

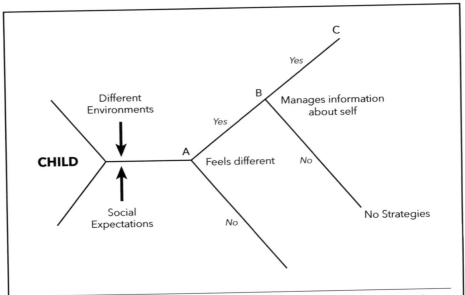

Figure 5.1. Information Management Model. From "Is being gifted a social handicap?" (p. 44) by L. J. Coleman and T. L. Cross, 1988, *Journal for the Education of the Gifted, 11.* Copyright 1988, The Association for the Gifted. Reprinted with permission of the author.

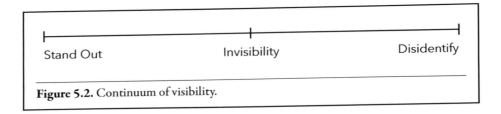

Figure 5.2. Continuum of visibility.

a test was easy, not volunteering answers, missing a few items on a test, and when asked about accomplishments, being noncommittal (Coleman, 1985).

The last goal on the continuum is to Disidentify with gifted students. An estimated 25% of gifted individuals who engage in social coping hold this goal (Cross et al., 1991). To that end, one can hang around groups of students who in the school would be stereotyped as not being gifted. Other social coping behaviors engaged in to reach this goal include telling jokes, claiming a test was difficult, feigning interest in small talk, making fun of other gifted kids, and going out for extracurricular activities for which one has little talent (Coleman, 1985).

In sum, due to the very complicated social environment of schools relative to giftedness, most gifted young people engage in social coping behaviors to create and maintain the social latitude to which they aspire. Most of the behaviors are relatively innocuous, although some are negative and a few possibly positive. Hiding oneself, avoiding interactions, and avoiding working on passions can be harmful in the social development of the gifted young person. Standing out somewhat brazenly as one who enjoys learning carries with it considerable social sanctions, as these gifted individuals are often made fun of or not included in social opportunities. Therefore, these behaviors may stifle social development. Some coping behaviors can have positive outcomes. For example, reading more in lieu of other experiences may become a lifetime recreation of choice, leading to increasing knowledge and enjoyment. When the environment is accepting of differences, including differences in academic ability, learners who are gifted and talented will not need to alter their behaviors to find the positive social experiences all children need.

Conclusion

Although they may be exceptional in their interests and abilities, gifted children are children first. All children need to feel connected to others, need opportunities to explore their interests, and need to find out what they can do (Deci & Ryan, 2000). Erikson's (1963) theory of psychosocial development applies to all learners, but it must be interpreted in the context of a child developing with exceptional abilities. Dabrowski's (1964) Theory of Positive Disintegration attempts to explain development of gifted individuals. The endogenous characteristics of asynchronous development, personality, perfectionism, excessive self-criticism, and multipotentiality are unique to this population. Only by recognizing the significance of their exceptionalities in context can educators adequately support the social and emotional development of students with gifts and talents.

Big Ideas

1. Gifted children will experience the same psychosocial crises as their nongifted peers. They may encounter these crises earlier.

2. Gifted children may relate their own experiences to the Theory of Positive Disintegration as they go through the stages of personality development.

3. All gifted children will exhibit some form of asynchronous development. The greater the asynchrony, the greater the challenges to their social and emotional development.

4. A higher proportion of gifted children than their nongifted peers has a tendency toward introversion. Their preference for reduced stimulation may be misunderstood by more extroverted peers and adults.

Big Ideas, *Continued.*

5. Being overly concerned with the perceived opinions of others affects the social and emotional development of gifted young people.

6. Multipotentiality can create a dilemma for the child, particularly when choices must be made to pursue one activity over other, equally attractive options.

7. Gifted children often receive mixed messages from teachers, counselors, and school administrators about their exceptional abilities.

8. Gifted children need positive social interactions; the Stigma of Giftedness Paradigm argues that they sometimes choose to manage the information others have about their exceptional abilities in order to have what they perceive as normal interactions.

Discussion Questions

1. Quite often people use the terms *social* and *emotional* as a single construct. How do you distinguish between the two? Are they equally important in the well-being of gifted students?

2. We have learned that people continue to develop over time. We have also learned of the construct of *asynchronous development*. What are some of the common ways in which students with gifts and talents are affected by asynchronous developmental patterns? How can these affect the classroom?

3. Have you ever received mixed messages from people about giftedness and gifted people? If so, how did you feel about it? Now, imagine a 15-year-old girl who faces these mixed messages on a daily basis. Add gender expectations, expectations associated with ethnicity, and the perceived expectations for consistent excellent performance in school. What steps might she take to create a reasonable life for herself?

4. Quite often adults talk about what they enjoy doing and are good at. For example, fishing, camping, cooking, sewing, athletic activities, and so forth are common hobbies. Often missing from this list are academic examples. Why might that be the case? What are some of the ramifications of this for the adults and for their children?

Discussion Questions, *Continued.*

5. Despite the numerous ways in which children vary (e.g., motivation, personality, passions, psychosocial development), some will argue it is in the students' interest to treat them exactly the same. Do you agree? Is sameness fairness? Is sameness equitable?

6. Everyone has to wait as part of existing within differing social contexts. How much waiting in classrooms is acceptable for students? Is the onus on the students to entertain themselves during periods of waiting in school? What are the long-term effects of spending much of your in-class time waiting for an appropriate assignment or opportunity?

7. Many adults think that students with gifts or talents are nerdy, some adults think that they are pushy, and still other adults think that they do not exist. If you were invited to serve on a panel during a meeting of faculty in a middle school, and your charge was to describe the daily experience of students with gifts and talents, what might you emphasize? What if you were to answer the same prompt, but in an assembly of middle school students of all abilities?

References

Ackerman, P. L., & Heggestad, E. D. (1997). Intelligence, personality, and interests: Evidence for overlapping traits. *Psychological Bulletin, 121,* 219–245.

Cohen, J., Onunaku, N., Clothier, S., & Poppe, J. (2005). *Helping young children succeed: Strategies to promote early childhood social and emotional development.* Washington, DC: National Conference of State Legislatures and Zero to Three.

Coleman, L. J. (1985). *Being gifted in school.* Menlo Park, NJ: Addison-Wesley.

Coleman, L. J. (2012). Lived experience, mixed messages, and stigma. In T. L. Cross & J. R. Cross (Eds.), *Handbook for counselors serving students with gifts and talents: Development, relationships, school issues, and counseling needs/interventions* (pp. 371–302). Waco, TX: Prufrock Press

Coleman, L. J., & Cross, T. L. (1988). Is being gifted a social handicap? *Journal for the Education of the Gifted, 11,* 41–56.

Coleman, L. J., & Cross, T. L. (2000). Social-emotional development and personal experience. In K. Heller, F. J. Mönks, R. J. Sternberg, & R. S. Subotnik (Eds.), *International handbook of giftedness and talent* (2nd ed., pp. 203–212). Oxford, UK: Pergamon.

Coleman, L. J., Micko, K. J., & Cross, T. L. (2015). Twenty-five years of research on the lived experience of being gifted in school: Capturing the students' voices. *Journal for the Education of the Gifted, 38,* 358–376.

Cross, T. L. (1997). Psychological and social aspects of educating gifted students. *The Peabody Journal of Education, 72*(3–4), 181–201.

Cross, T. L., Coleman, L. J., & Terhaar-Yonkers, M. (1991). The social cognition of gifted adolescents in schools: Managing the stigma of giftedness. *Journal for the Education of the Gifted, 15,* 44–55.

Cross, T. L., & Cross, J. R. (in press). Suicide among students with gifts and talents. In S. Pfeiffer, M. Foley-Nicpon, & E. Shaunessy-Dedrick (Eds.), *American Psychological Association handbook of giftedness and talent.* Washington, DC: American Psychological Association.

Dabrowski, K. (1964). *Positive disintegration.* Boston, MA: Little, Brown.

Deci, E. L., & Ryan, R. M. (2000). The "what" and "why" of goal pursuits: Human needs and the self-determination of behavior. *Psychological Inquiry, 11,* 227–268.

Delisle, J. R., & Squires, S. (1989). Career development for gifted and talented youth: Division on Career Development (DCD) and The Association for the Gifted (TAG) position statement. *Journal for Education of the Gifted, 13,* 97–104.

DeYoung, C. G. (2011). Intelligence and personality. In R. J. Sternberg & S. B. Kaufman (Eds.), *The Cambridge handbook of intelligence* (pp. 711–737). New York, NY: Cambridge University Press.

Erikson, E. H. (1963). *Childhood and society* (2nd ed.). New York, NY: Norton.

Fletcher, K. L., & Speirs Neumeister, K. L. (2012). Research on perfectionism and achievement motivation: Implications for gifted students. *Psychology in the Schools, 49,* 668–677.

Genshaft, J. L., Greenbaum, S., & Borovsky, S. (1995). Stress and the gifted. In J. L. Genshaft, M. Bireley, & C. L. Hollinger (Eds.), *Serving gifted and talented students: A resource for school personnel* (pp. 257–268). Austin, TX: Pro-Ed.

Goff, M., & Ackerman, P. L. (1992). Personality–intelligence relations: Assessment of typical intellectual engagement. *Journal of Educational Psychology, 84,* 537–553.

Hewitt, P. L., & Flett, G. L. (1991). Perfectionism in the self and social contexts: Conceptualization, assessment, and association with psychopathology. *Journal of Personality and Social Psychology, 60,* 456–470.

Hewitt, P. L., Flett, G. L., & Turnbull-Donovan, W. (1992). Personality and suicidal intent. *British Journal of Clinical Psychology, 31,* 181–190.

Howley, C., Howley, A., & Pendarvis, E. (2017). *Out of our minds: Turning the tide of anti-intellectualism in American schools* (2nd ed.). Waco, TX: Prufrock Press.

Kerr, B. A. (1991). *A handbook for counseling the gifted and talented.* Alexandria, VA: American Association for Counseling and Development.

McCrae, R. R., & Costa, P. T., Jr. (1996). Toward a new generation of personality theories: Theoretical contexts for the five-factor model. In J. S. Wiggins (Ed.), *The five-factor model of personality: Theoretical perspectives* (pp. 51–87). New York, NY: Guilford.

Mendaglio, S. (2012). Overexcitabilities and giftedness research: A call for a paradigm shift. *Journal for the Education of the Gifted, 35,* 207–219.

Mendaglio, S., & Tillier, W. (2006). Dabrowski's theory of positive disintegration and giftedness: Overexcitability research findings. *Journal for the Education of the Gifted, 30,* 68–87.

Olszewski-Kubilius, P., & Kulieke, M. J. (1989). Personality dimensions of gifted adolescents. In J. L. VanTassel-Baska & P. Olszewski-Kubilius (Eds.), *Patterns of influence on talent development: The home, the self and the school* (pp. 125–145). New York, NY: Teachers College Press.

Rysiew, K. J., Shore, B. M., & Leeb, R. T. (1999). Multipotentiality, giftedness, and career choice: A review. *Journal of Counseling and Development, 77,* 423–430.

Sajjadi, S. H., Rejskind, F. G., & Shore, B. M. (2001). Is multipotentiality a problem or not? A new look at the data. *High Ability Studies, 12,* 27–43.

Sak, U. (2004). A synthesis of research on psychological types of gifted adolescents. *Journal of Secondary Gifted Education, 15,* 70–79.

Silverman, L. K. (2012). Asynchronous development: A key to counseling the gifted. In T. L. Cross & J. R. Cross (Eds.), *Handbook for counselors serving students with gifts and talents: Development, relationships, school issues, and counseling needs/interventions* (pp. 261–279). Waco, TX: Prufrock Press.

Sosniak, L. A. (1985). Becoming an outstanding research neurologist. In B. S. Bloom (Ed.), *Developing talent in young people* (pp. 348–408). New York, NY: Ballantine.

Speirs Neumeister, K. L. (2015). Perfectionism in gifted students. In M. Neihart, S. Pfeiffer, & T. L. Cross (Eds.), *Social and emotional development of gifted children* (2nd ed., pp. 29–39). Waco, TX: Prufrock Press.

Terman, L. (1925). *Genetic studies of genius: Vol. 1. Mental and physical traits of a thousand gifted children.* Stanford, CA: Stanford University Press.

Tillier, B. (1995). *The theory of positive disintegration by Kazimierz Dabrowski.* Retrieved from http://www.positivedisintegration.com/10concepts.html#ml

Tillier, W. (2009). Dabrowski without the theory of positive disintegration just isn't Dabrowski. *Roeper Review, 31,* 123–126.

Webb, J. T. (1993). Nurturing social-emotional development of gifted children. In K. A. Heller, F. J. Mönks, & A. H. Passow (Eds.), *International handbook of research and development of giftedness and talent* (pp. 525–538). Oxford, UK: Pergamon Press.

Zeidner, M., & Shani-Zinovich, I. (2011). Do academically gifted and nongifted students differ on the Big-Five and adaptive status? Some recent data and conclusions. *Personality and Individual Differences, 51,* 566–570.

CHAPTER 6

Cognitive Development of Giftedness and Talents

From Theory to Practice

Camelia Birlean and Bruce M. Shore

The principal goal of education is to create people who are capable of doing new things, not simply repeating what other generations have done—people who are creators, inventors, and discoverers. The second goal of education is to form minds which can be critical, can verify, and do not accept everything they are offered.—Jean Piaget as cited in Eleanor Duckworth (1964, p. 175)[1]

Essential Questions to Guide the Reader

1. What evidence exists in modern theories of learning and thinking about how gifted learning and thinking are different from learning and thinking for nongifted learners?

2. What does information-processing theory (also called expertise theory) add to IQ-based theory to improve instructional planning?

3. What does constructivist theory further add to information-processing theory that can enhance instruction that supports gifted learning?

4. What does social-constructivist theory add to basic constructivism that can enhance gifted education?

---

1   The opening quote is from Piaget as reported by Eleanor Duckworth, Canadian-born dancer and educator who studied with Jean Piaget in Geneva, later worked in the U.S., and translated Piaget's presentations on his visit to the United States. We replaced "men" in the published source with "people" to be inclusive and because the French word "hommes" can be translated equally accurately as "men" or "persons" or "people."

Cannot shed / our experiences / perspectives

When we plan a lesson or extend a learning unit for students who exhibit gifted behavior, how we organize that experience is influenced by what we, as teachers, understand giftedness to be. That understanding is our personal theory about how the pupils learn and think. For example, if we think giftedness means the ability to think more quickly or in larger chunks, we might move the lesson or unit more quickly through larger amounts of content, but we might not change what the teacher does and what the learner does. However, if our theory of giftedness includes, among other things, being better able to plan ahead, compare multiple approaches, self-evaluate, and be comfortable with not having a single or right answer to a problem, then we would likely prepare a very different kind of lesson or unit. Driven by such a theory, a unit might ask learners to decide what the topic means, come up with and compare different ways to approach the topic, and judge for themselves when they are on good paths before they come to conclusions.

Teachers hold many theories, for example, about how children develop socially and emotionally, how classroom behavior is shaped, and how nutrition is related to learning. This chapter focuses on cognitive theories and cognitive development, that is, on how children think and learn. All teachers, especially a teacher newly grappling with giftedness among his or her students, need to be well equipped with professionally defensible—not just personal—theories of learning and cognition. Good theories support good practice, whether it is in education, engineering, medicine, or any profession in which we hold the well-being of another person in our care.

This chapter has three main parts. The first part explores the importance of moving theories about high ability beyond what IQ tests measure; that does not mean throwing IQ out, but the IQ is horse-and-buggy educational technology, coined about a century ago when more people rode horses than rode in trains or cars, and virtually none had flown. Other professions add new knowledge and new practices to old, and educators should expect the same of our profession as teachers. This first section examines the progression from IQ-based theories of giftedness (also called *psychometric theories* because they are mostly about measuring a psychological quality) to information-processing theories (also called *expertise-based theories* because they try to explain how experts think and learn). Second, the chapter looks at the current most important theories about children's learning, namely constructivist, and several kinds of constructivist practices that work amazingly well with most learners and especially with those with potential for gifted performance. These theories are called *constructivist* because they focus on how learners create meaning from their experience. Those terms are explained in some detail, and examples are given of how the theoretical ideas impact teaching. Third, the chapter expands the idea of social-constructivist teaching practices. The term *social* was added because they describe the role of social interaction in creating meaning.

Teachers are sometimes challenged when they do things differently in their classrooms. "That is not how I learned in school!" we are told. Those comments reflect personal theories and personal experience. There is, however, a science of teaching and learning that goes beyond personal experiences, and this is an introduction to part of that science. Every real profession is built on science, including biology for medicine, physics and chemistry for engineers, and psychology, among others, for education. If educators use some of this material, they will be able to professionally defend their teaching choices, and students will thrive.

Learning scientists and cognitive psychologists study the development of human cognition, but they have focused particularly on typical or average populations. There is a smaller collection of research on cognitive performance in gifted education, but research specifically connecting cognitive development and gifted educational practice remains scarce. This chapter updates a selection of major theories of cognitive development in light of more current empirical research and connects this research to practices in gifted education.

Theoretical Perspectives on Cognitive Development of Giftedness and Talents

What distinguishes learning of gifted students from performance in other age peers? As the various theories are addressed, the explanation for high performance evolves, particularly about characteristics of high performance within school-age groups (K–12) and across various disciplines. This section asks what gifted performance looks like in mathematics, the humanities, and occasionally in science. It also explores key elements of instruction (e.g., pedagogical roles, models, and strategies) that stimulate, nurture, and enhance high-level thinking skills in students.

The Need to Explain High Performance Beyond IQ-Testing Theory

The IQ-based explanation for high performance highlights the idea that the general factor of intelligence, viewed largely as a stable innate ability, changes minimally from infancy to adulthood. The number of specific factors composing intelligence increases as a result of age only. For example, with older students it becomes relevant to distinguish among verbal versus spatial-mathematical abilities. Later, this can be further broken down into specific abilities such as musical, mechanical, linguistic, and other contributors. Although factor scores on psychometric tests likely increase with age, the presumable stability of IQ across the lifetime is controlled by psychometricians by adjusting for chronological age when calculating the IQ scores (Cassidy, Roche, & O'Hora, 2010). In other words, older students might get more answers correct on an IQ test, but, in effect, to get the quotient Q in IQ, it is divided by the age. The IQ number does not inform us about the useful information regarding what additional things an older learner knows or can do. As learners develop, they are expected to acquire more information more quickly, but the emphasis remains on efficient accumulation of accurate knowledge. Although very influential on educational policies, IQ theory has been "discredited by the discovery that IQ can be improved by the right kind of training" (Commentary, 2008, p. 645).

Other theories differ from IQ-testing theory in at least two ways. First, children's intellectual ability is not genetically set (more or less) for life, but determined by the interaction of genetics (nature) and also stimulation from the environment (nurture). This empowers both students and teachers, because teachers are in the business of providing stimulation from the environment. IQ-based theories implicitly constrain educators' impact. Students can, through deliberate, well-coached practice and motivation, use intellectual and creative tools and strategies to overcome their own deficiencies and to advance their learning. Teachers gain agency to stimulate, nurture, and enhance children's intellectual development through judicious use of environmental variables, such as stimulating learning materials and experiences and effective instructional strategies.

Second, cognitive psychologists and some researchers in the field of giftedness and talent have stressed the need to understand giftedness not only through intelligence models, but also in relation to disciplinary thinking—that is, thinking about real subject-matter content, not about behavior. Early "thinking skills" programs used in gifted and talented programs (e.g., de Bono's Cognitive Research Trust [CoRT], 1973; Meeker's Guilford-based Structure-of-the-Intellect [SOI], 1969) generally failed when they were divorced from content in which the skills needed to be applied. Cognitive psychologists correspondingly criticized teacher education for focusing on pedagogical methods (e.g., teacher's use of questions, assessment of student performance) independent of subject matter (Ball & McDiarmid, 1990). "Linking strong content to strong learning goals to strong pedagogical practice [becomes] paramount" within school systems extensively driven by high standards and accountability demands (Little, Feng, VanTassel-Baska, Rogers, & Avery, 2007, pp. 272–273). Researchers in learning and in giftedness (e.g., Austin & Shore, 1993; Shulman, 1986, 1987) connected cognitive development and content areas within or across specific disciplines or talent domains. The content domain (e.g., history, geography, poetry, chemistry, environment) is important because the ways of knowing and creating new knowledge and what qualifies as good evidence vary, as do the more apparent differences in the objects of curiosity and vocabulary. New knowledge and understanding in history are not acquired in exactly the same way as in astronomy, although there are common underlying principles of learning. Studying and understanding individual differences with respect to thinking processes within disciplines could assist educators in designing higher quality curriculum and assessment, not only to support learning at higher levels for gifted students, but also to improve the education of all students (Friedman & Shore, 2000). Thinking skills need to be appropriately contextualized for maximum impact.

Explaining High Performance From a Cognitive or Information-Processing Perspective

The explanation for high performance embedded within the information-processing model provides a basis for understanding the array of individual differences in mental processing (Sternberg, 1977). Siegler (1996), a pioneer of the information-processing view, proposed that, as children mature and their brains develop, they are better able to focus their attention, process information more quickly, and store more information in memory. They develop progressively better rules and strategies for problem solving and thinking logically (higher mental processes). From this perspective, students' performance on intelligence and aptitude tests is generally attributed to variation in (a) speed of processing, (b) problem solving, (c) amount and depth of knowledge, and (d) metacognitive skills such as planning, questioning, and solution monitoring. Experts display a highly competent level of performance, access relevant information from their long-term memory (LTM) more rapidly, identify novel and creative solutions to problems, make use of learned strategies more effectively and flexibly, and possess better metacognitive skills (Coleman & Shore, 1991; Rabinowitz & Glaser, 1985).

Here is an example of an idea for a very basic classroom language arts lesson, first using just an IQ-based approach that could also be called *traditional* and moving toward an information-processing approach. In a traditional approach, a lesson aimed at building children's working vocabulary around a reading selection could begin with the teacher creating a list of new words in the story, presenting that list before beginning, having the children look the words up in dictionaries and practice using the new words, and proceeding with the reading. For children who exhibit gifted performance, there may be more challenging words, and the text selection may be at a higher reading level. If, however, educators make good use of what the information-processing approach tells them about learners' thinking abilities, they could plan several adaptations. First, they can ask the learners to read the text before having new words listed. They can work in teams to find all of the new words (new to anyone on the team), find out what the words mean, use their enhanced memories and depth-of-knowledge skills to connect these new words to related words that they already knew (even in another language), explain how these words are similar or different, decide if they have found all of the important new words, and determine how they can improve their team's search process with the next reading selection. Each group can share one or two new words at a time with the class, and they can post their new words to a class blog. Notice that the teacher and students are engaged in very different roles in this second example. It is a different lesson plan because it is based on a different theory about how children learn and think, not just faster and more, but not ignoring (or insisting on) the possibility of faster and more. And it works!

Problem solving and problem generation in the gifted and talented context. In their extensive review of cognitive development of giftedness, Steiner and Carr (2003) discussed four important topics in information-processing research: (a) processing speed, (b) knowledge base, (c) metacognition, and (d) problem-solving and strategic abilities. This section particularly focuses on (d), but it is important to briefly explain metacognition and to note two qualifications about processing speed.

Metacognition. Metacognition essentially means thinking about one's own thinking. Experts in domains from chess to mechanics and other subjects, plus other professionals, are very good at doing this. For this to be relevant to giftedness, it is important to define smart as more than having a high IQ. Instead, it can be redefined as evolving expertise. Sternberg (2001) and Shore (Barfurth, Ritchie, Irving, & Shore, 2009; Pelletier & Shore, 2003; Shore, 2010) have done this explicitly. A simple example could include teachers thinking about what they will say and adjusting what to say by taking into account how others might respond, before speaking aloud. It can mean sketching an outline of an essay before starting to write, having a goal, and realizing while writing when the writing drifts from the goal.

Processing speed and execution speed. Processing speed (how quickly thoughts progress in the brain) is not the same as problem-execution speed (how quickly the learner finishes a task). Execution or performance speed is directly observable; processing speed is not. Furthermore, accuracy counts more than speed in predicting IQ among learners with high IQs (Lajoie & Shore, 1986). That means speed is not the most important part of a high IQ, even though IQ tests are timed and referred to as *speeded* or *power* tests, so speed of completion should not be the most important part of a lesson. The quality of the learner's thinking is more important. (Teachers know this implicitly, but pressure from the testing world challenges their confidence in this regard.)

The usual assumption about problem-execution speed is that it is generally higher in giftedness—that is, learners exhibiting giftedness complete school and other tasks more quickly. That assumption is flawed. In fact, this apparent rapidity is limited to the routine or trivial parts of problems; it is what is called an artifact, a byproduct, rather than a key result of assigning tasks that are too easy for the learners, insufficiently challenging, and uninteresting. Highly competent learners actually spend longer thoughtfully planning and evaluating their possible responses, sketching on paper, doodling electronically, and asking "What if?" in conversation or in their minds when solving complex or multistep problems (Barfurth et al., 2009). A teaching implication is immediately apparent: A lesson created or adapted to take giftedness into account should not merely go more quickly or cover more territory. Educators need to check the steps in the lesson. If the tasks are trivial or students might have previous practice or already know the material, then, of course, they will finish quickly. They will appropriately be bored, possibly act out, and make more work for their teachers. How can a teacher know if a problem or topic is sufficiently complex and challenging? One way is to provide problems that have multiple answers or no known answers. Also, use problems with more than one step—figure this out, use that information to consider another issue, and then decide if better information could have been available. With experience this becomes easier to do as a teacher. At any level of teacher experience, a good answer is simple: Ask the students. Gather a few tasks and ask if they regard any of them as interesting, complex, or challenging enough to be worthy of their careful thought and time. If not, ask them to reshape the tasks so that they are. When asked to improve a learning task, high-achieving students make it more complex and add levels of difficulty, whereas other learners prefer to add more of what we could call "bells and whistles" (Maniatis, Cartwright, & Shore, 1998). These examples emphasize the importance of students' thinking rather than the speed.

Problem solving and strategic abilities. The nature of problem solving and problem generation (that is, coming up with problems to solve or problem finding) has been connected to exceptional performance by numerous investigators (see Mann, 2006; Matsko & Thomas, 2014). For example, in mathematics, Tjoe (2015) examined the extent to which the aesthetic appreciation for mathematical beauty in problem solving (notably simplicity and originality as especially desirable) was paralleled between expert mathematicians and mathematically successful students. No direct relation was found between mathematicians' and mathematically successful students' aesthetic view. For the experts, the beauty of mathematics was a problem-solving prerequisite; they sought it even before engaging in the solution process. The students were, regrettably, primarily motivated to obtain a quick, correct response. Appreciation for beauty in mathematics, a priority for actual mathematicians, was not inherent in mathematical giftedness; it is a learned competence, shared, nurtured, and promoted within the professional community of mathematicians, apparently beyond the high school level. There is no reason to wait that long. The difference could also reflect the emphasis the students faced on solving large numbers of problems quickly and accurately. That's the "old" way. The implication for a 21st-century mathematics teacher, whether in grade 1 arithmetic or in calculus, is to pause and smell the beautiful flowers. Did you notice any interesting patterns in the petals? In the leaves? What is your favorite number, and what does it make you think of? Have you counted the number of different angles in a printed 1? Can you print a 5 using straight lines instead of curves so it has five angles? Look carefully and you might discover a secret code for where our printed numbers come from. Can you print 4 or a 6 or a 7 in a way that fits this same pattern? Why do you think a zero is round or oval rather than a rectangle? Bring some illustrated alphabet, counting, and calligraphy books (or set up some web links) and ask the students to design a beautiful 6 or pentagon and to post it. Extend the lesson to cryptography and send some secret messages—illustrated, of course. Can this lead to an art project or a multimedia demonstration or to a career the students never before considered?

Research supports those kinds of lesson ideas. Mann (2006) claimed that "teaching mathematics without providing for creativity denies all students, especially the gifted and talented students, the opportunity to appreciate the beauty of mathematics and fails to provide the gifted student an opportunity to fully develop his or her talents" (p. 236). It also robs mathematics of its hidden mysteries and excitement for all learners, even the youngest. Matsko and Thomas (2014) proposed a novel approach for promoting creative thinking skills and deep conceptual understanding by examining the relationship among mathematics, creativity, and motivation with students enrolled in a residential high school. In open-ended survey questions, students articulated clearly how their engagement in problem creation enhanced their metacognitive strategies, particularly reflections on the creative process. Participants connected meaningful events and experiences in their lives, implying for classroom practice that the "self-directed nature of problem creation is critical to the success of assignments" (Matsko & Thomas, 2014, p. 165). Once again, if educators ask advanced learners to help plan learning challenges, they will be more engaged, and they will learn to think like experts in the domain. That is why educators should not teach thinking skills in isolation. Students think about something and connect it to something else. More connections enhance learning.

Empirical research on how experts solve problems provides insights into how giftedness manifests itself within specific disciplines, but that research has not widely addressed differences among learners of varying abilities, with two exceptions. The first exception was a study by Austin and Shore (1993) who reported that high-performing college-level physics students' concept maps more closely resembled those of experts in the quality and number of links among key concepts. Their course material was not much different from a mechanics or electricity course that high-performing secondary students might take. Pelletier (1994) showed that high-performing secondary mathematics students, like experts, grouped mathematics questions on the basis of underlying mathematical constructs rather than on surface characteristics such as being a word, graphic, or formula problem. Therein lies another lesson idea. Teachers know generally about concept maps, but do not always fully exploit them. From these two studies we learn something new about how to use concept maps in a lesson or a unit, especially with high performers. After the teacher presents the list of concepts, ask the students to connect every pair of concepts in as many ways as possible and to explain every link in detail. Ask them if any of the concepts belong together in a group and to figure out a way to show that on their maps. Then, have students explain how groups can be connected. Can this be done in different ways? Then ask them to explain their maps to the class. Concept maps can be created in multiple subject areas. Recent research has demonstrated that simultaneously working in different subject areas has an enhanced benefit, increasing performance and understanding in both (Rich, Leatham, & Wright, 2013). Are the concept maps in different subjects similar or different in their overall shape and how so? Why or why not? (Here is a teachers' hint: <u>Different subjects organize knowledge differ-ently, but they all organize knowledge.</u>) These are not typical concept-map exercises, and they can occupy high-performing students for hours. And the learning sticks like the storied spaghetti on the ceiling.

The expert-performance approach (Ericsson, Roring, & Nandagopal, 2007) connects deliberate practice and superior performance in both high-performing and expert individuals. According to Sternberg (2001), such relations should not exclude innate contributions to individual differences; teachers are adding to knowledge, not destroying old knowledge unless it is wrong (known in the education world as a misconception); they really want to fix misconceptions, but they also need to remember that only the learner can create new meaning. The teachers can only set up situations that can help them do so. Learners who exhibit gifted performance, like domain experts, are

- highly capable of identifying and generating novel and important problems within the context of their domain of curiosity (Sternberg & Davidson, 1985) and creating new solutions to problems that go beyond the mere application of previously learned rules to achieve a goal;
- faster problem solvers on trivial or familiar tasks, but they spend more time in the planning stage on nontrivial problems (Barfurth et al., 2009; Sriraman, 2003);
- more flexible in their strategies and problem solutions and possess higher levels of metacognition and self-regulation (Coleman & Shore, 1991; Shore & Kanevsky, 1993; Shore, Koller, & Dover 1994); and
- possess a significantly greater amount of knowledge in various disciplines and make better use (application) of their knowledge than typical learners (Coleman & Shore, 1991; Steiner & Carr, 2003; Sternberg & Davidson, 1985).

Teachers need to capitalize on these differences.

Shore and Kanevsky (1993) questioned whether superior performance is attrib-utable merely to the students' precocity (they can do at a younger age what others do later) or "does it reflect fundamental differences in thinking processes?" (p. 134). If, indeed, gifted thinking is qualitatively different from other thinking, then a qual-itative differentiation of classroom instruction and curriculum is required. On the other hand, if the nature of this difference is purely quantitative, for example, only faster or more efficient thinking, or faster mental development, then more atten-tion should be paid to acceleration strategies including curriculum compacting. Of course, the ultimate answer can be some of both. To illustrate this some-of-both qual-ity, Coleman and Shore (1991) conducted a study of high school students grouped according to grades in mathematics and physics. High-performing students and experts appeared to think qualitatively differently from lower performing students, but their use of metacognition and prior knowledge was not exclusive. Rather, they displayed these qualities more often than the other group. All groups used similar processes but with different frequencies, so the differences are both qualitative and quantitative. Low-achieving students can learn higher order thinking skills (Zohar & Dori, 2003). Shore and Kanevsky (1993) and Austin and Shore (1993) elaborated these findings, indicating that gifted thinking reflects:

- possessing a greater knowledge base and greater skill in connecting this past knowledge to newly learned information (e.g., students show connections in concept maps),
- favoring challenging and complex tasks (e.g., students improve the assignment, making it harder for themselves!),
- spending more time planning, but carrying out problem solutions more quickly mainly because of automaticity in procedural knowledge (developed through deliberate practice) after creating a plan,
- engaging more often and effectively in self-regulatory processes (e.g., students think ahead and evaluate each step toward a better solution),
- using strategies more flexibly (e.g., students complete the task different ways or choose alternate paths when appropriate), and
- representing and categorizing problems more effectively and efficiently (e.g., students group the concepts on a map according to different criteria: aesthetics, familiarity, importance to daily life, esotericism).

Explaining High Performance From a Constructivist Perspective

Contemporary curricular reforms, in general, and in gifted education in particular, emphasize teaching for understanding with emphasis on the construction of strong content knowledge based on deep understanding, authentic assessment, and inquiry-based, hands-on approaches by classroom teachers across all subject domains (Aulls & Shore, 2008; Renzulli, 1994; VanTassel-Baska, 2014). "Curriculum that integrates higher-level processes and specific conceptual-thinking activities with strong content yields content gains as strong as or stronger than a more direct, knowledge-based structure for teaching to standards" (Little et al., 2007, p. 272). Hence, educational reforms in general education (Aulls & Shore, 2008; National Research Council [NRC], 2000, 2012; Palincsar, 1998; Québec, 2004, 2007), as well as in gifted education (Renzulli, 1994; Shore & Delcourt, 1996; VanTassel-Baska, 2014; VanTassel-Baska & Brown, 2007), unanimously encourage a constructivist perspective as the framework for institutional culture change and as a critical theory and philosophy of instruction for grades K–12. Constructivist theory, entailing the sociocognitive conflict theory of Piaget (1956) and the social-constructivist theory of Vygotsky (1978), both explained below, led to a reexamination of learning and teaching across content domains by studying how learners construct their understanding of a stable and regular world through personal and social experiences. In constructivist theory, learners create or construct their own meaning or understanding of everything they experience. Teachers cannot impose meaning (personal meaning is not the same as being able to recite a definition). Teachers do, however, create conditions that facilitate students creating their own meaning and also avoiding misconceptions.

Piaget's and Vygotsky's Perspectives and Their Implications for Gifted Education

Although recognition that learners construct their own understanding is one of Piaget's most important educational contributions, teachers are probably most exposed to Piaget's (1956) developmental theory about four stages of cognitive growth. These stages are presumed to build upon one another: As the child advances through a new stage, his or her repertoire of cognitive structures becomes more complex in the number of connections with other cognitive structures due to maturation, adaptation, and assimilation. Loewen (2006) suggested that the nature and composition of cognitive structures also change as learners advance through stages of cognitive development. For example, thinking abilities of a toddler (at Piaget's preoperational stage), although critical to future cognitive development, remain fundamentally different from those of an elementary school-age student (concrete-operational stage) or a teenager (formal-operational stage). Individuals at these different stages would likely think, act, or react very differently when presented with the same stimulus (e.g., an object to look at, a question, or an idea). Understanding children's thinking would, in turn, enable educators to match teaching methods to children's cognitive capabilities. Piaget's theory does address what processes occur within the child, notably that

(a) cognitive development proceeds in a relatively orderly and predictable pattern and only changes after certain genetically controlled neurological maturation occurs;

(b) children construct knowledge from their interactive experiences with the physical world through engagement in activity which, in turn, alters their thinking processes at the same time;

(c) children learn through the two complementary processes of assimilation (making new ideas fit into the ways they already understand) and accommodation (adjusting their understanding to fit the new information about the world) in order to achieve the process of equilibration—the balance of the two; and

(d) actual changes in thinking take place through the process of equilibration (in response to a cognitive conflict) that promotes progression toward more complex thought levels.

Only (b) directly informs what teachers do, namely, create targeted experiences for learners. Piaget's theories do not specifically guide educators about the range of actions they can implement to facilitate or enhance learners' cognitive development, that is, to help children progress from one stage to another (but see Constance Kamii's publications if interested to see how Piaget's theories can be translated into rich mathematics experiences for very young children).

Piagetian theorists within gifted education (e.g., Gross, 2000) attribute this cognitive transformation to age alone and do not refer to the individuals' precocious accumulation of knowledge, their experiences, or to the quality of their thinking processes: "The gifted progress through the stages at significantly accelerated rates, thus reaching the formal operation stage much earlier" (Gross, 2000, p. 182). Reaching the formal operational stage sooner may be a given, but acceleration alone is not enough for the advanced learner. Acceleration is, indeed, consistent with Piaget's stage theory. In addition, students need to learn through discovery and direct interaction with the environment, which enables them to explore, manipulate, observe, and talk with peers about what they have experienced. Another layer to Piaget's theory must be added, and this part of the theoretical puzzle came from Lev Vygotsky.

Vygotsky's theory (1978; originally published in Russian in the 1930s) is distinguished from Piaget's theory in a couple of ways. Vygotsky's theory focuses on the critical, active role that more knowledgeable persons (teachers, mentors, or peers) with particular skills and knowledge play in scaffolding the learner's intellectual growth. Their job is to facilitate the learner's transition from the zone of actual development (what they already know and can do) to the Zone of Proximal Development (ZPD; what they could know or do, but not yet on their own). Differently from Piaget, Vygotsky argued that to successfully nurture the learner's cognitive growth, the teacher is expected to carefully assess the learner's current level of ability and to create challenging tasks that are within the learner's zone of near or proximal development—the ZPD consists of tasks that the learner can achieve but only with assistance. The ZPD is the link between performing at one level and moving toward being able to work at a higher level. Students are further scaffolded (supported, guided, and assisted) in their learning and development through prompts, reminders, and encouragements at the right time and in the right amount. As students become more proficient with the task at hand, the scaffold is gradually faded (like the parent's hand letting go of the back of a 6-year-old's seat on a new bicycle) until they are fully empowered over their learning process and product. There is always a new challenge in the zone between being able to do things independently and not being able to do them at all. The teacher manages that in-between zone. The key to all cognitive growth in Vygotsky's social-constructivism theory is dialogue, including progress across Piagetian stages, in all those experiences. Dialogue can be between learners, between learners and teachers or parents, and in the learner's head as self-dialogue.

So, two powerful theoretical ideas come together: Learners must create their own understanding or meaning (Piaget), and they do so and progress in their sophistication to do so through opportunities for real-world experiences, scaffolding, and dialogue (Vygotsky). From a Vygotskyan perspective, enrichment and differentiation strategies are appropriate options to support and develop giftedness.

Studies focusing on the ZPD have examined the amount of scaffolding provided (Kanevsky & Geake, 2004). Learners with greater learning potential and broader ZPD generally require fewer scaffolds in that a broad ZPD builds on a stronger knowledge base, ability to self-manage in new and complex learning situations, better ability to keep a sense of direction of how much more they could do with scaffolding, and the ability to link ideas that may be quite diverse. A wider ZPD means a greater range of potential new mastery. A narrower ZPD needs more frequent teacher intervention and smaller steps.

Kanevsky's (1995) model explained the concept of learning potential as an interaction between an individual's intellectual characteristics, including general knowledge base, information processing efficiency, and metacognitive knowledge and control, and motivational characteristics. This interaction is, in turn, continuously influenced by contextual variables in the individual's learning environment (e.g., student-teacher relationship, peer influence, teaching methods, materials, assessment criteria, home environment). Vygotsky's emphasis on the social context for cognitive growth and constructing meaning clearly guides pedagogical planning: A lesson or unit without dialogue is lacking. Therefore, for all the complexity of this section so far on constructivism, there is a very simple message for every teacher and every lesson planned: Make time for dialogue, especially student-student dialogue, several times during the learning day. This is not a frill or an add-on. It is the process by which students advance the quality of their thinking.

A number of researchers, who either embrace a Vygotskyan view or a mix with a Piagetian view (e.g., Aulls & Shore, 2008; NRC, 2000, 2012; Palincsar, 1998; Québec, 2004, 2007; Renzulli, 1994; Threlfall & Hargreaves, 2008; VanTassel-Baska, 2014), asserted that cognitive development by any learners, but especially learners with high academic success or potential, does not progress smoothly. Also, learners achieve higher levels of cognitive functioning in different material and contexts more quickly (Gagné, 1970), not only because they consolidate the skills specific to one particular stage at a faster pace, but also because they construct and internalize these skills qualitatively differently than less high-performing age-peers. As a result, the difference in thinking at each stage becomes increasingly more distinct in both quantity (e.g., knowledge amount and speed of acquisition) and quality (e.g., use of

[handwritten margin note: Writing in the Dialogical Classroom (Fecho, 2011)]

processes and knowledge connections). Giftedness includes both precocity (quick and advanced thinking for the age) and actually qualitatively different thinking strategies. Interacting with others provides the opportunity to test and eventually change learners' thinking (Kanevsky & Geake, 2004). Therefore, acceleration and enrichment strategies, in conjunction with careful differentiation and social structuring of the learning situation, become viable curricular and instructional options for the cognitive development of gifted learners.

Constructivist-Based Practices for Effective Classroom Enrichment and Differentiation

The principles of enrichment (Reis, Gentry, & Maxfield, 1998) and differentiation (Tomlinson & Jarvis, 2009; Ward, 1961) complete and complement each other, fitting very well within the social-constructivist theory of teaching and learning. They draw on Vygotsky's proposition that cognition and affect mutually influence and enhance each other, culminating as "undifferentiated unity" (Kanevsky, 2011, p. 239).

In collaboration with students, the teacher should plan educational activities with students, giving them meaningful choices about topics, goals, or with whom they work (co-construction of curriculum), while carefully considering students' learning preferences within their ZPD. VanTassel-Baska and her collaborators (VanTassel-Baska & Brown, 2007; VanTassel-Baska & Stambaugh, 2006) suggested that simply advancing successful students to the next stage of the curriculum (acceleration or pacing) is not a sufficiently effective intervention. Careful consideration of the depth of content (e.g., projects and research), complexity of students' learning experiences (e.g., multiple higher level skills), challenging materials, and creativity (e.g., skills and habits of mind that support innovation) become equally important when differentiating curriculum for gifted learners (see Table 6.1). Added to this list is the need to provide opportunities for dialogue in all learning situations. And instructional differentiation should apply to the content or skills to be taught (what), to the process of teaching (how), as well as to the outcomes of teaching (product). All of these should align with the learner's needs, interests, and learning styles (Kaplan, 2007; Tomlinson, 1999).

Three broad areas overlap in constructivism, enrichment teaching, learning, and curricular differentiation (Bruner, 1960; Piaget, 1956; Vygotsky, 1978):

1. an inductive approach to instruction that allows for deep learning and cognitive advancement,

2. authentic learning placed at the heart of enrichment clusters that engage students in lifelong learning skills (e.g., critical thinking, problem solving)

Table 6.1

VanTassel-Baska and Stambaugh's (2006) Curriculum Differentiation Feature Checklist

	Curriculum Features
Acceleration	Fewer tasks assigned to master standards
	Standards-based skills assessed earlier or prior to teaching
	Standards clustered by higher order thinking skills
Complexity	Used multiple higher level skills
	Added more variables to study
	Required multiple sources
Depth	Studied a concept in multiple applications
	Conducted original research
	Developed a product
Challenge	Employed advanced resources
	Used sophisticated content stimuli
	Made cross-disciplinary application
	Made reasoning explicit
Creativity	Designed or constructed a model based on principles or criteria
	Provided alternatives for tasks, products, and assessments
	Emphasized oral and written communication to a real-world audience

simulating both thinking processes and emotions enacted by practicing professionals in the real world, and

3. collaborative learning shown to promote a deep understanding of the world through access to multiple views and perspectives and to enhance knowledge construction within the individual.

Each overlap should be explored separately.

An Inductive Approach: Inquiry-Based Learning and Questioning

Inductive teaching and learning assumes student-centered instruction in which learners take ownership over their own learning processes and products. There are no strategies designed solely to align with giftedness. However, some strategies have proven to be highly effective, including, but not limited to, the use of inquiry as a core strategy to promote and enhance learning, questioning, open-ended activities, independent investigation, and problem-based learning designed around ill-defined problems that are meaningful to students' needs and interests (Shore & Delcourt, 1996; VanTassel-Baska, 2014; VanTassel-Baska & Brown, 2007).

Inquiry. Because of successful learners' extensive curiosity about the world around them, inquiry-based teaching and learning (Aulls & Shore, 2008; Shore, Aulls, & Delcourt, 2008) and specifically the deliberate use of question-asking (VanTassel-Baska, 2014) are highly recommended as effective inductive approaches aimed to nurture and promote high-level thinking, helping students inquire and learn about the world around them in deep and meaningful ways. Inquiry has been described according to four models of inquiry instruction by Aulls and Shore (2008). In each of the models, the content of a course or curriculum (i.e., namely objectives, content, sequences, methods, and evaluation) interacts with the dimension of teacher and learner influence on what (content) and how (process) they learn during the process of curriculum enactment. Each model differs in the amount of control the teacher and student have, with the first model having the teacher as the authoritative, decisional power for both the content and direction of inquiry, while the last model emphasizes collaborative processes between the teacher and the students for both the content and process of inquiry.

Questioning. Questioning is a core part of inquiry-based instruction and an effective tool for promoting self-reflection and metacognition. This refers in part to the questions teachers ask but, more importantly, to the questions students ask. Such thinking skills facilitate the development of thinking habits, which in turn lead to further advancement of thinking while also motivating the learner to clarify misunderstandings they might have about the topic in question. VanTassel-Baska (2014) encouraged teachers to deliberately use questioning models when framing their questions for instruction. The most popular model is Bloom's taxonomy of cognitive objectives (updated by Anderson & Krathwohl, 2001) for creating learning objectives in order to scaffold learners' thinking in a systematic manner on a learning trajectory from low levels (e.g., remember and understand) to higher levels of thinking (e.g., analyze, synthesize, evaluate, and create). Thinking is deconstructed into a hierarchy of levels wherein the higher levels reflect an increase in the learners' ability to understand and interact with the content. Successful learners should be allowed to move through the low levels at a faster speed while spending considerable more time at the higher levels of the taxonomy (Davis, Rimm, & Siegle, 2011).

Authentic Learning

Authentic learning environments are core to constructivism and inquiry instruction, enabling students to go from being simply consumers to becoming producers of knowledge. They identify a real problem and attempt to solve it by (a) filtering relevant information and evidence from the irrelevant and (b) classifying, analyzing, synthesizing, and evaluating the information. The emphasis is more on the process of knowledge construction than on the final product. Four criteria are foundational to authentic, real-life problems (Renzulli, Gentry, & Reis, 2004). First, the problem

requires a frame of reference, referring to the learners' emotional or internal invest-
ment in addition to curiosity in the topic. Second, problems are ill-defined and open
(as opposed to structured or having known answers) with no preestablished solutions or formulas for solving the problem. Third, real-life problems call for novel
solutions that would likely have an impact on the community, causing a change in
attitude, action, or beliefs. Fourth, results of real-life problems are disseminated to
an authentic audience.

Collaborative Learning

In constructivist-driven instruction, differentiation, enrichment, collaboration,
and dialogue are essential to learning because social interaction is at the heart of
learning (Vygotsky, 1978). Benefits of collaborative learning have been connected
to student outcomes in various areas, such as higher motivation and achievement,
higher levels of engagement, and finally greater reasoning and transfer of content
(Fiddyment, 2014; Morgan, 2007; Renzulli et al., 2004). French, Walker, and Shore
(2011) furthered understanding about links between giftedness and students' preferences for collaborative work, cautioning that high-performing students prefer to
work with others only during complex learning situations that aligned with their
learning goals, and when their engagement in collaborative work was mutually effective for themselves and their peers. Otherwise, these learners preferred independent
work.

Other research points to the importance of homogeneous grouping for high-
performing students, at least some of the time, as opposed to mixed-cooperative
learning groups (Saunders-Stewart, Walker, & Shore 2013). This means providing
students with at least some opportunities to interact and work with peers at the
same performance levels, both intellectual and creative, so they can also obtain the
right amount of peer scaffolding to grow cognitively and maximize their learning
potential.

homogeneous grouping to benefit GIT

Conclusion

Teachers should work with contemporary theories and the best evidence
that aligns with their goals. However, not all theories or goals are equal in merit
for teaching. If educators want to teach a long list of facts accurately and quickly,
IQ-testing (psychometric) theory might work. If they want to teach thinking skills
unconnected to content that matters to the learner or society, stage theory on its
own could help them set the level and pace. This chapter has described a few ways
in which theory has evolved. The goal was to explore how these theoretical perspectives connect to gifted education and their instructional implications. Perhaps
the best available evidence generally supports a combined social-constructivist and

inquiry- or expertise-based approach (also see Robinson, Shore, & Enersen, 2006, for a summary of inquiry, giftedness, and best practices), but there is a time and a place at which one or another theory suitably helps to shape specific instructional decisions and practice. The success of instruction rests in finding a balance between students' overall needs and the required curriculum, while providing opportunities for authentic problems and collaborative and inquiry-based experiences.

Big Ideas

1. Although IQ provides one conception of giftedness, there are others that focus on the roles of experience versus fixed ability levels; this empowers teachers to design and implement learning experiences that help all students grow cognitively while empowering learners to share in responsibility for their learning and appreciate the need to connect thinking abilities to content within or across subject disciplines and to how new knowledge is created.

2. Gifted ways of learning and thinking are not exclusive to children who demonstrate high performance or high potential, but such children use cognitive processes that are used by adult experts sooner, more readily, more often, and more effectively. The main educational implication is that the balance in lesson and unit planning should shift toward providing opportunities and time for these thinking processes, not just getting to the right answers rapidly. Thinking well does not happen automatically, but good answers pursue good thinking.

3. Information-processing or expertise theory helps define good thinking processes based on studying how experts formulate and solve important, not trivial problems. Specific ideas for teachers to incorporate include guiding students to link new ideas to what they already know; working with students to identify, modify, and work with what students assess as challenging and complex tasks; spending time planning before acting; encouraging students to evaluate their progress at several stages during an activity; using different approaches for each task undertaken; and exploring if the answers can be expressed in different ways and in different relations to other knowledge.

Big Ideas, *Continued.*

4. Constructivist theory adds the important principle that learners create their own meaning out of their experiences and activities. Teachers can say what new concepts mean to others, but learners need to work it out for themselves or it becomes parroted knowledge. Sometimes learners adjust their thinking to new knowledge, but sometimes they create misconceptions if they try to force-fit new ideas into their already existing schema. An important implication for teachers is to help learners consider how their new learning meshes with what they already know. Piaget's ideas of stages also remind us to attend to the level of abstraction that students should grapple with. Can they articulate underlying principles, for example, without reference to specific instances?

5. Social constructivism adds two critical pieces of the learning puzzle. First, there is a zone between what students already know and can do independently, and what they cannot yet do, even with help. That Zone of Proximal Development (ZPD) is the teacher's domain of professional action. That is where students can be successful with help, such as breaking down the task into smaller or larger bits compatible with the student in question, reaching further ahead or taking smaller steps. Students can work with more or fewer abstract or concrete examples, staying close by or encouraging more unattended exploration. Second, social constructivism identifies the mechanism that moves students through the ZPD. Every lesson needs to provide opportunities for dialogue focused on the intended learning.

Discussion Questions

1. Cognitive views of giftedness have implications for what teachers do to support and promote gifted thinking in their classrooms. How would you support or oppose this statement citing evidence from the chapter?

2. Social constructivism is well supported in this chapter. What are your thoughts on this theory as you think about your own classroom?

3. Assuming you could and did implement some of these theoretical and evidence-based ideas in your lessons and units, that means student success will also be redefined as something in addition to a high score on a test. You are preparing for parent–teacher night and a meeting with a parent of an exceptionally high performing student. How might you describe this success in terms consistent with these theories?

> **Discussion Questions,** *Continued.*
>
> 4. Let's assume that the content of this chapter, or at least some of it, was new to you. As with policy, we are most comfortable making gradual change in teaching practice. So, what would be the first suggested teaching idea that you (or you and a teacher colleague—make this a dialogue) might try to implement in a lesson or unit in the next month or two? What would be the second adaptation? Third?

References

Anderson, L., & Krathwohl, D. (Eds.). (2001). *A taxonomy for learning, teaching, and assessing: A revision of Bloom's taxonomy of educational objectives* (Complete ed.). New York, NY: Longman.

Aulls, M. W., & Shore, B. M. (2008). *Inquiry in education (Vol. I): The conceptual foundations for research as a curricular imperative.* New York, NY: Erlbaum.

Austin, L. B., & Shore, B. M. (1993). Concept mapping of high and average achieving students, and experts. *European Journal for High Ability, 4,* 180–195.

Ball, D. L., & McDiarmid, G. W. (1990). The subject matter preparation of teachers. In R. Houston (Ed.), *Handbook of research on teacher education* (pp. 437–449). New York, NY: Macmillan.

Barfurth, M. A., Ritchie, K. C., Irving, J. A., & Shore, B. M. (2009). A metacognitive portrait of gifted learners. In L. V. Shavinina (Ed.), *International handbook on giftedness* (pp. 397–417). Amsterdam, Netherlands: Springer.

Bruner, J. S. (1960). *The process of education.* New York, NY: Vintage Books.

Cassidy, S., Roche, B., & O'Hora, D. (2010). Relational frame theory and human intelligence. *European Journal of Behavior Analysis, 11,* 37–51.

Coleman, E. B., & Shore, B. M. (1991). Problem-solving processes in high and average performers in physics. *Journal for the Education of the Gifted, 14,* 366–379.

Commentary. (2008). *Journal of Philosophy of Education, 42,* 645–646.

Davis, G. A., Rimm, S., & Siegle, D. (2011). *Education of the gifted and talented* (6th ed.) Boston, MA: Allyn & Bacon.

de Bono, E. (1973). *CoRT thinking.* Blandford, England: Direct Educational Services.

Duckworth, E. (1964). Piaget rediscovered. *Journal of Research in Science Teaching, 2,* 172–175.

Ericsson, K. A., Roring, R. W., & Nandagopal, K. (2007). Giftedness and evidence for reproducibly superior performance: An account based on the expert performance framework. *High Ability Studies, 18,* 3–56.

Fiddyment, G. E. (2014). Implementing enrichment clusters in elementary school: Lesson learned. *Gifted Child Quarterly, 58,* 287–296.

French, L. R., Walker, C. L., & Shore, B. M. (2011). Do gifted students really prefer to work alone? *Roeper Review, 33,* 145–159.

Friedman, R. C., & Shore, B. M. (2000). *Talents unfolding: Cognition and development.* Washington, DC: American Psychological Association.

Gagné, R. M. (1970). *The conditions of learning* (2nd ed.). New York, NY: Holt, Rinehart, and Winston.

Gross, M. U. M. (2000). Issues in the cognitive development of exceptionally and profoundly gifted individuals. In K. A. Heller, F. J. Mönks, R. J. Sternberg, & R. F. Subotnik (Eds.), *International handbook of giftedness and talent* (2nd ed.). Amsterdam, Netherlands: Elsevier.

Kanevsky, L. S. (1995). Learning potentials of gifted students. *Roeper Review, 17,* 157–163.

Kanevsky, L. S. (2011). Deferential differentiation: What types of differentiation do students want? *Gifted Child Quarterly, 55,* 279–299.

Kanevsky, L. S., & Geake, J. (2004). Inside the zone of proximal development: Validating a multifactor model of learning potential with gifted students and their peers. *Journal for the Education of the Gifted, 28,* 182–217.

Kaplan, S. (2007). Differentiation by depth and complexity. In W. Conklin & S. Frei (Eds.), *Differentiating the curriculum for gifted learners* (pp. 79–88). Huntington Beach, CA: Shell.

Lajoie, S. P., & Shore, B. M. (1986). Intelligence: The speed and accuracy trade-off in high aptitude individuals. *Journal for the Education of the Gifted, 9,* 85–104.

Little, C. A., Feng, A. X., VanTassel-Baska, J., Rogers, K. B., & Avery, L. D. (2007). A study of curriculum effectiveness in social studies. *Gifted Child Quarterly, 51,* 272–284.

Loewen, S. (2006). Exceptional intellectual performance: A neo-Piagetian perspective. *High Ability Studies, 17,* 159–181.

Maniatis, E., Cartwright, G. F., & Shore, B. M. (1998). Giftedness and complexity in a self-directed computer-based task. *Gifted and Talented International, 13,* 83–89.

Mann, E. (2006). Creativity: The essence of mathematics. *Journal for the Education of the Gifted, 30,* 236–260.

Matsko, V., & Thomas, J. (2014). The problem is the solution: Creating original problems in gifted mathematics classes. *Journal for the Education of the Gifted, 37,* 153–170.

Meeker, M. N. (1969). *SOI: Its interpretation and its uses.* Columbus, OH: Merrill.

Morgan, A. (2007). Experiences of a gifted and talented enrichment cluster for pupils aged five to seven. *British Journal of Special Education, 34,* 144–153.

National Research Council. (2000). *Inquiry and the national science education standards.* Washington, DC: National Academies Press.

National Research Council. (2012). *A framework for K–12 science education: Practices, crosscutting concepts, and core ideas.* Washington, DC: National Academies Press.

Palincsar, A. M. (1998). Social constructivist perspectives on teaching and learning. *Annual Review of Psychology, 49,* 345–375.

Pelletier, S. (1994). *Habilité, expertise, et catégorisation des problèmes mathématiques* [Ability, expertise, and categorization of mathematical problems]. Master's thesis, McGill University, Montreal, Quebec, Canada. Retrieved from http://digitool.library.mcgill.ca/R/-?func=dbin-jump-full&object_id=141124&silo_library=GEN01

Pelletier, S., & Shore, B. M. (2003). The gifted learner, the novice, and the expert: Sharpening emerging views of giftedness. In D. C. Ambrose, L. Cohen, & A. J. Tannenbaum (Eds.), *Creative intelligence: Toward theoretic integration* (pp. 237–281). New York, NY: Hampton Press.

Piaget, J. (1956). *The origins of intelligence in children.* (M. Cook, Trans.). New York, NY: International University Press.

Québec. (2004). *Québec education program: Secondary school education, cycle one.* Québec, Quebec, Canada: Ministère de l'Éducation du Québec. Retrieved from http://www.mels.gouv.qc.ca/DGFJ/dp/programme_de_formation/secondaire/pdf/qep2004/qepsecfirstcycle.pdf

Québec. (2007). *Reaffirming the mission of our school: A new direction for success. Report of the task force on curriculum reform.* Retrieved from http://www.learnquebec.ca/toolkit/documents/newdirections.htm

Rabinowitz, M., & Glaser, R. (1985). Cognitive structure and processes in highly competent performance. In E. D. Horowitz & M. O'Brien (Eds.), *The gifted and talented: Developmental perspectives* (pp. 75–98). Washington, DC: American Psychological Association.

Reis, S. M., Gentry, M., & Maxfield. L. R. (1998). The application of gifted education pedagogy to teachers' classroom practices. *Journal for the Education of the Gifted, 21,* 310–334.

Renzulli, J. S. (1994). *Schools for talent development: A practical plan for total school improvement.* Mansfield Center, CT: Creative Learning Press.

Renzulli, J. S., Gentry, M., & Reis, S. M. (2004). A time and a place for authentic learning. *Educational Leadership, 62,* 73–77.

Rich, R. J., Leatham, K. R., & Wright, J. A. (2013). Convergent cognition. *Instructional Science, 41,* 431–453. doi:10.1007/s11251-012-9240-7

Robinson, A., Shore, B. M., & Enersen, D. L. (2006). *Best practices in gifted education: An evidence-based guide.* Waco, TX: Prufrock Press.

Saunders-Stewart, K. S., Walker, C. L., & Shore, B. M. (2013). How do parents and teachers of gifted students perceive group work in classrooms? *Gifted and Talented International, 28,* 99–109.

Shore, B. M. (2010). Giftedness is not what it used to be, school is not what it used to be, their future, and why psychologists in education should care. *Canadian Journal of School Psychology, 25,* 151–199. doi:10.1177/0829573509356896

Shore, B. M., Aulls, M. W., & Delcourt, M. A. B. (Eds.). (2008). *Inquiry in education (Vol. II): Overcoming barriers to successful implementation.* New York, NY: Erlbaum.

Shore, B. M., & Delcourt, M. A. B. (1996). Effective curricular and program practices in gifted education and the interface with general education. *Journal for the Education of the Gifted, 20,* 138–154.

Shore, B. M., & Kanevsky, L. S. (1993). Thinking processes: Being and becoming gifted. In K. A. Heller, F. J. Mönks, & A. H. Passow (Eds.), *International handbook of research and development of giftedness and talent* (pp. 133–147). Oxford, England: Pergamon.

Shore, B. M., Koller, M. B., & Dover, A. C. (1994). More from the water jars: A reanalysis of problem-solving performance among gifted and nongifted children. *Gifted Child Quarterly, 38,* 179–183.

Shulman, L. S. (1986). Those who understand: Knowledge growth in teaching. *Educational Researcher, 15*(2), 4–14.

Shulman, L. S. (1987). Knowledge and teaching: Foundations of the new reform. *Harvard Educational Review, 57,* 1–22.

Siegler, R. S. (1996). *Emerging minds: The process of change in children's thinking.* New York, NY: Oxford University Press.

Sriraman, B. (2003). Mathematical giftedness, problem solving, and the ability to formulate generalizations: The problem-solving experiences of four gifted students. *Journal of Secondary Gifted Education, 14,* 151–165.

Steiner, H. H., & Carr, M. (2003). Cognitive development in gifted children: Toward a more precise understanding of emerging differences in intelligence. *Educational Psychology Review, 15,* 215–246.

Sternberg, R. J. (1977). *Intelligence, information processing, and analogical reasoning: The componential analysis of human abilities.* Hillsdale, NJ: Erlbaum.

Sternberg, R. J. (2001). Giftedness as developing expertise: A theory of the interface between high abilities and achieved excellence. *High Ability Studies, 12,* 159–179.

Sternberg, R. J., & Davidson, J. E. (1985). Cognitive development in the gifted and talented. In F. D. Horowitz & M. O'Brien (Eds.), *The gifted and talented: A developmental perspective* (pp. 37–74). Washington, DC: American Psychological Association.

Threlfall, J., & Hargreaves, M. (2008). The problem-solving methods of mathematically gifted and older average-attaining students. *High Ability Studies, 19,* 83–98.

Tjoe, H. (2015). Giftedness and aesthetics: Perspectives of expert mathematicians and mathematically gifted students. *Gifted Child Quarterly, 59,* 165–176.

Tomlinson, C. A. (1999). *The differentiated classroom: Responding to the needs of all learners.* Alexandria, VA: Association for Supervision and Curriculum Development.

Tomlinson, C. A., & Jarvis, J. M. (2009). Differentiation: Making curriculum work for all students through responsive planning and instruction. In J. S. Renzulli, E. J. Gubbins, K. S. McMillen, R. D. Eckert, & C. A. Little (Eds.), *Systems and models for developing programs for the gifted and talented* (2nd ed.; pp. 599–628). Mansfield Center, CT: Creative Learning Press.

VanTassel-Baska, J. (2014). Artful inquiry: The use of questions in working with the gifted. *Gifted Child Today, 37,* 48–50.

VanTassel-Baska, J., & Brown, E. (2007). Toward best practice. *Gifted Child Quarterly, 51,* 342–358.

VanTassel-Baska, J., & Stambaugh, T. (2006). *Comprehensive curriculum for gifted learners* (3rd ed.). Boston, MA: Allyn & Bacon.

Vygotsky, L. S. (1978). *Mind in society: The development of higher psychological processes* (M. Cole, Trans.). Cambridge, MA: Harvard University Press.

Ward, V. S. (1961). *Educating the gifted: An axiomatic approach.* Columbus, OH: Merrill.

Zohar, A., & Dori, Y. J. (2003). Higher order thinking skills and low-achieving students: Are they mutually exclusive? *The Journal of the Learning Sciences, 12,* 145–181.

The Basics for Advanced Learning

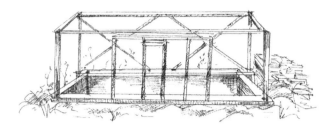

A strong foundation anchors the building in preparation for the next step: framing. The framing gives the building its shape, determines its size, establishes the number of floors, and ultimately provides a sturdy framework for the building. Strong and level, it directs the rest of construction.

The framework for the home may be made of wood and metal, but the framework for gifted education comprises which students are identified, what they learn, how we assess what they are learning, and the environment in which they live and learn.

This section has five chapters: "Identification," "Curriculum for Gifted Students: Developing Talent and Intellectual Character," "Learning Assessments for Gifted Learners," "Designing the Learning Environment for Gifted Students," and "The Learning Environment at Home: Parents and Families."

Myths

» **IQ is the only valid determiner of giftedness.** IQ is a valid determiner, but using multiple measures is best practice.

» **It is important to have gifted students in classes to be role models.** Gifted children need to be placed in classes where they can make continuous progress. Students don't relate to role models who are too different from themselves.

CHAPTER 7

Identification

Susan K. Johnsen

Not everything that can be counted counts, and not everything
that counts can be counted.—Albert Einstein

Essential Questions to Guide the Reader

1. How does the conception of giftedness influence identification practices?

2. How do the types and forms of assessments influence which students are identified as gifted and talented?

3. How might a school ensure that all students with gifts and talents are identified?

History of Identification

The history of the identification of gifted and talented students parallels the measurement of individual differences, particularly in the area of intellectual variations. Initially intelligence was viewed as comprising elementary cognitive processes such as reaction time and sensory discriminations (Cattell, 1890; Galton, 1883). Later, Binet and Simon (1905) assessed complex processes such as comprehension, judgment, and imagination to examine the full range of individual differences. The Binet scales were enthusiastically received in the United States and eventually translated into English and published by Terman in 1916 (i.e., the Stanford-Binet test). Terman's interest in "genius" led to his classic longitudinal study of 1,500 gifted children, *Genetic Studies of Genius* (Terman, 1925). In his study, children who scored above 140 on the Stanford-Binet test were identified as gifted. Hollingworth also used the Stanford-Binet to select highly gifted students for her school in New York City (i.e., those scoring in the top 1% of the population; Morelock & Feldman, 1997). The magnitude of the intelligence test score was therefore used to categorize gifted individuals as exceptionally gifted (IQ 150 and over) or profoundly gifted (IQ 180 and over; Webb, Meckstroth, & Tolan, 1982). Spearman (1927) supported the view that a common element existed between all cognitive processes measured on intelligence tests. He labeled this common element "*g*" for general intelligence and any variations as "s"—a two-factor theory. Based on these views and practices, the identification of gifted individuals was synonymous with performance on intelligence tests during the first half of the 20th century.

Beginning in the 1950s, with Guilford's address to the American Psychological Association regarding creativity (Guilford, 1950), the conception of intelligence became more multifaceted. Guilford (1967) proposed more than 120 independent abilities in his Structure of the Intellect model, and R. B. Cattell (1963) described two different *g* components: fluid intelligence (biological or genetically acquired) and crystallized intelligence (acquired through education.) After analyzing all of the different ability matrices, Carroll (1993) developed a three-stratum taxonomic structure in which *g*, fluid intelligence, is at the apex of a hierarchical structure of abilities followed by crystallized intelligence, general memory and learning, and other general processes (visual and auditory perception, retrieval, and speed). This taxonomic structure is central to the design of current intelligence tests.

Along with the conception of intelligence, identification has also been influenced by definitions of gifted and talented students. These definitions have paralleled the changing conceptions of intelligence. For example, Binet and Simon (1916) defined intelligence as the "ability to judge well, to comprehend well, and to reason well" (pp. 42–43). Terman (1916) suggested that intelligence is "an individual's ability to carry on abstract thinking" (p. 42). By 1972, the U.S. Office of Education provided a broader definition of gifted and talented students (Marland, 1972) that not only included general intellectual abilities but also specific academic aptitude, creative or productive thinking, leadership ability, visual and performing arts, and psychomotor ability. This definition was revised in 1993 but included essentially the same areas: "exhibit high performance capability in intellectual, creative, and/or artistic areas, unusual leadership capacity, or excel in specific academic fields" (U.S. Department of Education, 1993, p. 3). These federal definitions have influenced state definitions of gifted and talented students with most incorporating multiple areas: intelligence ($n = 38$), academic fields ($n = 24$), creativity ($n = 24$), and performing/visual arts ($n = 21$; National Association for Gifted Children [NAGC] & Council of State Directors of Programs for the Gifted [CSDPG], 2013). These broader definitions subsequently influenced the use of multiple criteria ($n = 25$) in the identification process with most states using varied assessments: intelligence tests ($n = 15$), achievement tests ($n = 16$), state-approved tests ($n = 14$), and nominations ($n = 7$). Along with these changing definitions, models have been created over the past 30 years to explain how gifted individuals develop their talents in achieving their full potential.

Current Views of Giftedness

Current researchers view giftedness as complex and multifaceted (Gagné, 1995, 1999; Renzulli, 1978; Subotnik, Olszewski-Kubilius, & Worrell, 2011; Tannenbaum, 1983). Abilities are not exhibited independently of the environment or other factors but rather are reciprocally influenced. For example, Renzulli (1978) viewed giftedness as the interaction among high levels of creativity, high levels of above-average intelligence, and high levels of task commitment. This interaction among the three clusters is necessary for creative and productive accomplishments. Similarly, Tannenbaum (1983) identified five factors that influence giftedness or outstanding performance: general ability (e.g., general intelligence), special ability (e.g., aptitude in a specific area), nonintellective facilitators (e.g., metalearning, commitment, strong self-concept, mental health, willingness to sacrifice), environmental influences (e.g., parents, classroom, peers, culture, social class), and chance. Gagné (1995, 1999) described not only multiple factors but also how gifts become developed into talents within different domains. Two sets of catalysts facilitate the talent development. Intrapersonal catalysts are described as genetic background and included physical (e.g., health, physical appearance) and psychological (e.g., motivation, personality, volition) factors. Environmental catalysts are surroundings (e.g., geographic, demographic, sociological), people (e.g., parents, teachers, siblings, peers), undertakings (e.g., programs for gifted and talented students), and events (e.g., divorce, changing schools, winning an award). More recently, Subotnik et al. (2011) described these factors as contributing to the development of eminence: general and domain specific abilities, task commitment, creativity, opportunity in the form of access to teaching and appropriate resources, psychosocial influences (motivation, opportunities taken, productive mindsets, psychological strength, social skills), and chance (financial resources, social and cultural capital, opportunities offered inside and outside of school).

These current conceptions of giftedness have influenced principles that provide the foundation for the identification process:

- *Giftedness is complex and multifaceted.* Theories, models, and recent research suggest that giftedness includes a set of interacting factors such as general intelligence, domain-related skills, creativity, and environmental and non-intellective factors such as self-regulation, self concept, commitment, interests, and mental health (Renzulli, 1999; Worrell & Erwin, 2011).

- *Gifts and talents are dynamic and developed over time.* Gagné (1999, 2004) emphasized the developmental nature of giftedness. He suggested that although individuals may have natural abilities placing them in the top 10% of their peer group, this gift needs to be developed into a talent through formal or informal learning. The result of talent development is exceptional performance (Subotnik et al., 2011). Giftedness is therefore a description of an individual's potential at a particular point in time (Pfeiffer, 2012).

- *Students exhibit their gifts and talents not only within a specific domain but also within an interest area* (Johnsen, 2008). For example, students whose gifts and interests are in science may not be recognized because identification instruments may assess the areas of English language arts and mathematics only. Because of the variation within the gifted and talented population, researchers suggest that domain-specific skills need to be assessed along with measures of general intelligence and then developed (Assouline & Lupkowski-Shoplik, 2012; Worrell & Erwin, 2011).

- *Giftedness is exhibited across all racial, ethnic, income levels, and exceptionality groups* (Johnsen, 2008). Although most states have definitions, policies, or rules that address the identification of gifted students from special populations, underrepresentation still occurs (Coleman, Gallagher, & Foster, 1994; Ford, Grantham, & Whiting, 2008; Worrell, 2003). Ford et al. (2008) estimated that African American students are underrepresented by about 51% and Hispanic students by about 42% in gifted programs. More equal representation across groups is enhanced when (a) definitions encompass a wider range of abilities (Pfeiffer, 2002), (b) professional development for teachers and parents is provided so that talents of more children from diverse backgrounds are recognized (Speirs Neumeister, Adams, Pierce, Cassady, & Dixon, 2007), and (c) tests fair to all populations in the identification process are used (Ryser, 2011a).

- *Early identification improves the likelihood that gifts will develop into talents* (Johnsen, 2008). Not being involved in appropriate educational opportunities early can result in domain-specific deficits that are not easily overcome (Subotnik et al., 2011). Researchers also report that when students from diverse backgrounds are identified early and attend schools and classes for gifted and talented students, they have higher achievement than those who are placed in general education classrooms with limited or no services (Borland, Schnur, & Wright, 2000; Cornell, Delcourt, Goldberg,

Table 7.1
National Standards Related to Identification

2013 NAGC-CEC Teacher Preparation Standards for Gifted and Talented Education
Beginning gifted education professionals use multiple methods of assessment and data sources in making educational decisions about identification of individuals with gifts and talents and student learning (NAGC-CEC 4.0, 2013)
Beginning gifted education professionals understand that some groups of individuals with gifts and talents have been underrepresented in gifted education programs and select and use technically sound formal and informal assessments that minimize bias in identifying students for gifted education programs and services (NAGC-CEC 4.1, 2013)
Beginning gifted education professionals collaborate with colleagues and families in using multiple types of assessment information to make identification and learning progress decisions and to minimize bias in assessment and decision-making (NAGC-CEC 4.3, 2013)
2010 NAGC Pre-K-Grade 12 Gifted Programming Standards: Student Outcomes
All students in grades PK–12 have equal access to a comprehensive assessment system that allows them to demonstrate diverse characteristics and behaviors that are associated with giftedness (NAGC 2.1, 2010)
Each student reveals his or her exceptionalities or potential through assessment evidence so that appropriate instructional accommodations and modifications can be provided (NAGC 2.2, 2010)
Students with identified needs represent diverse backgrounds and reflect the total student population of the district (NAGC 2.3, 2010)

& Bland, 1995; Franklin, 2009). Therefore, identification needs to begin as early as prekindergarten and comprehensively address a diverse range of characteristics.

Best Practices in Identification

Based on these principles and current conceptions of giftedness, researchers, psychologists, and educators have collaborated in identifying best practices for identifying students for gifted and talented programs (Council for Exceptional Children [CEC], 2010; Worrell & Erwin, 2011). This research literature has been used to develop standards and guidelines for developing and implementing identification procedures in schools (see Table 7.1) so that specific student outcomes are addressed (NAGC, 2010; NAGC & CEC, 2013).

Research-based practices that support these national standards relate to educating teachers and families about the characteristics of students with gifts and talents, developing environments where students are able to demonstrate their gifts and talents, establishing comprehensive identification procedures, using quality assessments, interpreting assessment results, and ensuring that the process minimizes bias and is equitable. If schools implement these practices, there is a greater likelihood that students with gifts and talents will be recognized and served.

Educate Teachers and Families

Teachers need to know the characteristics of students with gifts and talents. Without training, teachers are more likely to nominate students who reflect previously held conceptions of giftedness. They may believe that all gifted students are academically able (Hunsaker, Finley, & Frank, 1997), are from higher socioeconomic status groups (Guskin, Peng, & Simon, 1992), and are verbal and well mannered (Speirs Neumeister et al., 2007). These preconceptions often exclude diverse students from the identification process, such as English language learners (Esquierdo & Arreguín-Anderson 2012) or students from poverty (Peterson & Margolin, 1997).

Families need to be aware of the range of characteristics of students with gifts and talents, how to nurture their children's talents and interests, the importance of gifted education, and how to provide important information to the school about their child, such as completing nomination forms or collecting items for a portfolio of best work. Families need to understand the identification process, particularly those from lower income backgrounds who may not request nomination forms (Scott, Perou, Urbano, Hogan, & Gold, 1992), be reluctant to refer their children for assessment (Frasier, Garcia, & Passow, 1995), or not understand or approve behaviors associated with giftedness (Coleman & Cross, 2005). To increase the representation of special populations in the referral phase, schools need to send home information in a language that parents understand, include information about the gifted program at school orientations and special meetings, and make announcements through public and social media (Coleman, 1994; Dawson, 1997; Johnsen & Ryser, 1994; Reyes, Fletcher, & Paez, 1996; Shaklee & Viechnicki, 1995). Those families who have fewer financial resources may also need assistance in finding after-school and summer enrichment programs that offer scholarships to develop their children's talents (Johnsen, Feuerbacher, & Witte, 2007). In summary, family and educator support are extremely important in recognizing students with gifts and talents and providing them with early exposure to the talent domain, special services or learning outside of school, and quality education (Filippelli & Walberg, 1997; Olszewski-Kubilius, 2000; Subotnik, 1997; Williams, 2003).

Develop Environments That Provide Equal Access

If the goal of gifted education is to identify *all* students who need specialized curriculum and services to develop their potential, then educators need to design differentiated classroom environments where individual differences may emerge

(Hertzog, 2005; Worrell & Erwin, 2011). Individual differences exist in what students know and want to know (e.g., the knowledge and skills they are learning—the subject matter content and their interests), how quickly they learn the content (e.g., pacing and rate of learning), how they learn (e.g., preference for different types of activities), and the environment where they learn (e.g., individual, small group, community) (Johnsen, 2011). Teachers may differentiate by using pre-, ongoing, and summative assessments so that students do not have to review what they already know; organizing flexible groups around students' academic strengths and interests; using problem- or concept-based curriculum; adding depth and complexity to their learning experiences; providing variations and choices in assessments and assignments; and allowing students time to pursue their interests. Students who are placed in special education or in classrooms where teachers don't believe in gifted education should not be excluded from the identification process. Without this differentiation and attention to students from diverse backgrounds, teachers may not recognize all of the students with gifts and talents who need services.

Establish Comprehensive Identification Procedures Aligned to Student Characteristics

Identification procedures need to be comprehensive. To address this practice, school districts must look at their entire K–12 program to ensure that the identification procedures are in alignment with one another, with the program, and with the characteristics of the students (Johnsen, 2011; Worrell & Erwin, 2011). The assessments also need to be comprehensive so that students' talents and gifts may be recognized at any grade level and cohesive so that high performance at one level is predictive of high performance at another level. For example, if a school district has an accelerated mathematics program for students with gifts and talents, off-level assessments might be used beginning in kindergarten and aligned with end-of-course exams in various mathematics and advanced placement courses at the secondary level. These assessments would not only be aligned with math learning progressions but also designed so that they have similar difficulty levels (i.e., are equivalent). Students are then able to proceed smoothly and receive appropriate accelerated math programming. Assessments also need to be ongoing. Not all children will have the same educational opportunities and will not be able to demonstrate their potential until they have access to challenging, specialized curriculum or a gifted education teacher. Recognition of gifts and talents may occur at any point in the educational process.

Along with the alignment to the program, Louis, Subotnik, Breland, and Lewis (2000) emphasized how admission criteria need to be based on students' characteristics. They use the example of Juilliard's precollege program. Criteria include auditions, cutoff scores on a standardized test, and referrals from a network of outstanding teachers who serve as talent scouts. On the other hand, Hunter College Elementary School—whose students' characteristics include intellective traits such as general intelligence and abstract reasoning and nonintellective traits such as creativity, motivation, task commitment, and attention span—uses an intelligence test, a set of four problem-solving activities, and observations of children's interactions within a classroom setting.

Select and Use Quality Assessments

Assessments need to be aligned to the program and to the characteristics of the students. For example, if a school offers services for students with talents in the sciences, then the identification instruments would be different from those used for identifying students with potential in the arts. In addition, if the majority of students within the district are from special populations (e.g., English language learners, low income), then different types of assessments would need to be considered, such as those that are nonverbal or linguistically reduced. In all cases multiple criteria are needed because no single assessment is able to sample all of the behaviors demonstrated by the diverse population of gifted students (Johnsen, 2011). Multiple assessments include traditional intelligence and achievement tests, teacher checklists, portfolios, peer and self-nominations, auditions, interviews, parent questionnaires, products, activity checklists, and so on.

In selecting multiple instruments, these assessment qualities should be considered: variety of sources, qualitative and quantitative, out-of-level testing, bias, and technical adequacy.

- *Variety of sources.* Because not all students will exhibit their potential in the classroom, a variety of sources should be included during the identification process (Johnsen, 2011). These sources provide different perspectives of the same student and include teachers, families, peers, counselors, administrators, and community members.
- *Qualitative and quantitative.* Another way of gathering more information about the student is to use both qualitative and quantitative assessments. Qualitative assessments use words to describe the students' strengths and needs, while quantitative assessments use numbers (Ryser, 2011b). Qualitative assessments have the advantage of gathering information in more authentic contexts that might represent the student's talents and interests, such as products or performances, whereas quantitative assessments are more controlled so that results are consistent across testing administrations. When used together, they provide a broader view of the student's gifts and talents. In terms of specific assessments, researchers suggest that intellectual tests are good at predicting academic achievement but not sufficient (Neisser et al., 1996), creativity is best examined with the

academic domain (Park, Lubinski, & Benbow, 2007, 2008), products and performances are good at identifying potential (Tai, Liu, Maltese, & Fan, 2006; Wai, Lubinski, Benbow, & Steiger, 2010), and teacher rating scales are best for identifying psychosocial aspects (Worrell & Erwin, 2011).

- *Out-of-level testing.* Because some gifted students are performing above grade level in academic domains, off-level testing is needed to uncover what they don't know (Lupkowski-Shoplik & Swiatek, 1999). Group tests, state-mandated tests, and diagnostic achievement tests often do not have sufficient ceilings and shouldn't be used unless in combination with multi-level or out-of-level assessments (McIntosh & Dixon, 2005).

- *Minimize bias.* Special care needs to be taken to ensure that assessments minimize bias and are sensitive to cultural differences. When examining the test manual, educators need to look for (a) norms that are representative of the national population, (b) studies that compare performance differences between groups (e.g., minority, gender, disability), and (c) items that may have potential bias against particular groups (Ryser, 2011a). Some types of assessments such as performance and nonverbal measures may be better at identifying students from diverse backgrounds (Ryser, 2011a; VanTassel-Baska, Feng, & Evans, 2007) but need to be supplemented with other information (Worrell & Erwin, 2011). Worrell and Erwin (2011) suggested that preskills instead of developed skills might need to be assessed when testing students who are English language learners or from low-socioeconomic backgrounds. In addition, local norms might need to be developed if the school population is significantly different from the national norms (Lohman & Lakin, 2008).

- *Technically adequate.* Assessments need to meet the standards outlined by professional organizations in the measurement field (American Educational Research Association, American Psychological Association, & National Council on Measurement in Education, 2014). These standards describe the foundations underlying assessments, such as validity, reliability, and test fairness. Validity represents how well the assessment measures what it is supposed to measure. Reliability is defined by consistency within the assessment, over time, and across raters. Resources can assist educators in making informed decisions when selecting assessments (see *Mental Measurements Yearbook* and Robins & Jolly, 2011, for a review of quantitative assessments that are used in identifying gifted and talented students).

Organize and Interpret Assessment Results

Once identification information is gathered, the data need to be organized and interpreted by individuals who are familiar with the characteristics of gifted and talented students, the diversity of this group, and influences that might affect their performance. In addition, the identification committee needs to have knowledge about the psychometric qualities of measurements, different types of scores and how they compare with one another, the standard error of measurement, and limitations of assessments (Johnsen, 2011).

Different types of scores. Assessments provide different types of scores. Raw scores, which are the original numeric values, are transformed to other scores for comparison purposes: percentile ranks, standard or index scores, and grade equivalent scores.

Percentile ranks show the relative rank of how a student performed in relationship to other students who took the test. They should not be confused with percentages, which are simply the number of items that a student passed divided by the total number of items. A student who obtained a percentile rank of 95 performed better than 95% of the students who took the test. However, a difference between the 90th and the 95th percentile is not the same as a difference between the 50th and the 55th percentile because percentile ranks cluster heavily around the mean or average and are more sparsely distributed at the top and bottom.

Standard or index scores are based on the bell-shaped curve. They describe how well the student is performing above or below the average (or mean) for the group, which is at the top of the bell shape. The number that test developers use to indicate the mean will vary based on the type of standard score. For example, a z-score's average is described as a 0, a T-score's average is described as 50, and an IQ score's average is described as 100 (see Table 7.2). Similar to the different numbers used to describe average, how the distance is described above and below the mean (or standard deviation = SD) will also vary with the type of score. For example, z-scores have an SD of 1, T-scores have an SD of 10, and IQ scores have an SD of 15. Table 7.2 shows that a +1.00 under the z-score column, which is one standard deviation from the mean, is comparable to +60 under the T-score column, which is comparable to +115 under the intelligence quotients column. Given the percentile rank in the first column, one might interpret all of these scores by saying that the student performed better than 84% of the students who took the test. Table 7.2 also indicates that a +2.00 under the z-score column, which is two standard deviations from the mean, is comparable to +70 under the T-score column, which is comparable to +130 under the quotients column. All represent the 98th percentile; therefore, one might interpret these scores as saying that the student performed better than 98% of the students who took the test. One can continue in this fashion comparing scores at each level. Another good feature of standard scores is that standard deviations are of equal length across the entire bell-shaped curve. For example, the distance between an IQ score of 100 and 110 is the same as the distance between an IQ score of 130 and 140. Both equal 10 points. For this reason scores at all different points along the bell-shaped curve can be compared with one another and to percentile ranks

Table 7.2

Relationships Among Various Standard Scores and Percentile Ranks and Their Interpretation

Percentile Ranks	Intelligence Quotients	T-Scores	z-Scores	Stanines	Interpretation
99	150	83	+3.33	9	
99	145	80	+3.00	9	
99	140	77	+2.67	9	Very Superior
99	135	73	+2.33	9	
98	130	70	+2.00	9	
97	128	68	+1.75	8	
95	125	67	+1.67	8	Superior
94	123	65	+1.5	8	
84	115	60	+1.00	7	
81	113	58	+0.75	7	Above Average
75	110	57	+067	6	
63	105	53	+033	6	
50	100	50	0.00	5	Average
37	95	47	-0.33	4	
25	90	43	-0.67	4	
16	85	40	-1.00	3	
9	80	37	-1.33	3	Below Average

(see Table 7.2). Standard scores can also be compared to another group, which may be comprised of national, state, or local students. Sometimes local norms need to be developed if students in the school district are quite different than the national population (e.g., more students in poverty or more English language learners).

Grade or age equivalent scores are produced by examining each grade or age level's average raw score. Psychometricians then create a score using different types of statistical procedures. Because the scores are extrapolated and kindergarten students don't really take fifth-grade test items, a student in kindergarten performing at the fifth grade, sixth month (i.e., 5.6) on a math achievement test does not mean that she is solving math problems at a fifth-grade level. It simply means that she is solving math problems above grade level. Because knowledge acquired varies between grade levels and across ages, these scores should not be used in making placement decisions.

To summarize score comparisons, if a student were to score 130 on an intelligence test, perform at the 98th percentile on an off-level achievement test, and be ranked within the 9th stanine on a teacher checklist, how should her performance be described? One should state that the student was performing in the top 2% on all of the assessments. Notice that grade and age equivalent scores were not used since they are not comparable.

Standard error of measurement. Every test has error (i.e., the standard error of measurement [SEM]) that is based on the reliability or consistency of the test. A test score should therefore be viewed as an estimate of a student's actual performance, which falls within the upper and lower limits of the SEM. For example, if a test has an SEM of 3 points, then a standard score of 125 would be interpreted in this way: 68% of the time, a student's true score would fall within 122–128 (i.e., the superior range), a range of plus or minus one SEM or 3 points; 95% of the time, the true score would fall within 119–131 (i.e., the superior to very superior range), a range of plus or minus two SEM or 6 points; and 99% of the time, 116–134 (i.e., above average to very superior range), a range of plus or minus three SEM or 9 points (see Table 7.2).

Organization of information. Considering the varied characteristics of students with gifts and talents, the use of multiple assessments, comparable scores, and the standard error of measurement, the committee needs to carefully organize the information so that all information is considered, and the student's relative strengths and weaknesses can be determined. First, quantitative assessments should be considered equally in making decisions. Weighting of one assessment can occur when (a) the committee considers one instrument as more important than another (e.g., intelligence test as more important than a performance rating), (b) a source of information is used more than once (e.g., the teacher completes a checklist and also scores the product), and (c) a test is used as a gatekeeper (e.g., the student must make a certain cutoff score on a test before the rest of the information is considered). If all of the assessments are technically adequate, they should all be considered in the decision-making process (Johnsen, 2011). Second, qualitative information should remain descriptive so that it might be used to interpret the quantitative data and provide a more holistic view of the student. Third, scores from each assessment should be separated to view the student's best and weakest performances. The highest score is often indicative of a student's potential. Scores should never be summed and averaged into a single rating. This approach doesn't help identify the student's best performance or potential nor does it aid in future programming. It also doesn't consider measurement error. Fourth, the committee needs to understand that all assessments have limitations and may not sample the behaviors that would show a particular student's talent. Moreover the assessments may have some bias toward particular groups and may not be sensitive enough to identify those students who are performing above grade level or those who have disabilities that inhibit or mask performance. Finally, the committee should consider which students would benefit from gifted education programming and not limit who is served to a specific number or rigid cutoff score.

Minimize Bias Throughout the Process

The Office for Civil Rights (Trice & Shannon, 2002) provides guidelines for minimizing bias throughout the process. These guidelines relate to providing notice, referral and screening, evaluation and placement, and program participation. In providing notice, the purpose of the program, procedures, eligibility criteria, and the school district's contact person need to be simply and clearly explained to students, families, and others who might be involved in the identification process. Referral and screening criteria need to use multiple referral sources, be applied in a nondiscriminatory manner, and be related to the purpose of the gifted program. Teachers and other district staff need to have professional development regarding the characteristics of giftedness among underrepresented groups. Placement decisions are based on multiple criteria that are applied in a nondiscriminatory manner and are consistent with the purpose of the gifted program. Individuals involved in making decisions and interpreting assessment criteria are provided guidelines and training to ensure proper evaluation. Continued participation in the program is based on standards that are applied in a nondiscriminatory manner, are consistent with the program, and facilitate equal access for all students.

Example Case Study

One way that schools organize the data collected during the identification process is through a case study (see Figure 7.1). As can be seen in Figure 7.1, the assessment data are organized by phases (e.g., nomination/referral, screening, and selection), although the data might be organized by qualitative and quantitative information or another format.

In this case, the school offers programming in the core academic areas (i.e., math, science, social studies, and English language arts). There is a gifted education pullout teacher who supports the general education teacher in differentiating the classroom and also provides specialized curriculum in students' areas of strengths. During the screening and nomination phase, the counselor is responsible for collecting checklist information from a variety of sources (e.g., families, teachers, and the student). During the screening phase, quantitative data include checklists, achievement tests, and intelligence tests and are interpreted within ranges of performance. Along with percentile ranks and standard scores, the school inserts stanine scores because they are comparable and provide a range of performance, which takes into account some of the error in the assessments. Qualitative data collected include comments on checklists, interviews, and a portfolio of work. During the selection phase, the committee considers all of the information gathered from both phases in the identification process. The general education teacher, the gifted education teacher, the special education teacher, the family, the counselor, and the principal comprise the com-

Student: _Corina Fernandez-Garcia_   D.O.B.: _6-30-08_   ID#: _1523_   Date: _1-17-16_
Home School/Grade: _Ortega/Grade 2_ Language Spoken at Home: _Spanish_

I. Nomination/Referral Phase

Assessment	Score Obtained	Met Standard	Comments
Family Checklist (mother)	94th percentile SS 123 (8th stanine)	Yes	Math/Science (*see checklist*)
Counselor Checklist	98th percentile SS 130 (9th stanine)	Yes	Likes science; doesn't like class work (*see checklist*)
Teacher Checklist	81st percentile SS 113 (7th stanine)	No	Is distracted in class; doesn't do work (*see checklist*)
Achievement: Iowa Test of Basic Skills			
Reading	81st percentile SS 113 (7th stanine)	No	Above Average range
Math	95th percentile SS 125 (8th stanine)	Yes	Superior range
Science	99th percentile SS 135 (9th stanine)	Yes	Very superior range
Social Studies	75th percentile SS 110 (6th stanine)	No	Average range

II. Screening Committee Recommendation (*See committee members' signatures on back.*)

The Screening Committee has reviewed this student's data and has determined that he/she:
☑ Is recommended for additional screening.
☐ Is recommended and an exception is made because _____ .
☐ Is not recommended for additional screening.

III. Screening Phase

Interview	Exhibits characteristics (*see attached interview*)	Yes	Confirmed interests in science and her abilities in math
SAGES-2 Reasoning Math/Science LA/Social Studies	98th percentile SS 130 (9th stanine) SS 135 (9th stanine) SS 123 (8th stanine)	Yes	Very superior score on reasoning when compared to gifted sample
Portfolio of Work	Exhibits characteristics (*see attached artifacts*)	Yes	Science work shows interests and aptitudes

IV. Selection Committee Recommendation (*See committee members' signatures on plan.*)

Corina qualifies for services in the gifted classroom in science and math with differentiation in the general education classroom. Her interest in science needs to be developed further with a mentor.

Figure 7.1. Example case study.

mittee. All of the members must have received professional development in gifted education regarding the characteristics of gifted and talented students, particularly those from underrepresented populations, and gifted education.

In this particular case, each of the members reviewed the evidence before the committee met. They learned that the family had nominated their daughter for the gifted education program and completed the checklist. The background information indicated that Corina's first language was Spanish, and she began learning English in kindergarten in the school's bilingual program. She learned English rapidly and is now fluent and reading on grade level. She is a young second grader when compared to her peers because she was born in June, which may have influenced her performance on some of the tests if they did not provide age-related norms. There do appear to be discrepancies in the perspectives of the individuals regarding Corina's characteristics (e.g., the teacher's perspective versus family's perspective) and also in Corina's performance on achievement subtests. Her relative areas of strength appear to be in math with a strong interest in science. Upon reviewing the nomination/referral assessment data, the committee noted that Corina met the school district's standard (i.e., the 84th percentile or within the above-average to superior range) on the majority of the indicators, which was sufficient to recommend her for further assessment. During the screening phase, the counselor administered the nonverbal reasoning, language arts/social studies, and mathematics/science subtests of the Screening Assessment for Gifted Elementary and Middle School Students-2 (SAGES-2; Johnsen & Corn, 2001) because Corina appeared to be reading on grade level. She also knew that administering all of the subtests would provide the committee with comparisons to normal and gifted populations. The committee also interviewed Corina and reviewed a portfolio of her best work. Her interview and portfolio showed her talents and interest in math and science, and her performance on the SAGES-2 revealed her strengths in problem solving, mathematics and science, and overall learning potential. All of this information was considered in the committee's final recommendation, which was to place her in the gifted classroom for science and math, assist the general education teacher in differentiating the curriculum, and assist the family in nurturing her talents at home.

The case study format is based on best practices: (a) uses a variety of sources, (b) uses qualitative and quantitative assessments, (c) uses multilevel achievement tests that are designed for gifted students (e.g., SAGES-2), (d) uses nonverbal reasoning assessments along with verbal to minimize bias, (e) compares standard scores, (f) considers standard error of measurement, (g) organizes information to show students' strengths and weaknesses, and (h) presents all information for making decisions.

Development of Identification Procedures and Guidelines:

_____ Has the school developed clear guidelines regarding the identification of gifted and talented students?

_____ Are the guidelines aligned to gifted education programs and services?

_____ Are the guidelines aligned to gifted and talented students' characteristics, particularly those from underrepresented populations?

_____ Do the guidelines address informed consent, identification procedures, committee review, student retention, student reassessment, student exiting, and appeals procedures?

_____ Are the identification procedures comprehensive, spanning all grade levels and gifted education areas?

_____ Are the identification procedures cohesive, connected from one level to the next?

_____ Are the identification procedures ongoing, identifying students' gifts and talents throughout the school year?

Selection of Assessments:

_____ Are multiple assessments used during the identification process?

_____ Do the assessments provide both qualitative and quantitative information?

_____ Do multiple sources provide information?

_____ Are off-level tests used in determining achievement?

_____ Do assessments minimize bias and represent the local population?

_____ Are the assessments technically adequate (i.e., reliable and valid for the purposes of identification)?

Professional Development:

_____ Do educators and families receive information about characteristics of gifted and talented students, particularly those from diverse populations?

_____ Do educators and families understand the purpose and effects of gifted education?

_____ Do educators and families understand how to develop gifts and talents?

_____ Do educators and families understand the identification process?

_____ Do educators understand assessments, their use in the identification process, and their limitations?

Identification Process:

_____ Is identification information for families clear and in a language they would understand?

_____ Do classrooms provide opportunities for all students to express their gifts and talents?

_____ Do educators and families know how to collect assessment information?

_____ Do educators know how to adjust curriculum to learn about students' aptitude for learning?

_____ Do educators know how to interpret multiple assessments (e.g., compare scores, use standard error of measurement, examine relative strengths and weaknesses)?

Figure 7.2. Assessing the identification process.

Identification Process, *Continued:*

_____ Do educators organize data so that each student's relative strengths and weaknesses can be determined?

_____ Do educators use selection and placement criteria in a nondiscriminatory manner?

_____ Do educators collaborate with families in planning appropriate programming for gifted students?

_____ Is the programming plan aligned to each student's identified gifts and talents?

Student Outcomes:

_____ Do all students have equal access to the identification system (are all groups and schools equally represented in nomination and referral stages of the identification process)?

_____ Does each student have an opportunity to demonstrate his or her gift or talent?

_____ Do students in the gifted education program reflect the school district's population?

_____ Are all students who need gifted education services identified?

Figure 7.2. *Continued.*

Assessing Your School's Identification Process

In assessing a school's identification process, educators may want to use the checklist in Figure 7.2 to determine if they use best practices. These areas are addressed: development of identification procedures and guidelines, selection of assessments, professional development, identification process, and student outcomes.

Educators can use this checklist to assess strengths, to engage stakeholders in addressing any weaknesses, and in developing professional development for teachers, families, and others involved in the identification process. In responding positively to all of the statements on the checklist, a school has developed an identification procedure that is aligned to national standards and research-based practices.

Conclusion

Recognizing and identifying giftedness is critical to the development of each child's talents. Without this recognition, gifted students may not realize their potential. Definitions and conceptions of intelligence have influenced the ways that gifted and talented students are identified. Historically, giftedness was synonymous with intelligence. Performance on IQ tests indicated if an individual was gifted or not. Current researchers view giftedness as complex and more dynamic, interacting and reciprocally influenced by multiple factors: general ability, special ability, psychosocial factors, and the environment. Along with research, this developmental conception has influenced best practices in identification, which include educating teachers and families about the characteristics of students with gifts and talents, developing environments where students are able to demonstrate their gifts and talents, establishing comprehensive identification procedures, using quality assessments, interpreting assessment results, and ensuring that the process minimizes bias and is equitable. When schools use best practices, more students have access to gifted education programming and opportunities for developing their gifts and talents.

Big Ideas

1. The conceptions of gifted and talented students influence identification procedures.

2. The interaction of multiple factors influences the development of gifts and talents.

3. Identification of gifted students improves the likelihood that their talents will be developed.

4. Giftedness is exhibited across all diverse groups.

5. Multiple sources and types of assessments are needed to provide information about a gifted student's strengths in different domains and across varied environments.

6. Equal access needs to be considered at each stage in the identification process.

7. Identification needs to be comprehensive, cohesive, and ongoing.

Discussion Questions

1. Assume you have been appointed to a committee that will develop identification procedures for your school. You have been asked to assume a leadership role for selecting tests. What criteria will you use in selecting assessments?

2. You have noticed that the gifted education program does not represent the population of your district. What areas might you examine to address this challenge?

3. What topics might you include in a professional development workshop for teachers on identifying gifted students? For families?

4. Your school offers services to gifted and talented students in these areas: specific academic domains, leadership, and the visual and performing arts. What assessments might you use in identifying students for these services? Why would you use these assessments?

References

American Educational Research Association, American Psychological Association, & National Council on Measurement in Education. (2014). *Standards for educational and psychological testing*. Washington, DC: Author.

Assouline, S. G., & Lupkowski-Shoplik, A. (2012). The talent search model of gifted identification. *Journal of Psychoeducational Assessment, 30,* 45–59. doi:10.1177/0734282911433946

Binet, A., & Simon, T. (1905). Methodes nouvelles por le diagnostic du niveau intellectual des anormaux. *L'Année Psychologique, 11,* 191–244.

Binet, A., & Simon, T. (1916). *The development of intelligence in children* (E. S. Kit, Trans.). Baltimore, MD: Williams & Wilkins. (Original work published 1905)

Borland, J. H., Schnur, R., & Wright, L. (2000). Economically disadvantaged students in a school for the academically gifted: A postpositivist inquiry into individual and family adjustment. *Gifted Child Quarterly, 44,* 13–32.

Carroll, J. B. (1993). *Human cognitive abilities: A survey of factor-analytic studies.* New York, NY: Cambridge University Press.

Cattell, J. M. (1890). Mental tests and measurements. *Mind, 15,* 373–381.

Cattell, R. B. (1963). Theory of fluid and crystallized intelligence: A critical experiment. *Journal of Educational Psychology, 54,* 1–22.

Coleman, L. J. (1994). Portfolio assessment: A key to identifying hidden talents and empowering teachers of young children. *Gifted Child Quarterly, 38,* 65–69.

Coleman, L. J., & Cross, T. L. (2005). *Being gifted in school: An introduction to development, guidance, and teaching.* Waco, TX: Prufrock Press.

Coleman, M. R., Gallagher, J. J., & Foster, A. (1994). *Update report on state policies related to the identification of gifted students.* Chapel Hill: University of North Carolina at Chapel Hill, Gifted Education Policy Studies Program.

Cornell, D. G., Delcourt, M. A. B., Goldberg, M. D., & Bland, L. C. (1995). Achievement and self-concept of minority students in elementary school gifted programs. *Journal for the Education of the Gifted, 18,* 189–209.

Council for Exceptional Children. (2010). *Validation study resource manual.* Arlington, VA: Author.

Dawson, V. L. (1997). In search of the wild bohemian: Challenges in the identification of the creatively gifted. *Roeper Review, 19,* 148–152.

Esquierdo, J. J., & Arreguín-Anderson, M. (2012). The "invisible" gifted and talented bilingual students: A current report on enrollment in GT programs. *Journal for the Education of the Gifted, 35,* 35–47. doi:10.1177/0162353211432041

Filippelli, L. A., & Walberg, H. J. (1997). Childhood traits and conditions of eminent women scientists. *Gifted Child Quarterly, 41,* 95–103.

Ford, D. Y., Grantham, T. C., & Whiting, G. W. (2008). Culturally and linguistically linguistically diverse students in gifted education: Recruitment and retention issues. *Exceptional Children, 74,* 289–308.

Franklin, R. K. (2009). *A case study of a three-year pilot program on one district's attempt to increase the gifted identification of diverse elementary school students by having a talent development program* (Unpublished doctoral dissertation). Virginia Commonwealth University, Richmond.

Frasier, M. M., Garcia, J. H., & Passow, A. H. (1995). *A review of assessment issues in gifted education and their implications for identifying gifted minority students.* Storrs: University of Connecticut, The National Research Center on the Gifted and Talented.

Gagné, F. (1995). From giftedness to talent: A developmental model and its impact on the language of the field. *Roeper Review, 18,* 103–111.

Gagné, F. (1999). Gagné's differentiated model of giftedness and talent (DMGT) *Journal for the Education of the Gifted, 22,* 230–234.

Gagné, F. (2004). Transforming gifts into talents. The DMGT as a developmental theory. *High Ability Studies, 15,* 119–147.

Galton, F. (1883). *An inquiry into human faculty.* London, England: Macmillan.

Guilford, J. P. (1950). Creativity. *American Psychologist, 5,* 444–454.

Guilford, J. P. (1967). *The nature of human intelligence.* New York, NY: McGraw-Hill.

Guskin, S. L., Peng, C. J., & Simon, M. (1992). Do teachers react to "Multiple Intelligences"? Effect of teachers' stereotypes on judgments and expectancies for students with diverse patterns of giftedness/talent. *Gifted Child Quarterly, 36,* 32–37.

Hertzog, N. B. (2005). Equity and access: Creating general education classrooms responsive to potential giftedness. *Journal for the Education of the Gifted, 29,* 213–257.

Hunsaker, S. L., Finley, V. S., & Frank, E. L. (1997). An analysis of teacher nominations and student performance in gifted programs. *Gifted Child Quarterly, 41,* 19–24.

Johnsen, S. K. (2008). Identifying gifted and talented learners. In F. Karnes & K. Stephens, *Achieving excellence: Educating the gifted and talented* (pp. 135–153). New York, NY: Merrill Education/Prentice Hall.

Johnsen, S. K. (Ed.). (2011). *Identifying gifted students: A practical guide* (2nd ed.). Waco, TX: Prufrock Press.

Johnsen, S. K., & Corn, A. L. (2001). *SAGES-2: Screening assessment for gifted elementary and middle school students.* Austin, TX: Pro-Ed.

Johnsen, S. K., Feuerbacher, S., & Witte, M. M. (2007). Increasing the retention of gifted students from low income backgrounds in a university programs for the gifted: The UYP project. In J. VanTassel-Baska (Ed.), *Serving gifted learners beyond the traditional classroom: A guide to alternative programs and services* (pp. 55–79). Waco, TX: Prufrock Press.

Johnsen, S. K., & Ryser, G. (1994). Identification of young gifted children from lower income families. *Gifted and Talented International, 9*(2), 62–68.

Lohman, D. F., & Lakin, J. (2008). Nonverbal test scores as one component of an identification system: Integrating ability, achievement, and teacher ratings. In J. L. VanTassel-Baska (Ed.), *Alternative assessments for identifying gifted and talented students* (pp. 41–66). Waco, TX: Prufrock Press.

Louis, B., Subotnik, R. F., Breland, P. S., & Lewis, M. (2000). Establishing criteria for high ability versus selective admission to gifted programs: Implications for policy and practice. *Educational Psychology Review, 12,* 295–314.

Lupkowski-Shoplik, A., & Swiatek, M. A. (1999). Elementary student talent searches: Establishing appropriate guidelines for qualifying test scores. *Gifted Child Quarterly, 43,* 265–272.

Marland, S. P., Jr. (1972). *Education of the gifted and talented: Report to the Congress of the United States by the U. S. Commissioner of Education: Vol. 1.* Washington DC: U.S. Government Printing Office.

McIntosh, D. E., & Dixon, F. A. (2005). Use of intelligence tests in the identification of giftedness. In D. P. Flanagan & P. L. Harrison (Eds.), *Contemporary intellectual assessment* (pp. 504–520). New York, NY: Guilford Press.

Morelock, M. J., & Feldman, D. H. (1997). High-IQ, extreme precocity, and savant syndrome. In N. Colangelo & G. A. Davis (Eds.), *Handbook of gifted children* (2nd ed., pp. 439–459). Boston, MA: Allyn & Bacon.

National Association for Gifted Children. (2010). *NAGC Pre-K-Grade 12 gifted programming standards: A blueprint for quality gifted education programs.* Washington, DC: Author.

National Association for Gifted Children, & Council for Exceptional Children, The Association for the Gifted. (2013). *NAGC-CEC teacher preparation standards for gifted and talented education.* Retrieved from http://www.nagc.org/resources-publications/resources/national-standards-gifted-and-talented-education/nagc-cec-teacher

National Association for Gifted Children, & Council of State Directors of Programs for the Gifted. (2013). *2012–2013 State of the states in gifted education: National policy and practice data.* Washington, DC: Author.

Neisser, U., Boodoo, G., Bouchard, T. J., Boykin, A. W., Brody, N., Ceci, S. J., . . . Urbina, S. (1996). Intelligence: Knowns and unknowns. *American Psychologist, 51,* 77–101. doi:10.1037/0003-066X.51.2.77

Olszewski-Kubilius, P. (2000). The transition from childhood giftedness to adult creative productiveness: Psychological characteristics and social supports. *Roeper Review, 23,* 65–71.

Park, G., Lubinski, D., & Benbow, C. P. (2007). Contrasting intellectual patterns predict creativity in the arts and sciences: Tracking intellectually precocious youth over 25 years. *Psychological Science, 18,* 948–955.

Park, G., Lubinski, D., & Benbow, C. P. (2008). Ability differences among people who have commensurate degrees matter for scientific creativity. *Psychological Science, 19,* 957–961. doi:10.1111/j.1467-9280.2008.02182.x

Peterson, J. S., & Margolin, R. (1997). Naming gifted children: An example of unintended "reproduction." *Journal for the Education of the Gifted, 21,* 82–101.

Pfeiffer, S. I. (2002). Identifying gifted and talented students: Recurring issues and promising solutions. *Journal of Applied School Psychology, 19,* 31-50.

Pfeiffer, S. I. (2012). Current perspectives on the identification and assessment of gifted students. *Journal of Psychoeducational Assessment, 30*(1), 3–9. doi: 10.1177/0734282911428192

Renzulli, J. S. (1978). What makes giftedness? Reexamining a definition. *Phi Delta Kappan, 60,* 180–184, 261.

Renzulli, J. S. (1999). What is this thing called giftedness, and how do we develop it? A twenty-five year perspective. *Journal for the Education of the Gifted, 23,* 3–54.

Reyes, E. I., Fletcher, R., & Paez, D. (1996). Developing local multidimensional screening procedures for identifying giftedness among Mexican American border population. *Roeper Review, 18,* 208–211.

Robins, J. H., & Jolly, J. L., (2011). Technical information regarding assessment. In S. K. Johnsen (Ed.), *Identifying gifted students: A practical guide* (2nd ed., pp. 75–118). Waco, TX: Prufrock Press.

Ryser, G. R. (2011a). Fairness in testing and nonbiased assessment. In S. K. Johnsen (Ed.), *Identifying gifted students: A practical guide* (2nd ed., pp. 63–74). Waco, TX: Prufrock Press.

Ryser, G. R. (2011b). Qualitative and quantitative approaches to assessment. In S. K. Johnsen (Ed.), *Identifying gifted students: A practical guide* (2nd ed., pp. 37–61). Waco, TX: Prufrock Press.

Scott, M. S., Perou, R., Urbano, R., Hogan, A., & Gold, S. (1992). The identification of giftedness: A comparison of White, Hispanic and Black families. *Gifted Child Quarterly, 36,* 131–139.

Shaklee, B. D., & Viechnicki, K. J. (1995). A qualitative approach to portfolios: The early assessment for exceptional potential model. *Journal for the Education of the Gifted, 18,* 156–170.

Spearman, C. (1927). *The abilities of man.* London, England: MacMillan.

Speirs Neumeister, K. L., Adams, C. M., Pierce, R. L., Cassady, J. C., & Dixon, F. A. (2007). Fourth-grade teachers' perceptions of giftedness: Implications for identifying and serving diverse gifted students. *Journal for the Education of the Gifted, 30,* 479–499.

Subotnik, R. F. (1997). Talent developed: Conversations with masters in the arts and sciences: Vladimir Feltsman: Piano virtuoso and educational innovator *Journal for the Education of the Gifted, 20,* 306–317.

Subotnik, R. F., Olszewski-Kubilius, P., & Worrell, F. C. (2011). Rethinking giftedness and gifted education: A proposed direction forward based on psychological science. *Psychological Science in the Public Interest, 12*(1), 3–54.

Tai, R. H., Liu, C. Q., Maltese, A. V., & Fan, X. (2006). Planning for early careers in science. *Science, 312,* 1143–1144. doi:10.1126/science.1128690

Tannenbaum, A. J. (1983). *Gifted children: Psychological and educational perspectives.* New York, NY: Macmillan.

Terman, L. M. (1916). *The measurement of intelligence.* Boston, MA: Houghton Mifflin.

Terman, L. M. (1925). *Genetic studies of genius: Vol. I. Mental and physical traits of a thousand gifted children.* Stanford, CA: Stanford University Press.

Trice, B., & Shannon, B. (2002, April). *Office for Civil Rights: Ensuring equal access to gifted education.* Paper presented at the annual meeting of the Council for Exceptional Children, New York.

U.S. Department of Education. (1993). *National excellence: A case for developing America's talent.* Washington, DC: Author.

VanTassel-Baska, J., Feng, A. X., & Evans, B. L. (2007). Patterns of identification and performance among gifted students identified through performance tasks: A three-year analysis. *Gifted Child Quarterly, 51,* 218–231.

Wai, J., Lubinski, D., Benbow, C. P., & Steiger, J. H. (2010). Accomplishment in science, technology, engineering, and mathematics (STEM) and its relation to STEM educational dose: A 25-year longitudinal study. *Journal of Educational Psychology, 102,* 860–871. doi:10.1037/a0019454

Webb, J. T., Meckstroth, E. A., & Tolan, S. S. (1982). *Guiding gifted children: A practical source for parents and children.* Columbus, OH: Ohio Psychology Press.

Williams, F. (2003). What does musical talent look like to you? And what is the role of the school and its partners in developing talent? *Gifted Education International, 17,* 272–274.

Worrell, F. C. (2003). Why are there so few African Americans in gifted programs? In C. C. Yeakey & R. D. Henderson (Eds.), *Surmounting the odds: Education, opportunity, and society in the new millennium* (pp. 423–454). Greenwich, CT: Information Age.

Worrell, F. C., & Erwin, J. O. (2011). Best practices in identifying students for gifted and talented education programs. *Journal of Applied School Psychology, 27,* 319–340.

CHAPTER 8

Curriculum for Gifted Students

*Developing Talent and
Intellectual Character*

Todd Kettler

The real challenge for the future of curriculum in this field is the preparation of educators committed to the vision of curriculum as the core of what makes gifted education a worthwhile enterprise.—VanTassel-Baska (2004, p. xxxii)

Essential Questions to Guide the Reader

1. What characteristics of gifted learners drive modifications of pacing, depth, and complexity in the curriculum?

2. What are components of curriculum in gifted and talented education?

3. What evidence would one seek to validate that a curriculum is appropriate for gifted and talented students?

4. How can the goal of developing intellectual character influence curriculum and learning design in gifted education?

5. How might you defend VanTassel-Baska's assertion that curriculum is the core of what makes gifted education a worthwhile enterprise?

When the gifted students in Mrs. Kromer's third-grade class walk into the Regional Center for Advanced Academic Studies[1], they are beginning a learning adventure. The Regional Center is an elementary school for gifted students in grades 3–6. The English language arts curriculum reflects a carefully planned mix of the best curriculum design available for gifted learners. The students delve into advanced reading comprehension using Jacob's Ladder, a research-based approach to elevating the complexity of reading comprehension through advanced content and rigorous thinking skills. In addition, Mrs. Kromer engages the students in deep reading and discussion using the Junior Great Books series and shared inquiry approach. The third spoke of the reading program includes an independent reading program where students read books of their choice aligned to their independent reading level. Reading logs and reading journals allow the students to share their ideas and reflect on their reading preferences over time. Mrs. Kromer also models good reading and reflective thinking through class novel studies on challenging texts reflecting universal themes, great ideas, and enduring understandings.

In addition to the four-pronged approach to developing reading abilities, Mrs. Kromer immerses her third-grade students into an engaging vocabulary program designed specifically for gifted and advanced students that focuses on deep learning of vocabulary including Greek and Latin roots. The students are expected to integrate the vocabulary into writing assignments and oral communications. In addition, the students are introduced to sophisticated understanding of grammar and sentence structure beginning in third grade. The vocabulary and grammar are woven into the writing program with increasing complexity across grade levels, building students' capacities for writing narrative, expository, and argumentative texts.

The gifted curriculum at the Regional Center only begins in Mrs. Kromer's class. Each component of the four-pronged approach to reading, as well as the vocabulary, grammar, and writing programs, are aligned across each grade level from third grade through the end of middle school. The comprehensive gifted language arts program includes common terminology, increasing complexity, aligned assessment protocols, and plentiful teacher resources to develop engaging learning designs. Similarly well-defined curricula characterize mathematics, science, and social studies at the Regional Center.

The Regional Center is a good model for what gifted curriculum development looks like, but unfortunately, many gifted students attend schools with little or no articulation of a gifted curriculum. Some gifted students traverse the exact same curriculum as their general education counterparts. Other gifted students may be offered extensions and incidental differentiation, but occasional modifications and learning options fall short of the mission to develop advanced skills, expertise, and intellectual character in gifted students. Well-designed, clearly articulated, and

---

1   The Regional Center for Advanced Academic Studies is part of the Sandusky City Schools in Sandusky, OH (http://www.scs-k12.net). I appreciate their commitment to gifted education and their approval of this example.

tightly aligned learning experiences involving advanced content, complex thinking, and conceptual understandings ought to be the heart and soul of gifted education.

What Is Curriculum?

Curriculum is the intentional, systematic organization of learning experiences to accomplish desired student outcomes. Curriculum forms the foundation of educational practices. Ultimately curriculum ought to be theoretical and practical; it reflects both philosophy and learning science. A weak curriculum is characterized by disconnected activities leading to vague goals and outcomes. A strong curriculum is guided by models of learning design taking account of the characteristics of the learners, the educational context, and desirable educational goals. Above all, curriculum is about what should be taught and, just as importantly, why it should be taught (Null, 2011).

All curriculum design, including gifted and talented curriculum design, must begin with a clear understanding of goals or intended outcomes. Passow (1986) argued, "Without a clear conception of what we expect the gifted and talented students to achieve, what it is we want them 'to become' our curriculum efforts will be directionless" (p. 186). So, what do we want gifted and talented students to become? That may be the most important question gifted curriculum developers could ask; however, finding answers to the question is more difficult than one would imagine (Kettler, 2016). Some propose that we want gifted and talented students to become eminent in some field or domain (Subotnik, Olszewski-Kubilius, & Worrell, 2011). Renzulli (1982, 2012) has consistently argued that gifted and talented students need to become creative producers, and still others might contend that self-actualization is the outcome of gifted education (Grant & Piechowski, 1999).

All of those outcomes appear desirable, but do they present a clear conception of what we want gifted and talented students to become? A synthesis of existing goal statements suggests that there are two goals that accurately describe the outcomes of gifted education. First, gifted students will develop talent and expertise in one or more domains. Developing potential into talent has consistently been acknowledged as a goal of gifted education (Gagné, 1995; Subotnik et al., 2011). Talent development becomes increasingly domain-specific over time and requires significant allotment of discipline, commitment, and practice on the part of the learner. Research on the development of expertise also indicates domain-specific approaches where students gradually mimic the work of experts in a field or domain. For instance, this may involve approaches such as project-based learning and authentic assessments designed to replicate the work of professionals with increasing complexity across the upper grade levels.

The second goal of gifted education is the development of intellectual character. Intellectual character refers to habits of mind, patterns of thinking, and dispositions that both direct and motivate a person's thinking-oriented pursuits (Ritchart, 2002). Knowledge and skill development are incomplete without learning experiences to develop affective characteristics as well (Passow, 1986). Ideally gifted students would embody eight intellectual character traits as a result of participation in the gifted program: (a) intellectual humility, (b) intellectual courage, (c) intellectual empathy, (d) intellectual autonomy, (e) intellectual integrity, (f) intellectual perseverance, (g) intellectual curiosity, and (h) intellectual imagination. These traits guide curriculum development, instructional strategies, student reflection, and evaluation.

Four Components of Gifted and Talented Curriculum

Advanced Content

Accelerated standards. Content may be the most obvious component of any curriculum design. Although learning standards such as the Common Core State Standards, Next Generation Science Standards, or state standards provide the framework for curriculum, learning designers must select content to systematically accomplish the student outcomes delineated by the standards. Gifted and talented curriculum is distinguished from typical curriculum by advanced content (VanTassel-Baska, 2011; VanTassel-Baska & Stambaugh, 2006). Advanced content is characterized in two primary ways: (a) accelerated or above grade level and (b) enriched for increased depth and complexity. Curriculum design for gifted and talented students includes intentional and systematic differentiation applying a combination of acceleration and enrichment.

Developing a differentiated curriculum ought to include acceleration of learning standards. Gifted and advanced students often have mastered grade-level standards at the beginning of the academic year. Teaching to standards that students have already mastered leads to minimal or no academic growth, and it also creates a learning environment incapable of developing intellectual character and dispositions. Curriculum design in gifted education begins with some assessment of what content and skills students have already mastered. Many curriculum designers in gifted education assume advanced cognitive capacities typical of gifted learners that support above-grade-level content (see Table 8.1).

Content standards in gifted education are often accelerated so that students are learning knowledge and skills that are typically expected to be mastered one or more years later. For instance, Mofield and Stambaugh (2016) developed a series of gifted and talented language arts curriculum units for middle school students, and they used learning standards to define knowledge and skill expectations from grades 9 and 10. Thus, when a school adopts the *Perspectives of Power* curriculum (Mofield &

Table 8.1

Cognitive Traits Supporting Differentiated Curriculum

Traits	Description
Faster Processing	Gifted students typically process new information faster than general education peers on both simple and complex tasks.
Thorough Problem Solvers	Gifted students typically use a wider variety of problem solving strategies and generate more elaborate solutions than general education peers.
Metacognitive Strategies	Gifted students typically employ more metacognitive strategies to monitor and adjust their learning than general education peers.
Sustained Attention	Gifted students typically demonstrate longer and more thorough attention to learning tasks than general education peers.
Excellent Memory	Gifted students typically demonstrate superior memory and more efficient recall than general education peers.
Abstract Thinking	Gifted students typically think more abstractly and make more generalizations and connections within and across content than general education peers.
Curtailed Learning	Gifted students typically are more capable of learning new content with minimal or even no formal instruction compared to general education peers.
Complex Thinking	Gifted students typically demonstrate more sophisticated critical and analytical thinking skills than their general education peers.
Advanced Reading	Gifted students typically have advanced verbal skills including reading and vocabulary that allow them to read and comprehend more complex texts than general education peers.

Note. From "Critical Thinking Skills Among Elementary Students: Comparing Identified Gifted and General Education Student Performance," by T. Kettler, 2014, *Gifted Child Quarterly*, *58*, pp. 127–136. Copyright 2014 by National Association for Gifted Children. Reprinted with permission of the author.

Stambaugh, 2016) for use in a grade 7 gifted and talented language arts program, the gifted students are working on standards that are accelerated by two or three grade levels compared to typical grade 7 students.

Similarly, Kettler and Curliss (2003) demonstrated a tiered-objective model for creating differentiation in cluster-grouped mathematics classes. In the tiered-objective model, teachers create advanced content by scaling up objectives so that gifted and advanced students are working on the same concept but one or more grade levels above their peers. Developing curriculum with advanced content using accelerated standards yields an aligned approach that can be systematically implemented in a variety of settings.

Text complexity. Another approach to curriculum design with above-grade-level content is the selection of texts that are considered more complex with substantive content (Little, 2011). When designing language arts curriculum, literature selections should be advanced and substantive, yielding rich and rigorous reading experiences for gifted students. It is recommended (Hughes, Kettler, Shaunessy-Dedrick, & VanTassel-Baska, 2014) that literature selections be at least two reading levels above the student's grade. Thus, if in a typical language arts literature curriculum, texts like *To Kill a Mockingbird* and *The Odyssey* are scheduled for grade 9 students, those texts may be implemented in the grade 7 literature curriculum for the gifted and talented program. Advanced reading skills are developed through guided experiences using complex texts with advanced vocabulary and sophisticated themes and conflicts (Hughes et al., 2014). Gifted high school students ought to be reading complex literary and philosophical texts such as Plato's *The Republic* or Descartes' *Meditations on First Philosophy* as part of their curriculum.

When developing a social studies curriculum for gifted students, advanced texts may be primary documents, philosophical works, and jurisprudence documents such as Supreme Court majority and dissent opinions. For instance, a gifted curriculum for grade 8 United States history might include reading Thomas Paine's *Common Sense* and *The Rights of Man* as well as excerpts from *The Federalist Papers* by Alexander Hamilton and James Madison. These complex texts are capable of developing sophisticated reading skills, and they are also invaluable for developing deep conceptual understandings of the constitutional era in United States history. High school government curriculum for gifted students might include reading classic Supreme Court decisions and philosophical works that were influential in the development of democracy, such as John Locke's *Two Treatises of Government* and *A Letter Concerning Toleration* or John Stuart Mill's *On Liberty*. High school economics curriculum for gifted students may include regularly reading contemporary economics scholarship from *The Economist*. Complex and sophisticated texts are essential elements of the advanced content feature of gifted education curriculum.

Depth and complexity. The core curriculum can be differentiated for gifted and talented students through modifications for depth and complexity (Kaplan, 2009). In other words, the typical core curriculum of a school system can be transformed into advanced content through the addition of facets of depth and complexity. When adding depth to the curriculum, learning is designed with increasing difficulty, more divergence, and more abstraction. While adding depth takes content deeper, adding complexity makes content broader.

Eight elements of depth can transform typical content into advanced content (California Department of Education & California Association for the Gifted, 1994; Kaplan, 2009; see Table 8.2). Similarly, three elements of complexity can increase the breadth of study toward advanced content (see Table 8.3). In some cases, the typical curriculum may include one or more of the elements of depth and complexity. Such inclusion does not mean the typical curriculum is advanced; it is still the curriculum of the typical course of study. These elements of depth and com-

How do we develop the "want to"?

Table 8.2
Create Advanced Content by Adding Depth

Element of Depth	Description
Specialized Language	Each discipline contains specialized language that is used by experts in the discipline. Advanced content includes the introduction and use of specialized language in early stages of learning.
Details	Learning details of a topic leads to deeper understanding of the concept and increases opportunities for critical and creative thinking. Advanced content includes more details than typical grade-level content.
Patterns	Patterns can be found in all content areas, and the recognition of patterns allows students to make connections and draw inferences about causes and effects. Advanced content intentionally illuminates patterns.
Rules	Rules are the organizing structure of topics, phenomena, and disciplines. Advanced content emphasizes the structure of a discipline or a topic to allow for deeper understanding.
Ethical Issues	Each discipline contains dilemmas and controversial issues. Intentionally focusing on the ethical issues of an area of study can transform typical content into advanced content that is both rigorous and engaging.
Trends Over Time	Trends in an area of study are those changes that might be observed over time. For instance, the study of a short story might reveal changes over time in narrative structure and point of view. Advanced content includes trend analyses to better illuminate the present and predict the future.
Big Ideas	Advanced content goes beyond the facts, details, and concepts of the curriculum and also focuses on theories, principles, and generalizations that exist within as well as across disciplines.
Unanswered Questions	Ambiguity within an area of study is the germination of creativity. Advanced content may be built around unanswered questions requiring students to imagine, project, and generate possible explanations.

Note. Adapted from "Layering Differentiated Curricula for the Gifted and Talented," by S. N. Kaplan, in F. A. Karnes and S. M. Bean (Eds.), *Methods and Materials for Teaching the Gifted* (3rd ed., p. 116), 2009, Waco, TX: Prufrock Press. Copyright ©2009 by Prufrock Press. Adapted with permission.

Table 8.3
Create Advanced Content by Adding Complexity

Element of Complexity	Description
Multiple Perspectives	Many topics of study can be examined from multiple perspectives, and typical content can be transformed into advanced content when multiple perspectives are incorporated to create complexity.
Disciplinary Expansion	Content can be advanced when the topics of study expand beyond the typical discipline. A language arts curriculum can be expanded to a humanities curriculum and include studies related to religion, philosophy, and history. A mathematics curriculum can become more advanced when expanded to include coding, logic, and design.
Biography and Expertise	An area of study can be extended to include studies of those individuals whose expertise extended the field. An advanced mathematics curriculum may include an articulated focus on the contributions of great mathematics innovators over time. A curriculum may also be expanded to include studying contemporary experts and innovators in a field of study.

Note. Adapted from "Layering Differentiated Curricula for the Gifted and Talented," by S. N. Kaplan, in F. A. Karnes and S. M. Bean (Eds.), *Methods and Materials for Teaching the Gifted* (3rd ed., p. 117), 2009, Waco, TX: Prufrock Press. Copyright 2009 by Prufrock Press. Adapted with permission.

plexity ought to be thought of as a set of curriculum instruments to be orchestrated against the backdrop of the typical or core curriculum to transform what is typical into an advanced learning experience.

Advanced content is a foundational component of curriculum for gifted students. Curriculum managers as well as teachers ought to be able to point to accelerated standards, above-level texts, and/or elements of depth and complexity that clearly distinguish the gifted and talented curriculum from what is considered the typical or core curriculum.

Complex Thinking

The second component of gifted and talented curriculum is an emphasis on complex thinking. Curriculum for all students requires a taxonomy of thinking skills from basic comprehension to application and analysis. In fact, curriculum standards expect all students at various points in the learning sequence to think at the highest levels of complexity articulated in the revised Bloom's taxonomy (Anderson & Krathwohl, 2001). To be clear, the mark of a curriculum that is appropriate for gifted and talented learners is not the presence of complex thinking; rather, it is the prevalence, emphasis, and sophistication of complex thinking within the curriculum. For instance, all students are to think creatively even in the typical curriculum. All students may be taught to use the process of creative problem solving in the typical curriculum. The curriculum for gifted and talented learners ought to include more frequent opportunities and higher demands for quality in creative thinking.

Basic thinking skills include lower order cognitive processes such as identifying, recognizing, memorizing, and explaining. Complex thinking skills are associated with the concept of higher order thinking skills—those requiring more advanced cognition. There are five categories of complex thinking recommended for curriculum design in gifted education: (a) analytical thinking, (b) critical thinking, (c) creative thinking, (d) problem solving, and (e) inferential application (see Table 8.4). Curriculum for gifted and talented students ought to include ongoing opportunities for students to use complex thinking skills. Ideally, curriculum alignment would include a scope and sequence of each of the five skills over the kindergarten through grade 12 continuum. Complex thinking skills can be emphasized in combination with advanced content to create learning experiences that are sophisticated and rigorous; however, complex thinking skills could also be used with typical content to produce a moderately differentiated curriculum for gifted learners.

Curriculum design in gifted education should structure tasks and work so that student learning is connected to some product, performance, or exhibition that is authentic and valuable to the student (Schlechty, 2002). As students use complex thinking, they will engage in independent research, project-based learning, debates, seminar discussions, and other engaging methods of learning. The curriculum ought to lead students to work in ways similar to experts or professionals in a field. In this way, the curriculum emphasizes creative productivity developed through authentic products and performances (Renzulli, 1982). If gifted and talented students are to become creative producers, the curriculum should regularly call on them to practice productivity in a variety of ways that are consistently authentic and engaging.

Conceptual Understanding

More than half a century ago, Mortimer Adler (1958/1988) wrote a short essay published in the *Saturday Review of Literature* (November 22, 1958) titled, "What Is an Idea?" Interestingly, that essay has had a lasting effect on curriculum thinkers in gifted education. Adler wrote:

> In themselves and in relation to one another they comprise the configurations of the human mind, as intricate and varied in their crisscrossing patterns as the starry heavens. And like each individual star, every idea is a source of life and light which animates and illuminates the words, facts, examples, and emotions that are dead—or deadly—and dark within them. (p. 227).

Table 8.4
Emphasize Complex Thinking in Curriculum Design for Gifted Learners

Type of Thinking	Description	Examples
Analytical Thinking	Analytical thinking involves exercising judgment to compare, contrast, differentiate, illustrate, or articulate.	• Students compare democracy in ancient Greece, the middle ages, and contemporary United States. • Students articulate different sentence structures and how to use them effectively in writing.
Critical Thinking	Critical thinking is reflective thinking using principles of reasoning, logic, and evidence to analyze, evaluate, and construct consistent and coherent arguments, understandings, and judgments.	• Students engage in cross-examination debate on ethical topics in scientific research. • Students construct arguments and counterarguments on school uniforms.
Creative Thinking	Creative thinking is the generation of original ideas that are task-appropriate within the context of the discipline or field of study.	• Students generate ideas to apply water conservation at an elementary school. • Students create movie reviews to interpret classic and contemporary films.
Problem Solving	Problem solving involves defining a problem, generating potential solutions, evaluating and selecting a course of action, and implementing and evaluating the outcomes.	• Students identify problems associated with conducting local history research and propose solutions. • Students evaluate data sets and generate mathematical models capable of solving defined problems.
Inferential Application	Inferential application is applying what one knows about one situation to better understand another situation that is obviously similar.	• Students apply ecological systems concepts to better understand cultural constructs (e.g, religion, government). • Students apply literary criticism to understand scientific discourse.

Ideas are not facts. They are not collections of facts. Ideas are living, changing, and developing concepts that change people, inspire people, and perhaps destroy people. Working with a large research staff, Adler reviewed the greatest works of literature, philosophy, religion, and science and extracted what he termed "The Great Ideas" (p. 228). Building curriculum around great ideas introduces gifted students to dialogues of significance that have entertained generations of thinkers (see Table 8.5).

Gifted education has advocated concept-based curriculum for decades (e.g., Feldhusen, 1988; VanTassel-Baska, 1995, 1998; Ward, 1961). Concepts and ideas are abstract. They are not mastered; they are wrestled with, contemplated, and adored. Concepts and ideas require thinking and reflection. They bring meaning and significance to the content of disciplines. Avery and Little (2011) advocated concept-based curriculum because "we cannot function effectively in society without understanding concepts such as justice, authority, responsibility, and honor" (p. 125). What does it mean to emphasize conceptual understanding in curriculum for gifted and talented students?

Conceptual understanding is knowledge that connects what students are learning with individual experiences in the local context as well as universal concerns of the global community. Conceptual understandings are rich and complex; they guide actions, attention, and conviction as students mature. Thus, in its simplest rendering, conceptual curriculum connects to students' lives and pushes them to engage in internal and external dialogue to make sense of complex ideas.

Conceptual curriculum may be implemented in two ways. First, an entire course of study may be organized around a universal concept or conceptual question. For instance, a high school in Texas organized a four-course sequence of gifted and talented English language arts courses around compelling universal themes/questions. English I curriculum focused on the great idea of *one and many* using the overarching question, "Who am I?" English II curriculum focused on the great idea of *truth* with the overarching question, "What is truth?" English III curriculum was built around the great ideas of *reasoning* and *rhetoric* with the overarching question, "How can I change the world with words?" For the senior year, the gifted and talented English IV curriculum embraced the great idea of *courage* and the overarching question of "For what will I stand?" In developing those curricula, the gifted and talented curriculum staff selected materials and focused learning activities on the overarching questions. Discussion, reflection, and assessment continually returned to the great ideas and questions. For the culminating project in each course, the students had to answer the overarching question (e.g., What is truth?), and they had some options on how they could communicate their answers. They could create traditional essays, collections of poetry and/or prose, emergent genre projects, or multimedia presentations. A second way to implement a conceptual curriculum is through the use of unit-specific concepts. Often, the unit-specific concepts are derivatives of the great

Table 8.5

Great Ideas to Organize Curriculum for Conceptual Understanding

Adaptation	Ethics	Justice	Reason
Alienation	Evolution	Justification	Religion
Authority	Experience	Knowledge	Revolution
Beauty	Exploration	Law	Rights
Beliefs	Extinction	Liberty	Ritual
Cause	Faith	Loss	Science
Chance	Family	Love	Soul
Change	Fate	Loyalty	State
Citizen	Fear	Memory	Survival
Civilization	Freedom	Metaphor	Technology
Conformity	Friendship	Method	Temperance
Constitution	Good and evil	Morality	Theology
Courage	Growth	Myth	Time
Creativity	Habit	Narrative	Tolerance
Democracy	Happiness	Opposition	Tradition
Desire	Honor	Origin	Transformation
Discipline	Hope	Paradigm	Truth
Discovery	Humanity	Paradox	Tyranny
Duty	Idea	Pattern	Universal
Education	Identity	Peace	Unknown
Emotion	Imagination	Pleasure	Utility
Engineering	Immortality	Politics	Vice
Enigma	Information	Power	Virtue
Environment	Intelligence	Prudence	Will
Eternity	Invention	Reality	Wisdom

ideas. For instance, a number of outstanding gifted and talented curriculum units have been developed around broad concepts like relationships, power, systems, or patterns. An elementary school for gifted and talented students in Ohio recently developed units around even more specific concepts of friendship and diversity. The unit-specific concepts are integrated into the fabric of learning similarly to the course of study of universal concepts but on a smaller scale. The purpose of curriculum to emphasize conceptual understanding remains the same—connect students' lived experiences to complex ideas that illuminate the topics and standards of the curriculum.

Teaching and curriculum emphasizing conceptual understanding is further clarified through essential understandings—the enduring statements or generalizations that will be remembered when the facts and details fade. In the curriculum design process, conceptual understandings need to be articulated. For instance, the design team on a social studies curriculum unit focused on change may articulate the following three enduring understandings:

- Change sometimes hurts.
- Change can either result in better or worse outcomes.
- All change has a cause.

The enduring understandings are presented at the beginning of the unit, and students are asked to find exemplars to support these statements. Additionally, the curriculum may ask students or teams of students to generate additional enduring understandings about change and support them with argument and evidence.

Conceptual understandings push student learning beyond the rote and trivial. Curriculum emphasizing conceptual understandings can be rigorous and engaging yet also very personal for students. Even in mixed-ability classrooms, curriculum designed around big ideas and concepts can remove the learning ceiling (Roberts & Roberts, 2015) for gifted and talented students when combined with a culture of differentiation.

Develop Intellectual Character

To consistently develop and implement curriculum in gifted education, educators ought to begin with an understanding of what they want the gifted students to become (Passow, 1986). The fourth component of gifted curriculum is the intentional development of intellectual character (Ritchart, 2002), those traits that describe desirable dispositions within the context of deep learning and knowing (see Table 8.6). These traits ought to serve as the compass that keeps the curriculum focused and consistent. The traits are more than knowledge and skills. They are ways of being that combine integrity and virtue within the development of talent and expertise.

Intellectual character traits are the metacognitive, reflective facet of the gifted and talented curriculum. Both teachers and students in the gifted and talented program ought to be explicitly aware of the eight traits and what they mean. The traits may be visually represented in classrooms as they are ever-present reference points in thinking, learning, and reflection. For instance, in a grade 5 American History class, a teacher developed a unit on the development and adoption of the United States Constitution. The curriculum was rich in depth, focusing on big ideas such as a democracy, compromise, and unity. The curriculum also included an emphasis on complexity through the intentional consideration of multiple perspectives.

Table 8.6

Intellectual Character Traits Developed Through Gifted Education Curriculum

Intellectual Humility	Awareness of the limits of one's knowledge and the tendency toward egocentrism. Students with intellectual humility are aware of the potential bias, prejudice, and limitations of their viewpoints. Moreover, students with intellectual humility do not claim to know more than they actually know.
Intellectual Courage	Willingness to face and fairly address ideas, beliefs, or viewpoints with which one has strong negative emotions or with which one has not previously given serious attention. Students with intellectual courage do not passively and uncritically accept what they have learned. Students with intellectual courage are willing to admit that there may be truth in ideas that appear dangerous or absurd as well as acknowledge that some ideas strongly held in their social group may involve distortion or falsity. It takes intellectual courage to be a nonconformist when conformity contradicts well-reasoned positions.
Intellectual Empathy	Willingness to imagine oneself in the place of others in order to genuinely understand them. Intellectual empathy begins with consciousness of one's egocentric tendencies to identify truth with one's own beliefs or perceptions. Students with intellectual empathy are able to reason from premises, assumptions, and ideas other than their own. Additionally, students with intellectual empathy recall times past when they were mistaken in their conviction that they were right, and it is possible to similarly be deceived at present.
Intellectual Autonomy	Conviction to control one's own beliefs, assumptions, and inferences. Students with intellectual autonomy think for themselves without falling victim to group think tendencies. They analyze and evaluate beliefs using reason and evidence, and they question when questioning is appropriate and believe when belief is justified.
Intellectual Integrity	Commitment to be true and consistent in one's thinking. Students with intellectual integrity apply intellectual standards when they think and hold themselves to principles of reason and evidence. They are willing to admit discrepancies and inconsistencies in their own thinking when appropriate.
Intellectual Perseverance	Conviction to seek intellectual insights and truths even when such pursuits are difficult and frustrating. Students with intellectual perseverance stand firm in their use of reason even when others oppose rational principles. Students with intellectual perseverance understand and embrace the need to struggle with confusion and unsettled questions over time in order to achieve accurate understandings.
Intellectual Curiosity	Maintaining a desire to know more or understand something deeper. Students who are intellectually curious are not satisfied with shallow, surface-level explanations. Rather they seek complexity and deeper meaning in the ideas, principles, and narratives that they encounter. Students with intellectual curiosity consistently want to know more, raise new questions, and pose new problems.
Intellectual Imagination	Generating new ideas, questions, applications, and insights as a result of learning experiences. Students who have intellectual imagination seek new ways to understand and apply what they are learning. They imagine new possibilities, connections, and outcomes that others may not immediately conceive; moreover, they develop a disposition that each encounter may become an opportunity to create a new idea or extend an existing idea.

Note. Adapted from *Critical Thinking: Tools for Taking Charge of Your Learning and Your Life* (p. 3), by R. Paul and L. Elder, 2001, Upper Saddle River, NJ: Prentice Hall. Copyright 2001 by Prentice Hall. Adapted with permission.

Colonies came to the constitutional process with different perspectives and concerns. The teacher decided to have students reflect on intellectual character during the introduction of the unit. After using an engaging narrative to set the stage for the study of the constitutional process, she asked students to think about how they will need to use intellectual empathy during the course of this unit. Students wrote in their reflection journals several ways that intellectual empathy would be important while studying this topic. Then in pairs or triads, the students shared and compared ideas. The process culminated in a whole-class discussion of why intellectual empathy is important.

The American History example demonstrates how intellectual character traits can be used at the beginning of learning designs. In the example, the teacher selected the trait of emphasis that well-aligned with the content being studied (intellectual empathy). The traits could be part of the culmination of learning design as well. In a grade 7 language arts class, students were learning to construct arguments using specific rhetorical strategies. The content was advanced using accelerated English language arts standards on argumentative writing from grades 9 and 10. Students read and deconstructed examples of well-crafted arguments as part of the learning design. Students were placed in teams of two to prepare for formal debates using the arguments they constructed, and the topic of debate was the resolution that social media should be limited for students in early adolescence. At the culmination of the unit, the teacher asked the students to reflect on the eight intellectual character traits and write a personal reflection paper in which they select two or three of the intellectual character traits and describe how the learning and performance tasks in the unit help them develop those traits.

Intellectual character traits are the learner profile for the gifted and talented education program. The traits give direction to teachers and curriculum developers, but they are also tools routinely used with students for reflection and improvement. Students should learn to self-assess their development of intellectual character, giving specific examples. Teachers and parents can also provide narrative evaluations of the students' development of intellectual character.

Both experience and research (Semb & Ellis, 1994) suggest that much of what students learn in school is generally forgotten over time. Knowledge statements, facts, and details have a modest shelf life. However, curriculum is continually built upon content rich in these fleeting relics of education. Well-designed curriculum for gifted and talented learners should seek ways to take learning deeper into the core development of young people. As memory gradually purges itself of the quadratic formula, laws of physics, and the chronology of conquest and expansion, one might ask what is the learning that lasts? Intellectual character is meant to be the learning that lasts. Teaching to intentionally develop and sustain intellectual character among gifted and talented student populations ought to be the solid foundation on which advanced content, complex thinking, and conceptual understanding are designed.

Conclusion

Curriculum is at the core of gifted and talented education. It is the vehicle with which schools and teachers transition outstanding potential into exceptional talent and achievement. Curriculum can serve as a path for students' development of identity, passion, and conviction. The curriculum needs to be rich and rigorous, but most importantly, students ought to be able to see themselves, their families, and their histories in the curriculum. As they reflect upon who they are, they will begin to imagine who they can become.

The story of Mrs. Kromer's classroom that began the chapter exemplifies a school, a principal, and an administration that have intentionally placed curriculum at the heart of the gifted education program. Mrs. Kromer's students encounter an articulated curriculum focused on advanced content, complex thinking, and conceptual understandings. This year, the school began defining the intellectual character traits that will also benchmark the learning design. Mrs. Kromer and her fellow teachers are involved in the process, and they take pride and ownership of the learning design. They are continuously being trained, and the principal is committed to curriculum and instructional leadership for gifted kids. In the end, the students themselves reap the benefits of a commitment to theoretically sound gifted and talented curriculum.

Big Ideas

1. Curriculum is the intentional, systematic organization of learning experiences to accomplish desired student outcomes.

2. Without a clear understanding of our goals or what we want gifted students to become, our curriculum design efforts are meaningless.

3. Advanced content is at the heart of gifted and talented curriculum, and it is defined as above-grade-level content or content that is modified for increased depth and complexity.

4. Gifted and talented curriculum requires complex thinking, including analytical thinking, critical thinking, creative thinking, problem solving, and inferential application.

5. Conceptual understanding connects individual experiences to great ideas and universal concepts requiring contemplation, reflection, and response.

6. Gifted and talented curriculum should develop intellectual character in addition to the knowledge, skills, and concepts of the curriculum.

7. Curriculum, instruction, and the teachers who implement them are vital catalysts in the development of talent and exceptional achievement.

Discussion Questions

1. What types of training and guidance do teachers need in order to develop appropriate curriculum for gifted and talented students?

2. Gifted and talented curriculum requires resources that are different from the typical general education resources. How might a school select appropriate resources?

3. How might a school or teacher evaluate the effectiveness of a curriculum designed for gifted and talented students?

4. In what ways might the grouping of students influence the design and implementation of curriculum?

5. What type of instructional leadership from administrators is required for designing and implementing quality curriculum in gifted education?

References

Adler, M. J. (1988). *Reforming education: The opening of the American mind*. New York, NY: Macmillan. (Original work published 1958)

Anderson, L. W., & Krathwohl, D. R. (Eds.). (2001). *A taxonomy for learning, teaching, and assessing: A revision of Bloom's taxonomy of educational objectives*. Boston, MA: Allyn & Bacon.

Avery, L. D., & Little, C. A. (2011). Concept development and learning. In J. VanTassel-Baska & C. A. Little (Eds.), *Content-based curriculum for high-ability learners* (2nd ed.). Waco, TX: Prufrock Press.

California Department of Education, & California Association for the Gifted. (1994). *Differentiating the core curriculum and instruction to provide advanced learning opportunities*. Sacramento, CA: Author.

Feldhusen, J. (1988). Developing units of instruction. In J. VanTassel-Baska, J. Feldhusen, K. Seeley, G. Wheatley, L. Silverman, & W. Foster (Eds.), *Comprehensive curriculum for gifted learners* (pp. 112–150). Boston, MA: Allyn & Bacon.

Gagné, F. (1995). From giftedness to talent: A developmental model and its impact on the language of the field. *Roeper Review, 18,* 103–111.

Grant, B. A., & Piechowski, M. M. (1999). Theories of the good: Toward child-centered gifted education. *Gifted Child Quarterly, 43,* 4–12. doi:10.1177/00 1698629904300102

Hughes, C. E., Kettler, T., Shaunessy-Dedrick, E., & VanTassel-Baska, J. (2014). *A teacher's guide to using the Common Core State Standards with gifted and advanced learners in the English language arts.* Waco, TX: Prufrock Press.

Kaplan, S. N. (2009). Layering differentiated curricula for the gifted and talented. In F. A. Karnes & S. M. Bean (Eds.), *Methods and materials for teaching the gifted* (3rd ed., pp. 107–136). Waco, TX: Prufrock Press.

Kettler, T. (2014). Critical thinking skills among elementary students: Comparing identified gifted and general education student performance. *Gifted Child Quarterly, 58,* 127–136. doi:10.1177/001698621452208

Kettler, T. (2016). Curriculum design in an era of ubiquitous information and technology: New possibilities for gifted education. In T. Kettler (Ed.), *Modern curriculum for gifted and advanced academic students* (pp. 3–21). Waco, TX: Prufrock Press.

Kettler, T., & Curliss, M. (2003). Mathematical acceleration in a mixed-ability classroom. *Gifted Child Today, 26*(1), 52–56.

Little, C. A. (2011). Adapting language arts curricula for high-ability learners. In J. VanTassel-Baska & C. A. Little, (Eds.), *Content-based curriculum for high ability learners* (2nd ed., pp. 151–186). Waco, TX: Prufrock Press.

Mofield, E., & Stambaugh, T. (2016). *Perspectives of power: ELA lessons for gifted and advanced learners in grades 6–8.* Waco, TX: Prufrock Press.

Null, W. (2011). *Curriculum: From theory to practice.* Lanham, MD: Rowman & Littlefield.

Passow, A. H. (1986). Curriculum for the gifted and talented at the secondary level. *Gifted Child Quarterly, 30,* 186–191. doi:10.1177/001698628603000409

Paul, R., & Elder, L. (2001). *Critical thinking: Tools for taking charge of your learning and your life.* Upper Saddle River, NJ: Prentice Hall.

Renzulli, J. S. (1982). What makes a problem real: Stalking the illusive meaning of qualitative differences in gifted education. *Gifted Child Quarterly, 26,* 147–156. doi:10.1177/001698628202600401

Renzulli, J. S. (2012). Reexamining the role of gifted education and talent development for the 21st century: A four-part theoretical approach. *Gifted Child Quarterly, 56,* 150–159. doi:10.177/0016986212444901

Ritchart, R. (2002). *Intellectual character: What it is, why it matters, and how to get it.* San Francisco, CA: Jossey-Bass.

Roberts, J. L., & Roberts, R. A. (2015). Writing units that remove the learning ceiling. In F. A. Karnes & S. M. Bean (Eds.), *Methods and materials for teaching the gifted* (4th ed., pp. 221–255). Waco, TX: Prufrock Press.

Schlechty, P. C. (2002). *Working on the work: An action plan for teachers, principals, and superintendents.* San Francisco, CA: Jossey-Bass.

Semb, G. B., & Ellis, J. A. (1994). Knowledge taught at school: What is remembered? *Review of Educational Research, 64,* 254–279.

Subotnik, R. F., Olszewski-Kubilius, P., & Worrell, F. C. (2011). Rethinking gift-edness and gifted education: A proposed direction forward based on psychological science. *Psychological Science in the Public Interest, 12,* 3–54. doi:10.1177/1529100611418056

VanTassel-Baska, J. (1995). The development of talent through curriculum. *Roeper Review, 18,* 98–102.

VanTassel-Baska, J. (1998). *Excellence in educating gifted and talented learners* (3rd ed.). Denver, CO: Love.

VanTassel-Baska, J. (2004). Introduction to curriculum for gifted and talented students: A 25-year retrospective and prospective. In J. VanTassel-Baska & S. M. Reis (Eds.), *Curriculum for gifted and talented students* (pp. xxiii–xxxiii). Thousand Oaks, CA: Corwin Press.

VanTassel-Baska, J. (2011). An introduction to the integrated curriculum model. In J. VanTassel-Baska & C. A. Little (Eds.), *Content-based curriculum for high-ability learners* (2nd ed., pp. 9–32). Waco, TX: Prufrock Press.

VanTassel-Baska, J., & Stambaugh, T. (2006). *Comprehensive curriculum for gifted learners* (3rd ed.). Needham Heights, MA: Allyn & Bacon.

Ward, V. S. (1961). *Finding the gifted: An axiomatic approach.* Columbus, OH: Charles E. Merrill.

CHAPTER 9

Learning Assessments for Gifted Learners

Joyce VanTassel-Baska and Gail Fischer Hubbard

Learning is not attained by chance. It must be sought for with ardor and attended to with diligence.—Abigail Adams

Essential Questions to Guide the Reader

1. What is the purpose of learning assessments?

2. What is the role of traditional and nontraditional learning assessments in the education of advanced learners?

3. What are the crucial components of an effective learning assessment for the gifted?

4. What standards are applied within different types of assessments to judge learning?

5. How do we create a comprehensive approach to assessing advanced learning?

Assessment is an integral part of instruction. Formative assessment before instruction is a type of assessment that determines what an advanced learner already knows and is able to do. Formative assessment during instruction helps the teacher monitor and adjust the process of teaching and learning. Summative assessment after a period of instruction evaluates a student's success in understanding complex content, employing processes such as high-level thinking and problem solving, producing sophisticated or innovative products, and using the process of reflective metacognition. Wiggins and McTighe (2005) argued that the final culminating assessment should be the first component established in unit design to provide a framework for purposeful instructional activities. Regardless of how a unit or module of curriculum is constructed, assessment design is critical to effective teaching and learning.

Best Practice Applications of Learning Assessments

Four approaches to assessment may be used within the design of a unit to enhance the learning for gifted students. These assessment models may be used in both formative and summative ways to demonstrate high-level accomplishment of learning in specific content areas: standardized assessment; performance assessment, including high-stakes, external performance measures, and classroom pre-post performance assessments; product assessment; and portfolio assessment.

Standardized Assessment

Standardized achievement tests. The use of standardized achievement measures is a common approach employed to assess learning for everybody; however, standardized tests, by their very nature, are not good predictors of high- or low-level achievement. Because of the ceiling and floor effects of standardized testing, the results of these tests may not provide an accurate indication of performance for students who are gifted or for those who are developmentally delayed. Their usage has resulted in the underprediction of how much advanced students may know in a given area of learning (Ryser & Rambo-Hernandez, 2014).

Required state standardized tests. High-stakes summative assessment influences the shaping of classroom instruction. This is especially true of the end-of-year or end-of-course standardized tests required by each state. The New York State Regents examinations are one such example of standardized assessment. Other states developed statewide standardized assessments in response to the No Child Left Behind Act (NCLB, 2001). Under NCLB, all states established standardized assessments to test basic skills in reading, writing, and mathematics in grades 3–8 and end-of-course examinations in those subjects at the high school level. Although some state assessments included questions that required students to apply knowledge, many state assessments tested basic factual knowledge that required only one step for solution.

Given the inconsistency of state standards and assessments and the poor performance of students in the United States on international assessments such as the

Trends in International Mathematics and Science Study (TIMSS; National Center for Education Statistics, 2011), the National Governors Association Center for Best Practices (NGA) and the Council of Chief State School Officers (CCSSO) released the Common Core State Standards for English Language Arts and Mathematics (NGA & CCSSO, 2010a, 2010b). In response to the release of the Common Core State Standards, the trend in the development of state assessments (whether by state or consortium group) includes increased emphasis on these more advanced and performance-based assessment protocols. For example, the English language arts assessments may evaluate student comprehension of complex texts through assessment of student analysis of evidence from literary and informational texts, whereas in mathematics the emphasis may be on assessment of conceptual understanding through the application of key concepts to problem solving (VanTassel-Baska & Johnsen, 2015). Although these yearlong summative assessments are valuable in myriad ways, they are not necessarily useful for planning classroom instruction.

Off-level national assessments. For the past 40 years, the field of gifted education, led by the work of Julian Stanley, has used typical achievement tests with the gifted in two ways: (a) focusing on the top 2%–5% of the population on these tests to find promising learners in a given academic area and then administering a harder test (e.g., SAT, ACT) to find a better estimate of their true aptitude (this became known as talent searches), and (b) employing the advanced forms of these tests to assess advanced learning. Off-level achievement can be used to ensure that educators understand how advanced their learners may be (Brody & Mills, 2005; Warne, 2012).

Talent searches utilize off-level testing (e.g., such as the ACT or SAT for seventh graders and the PSAT 8/9 for fourth and fifth graders) to reveal the gifted student's capacity to have mastered content at levels 4 or more years beyond age-relevant curriculum. Such data then become useful for documenting the level of work of which a student is capable as well as the level of placement required for challenge. The use of off-level assessment for purposes of gauging learning may provide the best portrait of what students can do in an area of study, calling on educators to rethink traditional procedures for programming and placement of gifted students. The scenario featuring Barrett in Figure 9.1 illustrates this point.

The information gained from Barrett's being tested on the EXPLORE opened up a wide range of opportunities for him, both in and out of school. It provided his parents and his educators with data that could not be ignored in planning his educational future. Moreover, it provided a baseline for understanding *how* advanced he was and the implications of that reality. Many gifted students in our schools may not be quite as advanced as Barrett, but many are clearly ready for work 2 or more years beyond their placement. Using off-level learning assessment tools documents this readiness.

Barrett has been advanced in mathematics from the age of 2 when he memorized the house numbers on his street and begged his parents to play games with him related to the patterns that could be developed using those numbers. By age 5, he had mastered the basic computational facts and the principles of measurement. By age 7, he expressed interest in attending special math sessions held at the local university in the summer and learning chess. By age 9, he was enjoying work in probability and statistics.

Barrett was tested through Northwestern University's program on the EXPLORE test, given to students as young as he to determine advanced skill development. The results suggested he was functioning at the level of an eighth grader in mathematical knowledge and skills. Based on these results, his school intervened with an individually developed math program for him that focused on accelerating the Common Core math standards to the ninth-grade level, placing him in an Algebra 1 advanced course at the middle school, and providing him a mentor who would work with him once a week on mathematical topics of interest as well as monitor his current placement and level of work. Out of school, his parents decided to enroll him in Northwestern's fast-paced summer class in geometry and continue to search for other outside opportunities for him.

Figure 9.1. Scenario illustrating use of off-level assessment in mathematics.

The Iowa Tests of Basic Skills (ITBS), a standardized achievement test often used by school districts, assesses a broad range of skills in language, science, social studies, and mathematics. The test is typically employed two or more grade levels beyond student grade placement to assess advanced learning. Using it for a post-only analysis of where students are in a subject-based skill set may be both warranted and useful. Coupled with other end-of-instruction data, it may pinpoint important understanding of student mastery.

The use of off-level assessment may apply to other forms of assessment as well. For example, employment of sample tests from the Advanced Placement (AP) program may also be useful with middle and early high school students in specific areas of learning where they have shown advanced skills. The importance of getting an accurate picture of what individual students are capable of doing academically cannot be overestimated. Thomson and Olszewski-Kubilius (2014) noted that the use of these measures enhances our understanding of how to counsel students and parents in the talent development process, as well as provides educators cognitive profiles that are more useful for curriculum planning than other approaches to estimating learning levels of this population.

Performance Assessment

Performance assessments are open-ended with multiple correct responses rather than one correct answer. Performance assessment addresses important concepts in a given discipline and provides opportunities for students to engage with authentic questions that focus on high-level thinking and problem solving within that discipline (VanTassel-Baska, 2008, 2013).

In the classroom, performance assessments are designed to accept multiple responses supported by evidence as correct answers and to emphasize fluency and complexity over speed. Classroom performance assessment for advanced learners focuses on the exploration of advanced content, high-level thinking and problem solving, and the use of reflective metacognition to help students internalize their learning.

Effective performance-based assessments ensure that the assessment actually measures what it is intended to measure; established research-based protocols and rubrics enhance effective assessment as well. Although the use of performance tasks and assessment requires additional classroom time, the open-ended format, the support for articulation of thinking, and the resulting development of more complex responses make performance assessment particularly appropriate for advanced learners. An example of such an assessment is illustrated in Figure 9.2.

High-stakes, performance-based assessments of advanced-level courses. The hallmark secondary tests used to assess high-level learning may be seen as performance-based in their construction and utilization. These tests include the Advanced Placement (AP) Examinations, the Cambridge Programme Advanced International Certificate of Education (AICE) Examinations, and the International Baccalaureate Diploma Programme (IBDP) Examinations. These examinations require high school students to demonstrate in-depth conceptual understanding of the content of a given subject and the skills to analyze literary and informational text resources and to solve problems in mathematics and science. These secondary programs provide an important model for educators of the gifted in understanding the appropriate levels of assessment needed for advanced learners. All three programs emphasize in-depth analysis of complex informational and literary texts and high-level thinking. In addition, clear written responses to the questions are expected across genre. As assessment provides a foundation for planning instruction; understanding the assessment constructs for these advanced high school courses provides structure for the development of assessments for younger advanced learners.

Classroom-based, pre- and postassessments. The use of a pre-post performance assessment paradigm is highly useful in assessing both short- and long-term learning, especially in skill areas that are high level and articulated in the standards across years. Thus, such assessment data may be used by teachers across years to document ongoing student learning. In the case of gifted students, work in these areas is important to build foundational abilities in subjects like science, math, and writing. If the pre-post prompts are sufficiently challenging, they represent an opportunity for gifted students to show how much they know and can apply in a given domain. Such use of a pre-post assessment is illustrated in Figure 9.3.

Mrs. Wells has asked her fifth-grade students to weigh the pros and cons of buying an iPad or similar device they choose. Her students will record three reasons for and three against purchasing the iPad, justify one pro and one con answer in writing, analyze the pros and cons, arrive at a decision about the purchase, support the decision with evidence, and reflect upon the decision-making process. The end product will be a 5-minute persuasive speech before class peers.

Making a Decision	
Pro	**Con**
1.	1.
2.	2.
3.	3.
Justification for one pro answer:	Justification for one con answer:
Decision after analyzing the pros and cons:	
Justification supported by evidence for decision:	
Reflection: What was your decision? Why?	

Mrs. Wells will evaluate the decision-making process and the speech using the following rubric.

Performance Assessment Rubric				
Criteria	**1 (low)**	**2**	**3**	**4 (high)**
1. Student demonstrated higher level thinking in the analysis of pros and cons.				
2. Student supported decision with specific evidence.				
3. Student reflected on the decision-making process.				
4. Student presented a persuasive argument in a coherent manner that engaged the audience.				

Figure 9.2. Fifth-grade performance assessment scenario.

Preassessment in writing:
Should elementary students be restricted in the use of the Internet?
Compose a five-paragraph response that presents your position, provides reasons for that position, elaborates with evidence, and concludes the evidence-based stance. Your response will be judged on the following criteria: strong stance provided, solid reasons given, effective elaboration, integrative conclusion, and lack of mechanical problems (e.g., punctuation, usage, grammar).

Applications of the preassessment results:
The teacher decides to group the five best writers together as judged by the preassessment results for a weekly writing seminar that focuses on the gaps in their current capacity to handle persuasive writing, as well as to introduce advanced writing techniques for application in 30-minute, hands-on writing sessions. Advanced literature is used to stimulate student discussion as a basis for the writing. Monitoring of these students' progress occurs through the weekly timed writing assignments. Assessment of their learning after a 6-week period is a portfolio of their weekly pieces, assessed for organization, content, creativity, and mechanics. Depending on their level of growth, future work in writing is designed.

Postassessment in writing:
Should elementary students be allowed to accelerate their learning up to 3 years?
Compose a five-paragraph response that presents your position, provides reasons for that position, elaborates with evidence, and concludes the evidence-based stance. Your response will be judged on the following criteria: strong stance provided, solid reasons given, effective elaboration, integrative conclusion, and lack of mechanical problems (e.g., punctuation, usage, grammar).

Applications of the postassessment results:
The teacher regroups the best writers that emerge from this assessment along with those already working at the advanced level. The weekly seminar model continues. The teacher brings in a resident writer to address student-identified issues. The teacher, analyzing the writing standards, decides to advance the focus of the writing by integrating the requirements for the next two grade levels. Advanced literature is used to stimulate student discussion as a basis for the writing. Portfolios of weekly, in-class timed writing assignments are kept by students. Each student then adds a piece at the end of the portfolio that self-assesses progress in the aspects of writing addressed in the seminar, self-assesses each piece she has done, and conceptualizes what her needs are for future writing opportunities.

Figure 9.3. Scenario illustrating use of pre-post assessment in writing.

A pre-post design may be used at the classroom, school, or district level to assess growth and change in learning. It takes a mindful administrator to accomplish the cross district or school-based data collection and analysis. In individual classrooms, however, teachers can apply these principles fairly simply. For each subject to be taught, teachers should select a preassessment tool that will allow them to know the knowledge and skills that all gifted students are bringing to the classroom in that area. It is the most important skill set that a teacher should select for assessment. For example, three essentials might be a writing assessment, a science investigation assessment, and a math assessment that tap into ever-advancing problem sets. The results of these assessments may be used for grouping, curriculum adaptation, and gearing future assessments of learning. The postassessment should be a match to the preassessment in level of difficulty, format, and length of time for administration.

Product Assessment

Development of products provides multiple opportunities to differentiate instruction for gifted learners. Students can explore a chosen topic, issue, or idea in depth; can analyze complex advanced content using multiple resources; and can design an authentic product for an appropriate audience. Because product development encompasses so many critical elements of differentiation for gifted learners, creation and assessment of products are important components of gifted education curriculum and instruction (Moon, 2015; Renzulli & Callahan, 2008; Roberts & Inman, 2015).

Students may develop products that respond to specific requirements in a given unit of study. Although choice is important for gifted learners, the product still fulfills specific unit objectives. Such products should require a student to examine complex content in depth, employ high-level thinking (if possible, the type of thinking that would be used by a professional in the discipline), and prepare a product for an authentic audience. The product assessment should evaluate all of these components.

Students may self-select products and complete them as a team or independently. For example, Type III Enrichment activities from the Schoolwide Enrichment Model (Renzulli & Reis, 2014), in which students choose a real problem to investigate, is one example wherein students establish the goal of the project. The assessment of such products requires (a) assessment of the process of establishing the goal, (b) assessment of the focus of the product, and (c) the assessment of the product itself. Because developing product assessments that are both valid and reliable with interrater reliability can be challenging, adopting an established research-based rubric such as the Student Product Assessment Form (SPAF) is an effective and efficient approach for evaluating student project work (Renzulli & Reis, 1997).

Students may also develop products in response to an external competition such as National History Day and the Intel science competitions. The rubric for assessing the product is established by the sponsoring external agency. These rubrics, usually developed by professionals in a field, can be valuable models for constructing more routine products for the classroom.

Figures 9.4 illustrates the use of product assessments in a middle school classroom. The scenario illustrates the conceptualization of student projects followed by assessments of the research process and product presentation. Standards for writing, speaking, and listening have been addressed in the conceptualization of the project and in the development of the rubric.

Figure 9.4 also illustrates important components of using product-based assessment. First, the teacher has set the stage by conducting a brainstorming session, using a Need to Know Board to generate questions that students do not understand about governmental systems. Next, she has generated, in collaboration with students, the possible options that might be pursued for the research topic. She has left open to students, however, the final choice of topic and the mode of execution (e.g., dyads or independently). Both of these elements are important considerations in working with gifted learners—allowing for choice in tasks and work style. Next, the teacher has provided specifications for the project in respect to length of time, how the product will be judged, and the need for a specific number of resources to be cited. She also has included the rubrics for product choices. The inclusion of core rubrics that may be used for other student products and presentations helps students in developing the underlying process skills of conducting and presenting research. Finally, she has defined how she will engage in progress monitoring of her students to ensure their success as learners.

Portfolio Assessment

A portfolio is a purposeful and systematic collection of student work. Portfolio assessment uses examples of student work to show student growth over time. The process engages students in reflection on their own learning (Johnsen, 2008). This is especially true when the student includes a rationale for the selection of each piece.

Portfolios differ in purpose. One portfolio purpose might be to evaluate a student's progress over a given period of time, such as a marking period, a semester, or even a year. Examples of portfolios would include a collection of first-grade writings, each dated, to be reviewed to demonstrate student growth in writing or examples of third-grade problem solving in mathematics with dated student responses to indicate growth in mathematical reasoning.

Another portfolio purpose might be to evaluate student work against a specific list of requirements or goals. Student and teacher collaboratively select (or the student selects) examples of a student's best work to meet a specific requirement. An example of this portfolio would be the collection of a descriptive writing, a persuasive writing, and a creative writing to illustrate student success in meeting different

Students have been assigned a research project with various product options that relate to a prior study of various forms of government, including the concepts of democracy, monarchy, theocracy, and totalitarianism. Using the Need to Know Board as their tool for initial data collection, students reflect on their knowledge of governmental systems to date in the first column of the Need to Know Board.

Need to Know Board		
What Do I Know?	**What Do I Need To Know?**	**How Do I Find Out?**

After analyzing the results from the brainstorming discussion, students synthesize their interests for further knowledge into the following potential questions of interest in the second column of the Need to Know Board.

1. How does the concept of citizenship differ in different societies? How has the concept of citizenship changed throughout history?
2. What form of government offers its citizens the most benefits? What form offers the fewest benefits? Should citizens make all decisions of importance in a society? Why or why not?
3. How have societies ended up with the governmental models they have? How did these models evolve through the history and development of the society?
4. What are the distinctive differences among these four forms of government? What are the advantages and disadvantages of each form of government? What is the impact of these differences on world order?
5. If you were to change one aspect of our democracy, what would you change and why?

Each student is invited to choose from this list of questions or create her own question of interest. Working in dyads or alone, students have 2 weeks to complete the project paper and product of their choice.

Students will use the Research Process Assessment during the research process to develop the research paper, citing sources to support ideas throughout. No fewer than **five** sources should be cited and included in the reference section of the paper. The teacher will monitor the work as it is being done by conferences with students, comments on drafts, availability to answer questions, and providing resources in the classroom to consult on the topics selected. She will work with the media specialist to construct a list of online sources and print sources that will be helpful as students address their research questions.

Research Process Assessment				
1 = Poor representation and/or missing material; 2 = Fair representation of the process even though all aspects are included; 3 = Good representation of the process, responsive to the rubric requirements; 4 = Excellent representation of the process, showing clarity, accuracy, and comprehensiveness				
The student performs the following tasks:				
1. Identifies an issue or problem	1	2	3	4

Figure 9.4. Scenario illustrating the development and assessment of middle school student products in government.

Research Process Assessment				
2. Identifies point of view or arguments on issue	1	2	3	4
3. Formulates research questions	1	2	3	4
4. Gathers evidence through appropriate research techniques	1	2	3	4
5. Synthesizes data and presents it in meaningful ways	1	2	3	4
6. Draws conclusions and makes inferences	1	2	3	4
7. Determines implications and consequences related to the issue or problem identified	1	2	3	4
8. Provides appropriate citations to support research findings	1	2	3	4

Rubrics will be distributed for a product of the student's choice as they begin their research. For example, if a student chose an oral presentation, the following assessment would be used.

Oral Presentation Assessment			
1. The purpose of the presentation was clear.	Needs Improvement	Satisfactory	Excellent
2. The speaker included evidence to support the point of view taken.	Needs Improvement	Satisfactory	Excellent
3. The speaker showed in-depth knowledge of the subject.	Needs Improvement	Satisfactory	Excellent
4. The speaker employed logical reasoning to make a coherent presentation.	Needs Improvement	Satisfactory	Excellent
5. The speaker engaged the audience, using appropriate eye contact, adequate volume, and clear pronunciation.	Needs Improvement	Satisfactory	Excellent
6. The speaker used multimedia and/or visual displays.	Needs Improvement	Satisfactory	Excellent
Comment on the best part of this presentation:			
Suggestion for improvement:			

Figure 9.4. *Continued.*

writing standards in those three types of discourse. Figure 9.5 illustrates an approach to the development, assessment, and application of a portfolio focused on specific requirements in language arts.

The portfolio approach to assessment just described demonstrates the extent to which it puts students in charge of their own learning and shifts the accountability for that learning to them. Asking students to select the pieces for inclusion teaches them to evaluate using a given set of criteria and to make judgments within areas of the curriculum studied. Asking students to write an integration paper defending their choices, then describing how they will move their learning forward, sets the stage for ongoing student accountability. Finally, having students present the portfolio to their parents allows them to demonstrate their capacity to explain what they've learned and project future learning. Moreover, the portfolio approach allows the teacher to both judge and reflect on student learning. These data then enable her to construct more meaningful instruction for future learning experiences.

Discussion of Assessment Issues

Selecting an appropriate assessment is a challenging task. Some decisions are practical, such as cost and availability. For example, the use of an off-level standardized instrument requires both approval and resources to pay the cost of the instrument. Other practical considerations are the amount of time needed to develop an assessment and the use of already developed assessments rather than creating them.

Selecting Appropriate Assessments for Specific Purposes

The choice of assessment should be linked inextricably to the objectives or outcomes of a learning module. Assessment tools should meet the following criteria with respect to the purpose for which they are being used:

- *Does the assessment match the intent of the learner outcomes?* Assessment should mirror learner outcomes. For example, advanced learners need to develop high-level thinking skills. If the outcome is to enhance critical and creative thinking, then the assessment should be structured to measure growth in this area. Because thinking skills are lifelong with respect to development, a teacher should not expect the highest level of skills to be exhibited among students at any level. Rather the results of the assessment should be employed for instructional purposes in the next learning cycle.
- *Does the assessment address the scope of knowledge and skills of the learning sequence?* Often assessment tools are limited in scope, especially those that are performance-based, when the nature of the learning is broader and more complex. It is important that the scope of the assessment be considered. If the objectives of a unit of study call for advanced skill development in a

Ms. Gomez wants her students to show what they have learned in the language arts classroom across 9 weeks in school, so she has asked that they construct a portfolio of work completed to date. The portfolio's purpose is to highlight the best work that students have done in the following areas of language arts: writing, literature analysis and interpretation, research, language study, and oral presentations. The portfolio will contain at least 10 pieces in total that represent these outlined areas of study. Some pieces may be used to address more than one language arts area of learning. For example, a research project may represent both literary analysis and persuasive writing. Students may select their own criteria for inclusion but should consider the following qualifiers:

- it is the best I have done in this area of study,
- it shows my thinking,
- the artifact received positive feedback from my teacher,
- it is one I am proud of, and
- it shows my creativity.

After students have selected their pieces, they will write an explanation of what the collection represents in respect to their learning and how they expect to improve in these areas over the next 9-week period. Parents will be the audience. At a parent-teacher conference, students will present their portfolios to their parents and explain the pieces, including how and why they were selected and what they represent with respect to their learning to date.

The teacher will assess the students' portfolios, using the Rubric for Portfolio Assessment.

Rubric for Portfolio Assessment				
Criteria	1 (low)	2	3	4 (high)
1. Organization of the portfolio				
2. Piece matches the criteria				
3. Representation of language arts areas				
4. Integration commentary				
5. Creativity (e.g., aesthetic appeal of the portfolio, section introductions)				
6. Correct use of mechanics				

Major strengths of portfolio:

Major areas for improvement:

Figure 9.5. Scenario illustrating the development, assessment, and application of a student portfolio.

Teachers will use the results of the portfolio assessment task to answer the following questions about student growth in the class:

1. Overall, have students evidenced growth in all areas of language arts as seen in their pieces?
2. Is there consonance in the evaluation of the pieces (i.e., teacher and students)?
3. Do students demonstrate necessary metacognitive awareness of the portfolio tasks?
4. Are the plans for advancing their own learning viable?
5. Did their integration explanation demonstrate high-level thinking and synthesis of ideas?

Figure 9.5. *Continued.*

set of problem-solving skills, then the assessment should have the student demonstrate the integration of skills as in problem-finding, researching, and problem solution, including developing a plan of action, not just one of those skills.

- *Does the assessment focus on high-level skills and concepts?* Differentiated assessments call for the same features as a differentiated curriculum. They must be high level and conceptual, requiring articulation of the appropriate level of student learning.

Using Multiple Assessments

To monitor student performance and inform instruction, a teacher needs to collect assessment data across a learning cycle, using both formative and summative approaches. Each may employ the types of assessments described in this chapter. Figure 9.6 illustrates a possible use of multiple assessments. Using multiple assessments allows the teacher to see how authentic learning is occurring across the unit through several measures: (a) multiple student-generated lab reports (formative), (b) student feedback on progress (formative), and (c) pre-post data on overall growth in learning (summative). Moreover, the use of a standardized achievement test in science at the end of the year may also reveal the overall content learning (summative).

Integrating multiple assessments for purposes of providing a grade. Just as it is prudent to use more than one assessment to judge the extent of learning, so too it is important that the assessments fit together, providing a meaningful portrait of growth in the skills and concepts studied. When looking for growth in research skills, an educator could employ an assessment of research skills, metacognitive skills, and the product itself. These assessments provide an integrated picture of what students have learned at a given point in time as well as pointing out areas for future development. For example, a research skill set, organized on a Likert scale, may be a useful tool for the teacher or the student to use at three points during the learning

> **Outcome for student learning:** To develop scientific investigation skills
>
> **Assessments used by the teacher to be able to discern progress in learning:**
> 1. Pre-post use of the Fowler (1990) test to ascertain growth in specific research investigation skills
> 2. Lab experiment data that illustrate the ability to do scientific investigations
> 3. Self-assessment of progress on learning (metacognitive questions used at the beginning, middle, and end of a major unit)
>
> **Figure 9.6.** Scenario illustrating the use of multiple assessments.

experience: the beginning, the middle, and the end. This approach to integrating assessment data becomes highly manageable and coherent.

Relationship of Assessment and Instruction

Another issue that must be considered in assessment is its relationship to instruction. Formative assessment is assessment for learning, and summative assessment is assessment of learning (Chappius, Stiggins, Arter, & Chappius, 2005). Therefore, assessment may be used as a prelude to instruction as in a preassessment model. Results of that inform decisions about who is ready to learn the lesson as planned, who needs more support to reach the learning objectives, and who can already demonstrate the knowledge and skills and needs differentiated learning opportunities. Results of assessment may be used as the basis for further instruction. Assessment allows the teacher to think about learner growth at various points in time: before starting the learning experience, during the learning experience, and at the conclusion of it. The results are learning-centered, representing a challenge for the learner. They are also intertwined in any module of curriculum. Development of curriculum requires the definition of assessment strategies as a part of the design.

Communication With Students and Parents

Ultimately, learning assessments are important tools for communication with various groups. Assessment results become the starting place for a dialogue with students and parents. They should understand assessment results and what that means about student growth. Assessment results offer the basis for academic planning and development of talent. Teachers can help parents in making decisions about in-school and out-of-school options that might be appropriate, such as a competition or a special program. They also can counsel students and parents on social-emotional issues gifted students may face, given their advanced levels of functioning. In the area of school planning and career planning, use of learning assessment data is crucial. For example, young people can be counseled as early as seventh grade into a career path in science, technology, engineering, and mathematics (STEM) if their profile demonstrates compatible aptitudes, values, and interests (Webb, Lubinski, & Benbow, 2012).

Conclusion

This chapter has focused on a basic understanding of the role of assessment in gifted student learning. Four types of assessment teachers are likely to employ were described (i.e., standardized, performance-based, product, and portfolio). Scenario illustrations were included for the use of each type. Examples of each type of assessment that may be employed in programs for the gifted were discussed along with the issues that teachers must consider in selecting instruments for use.

Big Ideas

1. Learning assessments are an integral part of teaching and learning.

2. Learning assessments should be employed at three stages of the learning process: at the beginning to plan instruction based on student needs through preassessment (formative), at the midpoint to judge interim progress (formative), and at the conclusion to assess the degree of overall integrated learning (summative).

3. Multiple assessments must be considered to provide a meaningful portrait of learning.

4. Effective assessment types for advanced learners include off-level standardized tests and performance-based, product-based, and portfolio-based assessments.

5. Learning assessments should provide the rationale for offering above-level learning challenges for gifted learners.

6. Assessment data should be shared with students and parents at regular intervals to maximize understanding of learning progress and plan for future learning.

Discussion Questions

1. After reading the chapter, how has your thinking about assessment in relation to instruction changed?

2. What issues and problems do you see in using nontraditional assessments of learning with advanced students?

3. What advantages and disadvantages do you see in using the following types of assessment: traditional, performance-based, product, and portfolio?

References

Brody, L. E., & Mills, C. J. (2005) Talent search research: What have we learned. *High Ability Studies, 16,* 97–111.

Chappius, S., Stiggins, R. J., Arter, J., & Chappius, J. (2005). *Assessment for learning: An action guide for school leaders.* Portland, OR: Educational Testing Service.

Fowler, M. (1990). The diet cola test. *Science Scope, 13*(4), 32–34.

Johnsen, S. K. (2008). Portfolio assessment of gifted students. In J. VanTassel-Baska (Ed.), *Alternative assessments with gifted and talented students* (pp. 227–257). Waco, TX: Prufrock Press.

Moon, T. R. (2015). Alternative assessment. In J. A. Pucker & C. M. Callahan (Eds.), *Critical issues and practices in gifted education* (2nd ed., pp. 45–55). Waco, TX: Prufrock Press.

National Center for Education Statistics. (2011). *Mathematics and science achievement of U.S. fourth- and eighth-grade students in an international context.* Washington, DC: Author.

National Governors Association Center for Best Practices, & Council of Chief State School Officers. (2010a). *Common Core State Standards for English Language Arts.* Washington, DC: Author.

National Governors Association Center for Best Practices, & Council of Chief State School Officers. (2010b). *Common Core State Standards for Mathematics.* Washington, DC: Author.

No Child Left Behind Act, 20 U.S.C. §6301 (2001).

Renzulli, J. S., & Callahan, C. M. (2008). Product assessment. In J. VanTassel-Baska (Ed.), *Alternative assessments with gifted and talented students* (pp. 203–225). Waco, TX: Prufrock Press.

Renzulli, J. S., & Reis, S. (1997). *The Schoolwide Enrichment Model: A how-to guide for talent development* (2nd ed.). Mansfield Center, CT: Creative Learning Press.

Renzulli, J. S., & Reis, S. (2014). *The Schoolwide Enrichment Model: A how-to guide for talent development* (3rd ed.). Waco, TX: Prufrock Press.

Roberts, J. L., & Inman, T. F. (2015). *Assessing differentiated student products: A protocol for development and evaluation* (2nd ed.). Waco, TX: Prufrock Press.

Ryser, G. R., & Rambo-Hernandez, K. E. (2014). Using growth models to measure school performance: Implications for gifted learners. *Gifted Child Today, 37,* 17–23.

Thomson, D., & Olszewski-Kubilius, P. (2014). The increasingly important role of off-level testing in the context of the talent development perspective. *Gifted Child Today, 37,* 33–40.

VanTassel-Baska, J. (Ed.). (2008). *Alternative assessments with gifted and talented students.* Waco, TX: Prufrock Press.

VanTassel-Baska, J. (2013). Performance-based assessment: The road to authentic learning for the gifted. *Gifted Child Today, 37,* 41–47.

VanTassel-Baska, J., & Johnsen, S. K. (2015) Content acceleration: The critical pathway for adapting the common core state standards for gifted students. In S. G. Assouline, N. Colangelo, J. VanTassel-Baska, & A. Shoplik (Eds.), *A nation empowered* (Vol. 2, pp. 99–109). Iowa City: The University of Iowa, The Connie Belin & Jacqueline N. Blank International Center for Gifted Education and Talent Development.

Warne, R. T. (2012). History and development of above-level testing of the gifted. *Roeper Review, 34,* 183–193.

Webb, R. M., Lubinski, D. & Benbow, C. P. (2012). Mathematically facile adolescents with math-science aspirations: New perspectives on their educational and vocational development. *Journal of Educational Psychology, 94,* 785–794.

Wiggins, G., & McTighe, J. (2005) *Understanding by design* (2nd ed.). Washington, DC: Association for Supervision and Curriculum Development.

CHAPTER 10

Designing the Learning Environment for Gifted Students

Thomas P. Hébert

A great teacher continues to ask the question, "What can I do to make certain that each student in this classroom feels safe, valued, accepted, and challenged?"—Tomlinson (2008, p. 6)

Essential Questions to Guide the Reader

1. What theories guide educators in designing learning environments for gifted students?

2. How do teachers facilitate strategies to create supportive learning environments?

3. How do grouping practices influence the design of learning experiences for gifted students?

Sara Moore arrived in her fourth-grade classroom in early August. Refreshed from a relaxing summer that included a 2-week vacation at the beach, she was energized and looking forward to the start of school. She scanned the barren walls and furniture and decided they could wait. She would worry about the physical arrangement of the room later. She began her work of covering a shoebox with brightly colored paper. Her first task to prepare her classroom would be the design of Mrs.

183

Moore's Mailbox. As she worked with her craft materials, she reflected on her experiences with the classroom mailbox the previous year and smiled.

Sara had explained to her students that if they were to leave a letter in her mailbox, she guaranteed that they would find a letter from her in a sealed envelope the following morning. She initially had been deluged with notes from the children; however, she responded to all of them. Throughout the year, Sara received notes that helped her to understand how her students were feeling about their experiences in her classroom. The notes also provided her insight into the lives of her students beyond the classroom. She learned of team victories on the soccer field, family travels and camping trips, the arrival of new siblings, a parent's loss of employment, and more. Some letters were written as cries for help. She thought back to Marcus and the day she introduced him to the school's counselor after she read his note in which he shared his worries about his mother's battle with cancer. Sara realized that her mailbox became an important outlet for the children to share their personal lives with her when they needed support, encouragement, or a significant adult to listen to what was on their minds. As she continued to decorate the new mailbox, she pondered what she might learn from her students in the coming year. She wanted to continue designing a psychologically safe environment for her fourth graders. Determined to be an excellent teacher, Sara's years of working with bright children had helped to shape her philosophical views on the importance of designing student-centered classroom environments. She wanted to provide a place where students would feel comfortable being themselves and would feel at home as they enjoyed their fourth-grade experience. The theoretical literature described below reinforced Sara's approach to the design of learning environments.

Creating a Space

Sara Moore encountered the work of Parker Palmer (1993) who described teaching as creating a space. This struck Sara as a poetic metaphor until she understood that it describes everyday life. As Palmer explained, we understand what it means to run through an open field on a summer day, and we can compare that experience to traveling on a crowded rush-hour subway. On the crowded subway, we are hard-pressed to find a place to breathe and think; yet in an open field, we can also be open as our ideas and emotions emerge within us. According to Palmer, these experiences with space are parallel to our relationships with people in our lives. We know how it feels to be crowded by the urgency of deadlines and stressed by the competitiveness of colleagues. We have also experienced other times when colleagues collaborate effectively and people feel comfortable creating, inventing, and solving problems with enthusiasm and energy. We may also experience the same feelings with family and friends. We may have been overwhelmed by the expectations of those who are closest to us in contrast to other times when we feel accepted, supported, and appreciated for who we are as well as who we want to become. Palmer drew a parallel to schools:

> Similar experiences of crowding and space are found in education. To sit in a class where the teacher stuffs our minds with information, organizes it with finality, insists on having the answers while getting utterly uninterested in our views, and forces us into a grim competition for grades—to sit in such a class is to experience a lack of space for learning. But to study with a teacher who not only speaks but listens, who not only gives answers but asks questions and welcomes our insights, who provides information and theories that do not close doors but open new ones, who encourage students to help each other learn—to study with such a teacher is to know the power of a learning space. (pp. 70–71)

Palmer's (1993) learning space includes three significant characteristics: openness, boundaries, and an air of hospitality. Openness involves removing any barriers to learning. A teacher who wants to create an open learning space also must define and protect its boundaries, for such a space requires some structure. Without it, we openly invite confusion and chaos. A learning space also includes hospitality—being open to receiving each other and our new ideas. This space should be hospitable to make learning enjoyable but also provide room for students to experience the difficult challenges of learning, such as testing hypotheses, questioning false information, and dealing with mutual criticism.

Palmer's (1993) learning space is consistent with the work of William Purkey, a counselor educator whose research and philosophical approach have influenced the design of many gifted education classrooms. Purkey (1978) believed that good teaching involved a process whereby students are invited to see themselves as able, valuable, and self-directed, and a teacher's role is to encourage them to act according to these self-perceptions. The Invitational Learning concept, developed by Purkey and his colleagues, is a paradigm that provides educators with an approach for enriching the physical and psychological environments of schools and encouraging the development of the people who work there. Invitational Learning is centered on four guiding principles: respect, trust, optimism, and intentionality (Purkey & Novak, 2008; Purkey & Strahan, 2002). The foundation of invitational learning is *respect* for the unique value of each and every individual. Respect is evident when educators accept young people as they are, recognize their unlimited potential, invite them to take responsibility for their lives, and make appropriate decisions about their learning. *Trust,* the second key principle, recognizes the interdependence of human beings and guides teaching as a collaborative activity in which process is celebrated as much as product.

The third guiding principle, *optimism*, is the belief that human potential is endless and waiting to be discovered and nurtured. Optimistic teachers working with children have a vision of what is possible for their students to achieve. *Intentionality*, the fourth principle, refers to the ability to align perceptions with overt behaviors. Educators who are intentionally inviting consistently demonstrate integrity in their practice and remain dedicated to the reason many became teachers: an authentic appreciation of others and a desire to help students grow. They maintain personal dignity and self-respect alongside their respect for and trust in others, and they are deeply committed to caring for people (Hébert, 2011).

These four guiding principles are evident in Barbara Clark's (2013) design of a responsive learning environment. She maintained that all young people benefit from an "environment that is cognitively, physically, socially, and emotionally responsive to them" (p. 330). Clark described this environment:

> In a responsive learning environment, gifted students can pursue educational requirements and interests in depth and with a minimum of time limitations. They will no longer need to be held to the pace or achievement level of the class; they can be grouped flexibly with gifted students or other students as their learning needs require; or, when appropriate, they can work individually. All students can function as researchers, apprentices, or resident experts. The classroom becomes a laboratory for learning that is more closely related to the real world. (pp. 330–331)

According to Clark (2013), a responsive learning environment provides opportunities for the students to participate in a variety of instructional groupings such as total-group instruction, small-group instruction or problem solving, independent study, and recreational inquiry or reading. She maintained that the ambiance of the classroom should be inviting and comfortable and allow for plenty of movement and exploration with easy access to materials and resources for learning. There should be space for students to simultaneously engage in a variety of activities. Clark indicated that in such a setting young people can "learn responsibility and a sense of control when expectations and opportunities for choice, shared responsibility, and self-evaluation are a planned part of their day" (p. 333). The productive climate for learning is also supported with activities focused on social and emotional growth. Building and practicing affective skills are a consistent and significant part of the daily curriculum, and the emotional climate becomes warm and accepting. The design of such an environment—the open space as described by Palmer (1993)—will make the learning experience for students far more enjoyable and productive.

Designing Responsive, Differentiated, Inviting Classrooms

Sara Moore finished designing her classroom mailbox and headed to the teacher's lounge to purchase a soda. When she arrived, she was happy to see several of her colleagues. Sara joined Lamont and Celia in catching up on the latest news and sharing stories of summer travels. Sara's friends described the summer institute in gifted education they had enjoyed and were enthusiastic to pass on what they had learned. Lamont talked about specific strategies he learned to create a gifted-friendly classroom environment. He commented, "Sara, you know how I appreciated your classroom mailbox last year, so I made a point to attend workshops on addressing the social and emotional needs of our kids. I've stocked up on a variety of strategies that I'm sure you'll want to try." Celia was excited to chat about a plan for flexible grouping of students, and she spoke of different approaches to effectively address learning needs. Lamont and Celia mentioned that they had promised their principal they would facilitate an informational session with the faculty to share what they had learned. Sara was excited for them and looked forward to hearing more. The theoretical literature discussed below provides support for the instructional approaches that Lamont and Celia described.

As educators consider approaches to designing learning environments that support young people, it is important to bear in mind the diversity of 21st-century American classrooms. An appreciation for student differences becomes critical. In classrooms today, teachers meet advanced learners, students identified with learning difficulties, students whose first language is not English, students who underachieve for a variety of complex reasons, students from broadly diverse cultures and economic backgrounds, and students with widely varying interests and preferred modes of learning (Tomlinson et al., 2003). The challenge of serving academically diverse learners is an inevitable responsibility for regular classroom teachers; hence the design of differentiated classrooms must be taken seriously.

According to Tomlinson (2001), differentiated instruction provides multiple approaches to *content*, what students learn; *process*, how they go about making sense of ideas and information; and *product*, how they demonstrate what they have learned. She maintained that educators who effectively differentiate instruction recognize that different learners have differing needs; therefore, they proactively plan a variety of ways to arrive at learning. They operate on the premise that learning experiences are most successful when they are engaging, relevant, and interesting; therefore, educators tailor instruction for individual learners based on their knowledge of the different needs of students. Teachers who understand the need for teaching and learning to be a good match for students look for every opportunity to know their students better. Their instruction is rooted in assessment. They consider conversations with individual children, classroom discussions, student work, observation, and formal assessment as different ways to gather insights about what works best for each learner. What they discover about their students influences how they craft lessons in ways that help to build upon students' strengths. In the design of lessons, the instruction becomes a blend of whole-class, group, and individual instruction.

The way classrooms are designed reflects educators' philosophical views of how students learn. If the purpose of instruction is to provide young people opportunities to raise questions, to experiment, and to work collaboratively with others, then a classroom environment that will facilitate such interactions needs to be in place (Hunt & Seney, 2009). An educator's instructional approach will be strongly influenced by a school's philosophy on grouping students. Clark (2013) maintained that flexible grouping is critical for educators to be able to structure gifted students' experiences in order to best address their needs. She suggested that carefully planned grouping enables teachers to "provide advanced, appropriately paced, complex, and divergent materials and instruction to students who need such modifications to grow academically and intellectually" (p. 174). Roberts and Inman (2015) extended this position by calling attention to the need for teachers to be thoughtful in determining their intent for grouping students and their goals for the particular learning experience. With learning objectives in mind, the most appropriate grouping could be selected and facilitated. Clark and Roberts and Inman agreed that flexible grouping was especially beneficial for students. Clark expressed this succinctly:

> Flexible grouping will always be an important organizational strategy for teachers to use to effectively manage the many and varied needs of students within and among classrooms. As long as the major criterion for organizing learning, both homogeneous and heterogeneous grouping—flexibly practiced and carefully planned around the assessed needs, pacing, and learning patterns of students—will be necessary to ensure success for every learner. (p. 174)

Grouping

Sara Moore sat at the front of the seminar room on the day Lamont and Celia spoke with their faculty colleagues. Sara provided them an encouraging smile as she listened to what they had to offer. Having been scheduled for one hour in the professional development day, Lamont and Celia needed to deliver their new expertise succinctly. With that in mind, Celia presented what she had learned about facilitating a variety of grouping practices with gifted students.

In her introductory remarks, she pointed out several key issues for success noted by Roberts and Inman (2015). She explained that teachers must always have a strong rationale for grouping children. Once students are placed in different groups for instruction, all groups should be working on different tasks. The tasks should be equally challenging for all group members, and they are all to be held accountable for the task. Celia highlighted the importance of being flexible and using a variety of ways to group students. She pointed out that for some students grouping caused stress, and therefore giving children the opportunity to work alone was appropriate. She suggested that perhaps students might work individually on a task and then share the results in a small-group setting. She continued her presentation by high-lighting a variety of grouping practices that included cluster grouping, readiness or ability grouping, mixed-ability grouping, and various types of flexible grouping.

Cluster grouping involves grouping five to eight identified gifted students, usually those in the highest tier of ability in the grade-level population, in the classroom of one teacher who has been trained in how to teach highly able students. Proponents of cluster grouping argue that it is an effective way to meet both the cognitive and affective needs of gifted students. Teachers report that new leadership "rises to the top" in noncluster classes, for there are often students other than identified gifted students who welcome the opportunity to become new leaders in groups that no longer include the most advanced learners (Gentry, 2014).

Celia explained that with readiness or ability grouping, students are placed in classes or groups where course or lesson objectives are commensurate with student readiness or ability based on pretesting. Regardless of the grouping arrangement, making adjustments within the students' work remains key. Educators are reminded that purposeful placement of students in classes with well-articulated curriculum is not a quick fix because students will differ in their needs, abilities, and interests, and differentiation will be required to ensure continuous progress of all students (Roberts & Inman, 2015).

Celia cautioned her colleagues about mixed-ability grouping as she described the approach as a configuration that proved frustrating for almost all group members if the expectation was for all children to master a topic or skill. However, if the intention of the teacher was to develop communication and leadership skills, then this structured approach might be a good match.

The emphasis of Celia's presentation focused on the use of flexible grouping with gifted students. She encouraged her colleagues to consider flexible grouping according to student interests, learning style, readiness or achievement level, and gender.

In discussing grouping by interest, Celia explained that when teachers discover what their students are interested in, they are able to match topics in a unit of study to the students most interested in the topic. Regardless of ability level or learning style, those group members will work closely, investigating one aspect of the content they find intriguing. For example, military battle strategy buffs will be happy channeling their fascination with their selected topic as the class investigates the Civil War.

When students are grouped according to learning style, they will all be learning about the same content; however, they will do so based on the way they learn best. Although research does not conclusively link learning styles to achievement, using a variety of strategies to appeal to various learning styles increases engagement. For example, visual and auditory learners studying multiplication can be introduced to math programs that incorporate stories and provide pictures for learners to make connections. Retelling math stories to other group members may assist students in reaching mastery of multiplication facts (Roberts & Inman, 2015).

Celia discussed how teachers who pretest at the beginning of an instructional sequence often discover they have three readiness or achievement groups: those at grade level, those below, and those above. Students in the three groups will not need the same instructional activities, and differentiation becomes critical, for each and every student should be equally challenged and held accountable for learning. This grouping strategy is the one most likely to present challenge to advanced students. An educator is likely to see more growth using this strategy than the others.

Celia concluded her discussion by highlighting how grouping by gender may be used to encourage gifted middle school young women to ignore the males in class, be themselves, and celebrate their intelligences without fear of losing social capital. In a single-gender group, the young men in class may remain totally focused on hands-on construction activities without having to clown around and attempt to entertain the girls.

Pedagogical Strategies to Support Social and Emotional Needs

Following discussion and Celia's responses to questions posed by the faculty, Lamont continued the session offering pedagogical strategies that incorporate Purkey's (1978) four components of respect, trust, optimism, and intentionality. He began by introducing several strategies that may be used to establish relationships within the classroom at the beginning of the school year. He offered Business Cards, Wanted Posters, and Two-Word Poems. He also offered his colleagues several examples of interest inventories they might consider and concluded his presentation with Going to Boston, an activity designed to recognize and celebrate student strengths (Hébert, 2011).

In Business Cards, teachers explain to children how professionals have business cards that present an image to the world of what they are all about. They then share a collection of business cards and highlight how many of them send a very clear message. For example, a teacher might present a simple and elegant-looking card from a local bakery featuring gourmet cupcakes and explain to students how that card might appeal to someone shopping for elegant desserts for a special family celebration. After browsing through the collection of cards and studying how a card presents an individual's image, students are asked to reflect on a question: "What does a business card say about you?" Students are then provided large sheets of construction paper and time to design their personal business cards. When the cards are completed, students use them to introduce themselves to their classmates. Cards are displayed on the classroom walls for several weeks. The teacher's objective behind this activity is to help gifted students find friends. The science fiction buffs may find each other. The baseball card collectors will discover other sports junkies. The young women who design original step dance routines may discover other dancers. Through their common interests or passions, new friendships emerge. Students who are savvy in their knowledge of technology enjoy creating professional-looking cards, having them printed, and exchanging them amongst the group. Teachers can have students post their cards on the class website and begin to help them build important relationships. Such a nonthreatening activity enables teachers to begin building community during the opening days of school (Hébert, 2011).

Wanted Posters involves having children think about how they might advertise for a new friend by advertising their personal interests, hobbies, and passions. With a digital camera and a classroom set of individual snapshots, teachers have what they need to introduce each new member of the classroom community. An example of text from a seventh-grade Wanted Poster is provided below:

WANTED

Friends who love reading John Green novels, competing in gymnastics, enjoying slumber parties, and performing in theatrical plays and concerts.

Call Shantal
(555) 783-0235

Two-Word Poems on the first day of school can be fun. Students are paired with a partner and provided the time to get to know each other in quiet conversation. Once they have had enough time gathering information about each other's lives beyond the classroom, they are asked to write a two-word poem describing their classroom colleague. Each line of the poem is limited to two words. Classmates introduce their new friends by sharing their poems. Teachers may decide to have student artwork or personal snapshots accompany the poems for display. The following poem is an example of what might evolve from this activity:

Roderick Williamson
Great smile
Surfing dude
Rugged muscles
Baseball player
Yankees fan
Awesome guy!

Teachers who design gifted-friendly environments understand that acquiring as much information about their students as they can at the beginning of the school year will enable them to provide learning experiences that are aligned with their interests and passions. Important information can be acquired by conducting interest inventories. Several commercially available interest surveys have been popular in gifted education (see Renzulli, 1997). Winebrenner (2001) included a field-tested inventory in her work *Teaching Gifted Kids in the Regular Classroom,* as did Heacox (2002) in *Differentiating Instruction in the Regular Classroom.* Using interest inventories delivers a message to students that says, "I care about you and what you are interested in." Nugent (2005) recommended that educators consider developing their own questionnaires by asking questions of students regarding what they enjoy doing after school, what sports they enjoy, who are the important people in their lives, and how they feel about particular school subjects. With a bit of personal creativity, teachers can design useful surveys that will go a long way in uncovering helpful information for planning engaging curriculum and creating a supportive classroom community. The following are examples of questions that middle and high school teachers have incorporated in their inventories:

- What picture is on your screensaver on your computer? Or the background picture on your cell phone?
- You are stuck in the store as your mom's "this-will-only-take-a-minute" promise has turned into 45 minutes. So, to ease the frustration, you browse through the magazines. Which magazines are you most likely to pick up and flip through to see what's new this month?
- America is famous for being a melting pot of cultures. What is your ancestral background? Were your parents immigrants? Your great-grandparents? What are some family customs and celebrations that stem from your family's background? (Hébert, 2011)

Lamont described Going to Boston, an activity from the classic work of Canfield and Wells (1994) that classroom teachers can infuse at any time of the year to reinforce the strengths of students and celebrate their successes. In conducting this activity, the first student says, "I'm going to Boston with my suitcase, and in it I have my friendly personality." The student offers a personal characteristic or talent that he or she values. The next student then says, "I'm going to Boston, and in my suitcase I'm carrying Maria's friendly personality and my skills in cartooning." The third classmate says, "I'm going to Boston, and in my suitcase I'm carrying Maria's friendly personality, Jamal's skills in cartooning, and my talent for skateboarding." This continues until all students in the class have had their opportunity to add their special gift to the suitcase. Teachers in secondary classrooms may enjoy facilitating a variation of this activity for students in which they pack the suitcase with personal successes, asking them to identify their most outstanding success to date. A teenager may respond with "I'm going to Boston with my suitcase, and in it I have my acceptance letter to the Governor's Honors Summer Program." Another student may include her trophy from a recent state science fair. Young people enjoy Going to Boston, and when a student is humble and struggles to come up with a specific positive characteristic or strength, other students typically are ready to offer what they see as a strength in their classmate.

Lamont continued his discussion by highlighting the value of infusing affective curriculum into the classroom. According to Peterson (2016), an affective curriculum "is intended to help children and teens self-reflect, reflect about others, develop positive school relationships, learn expressive language, explore careers, self-regulate, make decisions and progress with developmental tasks" (pp. 308–309). This curriculum can be embedded into core academic curriculum and might include writing personal responses to literature, analyzing political leaders' value-laden responses to historical events, self-assessments of beliefs and values, affective insights through books, discussions of moral dilemmas, artistic responses to describing emotions, and using films to generate discussion of social and emotional concerns. Lamont concluded his discussion by directing his colleagues to additional helpful resources and highlighted the work of Ford and Trotman Scott (2016), Hébert and his colleagues (2014), and Peterson (2016).

Conclusion

Sara Moore provided both Lamont and Celia a warm hug following their session. She was excited with the "take-aways" she had acquired from her friends and promised to continue the conversation during lunch to discuss how she would implement the inspirational ideas they offered. She explained to her friends that with their help she looked forward to strengthening her skills in designing a warm, inviting, and safe learning environment for gifted students.

Big Ideas

1. Classroom environments should be places where all students feel psychologically safe, respected, and intellectually engaged.

2. The challenge of serving academically diverse learners is a critical responsibility for regular classroom teachers; therefore, the design of differentiated instruction must be taken seriously.

3. Students benefit from flexible grouping practices that address their diverse learning needs.

4. A productive classroom climate for learning is supported with activities focused on social and emotional growth.

Discussion Questions

1. What is the significance of the theoretical approach to education offered by Parker Palmer and William Purkey? How does an understanding of this theory support teachers in gifted education?

2. In what ways does Barbara Clark's model of a responsive classroom environment align with Carol Ann Tomlinson's approach to differentiated classrooms?

3. How might interest assessment influence a teacher's efforts in creating a supportive classroom environment?

4. What advice would you offer to a teacher who wants to infuse affective curriculum in several content areas?

5. How do the strategies described in the chapter support the social and emotional needs of gifted students?

6. Which approaches to flexible grouping have you facilitated in your classroom? Describe your experience.

References

Canfield, J., & Wells, H. C. (1994). *100 ways to enhance self-concept in the classroom* (2nd ed.). Boston, MA: Allyn & Bacon.

Clark, B. (2013). *Growing up gifted: Developing the potential of children at school and at home* (8th ed.). Boston, MA: Pearson.

Ford, D. Y., & Trotman Scott, M. (2016). Culturally responsive and relevant curriculum: The revised Bloom-Banks matrix. In K. R. Stephens & F. A. Karnes (Eds.), *Introduction to curriculum design in gifted education* (pp. 331–349). Waco, TX: Prufrock Press.

Gentry, M. L. (2014). *Total school cluster grouping and differentiation: A comprehensive research-based plan for raising student achievement and improving teacher practices* (2nd ed.). Waco, TX: Prufrock Press.

Heacox, D. (2002). *Differentiating instruction in the regular classroom: How to reach and teach all learners, grades 3–12.* Minneapolis, MN: Free Spirit.

Hébert, T. P. (2011). *Understanding the social and emotional lives of gifted students.* Waco, TX: Prufrock Press.

Hébert, T. P., Corcoran, J. A., Coté, J. M., Ene, M.C., Leighton, E. A., Holmes, A. M. & Padula, D. D. (2014). It's safe to be smart: Strategies for creating a supportive classroom environment. *Gifted Child Today, 37,* 95–101.

Hunt, B. G., & Seney, R. W. (2009). Planning the learning environment. In. F. A. Karnes & S. M. Bean (Eds.), *Methods and materials for teaching the gifted* (3rd ed., pp. 37–74). Waco, TX: Prufrock Press.

Nugent, S. (2005). *Social and emotional teaching strategies.* Waco, TX: Prufrock Press.

Palmer, P. J. (1993). *To know as we are known: Education as a spiritual journey.* San Francisco, CA: HarperCollins.

Peterson, J. S. (2016). Affective curriculum: Proactively addressing the challenges of growing up. In K. R. Stephens & F. A. Karnes (Ed.), *Introduction to curriculum design in gifted education* (pp. 307–330). Waco, TX: Prufrock Press.

Purkey, W. W. (1978). *Inviting school success: A self-concept approach to teaching and learning.* Belmont, CA: Wadsworth.

Purkey, W. W., & Novak, J. M. (2008). *Fundamentals of invitational education.* Kennesaw, GA: International Alliance for Invitational Education.

Purkey, W. W., & Strahan, D. B. (2002). *Inviting positive classroom discipline.* Westerville, OH: National Middle School Association.

Renzulli, J. S. (1997). *Interest-a-lyzer family of instruments: A manual for teachers.* Waco, TX: Prufrock Press.

Roberts, J. L., & Inman, T. F. (2015). *Strategies for differentiating instruction: Best practices for the classroom* (3rd ed.). Waco, TX: Prufrock Press.

Tomlinson, C. A. (2001). *How to differentiate instruction in mixed-ability classrooms* (2nd ed.). Alexandria, VA: Association for Supervision and Curriculum Development.

Tomlinson, C. A. (2008). Lessons learned from bright students about affect. In M. W. Gosfield (Ed.), *Expert approaches to support gifted learners* (pp. 4–9). Minneapolis, MN: Free Spirit.

Tomlinson, C. A., Brighton, C., Hertberg, H., Callahan, C. M., Moon, T. R., Brimijoin, K., . . . Reynolds, T. (2003). Differentiating instruction in response to student readiness, interest, and learning profile in academically diverse classrooms: A review of literature. *Journal for the Education of the Gifted, 27,* 119–145.

Winebrenner, S. (2001). *Teaching gifted kids in the regular classroom.* Minneapolis, MN: Free Spirit.

CHAPTER 11

The Learning Environment at Home

Parents and Families

Michael S. Matthews and Jennifer L. Jolly

> I asked Mom if I was a gifted child. She said they certainly wouldn't
> have PAID for me.—Calvin (Bill Watterson in *Calvin & Hobbes*)

Essential Questions to Guide the Reader

1. What do we know from the research on parenting gifted students?

2. How can teachers and schools build positive relationships with parents of gifted learners?

3. How can parents of gifted learners build positive relationships with teachers and schools?

4. What alternatives do parents have if they feel their child's needs still are not being met in the available school settings?

The key roles that parents play in their child's academic and social-emotional development are widely recognized. However, far less is known about how parents' roles and responsibilities may influence the development of students of high academic potential, or of children formally identified as academically gifted and talented. In extreme cases, some parents may single-mindedly devote all of their time and attention to their child's growth and development, while other parents may almost completely default on any responsibility for raising their offspring. Both

197

ends of the parenting continuum may be unhealthy, or worse, in terms of the outcomes they yield with regard to the child's ultimate accomplishments and mental health. This chapter addresses some of the questions surrounding parenting and the gifted child.

Historical View of Parenting Gifted Children

Early scholarly attention on parent and family influences began, at least in Europe, with Francis Galton's (1869) seminal work *Hereditary Genius: An Inquiry Into Its Laws and Consequences*. Although others previously had considered these issues, Galton noted, "I may claim to be the first to treat the subject in a statistical manner" (p. vi). Working from the idea of "eminence," which Galton suggested could be defined as approximately the top 1 in 4,000 persons in achievement or accomplishment, he developed the idea that greatness was in large part hereditary rather than environmental in origin. While recognizing the "common opinion that great men have remarkable mothers" (p. 329), he explained this away as being due to the fact that eminent men simply were more likely to praise their family members than other men were.

Galton (1869) further asserted that "the precocious child is looked upon as a prodigy [by his parents] . . . and he is pushed forward in every way by home influences, until serious harm is done to his constitution" (p. 331). This idea that precocious development would lead to problems, or "early ripe, early rot," persisted as the prevailing view about gifted students for the next several decades until it was challenged by Terman's findings in the 1920s and 1930s. Thus, although Galton may have been the first to consider parental influences through a scholarly, mathematical lens, he was perhaps unable to rise beyond the biases of his times to acknowledge the importance of familial influences on children's development.

Hollingworth (1926), also influenced by the work of Galton and the principles of heredity, worked toward a further understanding of familial influence on the development of children's abilities through her case studies of the education and development of children of extremely high IQ. Of particular interest to this chapter, she observed that parents of gifted children tended to have fewer children when compared to families with children of average or below-average intelligence (Hollingworth, 1929), allowing a greater amount of time to cultivate the child's gifts and talents. Following the work of Terman and Hollingworth, it appears that several decades followed in which there was little scholarly interest on the topic of parenting and gifted children.

Parent Understanding of Giftedness and the Gifted Label

In recent years, scholars have sought to understand public perceptions of giftedness and the gifted label, in part due to the stigma that often accompanies this label. Studies of the perceptions of teachers and students have only recently been extended to include parents, but findings seem broadly similar across stakeholders: The term *gifted* carries problematic associations in many settings.

In a seminal early study, Tannenbaum (1962) found that academic brilliance was viewed in a more negative light by adolescents when it was associated with studiousness and nonathletic characteristics. Other more recent studies (Carrington, 1996; Cramond & Martin, 1987; Lee, Cramond, & Lee, 2004) have confirmed and extended this finding to perceptions of teachers in both the U.S. and South Korea, and to adolescents in Australia, suggesting that the stigma attached to students perceived as having high academic ability yet lacking athleticism may be widespread.

Perceptions of the gifted label have been studied by a variety of scholars, and their work has identified both positive and negative associations tied to the notion of giftedness (Colangelo & Brower, 1987; Cornell, 1983, 1989; Dweck, 2000; Kerr, Colangelo, & Gaeth, 1988; Makel, 2009; McCoach & Siegle, 2007). In one example of this work, Makel (2009) found that students and parents held similar attitudes toward giftedness prior to the identification process, but nonidentified students and their parents reported lower attitudes toward giftedness following the identification process. Although suggestive, this study had a small sample size. More recently, Matthews, Ritchotte, and Jolly (2014) asked 138 parents of gifted learners about their usage of the term *gifted*. These authors found that approximately half of these parents felt they or their children would be judged negatively by others if they used the term; in many cases these parents used different terms in place of the word gifted, while parents of twice-exceptional children described their child's disability first before acknowledging their child's areas of giftedness. Peters, Matthews, McBee, and McCoach (2014) have recommended that the term gifted should be abandoned in favor of alternative terms that have fewer negative connotations, and that schools should label services rather than labeling individuals; they recommended the term *advanced academics* for this purpose.

Despite these notable drawbacks to the gifted label, labeling remains widely practiced because of its utility in matching students to appropriate programming, and because of the role labels play in the allocation of funding for specific educational programs and services. Parents should keep in mind the potential drawbacks of the gifted label, while also recognizing its utility in discussing and advocating for the educational needs of their child. It is important that in the study by Matthews et al. (2014), a minority of the parents, about one in three respondents, reported using the word gifted purposefully. These parents viewed their use of the term as an opportunity to educate other parents about giftedness as an important aspect of individual differences and what it means to be gifted, to dispel myths about giftedness, to celebrate their children's accomplishments, and to advocate for the needs of gifted learners beyond those of their own children.

Achievement and Parents' Influence

Parents' influence on the achievement of their child can be profound. Complicating an understanding of this issue are ongoing philosophical debates regarding the relationship between potential and achievement; these tensions are visible most specifically surrounding beliefs about whether high achievement is independent of genetic endowment. This perspective is evident in the "tiger mom" perspective on parenting (Chua, 2011) that is prevalent in Chinese and some other Asian cultures; in this view, hard work and parenting are prioritized as sources of academic success (Jolly & Matthews, 2012, 2014). Chua (2011) observed that this perspective is neither limited to parents who are ethnically Chinese nor adopted by all who are, but, when followed, it holds that if a child fails to achieve academic excellence, it is *only* because the parents are not doing their duty. Thus, parents may, and, in fact, should use harsh childrearing tactics, including name-calling or threats, so long as these achieve the desired result of their child being the top achiever in every valued area. Chua (2011) contrasts this with a Western (or perhaps more specifically, American) view of parenting, one in which the child's self-esteem appears to be valued as the most important outcome. Dazed by the glare of some of the book's depictions of her approach, readers of Chua's book sometimes overlook that the author also meant it to convey her own evolving perspective on parenting, including ultimately her partial retreat from the strict disciplinarian view held early on in her parenting practice. Although some traditionally minded parents may follow this strict approach, many parents would be uncomfortable with pushing their child in this manner. Indeed, in a more scholarly study of parenting, Wu (2008) observed in her study of Chinese American families' influence on talent development that these parents were confident about their children's future, that being a good parent was taken very seriously, and that these parents over time had combined both Chinese and Western parenting practices.

If parents view effort as the sole factor leading to academic and life success, then any failure or lack of achievement by their child becomes solely the child's fault, even if the parents' failure is viewed as an additional or enabling factor. This is a heavy burden to place on anyone, whether the person in question is a parent or especially a child. In seeking a more balanced perspective on the issue of nature versus nurture, it can be instructive to think about sports as an analogue of academic achievement. The desire for a football career by motivational speaker Rudy Ruettiger, as depicted in the film *Rudy* (Fried, Woods, & Anspaugh, 1993), showed clearly that even an almost superhuman degree of effort may be insufficient to make up for a distinct lack of physical endowment in the context of American college football. Similar arguments could be made in basketball and in most other sports; see, for example, Gladwell (2008) for an interesting perspective on how this plays out in the sport of ice hockey. In an analogous way, for the child who lacks the necessary genetic endowment, perhaps no amount of forced studying can produce a genius. However, success by some definition can almost always be achieved through extraordinary effort. The crucial yet unknown element is exactly where this balance between ability and effort is located; it likely is in a different place in each domain of human endeavor.

There are other relevant examples in the popular press that also may be instructive about the relationships between parenting and talent development. Adragan DeMello was pushed to graduate from college at age 16, but by age 23, he had recast this experience as having been a form of child abuse (CBS News.com Staff, 2000). The story of the Polgár family and these parents' successful efforts to make their three girls into chess prodigies is another example, but one that also highlights the likely role of genetic differences in exceptional achievement; although all three sisters became experts in the domain of chess, only one of the three consistently has achieved at the very highest, world-championship level of the game (Flora, 2005). Gladwell (2008) also discussed the role of effective parenting (or the lack thereof) in the story of Chris Langan, who despite a stratospheric IQ score, was unable to succeed academically because he was not raised to develop the associated noncognitive abilities that are vital to achieving successful academic outcomes.

As these varied examples illustrate, both genetics and environmental (especially parenting) influences likely play a role in the child's ability to achieve academic and life success. One other vital piece of the puzzle is how success should be defined; should achieving to one's full potential in a professional career be the only relevant measure of success, or can other achievements such as personal fulfillment, time for leisure activities, a rich family life, and the like also be considered successful outcomes? This question probably has been posed for at least a century, since Terman's study began, and there is still no consensus as to its answer. Ultimately it must be answered based on one's philosophy of life, but the existence of a variety of possible answers also illuminates ongoing debates in gifted education regarding the very nature or definition of eminence, whether eminence is the only or even the most appropriate goal of gifted education, and even whether gifted education services are the best way to achieve eminence or other desired outcomes for high-ability children—a goal that historically has proved elusive.

A middle road is most appropriate for most parents of high-ability youth. Excellence is an appropriate goal for our children, but eminence likely is not, due in part to the key role of chance factors in determining who does or does not become eminent. Excellence requires devoting a majority of time to parenting, but not to the single-minded extent that some retrospective studies and biographies suggest is needed for a child to have even a small chance of achieving eminence.

Parents of young gifted children engage in different behaviors compared to parents of nonidentified children, and these behaviors appear to exert a considerable influence on the child's academic and social growth during this stage of development. Mothers and fathers have been observed to promote independence, encourage responsibility, and offer their young gifted child unconditional love and support. They also provide academically centered activities and engage their child in play to promote reading, oral language, and fine motor skills, while not overregulating their child's play activities. Parents also value the inquisitiveness and unique perspective of their gifted child to a greater degree than parents of typical children do (Jolly & Matthews, 2014), and allow their children to be decision makers when this is appropriate, although the direction of any causal relationship that may exist here has not yet been demonstrated. Parents of gifted learners also are aware of their child's capability and drive, and recognize differences in these areas between their child and other, typically developing children.

Building Positive Relationships Between Parents and Schools

Parents, Gifted Programming, and Schools

Once children are identified as gifted, schools and parents must work together to ensure that appropriate services are secured. However, parents have found that programming and services have been of uneven quality and availability. Parents did not always feel well educated themselves as to what went on in their child's gifted program. Despite lack of knowledge about services or dissatisfaction regarding programming, parents were always upset with the elimination of such services (Jolly & Matthews, 2012).

In Jolly and Matthews' (2012) review of the literature on parenting gifted children, they identified four main concerns parents held with regard to schools and their gifted children. Some parents believed that schools were incapable of fulfilling their child's academic needs, while others felt that the available programming options were inadequate. Teasing and bullying were important concerns voiced by parents, along with their children missing regular class time and having to make up missed work for pull-out programs. Those parents who managed to develop good working relationships and became involved with their child's schools reported experiencing better relationships with the school and teachers. This latter finding suggests that both parents and teachers need to reach out to one another and consciously cultivate relationships in order to successfully meet the educational needs of the gifted children in their care.

Parents as Advocates

Parents often find themselves in the role of advocate after experiencing some specific incident that serves as a catalyst for their intervention. Gallagher defined gifted education advocacy as "a set of activities designed to change the allocation of resources to improve opportunities for the education of gifted and talented students" (as cited in Robinson & Moon, 2003, p. 8). Parental engagement in schools should be encouraged, because of the direct link observed between parental involvement and student achievement and behavior (Bloom, 1985). However, parents sometimes find themselves trying to balance between being ardent advocates and cooperative allies with school leaders and teachers (Besnoy et al., 2015; Speirs Neumeister, Yssel, & Burney, 2013).

Advocacy can begin at the stage of identification and may continue as parents seek to ensure that their children are provided with appropriate programming and services that align with school and district policies and priorities (Grantham, 2005; Robinson & Moon, 2003). Parents also seek opportunities for their gifted child to gain acceptance as part of their advocacy efforts. This can include work at the local school or classroom level, all the way through to the state and national level with efforts to establish policy or legislation (Robinson & Moon, 2003). Finally, parents' final efforts as advocates may be to prepare their children to act as self-advocates as they transition to young adulthood, an act that is especially crucial for those students who are identified as being twice-exceptional (Douglas, 2004; Speirs Neumeister et al., 2013).

Extending Traditional Learning Options

When parents determine that traditional programming is not (or perhaps is not capable of) meeting the learning needs of their gifted child, there are a variety of other options available to meet their child's educational needs. Alternatives to attending the regular neighborhood school can be grouped into four general categories. These include specialized schools, early entrance programs, talent search programs, and homeschooling. Online coursework of various types may be offered within more than one of these categories. Each option is described below.

Specialized schools can exist either within the regular school building (a "school within a school" model) or in a separate facility. One of the most common forms of the specialized school is the magnet program, which provides a separate setting in which instruction may be tailored to a subgroup of learners (such as highly gifted students), a particular curricular focus such as dual-language immersion or

International Baccalaureate programming, or preparation for specific career fields such as engineering or performing arts. Specialized schools have the distinct advantage of enrolling a population of student peers who are more likely to be motivated to study the particular subject(s) the program emphasizes. These schools also may be more likely to refuse admission or remove any students who display ongoing behavior or attendance problems, yielding a better overall learning environment than in attendance-zoned neighborhood schools that are required to admit all students based on the happenstance of geographic residence.

Charter schools offer another form of specialized public school, and one that has become far more widely available in recent years. Charter schools may have the same kinds of foci as magnet schools, but rather than falling under the administrative authority of the local district and its elected school board, they are administered by a school-level board that often is drawn from among those parents whose children attend the school. Charter schools are given greater flexibility in the day-to-day management of the school in comparison to traditional public schools, but are also funded at a lower per-pupil allocation, so some services typically provided in traditional public schools (such as for specific special needs instruction) may not be available in this setting. Charter schools are allowed to hire some teachers who do not hold degrees in education, with both the positive and negative possibilities that this flexibility presents. Some charter schools may be run by for-profit corporations, in which case caution is advised because these organizations may incur high management fees that must come out of the overall budget allocated to the charter school students' education.

Parents considering placing their child in a specialized school should be aware that transportation may be more difficult, either due to the school's location (because these programs usually serve a larger geographical area) or because parents may be expected to provide some or all of the transportation that the district would normally provide if their child were attending a traditional neighborhood school. Charter schools in particular may not provide any transportation, requiring parents to provide all transportation for their child to and from school each day. Charter schools also may fail occasionally, sometimes midyear and especially if they are only recently established, while the unexpected closing of other types of public school is rare.

Dual-enrollment programs offer students at the high school level the chance to attend one or more college courses while still a high school student. One of the clear advantages of these programs is that they are often offered at a very reduced rate (or free in some districts), while the student receives college credit that can be applied toward a postsecondary degree. Another advantage is that by allowing for greater student choice in coursework, these programs can be highly motivating for students who may be reluctant or unwilling to participate in the more highly regimented academic routine of traditional high school programs. Dual enrollment can be offered at the middle school level as well.

Participation requirements vary, but often for dual-enrollment programs the student must have completed successfully all of the coursework offered at the high school in a given subject, such as math. In contrast, early entrance programs accept the student directly into college, in some cases without first having completed the high school diploma, and the student completes all coursework from then on at the college level.

Talent search programs offer above-grade-level testing to students whose scores have been at or above the measurement ceiling of grade-level tests (Lee, Matthews, & Olszewski-Kubilius, 2008; Matthews, 2008). Depending on how they perform on the off-level measure, students may qualify to participate in summer (Stanley & Stanley, 1986), weekend, or online educational programming offered at an academically advanced level. Many high-ability learners find talent search testing and programming to be highly motivating, especially if they come from a setting where they have encountered few intellectual peers of their own age or grade level. Some talent search educational programs are accredited, meaning students can transfer course credit back to their home school in order to progress more rapidly to graduation, achieve prerequisites for other more advanced courses, or free up time to take desired electives in music, the arts, athletics, or an additional language.

Homeschooling is just what it sounds like; parents teach their child primarily in the home setting, rather than sending the child to a school building. Although the parent bears the primary responsibility in the homeschool setting for ensuring the child's educational needs are met, in many cases the parent's own teaching efforts are supplemented though means such as educational cooperatives with other homeschooling parents, community events designed for homeschooled children, and online learning for specific coursework that is more advanced than the parent feels comfortable teaching on her own. Note the intentional use of the word *her*—the vast majority of homeschooling does involve the mother (rather than father) most directly in their child's education (Jolly & Matthews, 2017; Jolly, Matthews, & Nester, 2013).

Although other alternatives to the traditional public school also have grown noticeably, homeschooling in particular has grown quite dramatically in the United States over the past four decades, by a factor of more than 16,000% according to one recent estimate (Murphy, 2014). Approximately one and three-quarter million U.S. children are currently being homeschooled, representing more than 3% of the country's school-age population, although exact figures are difficult to determine due to the patchwork of regulations and reporting requirements that exist (Jolly et al., 2013). Regardless of the exact number, it is clear that large numbers of parents feel they themselves are better equipped than schools are to educate their children.

Parents may choose to homeschool their child for a variety of reasons. Jolly et al. (2013) traced the origins of the modern homeschooling movement from its roots in the counterculture of the 1960s as a means of both rebellion and of ensuring that children were exposed to parents' social and cultural values. This trend continued, but in the 1980s homeschooling became more associated with conservative Christians who sought to homeschool their children as a means of insulating them from societal values and practices that they perceived as being overly secular. Today religious values still provide the primary motivation for about one third of homeschooling families, while the rest are dissatisfied with public schools primarily due to perceptions of a poor learning environment, disagreement with the schools' curricula, or other related reasons. Gifted and high-ability children can be found among all of these groups, and although no data exist on this question, one may project that they are likely most common among those who have left school for curricular reasons.

Online learning opportunities have grown dramatically over the past few years, from humble origins in correspondence-based learning by postal mail, in parallel with the explosive growth of the Internet. Many states now offer some form of virtual school, often at the high school level, in which students can enroll for some or all of their coursework.

Because online learning options have seen rapid growth and change, rather than providing a detailed snapshot of this moving target, an example illustrates many of the characteristics common to these learning options. At the time of writing this chapter, the North Carolina Virtual Public School (http://www.ncvps.org) is the second largest state-led online school in the United States. Enrollment in NCVPS includes more than 55,000 students drawn from public, private, charter, and homeschool settings, representing all of the state's 115 school districts. Teachers in this online program are highly qualified, with nearly two thirds holding a master's degree and nearly half being National Board Certified. Crucially for gifted learners, some high school courses are available to middle school students through NCVPS. Readers who wish to learn more about online learning options such as NCVPS are encouraged to consult its website for the most up-to-date information and to search online to learn what additional online options currently may be available to students in their area.

Conclusion

Parents and their engagement in their child's learning are vital to the development of the gifts, skills, and potential of their children. Although it may not be possible (or advisable) to "train" parents in the same way that we provide professional development to teachers, there are still a number of things that teachers and schools can do to develop understanding and foster collaboration between schools, parents, and their children with gifts and talents. Alternatives to public education are becoming more widely available and better publicized every year, so it is vital for teachers and schools to do everything possible to foster a successful learning environment and strong family engagement for children with gifts and talents in order to retain these learners in the public school setting. Understanding the role of parents and parenting in the social and academic development of these children is an important step toward meeting this goal.

Big Ideas

1. Understanding the role parents play in the lives of gifted children is integral to talent development.

2. Parents may be reluctant to use the gifted label, may use it consciously to educate others, or may overuse it.

3. The traditional Chinese perspective on parenting and the child's achievement emphasizes the role of effort exclusively. Parenting practices from this perspective may be at odds with American cultural views that also emphasize an inherited component and the importance of the child's self-esteem.

4. Advocacy on behalf of gifted children is extremely important, due to the lack of legal protections for these learners.

5. Specialized schools, early entrance programs, talent search programs, homeschooling, and online coursework are some of the available alternatives that parents may choose for their child's education.

Discussion Questions

1. Given the swings in public perceptions of giftedness and parenting over the past 150 years, where do you think current perceptions fall? Where might they be headed next, and why?

2. What is your own experience with the gifted label as a child, adult, parent, and/or teacher, and how does this experience inform your use of the term?

3. What is more important for achievement: intelligence or hard work? Use examples to support your position on this question.

4. What approaches to advocacy do you think would be most effective in supporting the educational needs of gifted learners in your setting?

Discussion Questions, *Continued.*

5.   Choose a specific alternative to traditional learning that is available to children in your community. Research it and provide a report back to your colleagues or classmates, including your analysis of how well this alternative might meet the needs of a gifted child from your community.

References

Besnoy, K. D., Swoszowski, N. C., Newman, J. L., Floyd, A., Jones, P., & Byrne, C. (2015). The advocacy experiences of parents of elementary age, twice-exceptional children. *Gifted Child Quarterly, 59,* 108–123.

Bloom, B. S. (Ed). (1985). *Developing talent in young people.* New York, NY: Ballantine.

Carrington, N. G. (1996). I'm gifted, is that OK? The social rules of being gifted in Australia. *Gifted and Talented International, 11*(1), 11–15.

CBS News.com Staff. (2000, February 15). *What price genius? Father pushes 10-year-old college student* [news broadcast]. Retrieved from http://www.cbsnews.com/news/what-price-genius

Chua, A. (2011). *Battle hymn of the tiger mother.* New York, NY: Penguin Press

Colangelo, N., & Brower, P. (1987). Gifted youngsters and their siblings: Long-term impact of labeling on their academic and personal self-concept. *Roeper Review, 10,* 101–103.

Cornell, D. (1983). Gifted children: The impact of positive labeling on the family system. *American Journal of Orthopsychiatry, 53,* 322–335.

Cornell, D. (1989). Child adjustment and parent use of the term "gifted." *Gifted Child Quarterly, 33,* 59–64.

Cramond, B., & Martin, C. E. (1987). Inservice and preservice teachers' attitudes toward the academically brilliant. *Gifted Child Quarterly, 31,* 15–19.

Douglas, D. (2004). Self-advocacy: Encouraging students to become partners in differentiation. *Roeper Review, 26,* 223–228.

Dweck, C. S. (2000). *Self-theories: Their role in motivation, personality, and development.* Philadelphia, PA: Psychology Press.

Flora, C. (2005, July 1). The Grandmaster experiment: How did one family produce three of the most successful female chess champions ever? *Psychology Today.* Retrieved from https://www.psychologytoday.com/articles/200507/the-grandmaster-experiment

Fried, R. N., & Woods, C. (Producers), & Anspaugh, D. (Director). (1993). *Rudy* [Motion picture]. United States: TriStar Pictures.

Galton, F. (1869). *Hereditary genius: An inquiry into its laws and consequences* (2nd ed.). London, England: Macmillan. Retrieved from http://galton.org/books/hereditary-genius/text/pdf/galton-1869-genius-v3.pdf

Gladwell, M. (2008). *Outliers: The story of success.* New York, NY: Little, Brown.

Grantham, T. C. (2005). Parent advocacy for culturally diverse students. *Theory Into Practice, 44,* 138–147.

Hollingworth, L. S. (1926). *Gifted children: Their nature and nurture.* New York, NY: Macmillan.

Hollingworth, L. S. (1929). The production of gifted children from the parental point of view. *Eugenics, 2*(10), 3–7.

Jolly, J. L., & Matthews, M. S. (2012). A critique of the literature on parenting gifted learners. *Journal for the Education of the Gifted, 35,* 260–290. doi:10.1177/0162353212451703

Jolly, J. L., & Matthews, M. S. (2014). Parenting. In J. A. Plucker & C. M. Callahan (Eds.), *Critical issues and practices in gifted education: What the research says* (2nd ed., pp. 481–492). Waco, TX: Prufrock Press.

Jolly, J. L., & Matthews, M. S. (2017). Homeschooling: An alternative approach for gifted and talented learners? In C. M. Callahan & H. L. Hertzberg-Davis, *Fundamentals of gifted education* (2nd ed.). New York, NY: Routledge.

Jolly, J. L., Matthews, M. S., & Nester, J. (2013). Homeschooling the gifted: A parent's perspective. *Gifted Child Quarterly, 57,* 121–134. doi:10.1177/0016986212469999

Kerr, B. A., Colangelo, N., & Gaeth, J. (1988). Gifted adolescents' attitudes toward their giftedness. *Gifted Child Quarterly, 32,* 245–247.

Lee, S.-Y., Cramond, B., & Lee, J. (2004). Korean teachers' attitudes toward academic brilliance. *Gifted Child Quarterly, 48,* 42–53. doi:10.1177/0016986204048001 05

Lee, S.-Y., Matthews, M. S., & Olszewski-Kubilius, P. (2008). A national picture of talent search and talent search educational programs. *Gifted Child Quarterly, 52,* 55–69. doi:10.1177/0016986207311152

Makel, M. C. (2009). Student and parent attitudes before and after the gifted identification process. *Journal for the Education of the Gifted, 33,* 126–143.

Matthews, M. S. (2008). Talent search programs. In J. A. Plucker & C. M. Callahan (Eds.), *Critical issues and practices in gifted education: What the research says* (pp. 641–653). Waco, TX: Prufrock Press.

Matthews, M. S., Ritchotte, J. A., & Jolly J. (2014). What's wrong with giftedness? Parents' perceptions of the gifted label. *International Studies in Sociology of Education, 24,* 372–393. doi:10.1080/09620214.2014.990225

McCoach, D. B., & Siegle, D. (2007). What predicts teachers' attitudes toward the gifted? *Gifted Child Quarterly, 51,* 246–254. doi:10.1177/0016986207302719

Murphy, J. (2014). The social and educational outcomes of homeschooling. *Sociological Spectrum, 34,* 244–272.

Peters, S. J., Matthews, M., McBee, M., & McCoach, D. B. (2014). *Beyond gifted education: Designing and implementing advanced academic programs.* Waco, TX: Prufrock Press.

Robinson, A., & Moon, S. M. (2003). A national study of local and state advocacy in gifted education. *Gifted Child Quarterly, 47,* 8–25.

Speirs Neumeister, K., Yssel, N., & Burney, V. H. (2013). The influence of primary caregivers in fostering success in twice-exceptional children. *Gifted Child Quarterly, 57,* 263–274.

Stanley, J. C., & Stanley, B. S. (1986). High-school biology, chemistry, or physics learned well in three weeks. *Journal of Research in Science Teaching, 23,* 237–250.

Tannenbaum, A. J. (1962). *Adolescent attitude toward academic brilliance.* New York, NY: Bureau of Publications, Teachers College, Columbia University.

Wu, E. H. (2008). Parental influence on children's talent development: A case study with three Chinese American families. *Journal for the Education of the Gifted, 32,* 100–129.

Programming for Advanced Learning and Talent Development

The next important step in the building process is to get the building under a roof. Not only does the roof protect what has been built, but it also allows for the exterior to be mortared and bricked and the interior to be dry-walled and fitted for plumbing and electricity.

In gifted education, this roof symbolizes the overarching programming offered for gifted students. From enrichment and acceleration to differentiation, a variety of programming must be available to address the unique needs of students. Creativity and talent are developed through programming. Unlike the securely fastened roof on the building, the roof on gifted education is flexible; that ceiling must be removed at times in order for students to actualize their potential.

This section has five chapters: "Enrichment: In and Out of School," "Acceleration: Practical Applications and Policy Implications," "Differentiation," "Talent Development as a Framework for the Delivery of Services to Gifted Children," and "Creativity: Definitions, Interventions, and Assessments."

Myths

» **Acceleration hurts the child emotionally and socially.** When appropriately implemented, acceleration is the most effective and least costly of all services for learners with gifts and talents.

» **Tutoring other students is an excellent service option for gifted students; students really learn content when they teach it.** All children deserve to learn something new every day, including those with gifts and talents. A student who tutors has typically mastered the material; people cannot learn something they already know.

» **If a school offers Advanced Placement or gifted programming, classroom teachers do not need to worry about addressing gifted learners' needs.** Advanced students learn at a faster pace and with greater complexity in their areas of giftedness than other students. Services are needed in all learning environments.

CHAPTER 12

Enrichment

In and Out of School

Kristen R. Stephens

Satisfaction of one's curiosity is one of the greatest sources of happiness in life.—Linus Pauling

Essential Questions to Guide the Reader

1. In what ways does enrichment nurture the dispositions of a lifelong learner?

2. How do enrichment experiences support the cognitive and affective development of gifted and talented students?

3. What role does enrichment play in college and career planning for gifted and talented students?

4. In addition to enrichment experiences connected with the curriculum, how might gifted and talented students benefit from enrichment experiences that are extraneous to the curriculum?

5. What are some of the challenges gifted and talented students face in accessing enrichment opportunities both in and outside of school?

To *enrich* means to improve or enhance the quality of something (Enrich, n.d.). In the context of enrichment experiences for gifted and talented learners, this means going beyond what is traditionally offered in the general curriculum or examining an area of study in greater depth. As the quote by Linus Pauling suggests, satiating one's curiosity can be personally rewarding, and enrichment is one way students can explore areas of interest, seek answers to questions, and grapple with complex problems. Essentially, enrichment is a vehicle for driving students toward their potential and passions.

In this chapter, the key features and benefits of enrichment are explored. Considerations for planning enrichment experiences and an overview of selected program models that specifically address enrichment are shared. Finally, an overview of in- and outside-of-school enrichment opportunities is provided, concluding with an examination of the role of technology in the future of enrichment for gifted and talented learners.

Understanding Enrichment

Enrichment can be conceptualized and contextualized in several ways. Gubbins (2014) offered the following categories of enrichment:

- enrichment *through curricular units*,
- enrichment *as an extension* to the curriculum, and
- enrichment *as a technique* for differentiating curriculum.

Enrichment *through curricular units* refers to the development of separate units that expose students to topics of study and/or complex concepts that are often not explicitly included within the standard curriculum. For example, dinosaurs, the Egyptians, innovation, future studies, the stock market, and forensic science are areas that may not be addressed in the standard curriculum, but due to their high interest among students, teachers may design units around these topics to support student engagement and learning. In schools, such units are well-suited for pull-out programs where gifted and talented students are grouped together for a portion of the school day or week, or these units can be delivered through an independent study opportunity. Outside of school, these types of enrichment units are ideal for afterschool, Saturday, or summer enrichment programs.

When a deliberate connection is made between the enrichment experience and the curriculum, enrichment can be viewed as an *extension of the curriculum*, adding depth and/or complexity to better address the learning needs of gifted and talented students. These extensions often expose students to more depth and breadth of content and incorporate learning experiences that promote inquiry, creativity, problem solving, and high-level thinking.

Enrichment can also be viewed as a *technique for differentiating* the curriculum. For example, to adjust learning experiences pertaining to the Civil War, gifted students might consider the topic in greater depth through a conceptual lens (e.g., *oppression, culture,* or *conflict*); examine more sophisticated vocabulary (e.g., popular sovereignty, sectionalism, the Whig Party); or analyze the details associated with a particular battle, political speech, or casualty statistics. To add complexity, students might explore the multiple perspectives associated with the war (e.g., Confederate vs. Union soldier), make interdisciplinary connections (e.g., incorporation of biographies, examination of how the war changed American medicine), or analyze the changes that have occurred over time in American culture as a result of the Civil War.

Finally, Renzulli (1998) offered a potential fourth category of enrichment for consideration:

- enrichment as a *teaching and learning philosophy.*

Renzulli's Schoolwide Enrichment Model, discussed later in this chapter, provides a practical plan for guiding school improvement and reform efforts, thus creating schools that are "laboratories for talent development" (Renzulli, 1998, p. 111). This broad view of enrichment focuses on the interaction between students, teachers, and the curriculum and aims to enhance and improve existing structures within a school.

Although these categories of enrichment (Gubbins, 2010; Renzulli, 1998) vary in context, each approach to enrichment, whether used singly or in combination, is a powerful tool for addressing the learning needs of gifted and talented learners. Teachers should consider the needs of the gifted and talented students, the gifted education program model being utilized, the curricular requirements of their respective school, and any underlying teaching and learning philosophies when making decisions about how to best design enrichment experiences for students.

Key Features of Enrichment

Enrichment should be purposefully planned to address students' specific learning needs. One should not to be lured into a shallow or superficial view of enrichment. Enrichment should advance a learner's academic and intellectual talent and skills. If the experience does not achieve this goal, then it is not enrichment (Gallagher, 1964). With this in mind, it is important to note that enrichment *is not*

- more of the same, repetitive work;
- busy work, random worksheets, and puzzles;
- thinking skills taught in isolation;
- unstructured free time; or
- sporadic.

Authentic enrichment should be substantive—designed to meet an important educational need that has been identified. Enrichment *is*

- designed to extend learning,

- responsive to student needs,
- meaningful and relevant,
- planned and purposeful engagement, and
- consistent and ongoing.

The Relationship Between Enrichment and Acceleration

Enrichment and acceleration should not be viewed as mutually exclusive (see Chapter 13 for information on acceleration). The two, though differing in focus, do go hand-in-hand. Enrichment primarily addresses the depth and breadth of curricular focus, while acceleration refers to the pace one moves though the curriculum.

Enrichment experiences can be accelerated, and accelerated areas can also be enriched. For example, introducing an eighth-grade student to the math topic of *topology* could be considered enrichment in that it goes beyond what is typically addressed in the standard curriculum and adds rigor to the study of geometry and three-dimensional figures. Topology could also be considered acceleration in this instance as it introduces the topic earlier than is traditionally expected. Likewise, a fourth-grade student who has been accelerated to fifth-grade math might still participate in math enrichment to cultivate his or her interests in math or to incorporate more depth and complexity in the curriculum. For example, this student might investigate why the United States does not use the metric system or connect fractions with probability by designing a game that gives all participants an equal chance of winning. These examples would constitute enrichment within an accelerated environment.

For gifted students, adjusting the pace of instruction while also adding depth and complexity to the curriculum creates a learning environment that is appropriately challenging and engaging. Furthermore, large scale meta-analyses (a statistical method for combining results from multiple studies) reveal that enrichment programs (Rogers, 1991) and acceleration (Kulik, 1992) both have a positive effect on student achievement. It is essential that both enrichment and acceleration are considered when planning learning experiences for gifted and talented learners to ensure growth is made toward their potential.

Benefits for Gifted Learners

Gifted learners benefit from enrichment opportunities due to their ability to move through the curriculum at a more rapid pace, insatiable appetite for learning new things, and need to engage in learning experiences that are appropriately challenging. In addition to these academic benefits, enrichment also affords gifted learners the opportunity to engage with like-ability peers, connect their broad and varied interests, and develop those skills necessary to persist through a challenge.

There has been limited research on the effectiveness of enrichment programs for gifted students. This is due in part to the relatively small number of participants and the lack of a control or comparison group (Subotnik, Olszewski-Kubilius, & Worrell, 2011). Nonetheless, existing studies have found favorable outcomes for gifted students, including an increase in students' self-concept (Gubbels, Segers, & Verhoeven, 2014), interest in a content area (Caleon & Subramaniam, 2007), and attitude toward school (Zeidner & Schleyer, 1999). Additionally, enrichment programs have been found to positively effect peer relations (Cohen, Duncan, & Cohen, 1994) and assist gifted students with identity formation (Simpson, 2014). Table 12.1 provides additional information regarding the academic and psychosocial benefits of enrichment for gifted students.

Considerations for Planning Enrichment Experiences

Effective enrichment experiences require thorough planning and coordination, regardless of whether enrichment is to be offered at the classroom, school, or district level. Parents and teachers need to be aware of all the enrichment opportunities that are available for gifted students and also need to know how to match an enrichment program to the needs of the student. As schools plan enrichment experiences for gifted students, the following questions should be considered:

- Which theoretical model(s) will be used to design and shape the enrichment program?
- What is the purpose of the enrichment experience for students?
- Where and when will enrichment take place?
- Through what mode will enrichment be delivered (e.g., learning centers, independent study, pull-out, tiered assignments, cluster groups)?
- What is the planned duration and intensity of the enrichment experience?
- Who will facilitate the enrichment experience?
- What criteria will be used to determine participation?
- What are the expected student outcomes of the enrichment experience?
- How will the enrichment experience connect to the general curriculum?
- What additional resources will be needed?

In addition to these considerations, Kaul, Johnsen, Witte, and Saxon (2015) identified three critical components of a successful enrichment program: (a) courses that align with student interests, (b) parental support, and (c) a focus on the development of interpersonal relationships with mentors and peers.

Table 12.1
Benefits of Enrichment for Gifted Learners

Academic Benefits	Psychosocial Benefits
• Broadens and deepens understanding within the discipline • Exposes students to new topics and ideas typically not addressed in the standard curriculum • Fosters critical thinking and problem solving within authentic contexts • Stimulates the dispositions of a life-long learner by appealing to students' sense of curiosity • Moves learning forward for gifted learners; students have the opportunity to learn something new • Connects students in a more meaningful and respectful way with the curriculum	• Develops students' interests • Connects students with like-ability peers and those with similar interests and passions • Prevents boredom and frustration • Encourages academic risk-taking • Addresses multipotentiality by providing a "space" for students to connect a breadth of skills, strengths, and interests • Fosters task commitment and perseverance as students navigate challenging content and processes • Provides opportunities to enhance creativity thinking

Instructional Strategies That Support Enrichment

Many instructional strategies used to plan and implement differentiation in the classroom also provide structures to support enrichment for gifted students. A discussion of all pedagogical techniques or strategies that support enrichment would be outside the scope of this chapter, but a few offered by McIntosh (2014) follow.

Choice Menus or Boards

Choice menus or boards offer students alternative options in how they can demonstrate evidence of their learning and can be based on readiness, interest, or learning profile. They can be provided at the culmination of a unit of study or within the context of an independent study for students who are ready to extend their learning within a content/topic area. It is important that all choices on the menu or board are aligned with targeted learning goals. Figure 12.1 provides an example of a choice menu designed to extend gifted students' learning experiences within a unit of study on ecosystems.

Kaplan's Depth and Complexity Icons

Sandra Kaplan's prompts/icons provide a framework for adding depth and complexity to the content being taught. Kaplan (2005) acknowledged that depth and complexity focus students on "increasingly more difficult, divergent and

Learning Objective: Compare the characteristics of several common ecosystems.
Directions: Select one of the following areas to research and present your findings in a product of your choice.

Assess the ethical issues surrounding human interaction with an ecosystem (e.g., overhunting, deforestation, pollution, land conversion) *[Ethics]*	Analyze the patterns that exist within an ecosystem (e.g., cause and effect, cycles) *[Patterns, Trends]*	Hypothesize potential causes for the fluctuation of density in population within an ecosystem *[Unanswered Questions]*
Explore the importance of biodiversity to an ecosystem *[Patterns, Trends, Across Disciplines]*		Analyze the role of inter-dependence within an ecosystem *[Big Ideas]*
Examine the similarities and differences between terrestrial and aquatic ecosystems *[Details]*	Evaluate the role of balance (homeostasis) in maintaining an ecosystem over time *[Big Ideas, Related Over Time]*	Compare and contrast varying perspectives regarding conservation policies (e.g., an owner of a timber company vs. a forest advocate) *[Multiple Perspectives]*

Figure 12.1. Choice menu on ecosystems (fifth-grade science).

abstract qualities of knowing a discipline or area of study" (p. 116), and thus serve to enrich the learning experience for gifted students. Depth icons include Language of the Discipline, Details, Patterns, Trends, Big Ideas, Rules, Unanswered Questions, and Ethics. The dimensions of complexity include Related Over Time, Across Disciplines, and View from Multiple Perspectives. In Figure 12.1, each learning experience within the choice menu has been labeled according to the icon of focus.

Problem-Based Learning (PBL)

PBL is a learner-centered instructional approach that requires students to conduct research and integrate and apply their knowledge and skills to solve an "ill-structured" problem. Stepien and Gallagher (1993) stated that "learners probe deeply into issues searching for connections, grappling with complexity, and using knowledge to fashion solutions" (p. 26). PBL fosters self-directed study, collaboration, effective communication, and justification of solution, providing an enriching learning experience for gifted students. Gallagher (1997) emphasized that "it is not just a problem-solving strategy; it is also good curricular material" (p. 338) that is necessary to address goals. In addition, PBL fosters the development of metacognitive skills by making students more aware of their thinking processes, heightening intrinsic interest, allowing for multidisciplinary connections and perspectives, supporting concept-based learning, and helping students adapt to change as they seek solutions and reformulate the problem (Gallagher, 1997). Figure 12.2 contains an example of an ill-structured problem from William & Mary's problem-based science unit, *Something Fishy: Exploring an Aquatic Ecosystem* (Center for Gifted Education, 2007).

Passion Projects

Passion projects are a tool that affords students the opportunity to share their intense interests with others while also enhancing or extending a unit of study. Cash (2011) recommended using passion projects as an anchoring assignment, an individual assignment, or to replace another unit project to create a better "fit" for gifted learners. Such projects provide students with opportunities for meaningful research in areas that may fall outside of the curriculum and can be quite ambitious (e.g., raising money for cancer research, improving conditions for animals in the community). They can also effectively support many of the affective characteristics of gifted students (e.g., keen sense of justice, altruism).

Program Models to Support Enrichment

Bain, Bourgeois, and Pappas (2003) found that although teachers are aware of the various theoretical models to guide instruction and programming for gifted learners, few actually use the models; thus, there seems to be a missing link between theory and practice. A program model can serve as a framework for developing enrichment opportunities within the context of the total school community. Program models that specifically have enrichment as a central component include Enrichment Triad Model (Renzulli, 1976), Schoolwide Enrichment Model (Renzulli & Reis, 1985), Purdue Three-Stage Enrichment Learning Model (Feldhusen & Kolloff, 1978), Autonomous Learner Model (Betts, 1985), and Self-Directed Learner Model (Treffinger, 1975). It should be noted that curriculum models that address enrichment are not included, as these extend beyond the scope of this chapter and are addressed elsewhere in this text.

Enrichment Triad Model

Building on his Three-Ring Conception of Giftedness (see Gubbins, 2010), Joseph Renzulli (1976) developed the Enrichment Triad Model. The model designates three types of enrichment:

Julie and Josh Miller's grandfather has come back to Virginia for one of his periodic visits. While eating with the family in Sam's Restaurant in the Phoebus section of Hampton, Grandfather Miller is very upset to find that sea trout is no longer on the menu.

"I came here to eat sea trout because Sam is the only one who can prepare it the way it should be cooked! Let me talk to Sam about this!" exclaims Grandfather Miller. When informed that Sam is on vacation in Florida, Grandfather becomes more angry and it is with great effort that the Millers convince him to settle for flounder stuffed with crab meat instead of sea trout.

Julie and Josh are understandably upset by these events. Wondering why sea trout is not available for their grandfather, they decide to investigate.

You are Julie and Josh's science teacher; they are your favorite students. They've come to ask for your help in their investigation. How can you help Julie and Josh?

Figure 12.2. Something Fishy initial problem (grades 6–8). From Center for Gifted Education (p. 44), *Something fishy: Exploring an aquatic ecosystem* (2nd ed.), 2007, Dubuque, IA: Kendall/Hunt. Copyright 2007 by Kendall/Hunt. Reprinted with permission.

- *Type I: General exploratory activities* are introduced that motivate and prepare students for engagement in a topic. During this stage, teachers might arrange guest speakers, field trips, or a film viewing or form an enrichment cluster by interest.
- *Type II: Group training activities* support the development of thinking and feeling processes. During this stage, students would engage in creative thinking, critical thinking, and problem solving. They would also hone their research, communication, and learning-how-to-learn skills, as well as any other skills associated with the methods of the discipline.
- *Type III: Individual and small-group investigations of real problems* provide students with the opportunity to pursue a self-selected area of interest. At this stage, students will apply their knowledge and skills and develop an authentic product that demonstrates their learning. Planning, organization, time management, task commitment, and decision making are just a few skills that students will apply during Type III enrichment.

Of the three, about 50% of student time should be spent in Type III enrichment experiences. Figure 12.3 provides an example of what the Enrichment Triad Model might look like in action.

Schoolwide Enrichment Model

Using the Enrichment Triad Model as its core, the Schoolwide Enrichment Model (SEM; Renzulli & Reis, 1985) details how enrichment experiences might

Type I	Type II
• Invite a local poet to class to read her poems and discuss her writing process. • Watch a video of a poetry slam. • Share song lyrics with poetry elements addressed in the curriculum. • Take a nature walk to find inspiration for a poem.	• Read different styles of poetry. • Examine how figurative language is used in poetry. • Analyze how choice of words impacts the meaning and tone of a poem. • Rehearse presenting a poem to an audience. • Research how a poet's life experiences may have influenced his or her art.

Type III
- Compose your own poem.
- Perform an original poem at a poetry slam.

Figure 12.3. Fourth-grade poetry unit using Enrichment Triad Model.

be structured at a more macro (i.e., school) level. Focusing on both academic and creative-productive giftedness, a broader talent pool of students is identified to participate in Type I and Type II learning experiences with the opportunity to "revolve into" (Renzulli & Renzulli, 2010, p. 146) Type III experiences. The SEM incorporates (a) informal and formal methods to determine the interests and learning styles of students, (b) curriculum compacting and other curricular modifications to streamline the curriculum and avoid unnecessary repetition, and (c) enrichment organized around Type I, II, and III learning experiences.

Purdue Three-Stage Enrichment Learning Model

Originally designed for use in pull-out programs, the Purdue Model consists of three distinct stages that move students from simple to complex thinking experiences. Students progress sequentially through all the stages (Moon, Kolloff, Robinson, Dixon, & Feldhusen, 2009):

- *Stage 1*: Students master core content and skills. Teachers lead critical and creative thinking exercises and provide instruction on targeted skills.
- *Stage 2*: The pace and challenge intensifies as students engage in inquiry related to the curriculum. Strategies used at this stage include problem solving, inductive and deductive reasoning, and analysis of arguments and concepts.
- *Stage 3*: Students apply their knowledge to real problems through independent investigations, self-directed inquiry, and the development of products.

The Purdue Model for secondary students has 11 components that support both enrichment and acceleration and can be used as a framework for organizing learning experiences for gifted high school students: (a) counseling services, (b) seminars, (c) AP courses, (d) honors classes, (e) math/science acceleration, (f) foreign languages, (g) arts, (h) cultural experiences, (i) career education, (j) vocational programs, and (k) extraschool instruction.

Autonomous Learner Model

The Autonomous Learner Model (ALM; Betts, 1985) is designed to equip students with the skills needed to initiate and direct their own learner. The ALM comprises five stages, each with focused learning experiences:

- *Orientation*: Understanding of self; theories and definitions of giftedness, talent, intelligence, and creativity; focus on personal development and group-building activities.
- *Individual Development*: Developing inter/intrapersonal, organizational, and other learning skills; use of technology to learn; college and career involvement.
- *Enrichment*: Using a variety of skills to find new knowledge; short-term and ongoing explorations and investigations, cultural activities, service learning, and field trips.
- *Seminars*: Working together in small groups; focused on general interest, controversial topics, authentic problems, and advanced knowledge.
- *In-Depth Study*: Engaging in individual and group projects, mentorships, presentations, and assessment.

The ALM can be used in a variety of contexts to support enrichment for gifted learners (e.g., small groups, regular classroom, individual course, within existing curricular areas).

Self-Directed Learner Model

Treffinger's (1986) Self-Directed Learner Model scaffolds learning across three levels, each with an increasing level of autonomy.

- *Level I*: Teacher provides students with a list of potential research topics and structures and supports the student throughout the research process through project completion.
- *Level II*: Teacher and student make decisions together regarding topics to research, mutually agree on project requirements, and select methods for how the final project will be assessed.
- *Level III*: Students have the freedom to choose their own topics and now have the skills necessary to effectively plan, manage, and conduct their own research through completion.

The Self-Directed Learner Model works well with independent study, small-group, and whole-class projects and ensures that students are developing the prerequisite skills necessary to become a lifelong learner.

Summary of Models

According to Sally Reis (2009), most models and theories pertaining to enrichment are

> interest-based; integrate advanced content, processes, and products; include broad interdisciplinary themes; foster effective independent and autonomous learning; provide individualized and differentiated curriculum and instruction; develop problem-solving abilities and creativity; and integrate the tools of the practicing professional in the development of products. (pp. 324–325)

All of these characteristics highlighted by Reis are addressed across the models described above. These program models provide systematic frameworks for developing new enrichment programs or for enhancing existing ones.

In-School Enrichment

For the purpose of this chapter, *in-school* enrichment opportunities are defined as those learning experiences affiliated with and/or sponsored by the school. Such enrichment may occur during or after school hours, but the school and/or district is the main organizing body.

When designing in-school enrichment options, the needs of students—both academic and psychosocial—should be considered. Ideally, a continuum of enrichment options should be available to address identified student needs. All available enrichment opportunities should be reviewed annually to ensure alignment with the needs of the students, the curricular standards, and the school and/or district missions. Although available enrichment options may vary from school to school, the quality and quantity of enrichment opportunities afforded to students should be consistent across schools to ensure equity of opportunity.

In-school options can be classified into two categories: (a) delivery format and/or pedagogies, and (b) commercial programs/curriculum.

Delivery Format and/or Pedagogies

There are many methods for providing enrichment to gifted students in school. Some require minimal time and preparation on the part of the teacher (e.g., independent study, learning centers), while others require more significant planning and coordination with the broader community (e.g., service-learning, mentorships). Following are descriptions of some of the various options.

Pull-out/resource room. Students are "pulled out" of the general education classroom to attend class with like-ability peers. These enrichment experiences can provide opportunities to extend or replace the general curriculum.

Independent study/learning contracts. Students engage in independent research that is either self-selected or negotiated with the teacher. Research topics may serve to extend the general curriculum or relate to an area of interest.

Learning centers. Students have the opportunity to engage in learning experiences that stretch their capabilities within a particular content area or allow them to examine areas of high interest within a discipline. Centers can be tiered to best meet the learning needs of students or serve as an anchor activity for students.

Field trips. Visits to historical sites, museums, and other cultural centers provide students with experiences that enhance engagement with the curriculum and deepen understanding. Traditional field trips are typically off the school site, but technology now allows for many virtual trip options (e.g., Live From Antarctica 2 [http://passporttoknowledge.com/antarctica2/main/t_index.html], The Nine Planets Solar System Tour [http://nineplanets.org], 4-H Virtual Farm [http://www.sites.ext.vt.edu/virtualfarm/main.html]). Some useful sites for field trip ideas, instructional resources, and fundraising tips are the Field Trip Factory (http://www.fieldtripfactory.com) and ClassTrips.com (http://www.classtrips.com).

Service learning. Connecting the curriculum with service to the community provides students with the opportunity to apply their knowledge and skills in a meaningful and rich context. Many of the social-emotional characteristics of gifted learners (e.g., compassion, sense of social justice, altruism) are also addressed through service learning (Stephens, Malone, & Griffith, 2016). Academic learning is a central component to service learning with a reciprocal relationship between the student and the recipient of the service—both parties receive benefit.

Simulations. These provide opportunities for students to role-play and problem solve while applying content knowledge, employing critical and creative thinking skills, working collaboratively, and considering multiple perspectives around important issues. Popular simulation topics include the stock market, Oregon Trail, outbreaks/pandemics, and the Continental Congress. See Interact (http://www.interact-simulations.com) for an array of commercially prepared simulations across grade levels and content areas.

Mentorships/internships. Students are connected with experts in their fields of interest and authentically acquire advanced content knowledge and skills within the discipline while tackling timely problems. In addition, students gain valuable information about career and college planning. (Additional information about mentorships/internships can be found under Outside-of-School Enrichment.)

Clubs. Students with shared interests meet to engage in discussion and/or activities related to a selected topic. LEGOs, chess, robotics, theatre, books, computer coding, the environment, yoga, and debate are just a few topics around which clubs might be formed. Clubs can meet before or after school, as an elective course, or on weekends. A teacher or parent facilitates club meetings and events.

Commercial Programs/Curriculum

Many schools participate in commercially available enrichment options. Some of these programs are fee-based, and all will require a teacher within the school to take the lead on planning and organizing the experiences for students (i.e., faculty sponsor). Parents can also be a great resource for coordinating efforts around these enrichment experiences.

Junior Great Books. Established in 1962, the Junior Great Books program was originally designed as an extracurricular program to encourage children to read and discuss books (Will, 1986). The inquiry-based nature of the program makes it particularly well-suited for gifted and talented students as they engage in critical thinking and writing. In addition, the texts have not been modified or simplified, so students are reading exactly how the author intended with rich vocabulary and syntax. Great Book products are available for grades K–12 and include fiction, nonfiction, and poetry. Visit http://greatbooks.org for additional information.

Battle of the Books. A voluntary reading incentive program, Battle of the Books is designed for students in grades 3–12. The book list (which changes each year) is shared with those students interested in participating. There are short (10 titles), medium (20 titles), standard (30 titles), and elite (36 titles) book lists organized by grade level that can be selected based on the veracity of the reader. Students are organized in teams for a final day-long competition or "battle" and receive points for answering questions about the books. Students benefit by having the opportunity to engage with others who share their love of reading and to talk about the books they have read. The school must have several copies of each book on the list available, and ordering wholesale from the distributor is recommended. For additional information visit, http://www.battleofthebooks.org.

Odyssey of the Mind (OM). Designed for students in Kindergarten through college, OM is a creative problem-solving program with competitions held at the local, state, and world levels. In addition to problem solving, students learn team-building and creative thinking skills. Five new competitive problems are introduced each year, and these problems typically take teams weeks or even months to solve. Problems are varied—some are technical while others might be more artistic- or performance-based. Schools must obtain a membership for teams to participate, and each school membership entitles the school to one team per problem per division in competition. Two sample OM problem synopses can be found in Figure 12.4. For additional information about Odyssey of the Mind, visit http://www.odysseyofthemind.com.

No-Cycle Recycle:
Teams will build, ride on, and drive a no-cycle, recycling vehicle. It will pick up discarded items, adapt them in some way, and then deliver them to places to be re-used. The vehicle must travel without pedaling for propulsion. In addition, the driver will have an assistant worker riding on the vehicle that will help process the trash items being repurposed. They will make an unplanned stop along the way to perform a random act of kindness.

Classics . . . Aesop Gone Viral:
Teams will create and present an original performance about a fable gone "viral." The problem will include a list of fables attributed to Aesop. Teams will select one and portray it, and its moral, as going viral—that is, being shared throughout the community and beyond. The performance will be set in a past era and include a narrator character, an artistic representation of the fable's moral, and a character that makes a wrong conclusion about the moral and is corrected.

Figure 12.4. Sample Odyssey of the Mind problems. From *2015–2016 Long-Term Problems Synopses* by Odyssey of the Mind, 2015, retrieved from https://www.odysseyofthemind.com/materials/2016problems.php#p1. Copyright 2015 by Odyssey of the Mind. Reprinted with permission.

Future Problem Solving Program International (FPSPI). Founded in 1974 by E. Paul Torrance, FPSPI engages students in creative problem-solving opportunities and competitions. Affiliate programs also exist at the state level. Individual and team competitions are available as well as a noncompetitive option. Team sizes vary based on component (i.e., global issues, community problem solving), and each team must have a designated coach. See Figure 12.5 for a sample FPSPI problem. For more information, visit http://www.fpspi.org.

Destination Imagination (DI). DI hosts team-based competitions that encourage the development of creative and critical thinking, problem solving, and team building. Competitions are administered through state and country affiliates, with seven new challenges being introduced each year. Challenges are aligned with the curriculum with a focus on STEM education. Teams consist of 2 to 7 members, and each team is charged a fee. During competition, teams solve two types of challenges: team challenges and instant challenges (quick challenges that reward teams for their teamwork). Each challenge is assessed by volunteer judges. Figure 12.6 contains a preview of a 2015–2016 Destination Imagination challenge. Visit http://www.destinationimagination.org to learn more.

Math Olympiads. Focusing on math problem solving, Math Olympiads provides a contest for teams of up to 35 students in grades 4–8. Only schools or homeschool associations can participate for a fee, and each team must have a PICO (Person in Charge of the Olympiad Team). Schools host five monthly contests from November to March. Each problem requires mathematical problem solving and

Disappearing Languages:

Language is the soul of a culture. The survival of a culture may depend on the language used for rituals and to describe cultural ideas, beliefs, and understandings. What is the impact on culture when its language disappears? By some estimates, of the six thousand languages left on Earth, 90% are expected to disappear or be endangered before the end of this century. In New Zealand, government and community initiatives are trying to revive the language of indigenous people, but even so it is in a precarious state. Many indigenous peoples around the globe don't have support to prevent their language from disappearing. Will anyone be able to read the rich literature embodied in the disappearing languages in the years to come? What oral traditions will be lost? What responsibilities, if any, do governments, institutions, and communities have towards preserving endangered languages?

Figure 12.5. Sample problem from FPSPI. From *FPSPI Topics* by Future Problem Solving International, n.d., retrieved from http://www.fpspi.org/topics.html. Copyright by Future Problem Solving International. Reprinted with permission.

Musical Mashup

Structural:
Hold it together and let it play out in this musical mashup.

Points of Interest:
- Design and build a structure that both supports weight and is a musical instrument.
- Play a musical solo using the structure as a musical instrument.
- Tell a story with at least one musical character.
- Integrate the story with the weight placement testing of the structure.
- Create and present two Team Choice Elements that show off the team's interests, skills, areas of strength, and talents.

Figure 12.6. Destination Imagination challenge. From *2015–16 Challenge Previews* by Destination Imagination, 2015, retrieved from http://www. destinationimagination.org/challenge-program/2015-16-challenge-previews. Copyright 2015 by Destination Imagination. Reprinted with permission.

has a designated time limit. Figure 12.7 details a sample contest problem. For more information about Math Olympiads visit http://www.moems.org.

MATHCOUNTS. A program that supports critical thinking and problem solving and strives to make teaching and learning math fun, MATHCOUNTS offers several programs including a middle school math competition, a national math club, a math video challenge, and a fund-raising solve-a-thon. Visit https://www.mathcounts.org for sample problems, posters, and videos (MATHCOUNT minis) by *The Art of Problem Solving*'s Richard Rusczyk, and additional program information.

Outside-of-School Enrichment

Outside-of-school enrichment options are those that parents/guardians must seek out for their children and are independent of the school. Teachers should alert parents to national, state, and community-based programs that serve to nurture students' strengths and interests.

Competitions

Competitions are a great way for students to connect with others of similar abilities and shared passions. Numerous organizations support competitions across nearly every discipline, some with substantial awards. See Karnes and Riley's (2013) book, *The Best Competitions for Talented Kids*, for a comprehensive listing of competitions.

Weekend and Summer Programs

Colleges and universities; museums; and other state, national, and community-based organizations offer weekend and summer enrichment and acceleration programs for gifted students with both commuter and residential options. Although cost may be prohibitive for some, many programs do offer merit- and/or need-based financial aid.

Talent search programs. Perhaps the most well-established programs are those offered by the various regional talent search organizations: Duke Talent Identification Program (http://tip.duke.edu), Johns Hopkins Center for Talented Youth (http://cty.jhu.edu), Center for Talent Development at Northwestern (http://www.ctd.northwestern.edu), and the Center for Bright Kids (https://www.centerforbrightkids.org). All provide an array of program (e.g., travel/field study, leadership, service learning) and delivery format options (e.g., online, weekend) to support their signature talent search programs. Although initially serving middle and high school students, most of these programs have now expanded to meet the

---

Time: 5 minutes
The only way that 10 can be written as the sum of 4 different counting numbers is
1 + 2 + 3 + 4. In how many different ways can 15 be written as the sum of 4 different
counting numbers?

Figure 12.7. Sample Math Olympiads problem: Grades 4–6. From *Mathematical Olympiads: Division E, Contest 4* by Math Olympiads, 2009, retrieved from http://www.moems.org/sample_files/SampleE.pdf. Copyright 2009 Math Olympiads. Reprinted with permission.

---

needs of gifted elementary school students. Approximately 16,000 students participate each year in summer programs offered though the various talent searches (Lee, Matthews, & Olszewski-Kubilius, 2008).

Governor's schools. Another option for the summer is attending a governor's school for gifted high school students. These highly selective programs provide access to rigorous curriculum, and tuition is kept as low as possible with partial or full fee support from the state's legislature. According to the National Conference of Governor's Schools (n.d.), approximately 23 states have a governor's school, with about 15–20 of these offering summer programming. For a listing of governor's school programs by state visit http://ncogs.org/index.php/programs-by-state.

Other programs. Providing a comprehensive listing of available programs here would be too voluminous; however, there are several websites that have compiled information on summer and weekend programming options. See the National Association for Gifted Children's Gifted and Talented Summer Resource Directory at http://giftedandtalentedresourcesdirectory.com and the Davidson Institute's list of summer programs by topic area at http://www.davidsongifted.org/db/Articles_id_10370.aspx.

Mentorships/Internships

When a student is ready to learn more advanced content, explore career pathways, or engage in a discipline through authentic research and interactions with experts, a mentorship or internship may be appropriate. This enrichment option is typically sought by high school students, but even younger students can benefit from experiences in the field and engagement with content experts. With technology, connecting students to all kinds of experts is now possible (Siegle, 2003; see Technology and Enrichment). Some colleges and universities and businesses have formal mentoring and internship opportunities; however, parents and teachers can also explore their community for possible mentoring/internship experiences for gifted students. The National Mentoring Partnership (http://www.mentoring.org) maintains a national database of youth mentoring programs to help connect mentors and mentees.

Technology and Enrichment

With the advancement of technology, enrichment options for gifted learners continue to broaden. From online learning courses to e-mentoring, and more, the possibilities seem limitless.

Online Learning

Many programs offer online learning opportunities so that students can participate regardless of their location. A few such programs follow.

- *Gifted LearningLinks*—Enrichment courses for students in grades 3–8 are offered through the Center for Talent Development at Northwestern University. Sample course titles include Online Writing Workshop; Google Geography; Campaign Trail: Polls, Policy & Persuasion; Mysteries of the Deep; Latin; Stock Market Experience; and Interactive Websites. Visit http://www.ctd.northwestern.edu/program_type/online-programs for additional information.
- *Stanford Education Program for Gifted Youth (EPGY)*—EPGY offers tutor-supported and independent study online courses across disciplines for students in grades K–12. Visit https://giftedandtalented.com to view course selections and tuition information.
- *The Summer Institute for the Gifted (SIG)*—SIG offers 8-week enrichment courses for students ages 7–12 on a wide range of topics. Students must meet eligibility requirements in order to participate. Sample courses include Be a Pet Vet (ages 7–8), The Entrepreneur in You (ages 9–10), Fun With Newtonian Physics (ages 11–12), and Symbols and Myths: What's Behind the Story? (ages 9–12). Visit http://www.giftedstudy.org/beyond/online for additional information.

e-Mentoring

Technology also makes finding a suitable mentor for gifted students more feasible, with physical proximity and time considerations no longer being limiting factors in pairing mentor and mentee. E-mail, Skype, and other web conferencing platforms make it possible for students to connect with experts all over the world in every area of endeavor.

The Internet

The Internet supports enrichment by providing access to a huge amount of information, images, and videos. Students can explore primary source documents, examine multiple perspectives around issues through readings and online discussions, create a blog to record and share their thoughts, and network with others who share their interests. The Internet provides students the world at their fingertips.

Internet safety (see Eckstein, 2009), new literacy skills (see Henry, 2006), and effective integration of technology in the classroom (see Besnoy, 2007) are a few issues related to technology that will need to be navigated with care; however, the academic and psychosocial benefits of using technology for gifted students may outweigh these concerns—especially for those students who have exhausted other forms of enrichment within their school or community.

Conclusion

Gagné (2015) acknowledged the recent resistance by educators to use the term *enriched* due to "perceived political pressures or public stereotypes (e.g., a non-enriched curriculum is a 'poor' curriculum)" (p. 287); however, the concept of enrichment should endure, as it is the most accurate description of the type of differentiation that advanced learners need. Without enrichment opportunities, gifted students are in danger of being unchallenged, which may lead to underachievement and total disengagement from the learning process.

Do all learners benefit from some form of enrichment? Possibly, but for gifted students, enrichment ensures engagement in learning experiences within their zone of proximal development and provides respectful learning experiences that advance their academic growth while nurturing their passions. For them, enrichment may be the difference between *being* and *becoming*.

Big Ideas

1. Enrichment addresses both the academic and psychosocial needs of gifted students.

2. Enrichment supports student engagement in the learning process.

3. Opportunities for enrichment foster the development of learning-to-learn skills and the dispositions of a lifelong learner.

4. Enrichment helps connect gifted students with others who share similar abilities and passions.

5. Enrichment can occur at different intensities within a variety of contexts.

6. The relationship between enrichment and the curriculum can be conceptualized in a variety of ways.

7. Enrichment and acceleration are not mutually exclusive.

Big Ideas, *Continued.*

8. Systematic frameworks exist to support the implementation of enrichment.

9. Technology has enhanced and broadened the availability of enrichment opportunities.

Discussion Questions

1. In what ways does access to enrichment opportunities contribute to inequities in schools?

2. What is the value of enrichment opportunities for gifted learners?

3. What are the similarities and differences among the different program models that support enrichment?

4. How has technology changed enrichment options for students?

5. What are some of the positive and negative connotations associated with the concept of enrichment?

References

Bain, S. K., Bourgeois, S. J., & Pappas, D. N. (2003). Linking theoretical models to actual practices: A survey of teachers in gifted education. *Roeper Review, 25,* 166–172.

Besnoy, K. (2007). Creating a personal technology improvement plan for teachers of the gifted. *Gifted Child Today, 30*(4), 44–48.

Betts, G. T. (1985). *Autonomous Learner Model for the gifted and talented.* Greeley, CO: Autonomous Learning Publications and Specialists.

Caleon, I. S., & Subramaniam, R. (2007). Augmenting learning in an out-of-school context: The cognitive and affective impact of two cryogenics-based enrichment programmes on upper primary students. *Research in Science Education, 37,* 333–351.

Cash, R. M. (2011). *Advancing differentiation: Thinking and learning in the 21st century.* Minneapolis, MN: Free Spirit.

Center for Gifted Education. (2007). *Something fishy: Exploring an aquatic ecosystem* (2nd ed.). Dubuque, IA: Kendall/Hunt.

Cohen, R., Duncan, M. K., & Cohen, S. L. (1994). Classroom peer relations of children participating in a pull-out enrichment program. *Gifted Child Quarterly, 38,* 33–37.

Destination Imagination. (2015). *2015–16 challenge previews*. Retrieved from https://www.destinationimagination.org/challenge-program/2015-16-challenge-previews

Eckstein, M. (2009). Enrichment 2.0: Gifted and talented education for the 21st century. *Gifted Child Today, 32*(1), 59–63.

Enrich. (n.d.). In *Merriam Webster's Online*. Retrieved from http://www.merriam-webster.com/dictionary/enrich

Feldhusen, J. F., & Kolloff, P. B. (1978, September/October). A three-stage model for gifted education. *Gifted Child Today, 1,* 3–5, 53–57.

Future Problem Solving International. (n.d.). *FPSPI topics*. Retrieved from http://www.fpspi.org/topics.html

Gagné, F. (2015). Academic talent development programs: A best practices model. *Asia Pacific Education Review, 16,* 281–295.

Gallagher, J. J. (1964). *Teaching the gifted child*. Boston, MA: Allyn & Bacon.

Gallagher, S. A. (1997). Problem-based learning: Where did it come from, what does it do, and where is it going? *Journal for the Education of the Gifted, 20,* 332–362.

Gubbels, J., Segers, E., & Verhoeven, L. (2014). Cognitive, socioemotional, and attitudinal effects of a Triarchic Enrichment Program for gifted children. *Journal for the Education of the Gifted, 37,* 378–397.

Gubbins, E. J. (2010). Three rings, three enrichment activities, three decades earlier. *Gifted Education International, 26,* 157–168.

Gubbins, E. J. (2014). Enrichment. In J. A. Plucker & C. M. Callahan (Eds.), *Critical issues and practices in gifted education* (2nd ed., pp. 223–236). Waco, TX: Prufrock Press.

Henry, L. A. (2006). SEARCHing for an answer: The critical role of new literacies while reading on the Internet. *Reading Teacher, 59,* 614–627. doi:10.1598/RT.59.7.1

Kaplan, S. (2005). Layered differentiated curricula for the gifted and talented. In F. A. Karnes & S. M. Bean (Eds.), *Methods and materials for teaching the gifted* (2nd ed., pp. 107–131). Waco, TX: Prufrock Press.

Karnes, F., & Riley, T. (2013). *The best competitions for talented kids: Win scholarships, big prize money, and recognition*. Waco, TX: Prufrock Press.

Kaul, C. R., Johnsen, S. S., Witte, M. M., & Saxon, T. F. (2015). Critical components of a summer enrichment program for urban low-income gifted students. *Gifted Child Today, 38,* 32–40.

Kulik, J. A. (1992). *An analysis of the research on ability grouping: Historical and contemporary perspective: Research-based decision making series*. Storrs: University of Connecticut, The National Research Center on the Gifted and Talented.

Lee, S., Matthews, M. S., & Olszewski-Kubilius, P. (2008). A national picture of talent search and talent search educational programs. *Gifted Child Quarterly, 52,* 55–69.

Math Olympiad. (2009, February 3). *Mathematical Olympiads: Division E, Contest 4.* Retrieved from http://www.moems.org/sample_files/SampleE.pdf

McIntosh, J. (2014). Differentiation: Demolishing ceilings. In M. Gentry (Ed.), *Total school cluster grouping and differentiation* (2nd ed., pp. 99–120). Waco, TX: Prufrock Press.

Moon, S. M., Kolloff, P. A., Robinson, A., Dixon, F., & Feldhusen, J. F. (2009). The Purdue Three-Stage Model. In J. S. Renzulli, E. J. Gubbins, K. S. McMillen, R. D. Eckert, & C. A. Little (Eds.), *Systems and models for developing programs for the gifted and talented* (2nd ed., pp. 289–322). Waco, TX: Prufrock Press.

National Conference of Governor's Schools. (n.d.). *Programs by state–NcoGS.* Retrieved from http://ncogs.org/index.php/programs-by-state

Odyssey of the Mind. (2015). *2015–2016 long-term problems synopses.* Retrieved from http://www.odysseyofthemind.com/materials/2016problems.php

Reis, S. M. (2009). Enrichment theories. In B. A. Kerr (Ed.), *Encyclopedia of giftedness, creativity, and talent* (pp. 322–325), Thousand Oaks, CA: Sage.

Renzulli, J. S. (1976). The Enrichment Triad Model: A guide for developing defensible programs for the gifted and talented. *Gifted Child Quarterly, 20,* 303–326.

Renzulli, J. S. (1998, October). A rising tides lifts all ships: Developing the gifts and talents of all students. *Phi Delta Kappan, 80,* 104–111.

Renzulli, J. S., & Reis, S. M. (1985). *The Schoolwide Enrichment Model: A comprehensive plan for educational excellence.* Mansfield, CT: Creative Learning Press.

Renzulli, J. S., & Renzulli, S. R. (2010). The Schoolwide Enrichment Model: A focus on student strengths and interests. *Gifted Education International, 26,* 140–157.

Rogers, K. B. (1991). *The relationship of grouping practices to the education of the gifted and talented learner: Research-based decision making series.* Storrs: University of Connecticut, The National Research Center on the Gifted and Talented.

Siegle, D. (2003). Technology: Mentors on the Net: Extending learning through telementoring. *Gifted Child Today, 26*(4), 51–54.

Simpson, J. (2014). A case study on enrichment seminar and gifted students. *Gifted and Talented International, 29*(1), 63–77.

Stephens, K. R., Malone, D., & Griffith, A. P. (2016). Service-learning in gifted education: Addressing cognitive and affective domains. In K. R. Stephens & F. A. Karnes (Eds.), *Introduction to curriculum design in gifted education* (pp. 281–305). Waco, TX: Prufrock Press.

Stepien, W., & Gallagher, S. (1993). Problem-based learning: As authentic as it gets. *Educational Leadership, 50*(7), 25–28.

Subotnik, R. F., Olszewski-Kubilius, P., & Worrell, F. C. (2011). Rethinking gifted-ness and gifted education: A proposed direction forward based on psychological science. *Psychological Science, 12,* 3–54.

Treffinger, D. J. (1975). Teaching for self-directed learning: A priority for the gifted and talented. *Gifted Child Quarterly, 19,* 46–59.

Treffinger, D. J. (1986). Fostering effective, independent learning through individualized programming. In J. S. Renzulli (Ed.), *Systems and models for developing programs for the gifted and talented* (pp. 429–460). Mansfield Center, CT: Creative Learning Press.

Will, H. (1986). Junior Great Books: Toward a broader definition of the more able learner. *Gifted Child Today, 9*(1), 6–7.

Zeidner, M., & Schleyer, E. (1999). The effect of educational context on individual difference variables, self-perceptions of giftedness, and school attitudes in gifted adolescents. *Journal of Youth and Adolescence, 28,* 687–702.

CHAPTER 13

Acceleration

*Practical Applications and
Policy Implications*

Susan Assouline and Ann Lupkowski-Shoplik

And therein lies the paradox. When you don't believe in something, you demand nearly perfect evidence. If you are comfortable with an educational intervention, anecdotal evidence is plentiful and sufficient. When it comes to acceleration as an intervention, we do have consistently robust research evidence. However, that is not enough to put acceleration into common practice.—Assouline, Colangelo, and VanTassel-Baska (2015, p. 14)

Just do it.—Mason Carter, skipped sixth grade with additional acceleration in math

Essential Questions to Guide the Reader

1. What is the relationship between the intervention of acceleration and gifted education?

2. What is the role of the gifted education professional with respect to advocacy of accelerative interventions?

3. How does research inform both practice and policy?

Introduction and History of Acceleration in the United States

Acceleration is an educational intervention based on progress through an educational program at ages younger or at rates faster than typical (Pressey, 1949). Despite our long-term awareness of this intervention, its implementation and understanding remain enigmatic. This chapter should provide a better understanding of acceleration in order to remove some of the mystery associated with it.

Pressey's post-World War II definition continues to serve the gifted education community well into the 21st century. This likely may be due to forces shaping society following World War II that continue to impact us. Two forces salient to the history of acceleration as well as current educational practice, that also have relevance for future consideration, include workforce development and our global standing with respect to educating students, especially in the areas of science, technology, engineering, and mathematics (STEM). Both of these topics also are grounded in our early history, which includes the establishment of public education.

Acceleration in the 18th, 19th, and 20th Centuries: The One-Room, Ungraded School

Even before its founding, the population of the United States was predominately rural, a circumstance that came to define the structure of many of our public institutions, including schools[1]. In particular, schools were created to meet the needs of their students, which at the time focused on an understanding of religion with the Bible as the main text; most decisions about education were locally determined. In today's public schools, the Bible has been replaced by secular content; however, local decisions, usually made by individuals on publically elected school boards, remain constant. Local decision making may have been due to early disparity in available funding for resources, including buildings. These disparities are common today. Colangelo et al.'s (1999) description of the impact of the federal Land Ordinance of 1785 (funds that were allocated to school buildings via land sales) is as relevant today as it was more than 200 years ago: "Some communities mustered more funds and materials than others, but rural schools across the young country shared many of the same shortcomings: poorly trained teachers, out-of-date materials, and dilapidated buildings" (p. 6).

Fast-forward to the early part of the 20th century where one half of the student population was enrolled in one of the one-room schools scattered across the county (Colangelo et al., 1999). By definition, these schools contained students of all grades

---

1   For a comprehensive discussion of gifted education in rural schools, see *Gifted Education in Rural Schools: A National Assessment* by Colangelo, Assouline, and New (1999), the first volume of a three-part series on gifted education in rural schools written and published by the Belin-Blank Center.

and ages in one room, which meant the need for extensive differentiation, including adjusted pacing, on the part of the teacher. Even without formally acknowledging the fundamental educational concept of individual differences (i.e., differences in psychological attributes such as cognitive ability), teachers in one-room schools responded to the learning needs of individual students by adjusting the curriculum content as well as the pace. Within the one-room school setting, there was little that would prevent the teacher from recognizing student potential and allowing the student to progress through the curriculum at an appropriate pace. Therefore, acceleration could happen very easily, as in the case of precocious young students who were allowed to move up a few rows to sit with older students if they were ready to study advanced lessons.

School reform, typically associated with current advances in curriculum or school policy, is a well-established pattern for schools and pedagogy. An early school reform, the common school movement, occurred in the late 1800s. By the mid-1900s, educators taught in schools where a standard curriculum was presented by a qualified teacher to a group of same-aged students at the same pace, no matter what the students' learning needs were. The midpoint of the 20th century represents a temporal juncture at which societal forces impact the broader topic of academic acceleration as an educational intervention.

Acceleration Pre- and Post-World War II: Early Entrance Into Postsecondary Institutions

Ironically, the history of acceleration in the U.S. initially focused on entrance into postsecondary institutions prior to the age of 18 (Pressey, 1949). Pressey (1949) cited the title of Harvard President Eliot's address to the 1888 National Education Association, "Can School Programs Be Shortened and Enriched?" as evidence of a focus on the need to "save time" (p. 5). What does it say about the current state of education when passionate arguments in favor of acceleration (see Assouline, Colangelo, VanTassel-Baska, & Lupkowski-Shoplik, 2015, or Colangelo, Assouline, & Gross, 2004) echo so strongly the arguments from the 19th and 20th century? For example, in reviewing the research evidence on early entrance to college, Pressey (1949) concluded, "the evidence was practically unanimous that younger entrants were most likely to graduate, had the best academic records, won the most honors, and presented the fewest disciplinary difficulties" (p. 7). These research findings mirror the findings reported by many current researchers including Lubinski (2004), Wai (2015), and McClarty (2015).

The 20th century wars were devastating times of crisis. Yet, in times of crisis, Americans typically respond by recognizing the need for technological and educational innovation. Colangelo, Assouline, and Gross (2004) offered a succinct summary of the impact of the war years on acceleration as an academic innovation, including programming initiated by three postsecondary institutions (Ohio State, University of Illinois, and University of Chicago) to enroll younger students. In the early 1950s, the Ford Foundation provided scholarships to young students so that they could enroll in college prior to joining the military.

Although the Ford Foundation's scholarship initiative for young students was successful, it was eventually discontinued. One of the Ford Foundation's most significant educational innovations was the establishment of the College Board's Advanced Placement Program (AP) in the mid-1950s. The expansion and increased accessibility of AP is notable because AP is an important form of acceleration for secondary students, and it is now widely used throughout the United States. As reported in the 2014 10th Annual AP Report to the Nation (College Board, 2014), more than one million students took more than 3 million AP exams in one or more of the 34 content areas available. It is wonderful that more than a million students benefit from the AP program; however, several hundred thousand more students would qualify and benefit, yet the program is not available to them for myriad reasons, including lack of trained teachers and appropriate school resources.

Acceleration and Gifted Education

Although related both philosophically and practically, acceleration as an educational intervention is not synonymous with gifted education. The most important connection between the two is the teacher or coordinator of gifted education who is most likely to be aware of accelerative opportunities within the broad context of gifted educational opportunities. The biennial *State of the States in Gifted Education: Policy and Practice Data*, generated by the National Association for Gifted Children (NAGC), in collaboration with the Council of State Directors of Programs for the Gifted (CSDPG), makes salient this distinction in multiple ways. For example, in the 2014–2015 report (NAGC & CSDPG, 2015), about 80% of reporting states (*n* = 42) report a mandate related to gifted and talented education; yet only 13 of the reporting states had policy specifically permitting acceleration strategies. The percentage of states allowing for one or more of the various forms of acceleration varied tremendously:

> Among individual acceleration options, 13 states had policy that specifically did not permit early entrance to Kindergarten (a form of acceleration), while seven states specifically permitted it and 19 left it to LEA [Local Education Authority, i.e., school district] . . . Twenty-eight states had policy specifically permitting dual enrollment as a form of acceleration . . . twenty-two states had policy that specifically permitted middle school students to be dually/

concurrently enrolled in high school. (NAGC & CSDPG, 2015, p. 13)

Even though the implementation of gifted education (e.g., enrichment pull-out programs at the elementary level) has remained largely unchanged (Callahan, Moon, & Oh, 2013), the application of acceleration as an intervention has evolved. The 2014–2015 State of the States (NAGC & CSDPG, 2015) reflects a decade of significant changes in the area of acceleration, likely due in large part to the 2004 publication of the watershed report, A *Nation Deceived: How Schools Hold Back America's Brightest Students* (Colangelo et al., 2004). As indicated in the opening pages of that report:

> It is often difficult to make strong generalizations about research in education since, so often, scholars present contradictory findings. In fact, many educational interventions have been implemented with a flimsy research basis or no research at all. Acceleration stands as a striking exception to the rule. For example:
> - Acceleration has been well researched and documented.
> - Acceleration is the best educational intervention for high-ability (gifted) students.
> - Acceleration is consistently effective with gifted students.
> - Acceleration is highly effective for academic achievement.
> - Acceleration is usually effective in terms of social-emotional adjustment. (Colangelo et al., 2004, p. 2)

The fact that academic acceleration is the most well-researched academic intervention in terms of effectiveness, yet the most underused in practice and policy, defies logic. Considering that it is also highly cost effective—in that there is seldom any cost involved—should make it a high priority when planning services. A primary goal of the Colangelo et al. (2004) report was to initiate a national conversation to address the major excuses for holding back our brightest students. The 12 major excuses and their responses are listed in Table 13.1.

Forms of Acceleration

Implementation of acceleration occurs in a variety of ways and can focus on the individual student, small groups, or whole classes. Table 13.2 presents 20 types of acceleration described by Southern and Jones (2015). The forms listed are neither exhaustive nor mutually exclusive in that students may experience several forms during an academic career. Included in the table are common accelerative interventions such as whole-grade acceleration and single-subject acceleration, as well

Table 13.1

Twelve Reasons Why Acceleration Isn't Accepted in America's Schools

Excuses Given for Not Accelerating Students	Response to the Excuses
Teachers lack familiarity with acceleration.	Although more educators are familiar with the research, the majority of educators do not learn about it in their preservice educational training.
Confidence about acceleration as an intervention is low.	The evidence regarding the benefits of acceleration is overwhelming; however, because educators don't know about it, they aren't comfortable with it as an intervention.
Acceleration runs counter to personal beliefs.	The implicit belief is that "kids should be with their peers," and *peer* refers to an age-group, not an interest or aptitude.
Academic placement should be based on age.	Gifted students are more academically and socially-emotionally advanced. Placement should be based on readiness.
Doing nothing is better than being sorry.	Choosing to not accelerate, even though the evidence points to readiness, is making a choice for boredom and disengagement from school.
Acceleration is not taught in preservice teacher training.	College of Education faculty respect research; the two publications (*A Nation Deceived* and *A Nation Empowered*) offer the research evidence that supports acceleration.
It's not good to push kids.	Acceleration is allowing students to move at an appropriate pace and learn what they are ready to learn.
It's hard to make new friends.	Many bright students are inclined to interact with older students, and acceleration broadens the friendship group.
It's not fair for the other kids in the class.	This is a confusion of equity with sameness (i.e., all students have the same curriculum at the same time). Equity refers to equal access to challenging material no matter the age of the student.
Other students in the class will have lower self-esteem.	Educators are highly sensitive to the feelings of their students, which is an important characteristic of a successful teacher; however, students are familiar with seeing age-peers progress at different rates in many settings, such as sports and music.
There will be gaps in basic knowledge.	Accelerated students are quick learners, and any gaps quickly disappear.
There have been unsuccessful cases.	There are unsuccessful cases, but the numbers have been exaggerated and the reasons vary. Excellent planning can minimize unsuccessful situations. Finally, it's rare to read about academic success.

Note. Adapted from *A Nation Deceived: How Schools Hold Back America's Brightest Students* (Vol. 1, pp. 6–9) by N. Colangelo, S. Assouline, & M. U. M. Gross, 2004, Iowa City: The University of Iowa, The Connie Belin & Jacqueline N. Blank International Center for Gifted Education and Talent Development. Copyright 2004 by The University of Iowa, The Connie Belin & Jacqueline N. Blank International Center for Gifted Education and Talent Development.

Table 13.2

Forms of Acceleration

1. Early admission to kindergarten	11. Extracurricular program
2. Early admission to first grade	12. Distance learning courses
3. Grade-skipping	13. Concurrent/dual enrollment
4. Continuous progress	14. Advanced Placement
5. Self-paced instruction	15. International Baccalaureate program
6. Subject-matter acceleration/partial acceleration	16. Accelerated/honors high school or residential high school on a college campus
7. Combined classes	17. Credit by examination
8. Curriculum compacting	18. Early entrance into middle school, high school, or college
9. Telescoping curriculum	19. Early graduation from high school or college
10. Mentoring	20. Acceleration in college

Note. See Southern and Jones (2015), pages 9–18, for complete definitions for each form.

as some types that are more nuanced. For example, concurrent/dual enrollment at the high school level, AP, and the International Baccalaureate (IB) program represent nuanced accelerative opportunities for high-ability high school students. Concurrent/dual enrollment, where a high school student takes a college course, can be tailored to fit the student's local options (students who live in university communities may take a university-level class; other students may have a community college available). IB is a specialized highly rigorous educational program, available at the middle school and high school level. Students who perform well on the IB exams may earn advanced standing at selected universities worldwide. AP coursework is also part of a program that includes specialized teacher training and a standardized examination. AP and IB are similar in that both may result in advanced standing in college or university; however, an AP course is by definition college-level content taught to high school students, which makes it accelerative.

What the Research Says About the Forms of Acceleration

Current research findings were summarized in Volume 2 of *A Nation Empowered* (Assouline, Colangelo, VanTassel-Baska, & Lupkowski-Shoplik, 2015). Researchers indicate that few problems are experienced with acceleration, and those that occur are typically attributed to incomplete or poor planning (Southern & Jones, 2015); acceleration produces significant academic gains regardless of the type of acceleration utilized (Rogers, 2015); and acceleration produces small-to-moderate social/emotional gains for gifted students (Rogers, 2015). Longitudinal studies indicate that students have few regrets about their acceleration (Wai, 2015). Perhaps some of the most compelling findings come from those longitudinal studies that indicate accelerated students are more successful than same-age peers of similar ability who did not accelerate (Wai, 2015), and they also demonstrate advantages over older peers of similar ability who began their careers at the same time (McClarty, 2015). In fact, accelerated students show higher rates of productivity, work in more prestigious occupations, are more successful, earn more money and increase their incomes faster than older, similar-ability peers who were not accelerated (McClarty, 2015).

The bottom line? Acceleration provides *immediate benefits* in terms of students experiencing increased engagement in school, earning higher grades, and pursuing more challenging courses, as well as *long-term benefits* in terms of career advancement and life satisfaction. The findings are consistently positive across many different research studies and with a variety of research subjects.

Although the research is overwhelmingly positive, decisions about individual students must still be made with a focus on the success of the individual, which engenders caution. It may be unrealistic to expect a research study to report that 100% of accelerated students report successful experiences, but educators and parents want to do everything in their power to make that percentage as high as possible when thinking about individual students. Rather than feeling immobilized by the fear of making the wrong decision, it is important to take advantage of the tools available to help consider the options systematically and base decisions upon relevant research findings.

Implementation of Acceleration

Acceleration and Its Implementation Outside of Schools

Historically, many accelerative programs were conducted outside of the school setting, such as the early entrance to college programs and college scholarship programs mentioned above. No outside-of-school program for gifted students is as successful or as ubiquitous as the university-based talent search programs founded by Julian Stanley in 1971 (Assouline & Lupkowski-Shoplik, 2012; Brody, 2009; Lupkowski-Shoplik, Benbow, Assouline, & Brody, 2003; Olszewski-Kubilius, 2015). Joyce VanTassel-Baska posited that Stanley's talent search model is the genesis of every form of acceleration, and acceleration needs to be the starting point for any gifted program (personal communication, July 26, 2016).

As part of the talent search, high-achieving students take an above-level test (one that is developed for older students); students earning high scores are invited to accelerative programs during the summer, on weekends, and through online programs. For example, students can complete one or more courses (such as Algebra I) in a 3-week period in the summer. Students participate in diagnostic testing to establish what they do and do not know and spend time in the course studying material that is new to them. Because they are gifted learners, by definition, they are able to learn the material more quickly. Studies show they learn and retain the material well and continue seeking advanced courses as they move along into their high school careers (Lupkowski-Shoplik et al., 2003).

As previously mentioned, the talent search programs began in the 1970s, and by the 1980s students throughout the country had access to these accelerative opportunities (Stanley, 2005). Literally millions of gifted students have benefitted from these opportunities over the years. In many cases, students participating in talent search programs were able to receive local school credit for the work they had completed. In other cases, they were unable to receive that credit. Decisions about credit were up to the local schools. Stanley (2005) called his approach "benignly insidious" (p. 11) because he hoped the fact that students were participating in outside-of-school programs would eventually have an impact on local school programs; in the meantime, the individual talented students' needs were being well-served. Over the past 45 years, talent search programs provided a substantial portion of the research on the impact of acceleration on talented youth (see, for example, Wai, 2015).

Acceleration and Its Implementation Within Schools

The vast majority of talented students' needs should be addressed during their time in school. Talented students might experience accelerative opportunities by participating in special programs or by accelerating individually. Some students are able to participate in well-organized accelerative programs, while others are able to accelerate on their own. An example of a comprehensive accelerative program is UMTYMP, the University of Minnesota Talented Youth Mathematics Program (http://mathcep.umn.edu/umtymp), which provides subject-matter acceleration systematically to students in the Minneapolis/St. Paul area. Individual schools might provide similar programs, such as in the mentor-paced program at the Southern Valley School District described in *Developing Math Talent* (Assouline & Lupkowski-Shoplik, 2011, pp. 197–199).

If a specific program isn't currently available, regular classroom teachers and gifted specialists can play a role in discovering and developing academically talented youth who need accelerative opportunities. Grade-level testing and above-level testing may help to identify students ready for more challenging curriculum and/or subject acceleration. Preassessing students on the specific topic or unit helps to identify who has already mastered the material and is ready to move on. Teachers can compact the curriculum. Educators might challenge these students in the regular classroom or gifted program by providing higher level content on a daily basis, such as extension activities provided by the textbook publisher or advanced activities provided by content-based competitions (e.g., the Mathematical Olympiads for Elementary and Middle Schools, http://www.moems.org). Regular classroom teachers can group students by ability within the classroom and differentiate activities on a daily basis. Gifted specialists or regular classroom teachers might also provide support for a student who is participating in an online, accelerative course or work with administrators to determine a higher level placement in a specific subject in their school.

In contrast to an organized program that addresses subject-matter acceleration, individual students and their families might be able to coordinate with their schools and skip one or more grades in school (see Assouline, Colangelo, & VanTassel-Baska, 2015, for case study examples of this approach). The Iowa Acceleration Scale (IAS; Assouline, Colangelo, Lupkowski-Shoplik, Forstadt, & Lipscomb, 2009) is a tool useful for evaluating the appropriateness of whole-grade acceleration. The IAS structures the discussion about acceleration and facilitates a team-based approach to considering all aspects of a student's development important to a grade-skipping decision: academic, social-emotional, physical, educational context, and so forth. After a team works through the various sections of the IAS, members can feel confident they have considered the important factors in making a good decision. The IAS is not a test for students, but a tool for educators and families to use as they work through the issues surrounding a decision for a student to skip a grade. See Lupkowski-Shoplik, Assouline, and Colangelo (2015) for more details about this tool and its implementation.

Adapting an Outside-of-School Model for Use In Schools

The talent search model (described above) has offered, outside of the typical school setting or gifted education classroom, challenging accelerative opportunities to countless numbers of academically talented students through its testing programs, summer and weekend classes, and other opportunities designed to bring talented students together and allow them to move ahead through rigorous coursework at an appropriate pace. In an attempt to provide similar opportunities to larger numbers of students as well as to offer these opportunities to students throughout the school year (rather than only on weekends and in the summer), the University of Iowa's Belin-Blank Center established above-level testing via the talent search model for high-potential and/or high-achieving fourth through sixth graders in their schools. This in-school testing program uses I-Excel[2] as a gateway to classroom differentiation; challenging courses offered online; and/or high-interest, challenging programs on-site at the University of Iowa and in other locations.

Educators have a prominent role in the process because they partner with the Belin-Blank Center to establish a testing session during the school day (or on week-

---

2   I-Excel licenses content developed by ACT that was designed to measure academic progress of junior high students. From that content, Belin-Blank has been identifying the academic talents of bright students in grades 4–6 for more than 20 years.

ends). The test, I-Excel, is an online, above-level test first used in 2016. Comprising eighth-grade content in science, math, English, and reading, I-Excel uses an online platform developed by the Belin-Blank Center. Thus I-Excel is a talent search instrument, administered in schools by teachers to high-potential and/or high-achieving students in grades 4–6. IDEAL Solutions is the automated system that assists educators in interpreting I-Excel test results and in selecting appropriate program options for the students (see http://www.i-excel.org for more information). The ultimate goal is for educators to learn about and employ successful talent search model techniques during the school day, so all gifted students may experience more challenge all day, every day.

Professional Development for Teachers, Counselors, and Support Staff

The bedrock of successful implementation of any of the multiple forms of acceleration (see Table 13.2) is the training of school personnel, especially teachers and counselors. It is still rare to have acceleration taught in colleges of education. Therefore, classroom teachers or school counselors often learn about acceleration on the job, just as they learn about other educational options or innovations for students offered by their school or district. They may learn by trial and error or, if they are in a progressive district, through a school or district in-service. Some postsecondary institutions, especially those with gifted education centers, offer graduate courses aimed specifically at providing a comprehensive approach to academic acceleration.

Croft and Wood (2015) made a strong case for the explicit examination of professionals' attitudes and perceptions about individual biases associated with the practice of acceleration. Croft and Wood offered a comprehensive model of professional development that recognizes the role of the change process in addressing an educator's attitudes or practice surrounding acceleration. Their model includes the opportunity for reflection on current attitudes while also presenting research-based content and evidence-based applications.

Bridging the Impasse Between Research and Practice: Policy

Education is an especially complicated field. Almost every adult has had exposure to classroom learning and thus, has implicit biases and attitudes about curriculum and methodology. Professional educators (e.g., teachers, principals) as well as educational support professionals (e.g., counselors, speech pathologists, school psychologists) have to navigate a complex, nuanced, and highly public practice. Ideally, educators will be motivated to seek out research that will inform their practice. Indeed, they are in the best position to bridge the impasse that currently exists between the research, which presents a robust case for including one or more of the many forms of acceleration in the classroom, and the actual practice.

Policy can provide the structure to bridge the impasse between research and practice. VanTassel-Baska (2015) offered a very comprehensive discussion regarding the role of policy, especially in light of the absence of federal legislation for gifted education or academic acceleration. Policy will assist all stakeholders by eliminating inconsistencies in practice, which are a direct result of the local control for decision upon which many school districts were established. VanTassel-Baska (2015) suggested that the primary purpose, as well as the measure of success, for any policy is whether it "protects student's rights and opportunities" (p. 43). The research informs educators regarding the student's learning and social-emotional needs, and well-informed educators can use policy to bolster their professional practice, ensuring that all students are engaged in the learning process.

Conclusion

This chapter has presented an overview of the history of academic acceleration in gifted education, as well as how it is currently applied in the school building and outside of school. Several major points can be gleaned from the chapter, shared as follows.

Big Ideas

1. Research clearly demonstrates the effectiveness of academic acceleration for gifted students. Acceleration works. It is the most effective intervention for gifted students.

2. Acceleration comes in 20 different forms, and these forms can be used in a variety of ways to meet the needs of individual students.

3. Several tools are available for educators to use to make informed decisions about the different forms of acceleration.

4. Perhaps the greatest concerns about acceleration focus around the social-emotional and psychological effects. Research indicates that, when students are carefully chosen for acceleration, the nonacademic effects are small or negligible, and they are in a positive direction. In other words, the concerns about negative effects are unfounded.

5. If we truly are to make data-driven decisions and implement evidence-based practice, acceleration should be the first intervention we use when designing programs and opportunities for gifted students.

Big Ideas, *Continued.*

6. The university-based talent search programs have provided superb resources for academically talented students. Additionally, they have established a solid research base and support for academic acceleration. Some of the options developed by the talent searches are now becoming available within schools.

7. Acceleration is rarely taught in colleges of education, so postgraduate professional development for teachers and counselors is vital. In addition to teaching specific techniques and research findings about acceleration, it is also important to explicitly examine professionals' attitudes and biases concerning acceleration.

8. In the absence of federal legislation for gifted education or academic acceleration, policy provides a needed bridge between research and practice. Policy is useful in making practice consistent across location and time.

Discussion Questions

1. What misconceptions did you have about acceleration before reading the chapter?

2. What are the most important points for regular classroom teachers and administrators to understand about academic acceleration for gifted students?

3. How can teachers advocate effectively for acceleration?

4. How can educators facilitate the implementation of accelerative strategies in their schools and districts?

5. Think of a child you know who could have benefitted from acceleration. What type(s) of acceleration would have worked and why?

References

Assouline, S. G., Colangelo, N., Lupkowski-Shoplik, A., Forstadt, L., & Lipscomb, J. (2009). *Iowa Acceleration Scale manual: A guide for whole-grade acceleration K–8.* Tucson, AZ: Great Potential Press.

Assouline, S. G., Colangelo, N., & VanTassel-Baska, J. (2015). *A nation empowered: Evidence trumps the excuses holding back America's brightest students* (Vol. 1).

Iowa City: The University of Iowa, The Connie Belin & Jacqueline N. Blank International Center for Gifted Education and Talent Development.

Assouline, S. G., Colangelo, N., VanTassel-Baska, J., & Lupkowski-Shoplik, A. (Eds.). (2015). *A nation empowered: Evidence trumps the excuses holding back America's brightest students* (Vol. 2). Iowa City: The University of Iowa, The Connie Belin & Jacqueline N. Blank International Center for Gifted Education and Talent Development.

Assouline, S. G., & Lupkowski-Shoplik, A. (2011). *Developing math talent.* Waco, TX: Prufrock Press.

Assouline, S. G. & Lupkowski-Shoplik, A. (2012). The talent search model of gifted identification. *Journal of Psychoeducational Assessment, 30*(1), 45–59.

Brody, L. E. (2009). The Johns Hopkins Talent Search Model for identifying and developing exceptional mathematical and verbal abilities. In L. V. Shavinina (Ed.), *International handbook on giftedness* (pp. 999–1016). New York, NY: Springer.

Callahan, C. M., Moon, T. R., & Oh, S. (2013). *Status of elementary gifted programs.* Charlottesville: University of Virginia, Curry School of Education, National Research Center on Gifted and Talented.

Colangelo, N., Assouline, S. G., & Gross, M. U. M. (2004). *A nation deceived: How schools hold back America's brightest students* (Vol. 1). Iowa City: The University of Iowa, The Connie Belin & Jacqueline N. Blank International Center for Gifted Education and Talent Development.

Colangelo, N., Assouline, S. G., & New, J. K. (1999). *Gifted education in rural schools: A national assessment.* Iowa City: The University of Iowa, The Connie Belin & Jacqueline N. Blank International Center for Gifted Education and Talent Development.

College Board. (2014). *The 10th annual AP report to the nation.* New York, NY: Author. Retrieved from https://research.collegeboard.org/programs/ap/data/nation/2014

Croft, L., & Wood, S. M. (2015). Professional development for teachers and school counselors: Empowering a change in perception and practice of acceleration. In S. G. Assouline, N. Colangelo, J. VanTassel-Baska, & A. Lupkowski-Shoplik (Eds.). *A nation empowered: Evidence trumps the excuses holding back America's brightest students* (Vol. 2, pp. 87–98). Iowa City: The University of Iowa, The Connie Belin & Jacqueline N. Blank International Center for Gifted Education and Talent Development.

Lubinski, D. (2004). Long-term effects of educational acceleration. In N. Colangelo, S. G. Assouline, & M. U, M. Gross (Eds.), *A nation deceived: How schools hold back America's brightest students* (Vol. 1, pp. 23–37). Iowa City: The University of Iowa, The Connie Belin & Jacqueline N. Blank International Center for Gifted Education and Talent Development.

Lupkowski-Shoplik, A., Assouline, S. G., & Colangelo, N. (2015). Whole-grade acceleration: Grade-skipping and early entrance to kindergarten or first grade. In S. G. Assouline, N. Colangelo, J. VanTassel-Baska, & A. Lupkowski-Shoplik (Eds.), *A nation empowered: Evidence trumps the excuses holding back America's brightest students* (Vol. 2, pp. 53–71). Iowa City: The University of Iowa, The Connie Belin & Jacqueline N. Blank International Center for Gifted Education and Talent Development.

Lupkowski-Shoplik, A., Benbow, C. P., Assouline, S. G., & Brody, L. E. (2003). Talent searches: Meeting the needs of academically talented youth. In N. Colangelo & G. A. Davis (Eds.), *Handbook of gifted education* (3rd ed., pp. 204–218). Boston, MA: Allyn & Bacon.

McClarty, K. (2015). Early to rise: The effects of acceleration on occupational prestige, earnings, and satisfaction. In S. G. Assouline, N. Colangelo, J. VanTassel-Baska, & A. Lupkowski-Shoplik (Eds.), *A nation empowered: Evidence trumps the excuses holding back America's brightest students* (Vol. 2, pp. 171–180). Iowa City: The University of Iowa, The Connie Belin & Jacqueline N. Blank International Center for Gifted Education and Talent Development.

National Association for Gifted Children, & Council of State Directors of Programs for the Gifted. (2015). *State of the states in gifted education 2014–2015.* Washington, DC: Author.

Olszewski-Kubilius, P. (2015). Talent searches and accelerated programming for gifted students. In S. G. Assouline, N. Colangelo, J. VanTassel-Baska, & A. Lupkowski-Shoplik (Eds.), *A nation empowered: Evidence trumps the excuses holding back America's brightest students* (Vol. 2, pp. 111–121). Iowa City: The University of Iowa, The Connie Belin & Jacqueline N. Blank International Center for Gifted Education and Talent Development.

Pressey, S. L. (1949). *Educational acceleration: Appraisals and basic problems* (Bureau of Educational Research Monographs, No. 31). Columbus: Ohio State University Press.

Rogers, K. B. (2015). The academic, socialization, and psychological effects of acceleration: Research synthesis. In S. G. Assouline, N. Colangelo, J. VanTassel-Baska, & A. Lupkowski-Shoplik (Eds.), *A nation empowered: Evidence trumps the excuses holding back America's brightest students* (Vol. 2, pp. 19–29). Iowa City: The University of Iowa, The Connie Belin & Jacqueline N. Blank International Center for Gifted Education and Talent Development.

Southern, W. T., & Jones, E. D. (2015). Types of acceleration: Dimensions and issues. In S. G. Assouline, N. Colangelo, J. VanTassel-Baska, & A. Lupkowski-Shoplik (Eds.), *A nation empowered: Evidence trumps the excuses holding back America's brightest students* (Vol. 2, pp. 9–18). Iowa City: The University of Iowa, The Connie Belin & Jacqueline N. Blank International Center for Gifted Education and Talent Development.

Stanley, J. C. (2005). A quiet revolution: Finding boys and girls who reason exceptionally well and/or verbally and helping them get the supplemental educational opportunities they need. *High Ability Studies, 16*(1), 5–14.

VanTassel-Baska, J. L. (2015). The role of acceleration in policy development in gifted education. In S. G. Assouline, N. Colangelo, J. VanTassel-Baska, & A. Lupkowski-Shoplik (Eds.), *A nation empowered: Evidence trumps the excuses holding back America's brightest students* (Vol. 2, pp. 43–52). Iowa City: The University of Iowa, The Connie Belin & Jacqueline N. Blank International Center for Gifted Education and Talent Development.

Wai, J. (2015). Long-term effects of educational acceleration. In S. G. Assouline, N. Colangelo, J. VanTassel-Baska, & A. Lupkowski-Shoplik (Eds.), *A nation empowered: Evidence trumps the excuses holding back America's brightest students* (Vol. 2, pp. 73–83). Iowa City: The University of Iowa, The Connie Belin & Jacqueline N. Blank International Center for Gifted Education and Talent Development.

CHAPTER 14

Differentiation

Tracy Ford Inman and Julia Link Roberts

We look for differences not to label but to address the differences.
—Margaret Sutherland

Essential Questions to Guide the Reader

1. Why is it important to differentiate instruction for advanced learners?

2. How can an educator establish a culture that supports and develops effective differentiation?

3. Why is planning a necessary step before preassessment?

4. Why is effective differentiation impossible without preassessment?

5. What roles do content, process, product, and assessment play in effective differentiation?

6. How does a teacher use students' readiness levels, interests, and learning profiles in differentiating instruction?

7. What are commonalities in the sample models for differentiating?

History of Differentiation

The one-room schoolhouse common to America in the 1800s and early 1900s provided an example of diiferentiation—different assignments for students based on what they knew and were ready to learn. In *Understood Betsy* (Fisher, 1917), the main character, a third grader who attended a one-room school, explained her thoughts about school:

> You aren't any grade at all, no matter where you are in school. You're just yourself, aren't you? What difference does it make what grade you're in? and What's the use of your reading little baby things too easy for you just because you don't know your multiplication table? (pp. 101–102)

Betsy certainly understood the main point concerning the need for differentiated instruction matched to what she knew and was able to do rather than instruction based on the year she was born.

Over time, some teachers (like Betsy's) have personalized instruction for students, while others have taught classes as though all students were at the same point in their learning. Differentiation has long been a focus in exceptional education and has more recently become a major topic in general education. An academic discussion of differentiation for gifted learners was the focus at the First Curriculum Leadership Training Institute held in 1982. In the printed proceedings from the conference, Kaplan (1982) stated, "Differences in *means*—i.e., the way in which ends are achieved—represent variations in the practices by which curricula for different types of gifted and talented learners may be constructed, and hence, differentiated" (p. 58). Passow (1982b) acknowledged that, "gifted/talented individuals come in a vast variety of sizes and shapes. Since giftedness is not a unitary trait, the needed differentiated curricula will vary considerably. Many differentiated approaches are needed" (p. 36).

In summarizing the work of the conference, Passow (1982a) provided the *would*, *could*, and *should* litmus test for education of the gifted:

> *Would* all children want to be involved in such learning experiences?
> *Could* all children participate in such learning experiences?
> *Should* all children be expected to succeed in such learning experiences? (p. 12)

These questions guide the educator in determining if the learning experience is appropriate for the gifted and talented student or whether it is equally appropriate for all. Answering no to any one of these questions likely indicates that learning experience should be provided for some but not all students: In other words, differentiation would be appropriate.

Definition: Differentiation

As programming for advanced learners, differentiation, in the broad sense, includes both enrichment and acceleration (see Chapters 12 and 13). In a more narrow sense, the National Association for Gifted Children (NAGC, n.d.) defined it as "modifying curriculum and instruction according to content, pacing, and/or product to meet unique student needs in the classroom" (para. 21). Note the root of the word: *different*. Effective differentiation is more than just different; rather, it is different with a purpose, and that purpose is making the learning experiences meaningful to students. Effective differentiation, then, is "the match of the curriculum and learning experiences to learners . . . to facilitate ongoing continuous progress for all students" (Roberts & Inman, 2015b, p. 5).

Rationale for Differentiation

Students of the same age differ in skill levels and in what they already know about specific areas of content. Teaching an entire class as one homogeneous group misses the opportunity for many students to make continuous progress. Therefore, it is imperative to differentiate, even if a teacher has a class of gifted students, as these students will bring different experiences, interests, and levels of readiness to each unit of study. After all, all children come to school to learn new things every day, and *all children* includes those who are gifted and talented.

Teachers realize the importance of differentiation, but they tend not to differentiate. Archambault et al. (1993) found that teachers use one lesson plan to teach even though they voice the importance of differentiation; 10 years later, a follow-up study had the same results (Westberg & Daoust, 2003). One factor affecting the lack of differentiation is that teachers simply are not trained to do it. The New Teaching Center conducted the Teaching, Empowering, Leading, and Learning (TELL) survey across 20 states, questioning educators and administrators on a variety of subjects, including professional development needs. A large percentage of teachers indicated that they need training on differentiation in order to teach their students more effectively, as these four randomly selected states indicate: Colorado, 55% (TELL Colorado, 2015); Kentucky, 57% (TELL Kentucky, 2015); Maryland, 48% (TELL Maryland, 2015); and Tennessee, 57% (TELL Tennessee, 2015). When teachers do have training, it tends to be focused on differentiating for exceptional students on the other end of the spectrum, not high-ability or gifted and talented students.

Other reasons for not differentiating abound: lack of time, lack of resources, few role models, concerns with classroom management, the myth that gifted young people will be fine on their own, limited support from administrators, and more. Note these reasons all focus on the teacher. Why then should teachers differentiate in their classrooms? Continuous progress, student motivation, and learning top the list along with fairness and equity of opportunity. Who is the focus here? The student (Roberts & Inman, 2015b). Because students and their continuous progress are the main reasons schools exist, it is not surprising that the NAGC (2010) Pre-K–Grade 12 Gifted Education Programming Standards include differentiation in the Curriculum Planning and Instruction Standard. Johnsen (2012) elaborated: "Educators (a) develop comprehensive, cohesive programming for students with a variety of gifts and talents that is based on standards, incorporate differentiated curricula in all domains, and use a balanced assessment system (Kitano, Montgomery, VanTassel-Baska, & Johnsen, 2008; Tomlinson, 2004; Stiggins, 2008; VanTassel-Baska, 2004)" (p. 14).

Principles to Guide Effective Differentiation

For the greatest impact on learning, a differentiated assignment is not just different; rather, it matches the students' levels of readiness to engage in learning on a particular topic or concept (although differentiation may also match interest or learning profile of the learner). Effective differentiation facilitates continuous progress for all students, including gifted and advanced learners.

Key principles of effective differentiation for advanced learners include the following:

- establishing a climate in the classroom that supports learning with students engaged in various learning experiences;
- planning and implementing a management system for procedures (e.g., grouping, record keeping, and materials);
- starting with solid content;
- determining what students must know, understand, and be able to do before engaging in other planning;
- using preassessment as well as other formative assessments (e.g., feedback) as guides to match learning experiences to learners and clusters of learners;
- planning learning experiences that vary the process (i.e., cognitive activity) in which students engage to learn about the content;
- implementing learning experiences that ensure an appropriate level of challenge for all students, knowing that one level of challenge for a class is seldom challenging for all; and
- recognizing that summative assessment provides information regarding student learning and allows for planning of future learning experiences.

Culture

The climate or culture of a classroom has one of the most powerful effects on student achievement, specifically in the areas of group cohesion, well-managed classrooms, and peer support and influence, according to Hattie's (2012) meta-analyses of 800 educational studies. An inviting climate encourages risk and views all participants as learners (including the teacher). Hattie (2012) argued that making learning "exciting, engaging, and enduring" (p. 34) produces the most powerful effects in achievement. Culture directly affects achievement.

In order to create a classroom environment conducive to effective differentiation, several principal components must be intentionally developed and nurtured: respecting diversity of learners, maintaining high expectations, and generating openness (Roberts & Inman, 2015b). Each member of the learning community needs to not only acknowledge differences but also respect that diversity. This pertains to everything from race, religion, and general background to learning profile and interest. High expectations should be set for both students and teacher; of course, for students, those expectations should be appropriately high based on individual need—think Vygotsky's (1978) Zone of Proximal Development. Risk-taking and growth mindset (Dweck, 2006) should be celebrated. A differentiated classroom should generate openness, thus encouraging both teacher and students to be open to a variety of things. These include being open to new ideas, understanding the idea that assessment drives instruction, realizing that pace of instruction should differ for students, capitalizing on teacher strengths, encouraging student choice and input, contemplating unconventional ways to learn, understanding the concept that routines and procedures simplify instruction, and more (Roberts & Inman, 2015b). Cash (2011) added the importance of creating a "brain-compatible learning environment" (p. 46) that includes a safe learning environment, stimulation of all five senses, opportunities for physical action and connections to be made with past learning, and the provision of relevant and timely feedback.

Questions That Lead to Effective Differentiation

When creating effectively differentiated learning experiences, the educator must address three important questions:

1. *Planning Question*—What do I want students to know, understand, and be able to do?
2. *Preassessing Question*—Who already knows, understands, and/or can use the content or demonstrate the skills? Who needs additional support in order to know, understand, and/or demonstrate the skills?

3. *Differentiation Question*—What can I do for him, her, or them so they can make continuous progress and extend their learning? (Roberts & Inman, 2015b, p. 11)

Most educators answer the first one well, relying on standards, programs of study, and the like. The second question, however, is not always asked—and sometimes, when it is, the answers are ignored, simply put in a folder and filed away. It proves much easier for educators to pull out the lesson they have already designed to meet the needs of the typical learner. The information gathered from Question 2 should guide Question 3.

Hattie (2012) posed his questions this way:

> Teachers and students need to *know the learning intentions* and the criteria for student success for their lessons, know *how well they are attaining* these criteria for all students, and know *where to go next* in the light of the gap between students' current knowledge and understanding of the success criteria of "Where are you going?", "How are you going?", and "Where to next?" (p. 22)

Roberts and Inman's (2015b) practical questions (listed previously) encourage teachers to base instruction on those findings.

Importance of Assessment

Simply stated, differentiation without assessment is not only ineffective—it also isn't differentiation. When an educator varies learning experiences for students, those professional decisions must be data-driven. The teacher must ascertain appropriate starting points for students (i.e., preassess) just as he needs to make periodic checks to determine learners' needs and the effectiveness of the methods so that students can make continuous progress. The educator then adjusts complexity, content, learning experiences, pace—any number of variables—to address learners' needs and advance learning. Chappuis, Stiggins, Arter, and Chappuis (2005) called this assessment *for* learning (i.e., formative assessment). Studies have indicated clear gains in student achievement when formative assessment is utilized effectively—as much as a 35% increase (Black & Wiliam, 1998). Also important is assessment *of* learning (i.e., summative assessment), which indicates student understanding of a concept or skill at a given point in time (e.g., a grade in a grade book). Assessment of learning certainly has a place in the educational process, but assessment for learning guides the actual learning and encourages continuous progress (Tomlinson & Moon, 2013). NAGC's (2010) Pre-K–Grade 12 Gifted Education Programming Standards made assessment one of the six standards, including assessment of the learning progress and outcomes: "Students with gifts and talents demonstrate advanced and complex learning as a result of using multiple, appropriate, and ongoing assessments" (p. 2). For example, an educator teaching a unit keeping this standard in mind could assess in the following ways: preassess content knowledge via end-of-unit exam (formative/preassessment), student-created learning logs (formative), peer feedback and student reflection (formative), and end-of-unit exam (summative for grade and also indicating growth when compared to the pretest).

Preassessment

As mentioned in the three questions, preassessment determines what a student already knows, understands, and is able to do, as well as whether additional support is needed in order for her to know and understand content or demonstrate the skills. An educator cannot possibly make appropriate modifications in the learning experiences if he has not determined the student's level of readiness, strengths, or interests. McTighe and O'Connor (2005) presented a medical analogy to stress the importance of preassessment: "Diagnostic assessment is as important to teaching as a physical exam is to prescribing an appropriate medical regiment" (p. 14). None of us would (or should) trust a physician who makes blind diagnoses, perhaps relying on typical ailments or issues for people our age. Nor should students trust educators who blindly create learning experiences, perhaps relying on standards designed for typical readiness for students of a certain age or grade.

Preassessments vary in form and intent because they are based on the unit or lesson to be taught. Ideally the preassessment mirrors the aspect to be differentiated. For instance, if the match will be the complexity of thought regarding civil liberties, then a preassessment based on levels of readiness would be appropriate. If student learning is based on which aspects of the unit most intrigue them, then an interest inventory is in order. For advanced learners, one of the most critical areas to preassess for continuous progress is level of readiness for learning a particular concept or standard. Students cannot learn what they already know, so, by determining what is already known, the educator can modify instruction to focus on the concepts yet to be mastered. Preassessments can target levels of readiness, interests, learning profiles, familiarity with products, and more. Examples include end-of-unit exams, open-ended questions, K-W-L charts, T-W-H charts (Roberts & Roberts, 2011), graphic organizers such as mind maps (Buzan, 1983) or Venn diagrams (Kanevsky, 2003), five hardest questions (Winebrenner, 1992), and more. If used to differentiate for specific students, preassessments should be individual and written in order to make defensible modifications. Students should understand that preassessments are not graded—they are simply tools to help personalize learning. They should also know they are not expected to know the material beforehand. Oftentimes, a few minutes of preteaching can provide more accurate data for the educator, especially if the student has not seen the content since the last school year.

Formative Assessment

Preassessment actually falls into the category of formative assessment. Whereas preassessment serves a diagnostic role, formative assessment throughout the learning experiences allows the educator to modify instruction for optimal learning. Popham (2008) described this as "a process used by teachers and students during instruction that provides feedback to adjust ongoing teaching and learning to improve students' achievement of intended instructional outcomes" (p. 5). All students need appropriate challenge and academic stretch. Formative assessment may be individual and written, such as exit slips, nongraded quizzes, learning logs, or homework; they may also be group assessments or more informal, such as asking for a thumbs-up/thumbs-down from students to measure the overall pulse of the classroom's learning. Of course, the more individualized, the more accurate the modification of the teaching and learning.

Note the word *feedback* in Popham's (2008) description. Hattie (2008) discovered in his meta-analysis that feedback influences achievement. Wiggins (2012) stated that "feedback is information about how we are doing in our efforts to reach a goal" (p. 10). In order for feedback to be most effective, it should be learner-specific, occur soon after the performance or learning experience, focus on the most important concepts without being all-inclusive, and be ongoing (Inman & Roberts, 2016). Hattie and Timperley (2007) described a four-tiered model of feedback: feedback about the task, the processing of the task, self-regulation (i.e., self-evaluation or self-confidence), and the student as a person. Consider the term *feedforward* instead of *feedback* to understand the tremendous impact appropriate insight and criticism can have on student learning. Whether the feedforward comes from the teacher, other students, or student self-reflection, it can prove a powerful change agent.

Summative Assessment

Summative assessment distinguishes itself from formative in that it results in the determination of what has been learned at the culmination of a learning experience, lesson, or unit, ideally product-based or performance-based in nature. Because summative assessment focuses on mastery level of learning, it should reflect the learning objectives of the unit or lesson, thus directing the educator to plan learning experiences to facilitate students demonstrating those learning outcomes at high levels. Wiggins and McTighe (2005) suggested a backward design model wherein the assessments are created before the learning experiences.

The words *multiple* and *appropriate* embedded in the NAGC (2010) Pre-K–Grade 12 Gifted Education Programming Standards certainly come into play.

Appropriate means that the measurement matches the content and learning objectives, and, where possible, brings into play the student's strengths, learning profile, and/or interests. Just as differentiated instruction addresses learners' individualities, so should assessement (thus the term *multiple* in the standard). Educators should refrain from always using pen-and-paper exams. When several kinds of assessments are utilized, students can demonstrate mastery in myriad ways, such as performance-based or product-based (Tomlinson & Imbeau, 2010). In Chapter 9, VanTassel-Baska and Hubbard emphasized the critical nature of varied summative assessments for advanced learners. They suggested educators incorporate a range of assessments from performance-based and product-based to portfolios and standardized tests (especially in relation to Advanced Placement courses). In performance-, product-, or portfolio-based assessments, students should receive the rubric at the same time as the task so that it can guide the development of the performance, product, or portfolio (e.g., Renzulli and Reis's [2014] Student Product Assessment Form or Roberts and Inman's [2015a] Developing and Assessing Product [DAP] Tool).

Important to note is the misconception regarding differentiation and grading. Tomlinson and Moon (2013) argued that differentiation is not incongruous with grading. Issues in grading differentiated work typically stem from faulty grading practices, not the differentiation.

Components to Be Differentiated

Educators differentiate primarily through content, process, product, and assessment. Content refers to what the students are to know, understand, or be able to do. Process does not necessarily denote the process students use to learn (think "what the hands are doing"); rather, it describes the cognitive process used (think "what the mind is doing"). Products are the vehicles students use to demonstrate what they have learned, whereas assessment refers to the means the teacher uses to measure the learning. Tomlinson and Moon (2013) also included differentiation through affect/environment (i.e., classroom climate). Figure 14.1 illustrates this relationship with elements in learning experiences.

Content

A strong conceptually based curriculum provides the foundation for continuous learning in advanced students. (See Chapter 8 for a full discussion.) Curricula tied to universal themes or great ideas (Adler, 1988) prove abstract and therefore not able to be mastered. This is not true with most curricula, especially those that are content-based. A large curriculum compacting study (Reis et al., 1993) found that gifted students knew as much as 50% of the curriculum before school started; when that content was omitted, these students scored just as well as control students

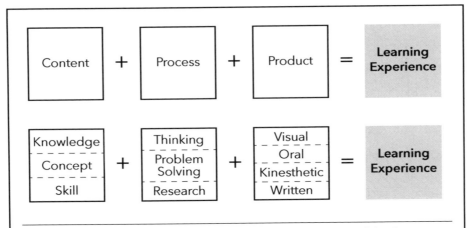

Figure 14.1. Elements of learning experiences. From "Writing Units That Remove the Learning Ceiling," by J. L. Roberts and R. A. Roberts in *Methods and Materials for Teaching the Gifted* (4th ed., p. 233), by F. A. Karnes and S. M. Bean (Eds.), 2015, Waco, TX: Prufrock Press. Reprinted with permission.

on achievement tests. Many advanced students have already mastered the content, thus making differentiation tantamount to success. Content can be basic or complex—most topics in an elementary science class (e.g., the cell) can have an entire graduate-level class taught on that one topic. Not only can a teacher differentiate content by going more in depth, but she can also have the student study a tangential area not typically covered in the unit (such as weaponry in the Civil War) or allow the student to continue to the next unit.

Process

Process is not what the child is doing to learn, such as reading a text versus interviewing someone. Rather, process refers to a child's brain: the level at which he is processing this material. For example, if a child does not fully understand how to add fractions, then he needs to start at very basic levels when beginning the addition of complex fractions (e.g., "What are complex fractions?"). A learner who knows how to add fractions is ready to begin applying what he knows about adding simple fractions to adding complex fractions and analyzing the difference. The child who has mastered adding fractions and can readily apply that mastery to complex fractions is ready for complex problems and predicting outcomes. Differentiation of process involves varying the sophistication of the minds-on part depending on how the child is ready to think about the concept. Differentiating learning experiences based on the revised Bloom's taxonomy (Anderson & Krathwohl, 2001) is one strong way to meet advanced learners' needs.

Product

When what the child is learning is more important than how she demonstrates it, differentiation of product works well. For example, if students are researching the French Revolution with the intent of understanding the social, economic, and political causes, then it may not matter to the teacher how the students show what they learned. Some may produce a PowerPoint presentation complete with embedded videos, while others may write an analytical essay. However, if an English teacher is teaching the essay, then student products should be essays. Professionals create products of all kinds, from the architect drawing a blueprint, to the sales representative pitching an idea through a Prezi, to a curator designing a museum exhibit. Student products must be held to high standards so that learners understand the expectations of professionals creating those products. Both teachers and students need guidance on criteria; one to develop the product and one to assess it. Products should be authentic and real world.

Assessment

Perhaps the hardest dimension to differentiate, assessment can be modified to match learner needs. Realize that learners with gifts and talents are also exceptional learners—they learn very differently from the norm. In order for students to experience academic growth, they must be assessed at a level that allows students to show that growth. Typically this means removing the learning ceiling (Roberts & Boggess, 2015) and utilizing multiple and appropriate assessments.

Considerations to Influence Differentiation Decisions

Whether an educator is differentiating content, process, product, or assessment, she can construct the varied learning experiences in several ways: readiness level, interests, or learning profile (Heacox & Cash, 2014; Roberts & Inman, 2015b; Tomlinson & Imbeau, 2010; Tomlinson & Moon, 2013).

Readiness Level

Hattie (2008), in his examination of 800 meta-analyses related to student achievement, found that "for grouping to be maximally effective materials and teaching must be varied and made appropriately challenging to accommodate the needs of students at their different levels of ability" (p. 95). That "appropriately challenging" decision stems from preassessment. An educator can differentiate readiness levels in numerous ways: varied reading level of texts, tiered assignments, small groups, compacting the curriculum, independent study, and pace.

Interests

A well-constructed interest inventory facilitates differentiation based on interests. These could be interests as related to the content or certain aspects of the content (or lack of interest—also important for an educator to know) as well as general interests in life. If a creative teacher can tap into a learner's outside interests, a hesitant student may be more willing to engage in the learning experience and an interested learner may be more engaged (see Reis & Siegle, 2002, as an example). Research links interest-based differentiation to "student motivation, productivity, and achievement . . . and appears to result in positive impacts on learning in both the long and short term" (Tomlinson, 2014, p. 200).

Learning Profile

Although not as well documented in terms of achievement growth (Tomlinson, 2014), learning profiles can be the basis for differentiation. A learner's profile consists of multiple aspects: Tomlinson and Imbeau (2010) listed gender, culture, intelligence preferences, and learning style. Work preference (group vs. individual) as well as product preference (Kettle, Renzulli, & Rizza, n.d.) could also be added. Be careful in utilizing this approach too often. Multiple meta-analyses of the last 40 years of research concur: "there is no adequate evidence base to justify incorporating learning styles assessments into general education practice" (Marshik, 2015). Inventories about learning styles and intelligence preferences and lessons developed from those should be used with caution. Remember that

> the goal of learning-profile differentiation should be to create more ways for students to take in, engage with, explore, and demonstrate knowledge about content, and then to help students develop awareness of which approaches to learning work best for them under which circumstances, and to guide them to know when to change approaches for better learning outcomes. (Tomlinson & Moon, 2013, p. 11)

Grouping

Effective differentiation calls for the preassessment to mirror the method of differentiation (i.e., content, process, product, and/or assessment) as well as the approach (i.e., readiness level, interests, or learning profile). The effectiveness of the differentiation also is dependent on grouping of learners evidenced by the preassessment. Whether these students are physically grouped together or simply received the same learning task, the learning experiences must differ from the other learners or groups. Groups and their learning experiences must be intentionally planned. Educators should ask themselves, "Why is this student or group of students learning this content in this way?" Table 14.1 lists grouping options based on both ability and performance. Please note the effect size, which indicates how large of an impact the treatment (i.e., grouping option) had on learning. An effect size of .6 would indicate students gain six additional months of learning when grouped that way as opposed to students who are not grouped. Of course, learning experiences must differ for the group.

Models of Differentiation

For this chapter, three models will be shared as samples of differentiating the curriculum for classroom instruction. These models were developed by Kaplan (2009), Tomlinson and Moon (2013), and Roberts and Inman (2013). The models have in common that they are conceptualized to help teachers match learning experiences to learner needs, including the needs of advanced learners; yet each model takes an individual approach to differentiation.

Kaplan Model

Kaplan (2009) conceptualized the Grid Model as

> a tool to generate differentiated curricular learning experiences to accommodate an entire heterogeneous class, small homogeneous groups, or individual students. The Grid can either supplement or replace the core curriculum unit or course of study by providing a single learning experience or an entire unit of study comprising a set of learning experiences. (p. 247)

Those learning experiences share common elements necessary for differentiation (see Figure 14.2). The Grid (see Figure 14.3) links those elements (i.e., content, process, and product) to an overarching theme as it provides the framework for creating differentiated learning experiences for advanced learners. In doing so, the Grid gives "greater sophistication to the existing core curriculum" (Kaplan, 2009, p. 247).

Table 14.1
Grouping Options

Grouping Option: Ability-Based	Brief Description	Research Summary	Academic Effect Size
Full-Time	Gifted students are placed in a full-time gifted class, gifted magnet school, a school-within-a school, or a special school	"clearly documents substantial academic gains and increases in motivation toward the subjects being studied. . . . their perceptions of challenge and social outlets are substantially improved" (p. 13)	Some studies show as much as 1 4/5 years of learning in a year's time. +.49 +.33
Cluster	5–8 students gifted in same area are grouped in the same class and receive differentiated learning experiences; rest of class is mixed ability	"substantial academic gains in achievement and . . . more positive attitudes toward learning" (p. 25); increased differentiation occurs; other students also benefit academically	+.62
Pull-Out	Students gifted in same area are pulled from class by a trained teacher to work on extensions of content, critical thinking skills, or creativity	"substantial improvement in skill development . . . more differentiated materials are provided to teachers than for those in other grouping situations, thereby requiring so much less personal effort" (pp. 16–17); students have higher self-concept	+.45 +.44 +.32
Cooperative	Gifted students are grouped together to work cooperatively on a task	"suggests possible achievement gains if and when the curriculum itself has been appropriately modified and differentiated. It does not seem to improve or harm self-perception or socialization. . . there is no support that mixed ability cooperative learning groups has any type of benefit for gifted students" (p. 19)	+.28

Table 14.1, *Continued.*

Grouping Option: Performance-Based	Brief Description	Research Summary	Academic Effect Size
Regrouping for Specific Instruction	Students in one grade are placed in classes based on achievement level in that subject; learning experiences are differentiated	High-performing students can make as much as 1 4/5 year's gain in a year's time, but curriculum must be accelerated	+.79
Cluster	5–8 top performing students in an area are grouped in the same class and receive differentiated learning experiences; rest of class is mixed ability	Little research on this form of cluster grouping	+.44
Within-Class/ Flexible	Teachers preassess and group students according to readiness to learn concept or skill; learning experiences are differentiated	Overall, research shows positive gains	+.34
Cooperative	High-performing students are grouped together to work cooperatively on a task	Students complain less of lack of challenge, feelings of exploitation, and loneliness	+.28
Cross-Graded/ Multiage	*Cross-graded:* "All grade levels teach a specific subject at the same time of day so that all students can participate at the level in the curriculum where they are currently functioning, regardless of age or actual designated grade level" (p. 35) *Multiage:* Students from three or more grade levels are placed in one class so they can work at own level	Positive for all learners; teachers more likely to accommodate differences; academic and leadership growth reported by teachers	+.45 +.46

Note. Research summaries and effect sizes stem from Rogers (2005) and Rogers (2014). Multiple effect sizes reflect multiple studies. Direct quotes, unless otherwise noted, come from Rogers (2005). From *Parenting Gifted Children 101: An Introduction to Gifted Kids and Their Needs* (pp. 78–84) by T. F. Inman and J. Kirchner. Waco, TX: Prufrock Press. Copyright ©2016 by Prufrock Press. Adapted with permission.

Defining the Elements to Differentiate the Curriculum

Content: specific means to accelerate, extend in depth and complexity, and/or focus or individualize the subject matter of the core or basic curriculum for gifted learners

Processes: introduction, reinforcement, and/or mastery of skill set
- basic skills fundamental to the disciplines
- productive thinking skills: critical, creative, problem solving, logic
- research skills and pre-existing references or inputs to investigate an area of study

Product: development of the authentic means of communication related to the work of the disciplines

---

Figure 14.2. Defining the elements to differentiate the curriculum. From "The Grid: A Model to Construct Differentiated Curriculum for the Gifted," by S. N. Kaplan. In *Systems and Models for Developing Programs for the Gifted and Talented* (2nd ed., p. 238) by J. S. Renzulli, E. J. Gubbins, K. S. McMillen, R. D. Eckert, and C. A. Little (Eds.), 2009, Waco, TX: Prufrock Press. Copyright 2009 by Prufrock Press. Reprinted with permission.

Tomlinson and Moon Model

Tomlinson and Moon's (2013) model on differentiation provides direction for planning and implementation (see Figure 14.4). This model describes principles for differentiation as well as guidance for the differentiation of content, process, product, and affect/environment. Tomlinson and Moon argued, "In a differentiated classroom, the teacher's aim is to make the classroom work for each student who is obliged to spend time there" (p. 4).

Roberts and Inman Model

Roberts and Inman (2013) presented the Effective Differentiation Model: An Instructional Model to Support Continuous Progress and Lifelong Learning (see Figure 14.5). At the center of the model are the Learner Outcomes, and the entire model is set upon the background of the classroom climate that allows differentiation to work well. The three pie-shaped pieces focus on content, process, and product, beginning with formative assessment and concluding with summative assessment. The goals of continuous progress and lifelong learning are central when planning for and implementing this model.

Dual Differentiation

In order to meet the needs of twice-exceptional learners, differentiation needs to support both the areas of disability and challenge in areas of giftedness. Twice-

Theme: Organizing elements to provide continuity to the curriculum.		
Big Idea: The statement of a generalization, principle, or theory that relates to the universal concept and is defined, verified, and supported by relating it to content within, between, and/or across disciplines.		
Process	**Content**	**Product**
The skills or competencies the gifted are expected to master beyond the fundamental, rudimentary, or basic skills include productive (logical, creative, problem-solving, and critical) thinking skills, research skills or the skills of accessing, interpreting, summarizing, and reporting information and the personalized skills particular to the individual aptitude of the gifted.	The subject matter selected for the curriculum reflects knowledge that is mandatory for all students to learn, knowledge that is commensurate with the level of conceptualization responsive to the gifted, and knowledge particular to the individual needs and interests of the gifted.	The forms of communication to reference a subject or the products by which the gifted summarize and transmit the knowledge they have assimilated and the skills they have mastered should include experiences in a variety of media, learning the technology and materials for appropriate and accurate production, and developing outlets for sharing and gaining feedback relative to the developed work.
Learning Experience: The intersection of the elements (content, processes, and product) constitutes the objective or learning experience that guides the teaching/learning process. Learning experiences are essentially fixed ends or the perceived anticipated outcome of teaching and/or learning. They provide the framework for units or courses of study, lesson plans, and independent study. The teacher and/or students use the learning experience to develop and plan the activities to attain this end.		

Figure 14.3. The Grid Model organization of elements to provide continuity of the curriculum. From "The Grid: A Model to Construct Differentiated Curriculum for the Gifted," by S. N. Kaplan. In *Systems and Models for Developing Programs for the Gifted and Talented* (2nd ed., p. 239) by J. S. Renzulli, E. J. Gubbins, K. S. McMillen, R. D. Eckert, and C. A. Little (Eds.), 2009, Waco, TX: Prufrock Press. Copyright 2009 by Prufrock Press. Reprinted with permission.

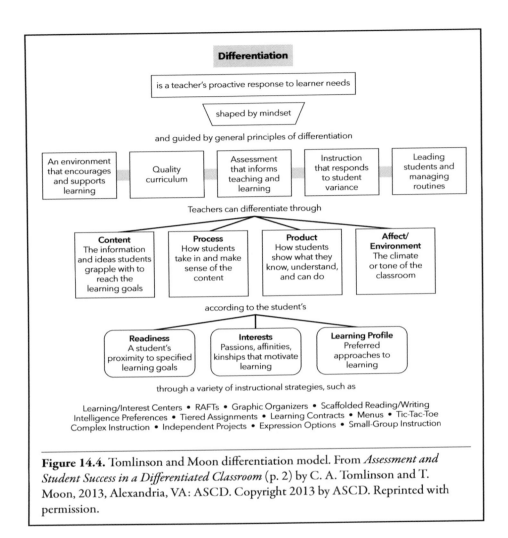

Figure 14.4. Tomlinson and Moon differentiation model. From *Assessment and Student Success in a Differentiated Classroom* (p. 2) by C. A. Tomlinson and T. Moon, 2013, Alexandria, VA: ASCD. Copyright 2013 by ASCD. Reprinted with permission.

exceptional students differ one from the other in their areas of disabilities and the areas of strength, making it very important to assess individual students and critical to plan to help them make continuous progress. The needs of young people with dual exceptionalities require dual differentiation (Baum, Cooper, & Neu, 2001). (See Chapter 22 for a thorough discussion of twice-exceptional learners.)

Conclusion

Much information about differentiation was developed in the field of gifted education, although general education includes differentiation in their current lexicon of topics. Often differentiation is included in teacher education courses or professional development for students who need more time and a more basic level for

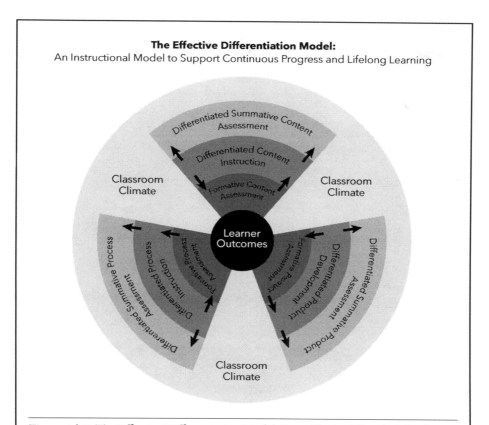

The Effective Differentiation Model:
An Instructional Model to Support Continuous Progress and Lifelong Learning

Figure 14.5. The Effective Differentiation Model. From *Teacher's Survival Guide: Differentiating Instruction in the Elementary Classroom* (p. 17) by J. L. Roberts and T. F. Inman, 2013, Waco, TX: Prufrock Press. Copyright 2013 by Prufrock Press. Reprinted with permission.

the content and process rather than for advanced or gifted learners. Differentiation is critical for advanced learners, too, if they are to make continuous progress.

Remember, differentiation is more than different. Effective or defensible differentiation matches learners' levels of readiness, interests, and learner profiles. Such differentiation allows for continuous progress (learning is why children and young people go to school) and develops lifelong learners.

Big Ideas

1. Solid content forms the base for planning to differentiate.

2. A culture conducive to effective differentiation must be intentionally developed and nurtured.

3. Determining what students already know and are able to do sets the bar for what will be motivating and energizing for students.

4. Assessment (formative—including preassessment—and summative) informs instruction.

5. The overall goal of differentiation is optimum growth based on appropriate levels of challenge.

Discussion Questions

1. What is your own definition of *differentiation?* Be sure to consider intent, principles, and components.

2. What is currently going on in your classroom and your school that supports and provides evidence of differentiation?

3. How would you design a mini-faculty presentation in which you argue that differentiation should be an important initiative in your school?

4. In what ways does your school's mission statement speak to differentiation in school, in particular, differentiation of advanced learners?

5. Which model of differentiation best resonates with you? Why?

6. Contrast differentiation with effective differentiation. What is the big difference in the two?

References

Adler, M. J. (1988). *Reforming education: The opening of the American mind.* New York, NY: Macmillan.

Anderson, L. W., & Krathwohl, D. R. (Eds.). (2001). *A taxonomy for learning, teaching, and assessing: A revision of Bloom's taxonomy of educational objectives.* New York, NY: Longman.

Archambault, F. X., Jr., Westberg, K. L., Brown, S. W., Hallmark, B. W., Emmons, C. L., & Zhang, W. (1993). *Regular classroom practices with gifted students:*

Results of a national survey of classroom teachers (RM93102). Storrs: University of Connecticut, The National Research Center on the Gifted and Talented.

Baum, S. M., Cooper, C. R., & Neu, T. W. (2001). Dual differentiation: An approach for meeting the curricular needs of gifted students with learning disabilities. *Psychology in the Schools, 38,* 477–490.

Black, P., & Wiliam, D. (1998). Inside the black box: Raising standards through classroom assessment. *Phi Delta Kappan, 80,* 130–148.

Buzan, T. (1983). *Use both sides of your brain* (Rev. ed.). New York, NY: Dutton.

Cash, R. M. (2011). *Advancing differentiation: Thinking and learning for the 21st century.* Minneapolis, MN: Free Spirit.

Chappius, S., Stiggins, R. J., Arter, J., & Chappius, J. (2005). *Assessment for learning: An action guide for school leaders.* Portland, OR: Educational Testing Service.

Dweck, C. S. (2006). *Mindset: The new psychology of success.* New York, NY: Ballantine Books.

Fisher, D. (1917). *Understood Betsy.* New York, NY: Henry Holt.

Hattie, J. (2008). *Visible learning: A synthesis of over 800 meta-analyses relating to achievement.* New York, NY: Routledge.

Hattie, J. (2012). *Visible learning for teachers: Maximizing impact on learning.* New York, NY: Routledge.

Hattie, J., & Timperley, H. (2007). The power of feedback. *Review of Educational Research, 77,* 81–112.

Heacox, D., & Cash, R. M. (2014). *Differentiating for gifted learners: Going beyond the basics.* Minneapolis, MN: Free Spirit.

Inman, T. F., & Kirchner, J. (2016). *Parenting gifted children 101: An introduction to gifted kids and their needs.* Waco, TX: Prufrock Press.

Inman, T. F., & Roberts, J. L. (2016). Authentic, formative, and informative: Assessment of advanced learning. In T. Kettler (Ed.), *Modern curriculum for gifted and advanced academic students* (pp. 205–236). Waco, TX: Prufrock Press.

Johnsen, S. K. (2012). *NAGC Pre-K–Grade 12 Education Programming Standards: A guide to planning and implementing high-quality services.* Waco, TX: Prufrock Press.

Kaplan, S. K. (1982). Curriculum development the culturally different gifted/talented: A perspective. In S. N. Kaplan, A. H. Passow, P. H. Phenix, S. M. Reis, J. R. Renzulli, I. S. Sato . . . V. S. Ward (Eds.), *Curricula for the gifted: Selected proceedings of the first national conference on curricula for the gifted/talented* (pp. 55–58). Ventura, CA: Ventura County Superintendent of Schools Office.

Kaplan, S. K. (2009). The grid: A model to construct differentiated curriculum for the gifted. In J. S. Renzulli, E. J. Gubbins, K. S. McMillen, R. D. Eckert, & C. A. Little (Eds.), *Systems and models for developing programs for the gifted and talented* (2nd ed.). Waco, TX: Prufrock Press.

Kanevsky, L. S. (2003). Tiering with Venn diagrams. *Gifted Education Communicator, 34*(2), 42–44.

Kettle, K. E., Renzulli, J. S., & Rizza, M. G. (n.d.). *My way . . . An expression style inventory.* Retrieved from http://www.prufrock.com/Assets/ClientPages/pdfs/SEM_Web_Resources/My%20Way.pdf

Marshik, T. (2015. April 2). *Learning styles & the importance of critical self-reflection* [TEDx Talks]. Retrieved from http://www.youtube.com/watch?v=855Now8h5Rs

McTighe, J., & O'Connor, K. (2005). Seven practices for effective learning. *Educational Leadership, 63*(3), 10–17.

National Association for Gifted Children. (2010). *Pre-K–Grade 12 Gifted Programming Standards.* Retrieved from http://www.nagc.org/resources-publications/resources/national-standards-gifted-and-talented-education/pre-k-grade-12

National Association for Gifted Children. (n.d.). *Glossary of terms.* Retrieved from http://www.nagc.org/resources-publications/resources/glossary-terms

Passow, A. H. (1982a). Differentiated curricula for the gifted/talented: A perspective. In S. N. Kaplan, A. H. Passow, P. H. Phenix, S. M. Reis, J. R. Renzulli, I. S. Sato . . . V. S. Ward, *Curricula for the gifted: Selected proceedings of the first national conference on curricula for the gifted/talented* (pp. 4–20). Ventura, CA: Ventura County Superintendent of Schools Office.

Passow, A. H. (1982b). The relationship between the regular curriculum and differentiated curricula for the gifted/talented. In S. N. Kaplan, A. H. Passow, P. H. Phenix, S. M. Reis, J. R. Renzulli, I. S. Sato . . . V. S. Ward, *Curricula for the gifted: Selected proceddings of the first national conference on curricula for the gifted/talented* (pp. 33–43). Ventura, CA: Ventura County Superintendent of Schools Office.

Popham, W. J. (2008). *Transformative assessment.* Alexandria, VA: Association for Supervision and Curriculum Development.

Reis, S., & Siegle, D. (2002). *If I ran the school: An interest inventory.* Retrieved from http://nrcgt.uconn.edu/wp-content/uploads/sites/953/2015/07/cc_ranschool.pdf

Reis, S. M., Westberg, K. L., Kulikowich, J., Caillard, F., Hébert, T., Plucker, J., . . . Smist, J. M. (1993). *Why not let high ability students start school in January? The curriculum compacting study* (RM93106). Storrs: University of Connecticut, The National Research Center on the Gifted and Talented.

Renzulli, J., & Reis, S. (2014). *The Schoolwide Enrichment Model: A how-to guide for educational excellence* (3rd ed.). Waco, TX: Prufrock Press.

Roberts, J. L., & Boggess, J. P. (2011). *Teacher's survival guide: Gifted education.* Waco, TX: Prufrock Press.

Roberts, J. L., & Inman, T. F. (2013). *Teacher's survival guide: Differentiating instruction in the elementary classroom.* Waco, TX: Prufrock Press.

Roberts, J. L., & Inman, T. F. (2015a). *Assessing differentiated student products: A protocol for development and evaluation* (2nd ed.). Waco, TX: Prufrock Press.

Roberts, J. L., & Inman, T. F. (2015b). *Strategies for differentiating instruction: Best practices in the classroom* (3rd ed.). Waco, TX: Prufrock Press.

Roberts, J. L., & Roberts, R. A. (2015). Writing units that remove the learning ceiling. In F. A. Karnes & S. M. Bean (Eds.), *Methods and materials for teaching the gifted* (4th ed., pp. 221–256). Waco, TX: Prufrock Press.

Rogers, K. B. (2005). *A menu of options for grouping gifted students.* Waco, TX: Prufrock Press.

Rogers, K. B. (2014, February). *Why would you group the gifted? Making it practical.* Keynote presented at the annual conference of the Kentucky Association for Gifted Education, Lexington, KY.

TELL Colorado. (2015). *Result details.* Retrieved from http://www.tellcolorado.org/results

TELL Kentucky. (2015). *Result details.* Retrieved from https://tellkentucky.org

TELL Maryland. (2015). *Result details.* Retrieved from http://www.tellmaryland.org/results

TELL Tennessee. (2015). *Result details.* Retrieved from http://telltennessee.org/results

Tomlinson, C. A. (2014). Differentiated instruction. In J. A. Plucker & C. M. Callahan (Eds.), *Critical issues and practices in gifted education: What the research says* (pp. 197–210). Waco, TX: Prufrock Press.

Tomlinson, C. A., & Imbeau, M. (2010). *Leading and managing a differentiated classroom.* Alexandria, VA: Association for Supervision and Curriculum Development.

Tomlinson, C. A., & Moon, T. R. (2013). *Assessment and student success in a differentiated classroom.* Alexandria, VA: Association for Supervision and Curriculum Development.

Vygotsky, L. S. (1978). *Mind in society: The development of higher psychological processes.* Boston, MA: Harvard University Press.

Wiggins, G. (September, 2012). Seven keys to effective feedback. *Educational Leadership, 70*(1), 10–16.

Wiggins, G., & McTighe, J. (2005). *Understanding by design* (2nd ed.). Alexandria, VA: Association for Supervision and Curriculum Development.

Westberg, K. L., & Daoust, M. E. (2003, Fall). The results of the replication of the Classroom Practices Survey replication in two states. *The National Research Center on the Gifted and Talented Newsletter.* Retrieved from http://nrcgt.uconn.edu/newsletters/fall032

Winebrenner, S. (1992). *Teaching gifted kids in the regular classroom.* Minneapolis, MN: Free Spirit.

CHAPTER 15

Talent Development as a Framework for the Delivery of Services to Gifted Children

Paula Olszewski-Kubilius, Rena F. Subotnik, Frank C. Worrell, and Dana Thomson

It is meaningless to be gifted in IQ. One has to be gifted in *something,* any specialty, excluding what is ephemeral, like tested intelligence. . . . If the mystery can be solved at all, the tactics have to begin with finding ways to assess specific aptitudes in *every* gifted young mind. But what *ought* to be does not always *come* to be.— Tannenbaum (2009, p. 514)

Essential Questions to Guide the Reader

1. How does the talent development framework compare to the traditional framework for gifted education?

2. What are the implications of a talent development framework for identification of giftedness?

3. What are the implications of the talent development framework for programming for gifted learners?

4. In what ways can the talent development framework address issues of equity and excellence in gifted education?

Recently, traditional approaches to gifted education and their usefulness in the current educational context of schools have been a source of wide discussion.

Talent development has been put forward as an alternative conceptual framework by several researchers, scholars, and practitioners (Dai & Chen, 2014; Horn, 2015; Subotnik, Olszewski-Kubilius, & Worrell, 2011), and other new frameworks (Peters, Matthews, McBee, & McCoach, 2014) have been proposed as well.

The phrase *talent development* is a frequent informal reference to gifted education practices or programs that support identifying the strengths of all individuals. In gifted education, the meaning of talent development focuses on identifying domain-specific abilities in all individuals *and* developing the talents of those who show exceptional abilities in response to instruction and coaching. This chapter will explore the meaning of talent development as a conceptual framework and its distinguishing and defining features; moreover, it will compare this conceptualization to more traditional views on giftedness. Implications of a talent development framework for educational practice in schools will also be discussed.

History of Talent Development

Although current discussions of talent development within gifted education seem to suggest that it is a new model, it actually has historical beginnings in the late 1980s and early 1990s as found in the writings of many distinguished individuals in the field, including Don Treffinger, John Feldhusen, Carolyn Callahan, Joe Renzulli, and others (see Schroth, Collins, & Treffinger, 2012). These leaders perceived a need for a shift in the field to "recognizing and nurturing students' talents rather than focusing primarily on identifying and labeling children as 'gifted'" (Schroth et al., 2012, p. 39). They collectively called for a broader conception of giftedness, beyond IQ, and a greater emphasis on finding and developing potential, particularly within typically underidentified and underserved groups of students.

Why is talent development as a framework for gifted education services gaining ground now despite having first been proposed more than 20 years ago? Contemporary research demonstrates the fluid nature of intelligence, especially the impact of increased opportunity (Dweck, 2012; Ericsson, Nandagopal, & Roring, 2005; Nisbett et al., 2012) on raising ability scores. The role of specific cognitive abilities in identifying talented individuals in specific domains has amply been supported in research (Park, Lubinski, & Benbow, 2007), and new research also points to the importance of other factors beyond ability in gifted performance (Farrington et al., 2012; Subotnik et al., 2011).

Another factor is the concern that traditional conceptions of giftedness do not respond to the changing demographics of the U.S. school population, nor do they address current concerns about racial and socioeconomic achievement and excellence gaps (Olszewski-Kubilius & Clarenbach, 2012; Plucker, Burroughs, & Song, 2010; Plucker, Hardesty, & Burroughs, 2014). Another is that within gifted education, despite a plethora of program models, low-income students, second language learners, and culturally and linguistically diverse students continue to be underrepresented (Olszewski-Kubilius & Clarenbach, 2012; Worrell, 2014, 2015).

Additionally, new research on several fronts, including within gifted education, has influenced interest in talent development. For example, several studies have demonstrated the efficacy of using gifted education practices and curricula with a broader range of learners, specifically students in high-poverty, Title 1 schools (Gavin, Casa, Firmender, & Carroll, 2013; Reis, McCoach, Little, Muller, & Kaniskan, 2011; VanTassel-Baska, Bracken, Feng, & Brown, 2009), when combined with appropriate scaffolding and support for learners. In order to respond to new research as well as continuing problems of underrepresentation, gifted education is seeking new approaches to identification and programming to identify and better serve more students with talents.

Comparison of the Gifted Child and Talent Development Frameworks

In order to highlight the distinctions between the traditional approach to gifted education that has historically dominated practice in the field and the talent development model of Subotnik et al. (2011), we draw on the work of others who have written about or compared conceptual models. These include the work of David Dai (Dai, 2011; Dai & Chen, 2014), who explicated three current perspectives on gifted education practice and research: talent development, the traditional gifted child approach, and the Response to Intervention framework; Matthews and Foster (2006), who distinguished between the mystery (traditional) and mastery models of gifted education; and Peters et al. (2014), who articulated an approach to gifted education called *advanced academics* that they distinguished from a more traditional high-IQ psychological approach to gifted education.

Views on Ability

Table 15.1 provides a comparison of the traditional approach to giftedness and the talent development framework on key dimensions. At the foundation of both perspectives is a shared belief in the existence and importance of individual differences in ability (Gottfredson, 1997). Gifted education, from any framework, is built upon a belief that these individual differences have implications for the education of children. This is a cornerstone of the field.

General and Specific Abilities

The traditional and talent development perspectives differ, however, in the relative importance placed on general ability (e.g., IQ) versus more specific abilities

Table 15.1
Comparison of Traditional Gifted Child Perspective With Talent Development Perspective

Concepts	Traditional Child	Talent Development
Over-riding perspective	• Primary emphasis on giftedness as a trait of an individual • Giftedness as "being"	• Primary emphasis on giftedness as a state one achieves with opportunity, practice, and study • Giftedness as "doing"
Ability	• Individual differences in ability are the basis for gifted education • Ability is all or none—you have it or you don't • Recognizes importance of level of ability within gifted population (e.g., highly gifted)	• Same, but sees ability as malleable, especially with the provision of opportunity • Ability is developmental and starts with potential, moves to competence then expertise and creative productivity in adulthood
General intelligence and domain specific ability	• General intelligence defines giftedness • Less concerned about domain-specific academic abilities • Recognizes specific ability in performing arts	• General intelligence is seen as important at younger stages of talent development and foundational for domain specific talent • Importance of general ability varies by domain of talent • Places greater emphasis on all domain-specific abilities, academic and performing arts • Assessment of domain-specific abilities, such as mathematical and verbal abilities, are increasingly important with development
Achievement	• An individual can be gifted irrespective of achievement	• Potential and ability defines giftedness in younger children • Outstanding achievement defines giftedness by secondary school
Psychosocial dimensions of talent	• Some social-emotional attributes seen as enduring characteristics of all gifted individuals and defining of and inherent within giftedness • Gifted students can have unique psychological needs	• Not inherent in being gifted • Characteristics result from interaction between gifted individual and environment, influenced by culture and opportunity • Psychosocial skills are critical to talent development and these change with domain of talent and stage of developed talent • Psychosocial skills are seen as malleable, coachable, and teachable

Table 15.1, *Continued.*

Concepts	Traditional Child	Talent Development
Psychosocial dimensions of talent, *Continued.*		• Emphasizes deliberate cultivation of psychosocial skills to support giftedness and high achievement within domains • Gifted students can have unique psychological needs
Educational programs	• All forms of acceleration, enrichment, specialized schools, outside-of-school programs • Often not continuous K–12 • Focused on general intellectual ability	• Same but should be designed within domains of talent/ability • Programs need to be different at different stages of talent development (e.g., exposure for young children, acceleration and enrichment for older children, mentorships and apprenticeships for secondary students and beyond)
Outcome of gifted education	• Focus is on responding to student's immediate needs for greater challenge, faster pacing, and intellectual peer group • Long-term outcome not often specified	• Cultivating domain-specific talents to a high degree • Moving students to the next level of talent development (i.e., developing potential into competency, competency into expertise, and expertise into creative achievement in adulthood)

Note. Adapted from "Talent Development as a Framework for Gifted Education," by P. Olszewski-Kubilius and D. Thomson, 2015, *Gifted Child Today, 38,* p. 52. Copyright 2015 Sage Publications. Reprinted with permission.

(e.g., mathematical, spatial, or verbal reasoning ability). In the traditional gifted child perspective, high intellectual ability defines giftedness, typically in the form of high scores on IQ or other general cognitive ability tests. In the talent development framework, general cognitive ability is foundational to the development and later emergence of more domain-specific abilities. Just as in sports, general athletic ability may signal the potential for exceptional athleticism, but it is less helpful in identifying talented basketball players than specific skills related to passing and dribbling. Analogously, by adolescence, measures of more specific abilities are better identifiers of talent and more predictive of future achievement within related domains than measures of general cognitive ability. For example, mathematical and spatial reasoning ability are related to achievement in science, technology, engineering, and mathematics (STEM) fields, while high verbal ability is predictive of achievement in the humanities and social sciences (Park et al., 2007; Wai, Lubinski, & Benbow, 2005, 2009). From the talent development perspective, general ability measures such as IQ scores may be helpful in the earlier stages of talent development, before differentiation of interests and abilities takes place, and in identifying potential in the absence of specific achievement—for example, for young children or children from poverty. However, "as one picks up domain knowledge and skills, the predictive power of general aptitude measures diminishes" (Dai, 2010, p. 58).

The talent development framework emphasizes that domains of talent, such as music, dance, sports, and academic fields, have unique trajectories (Subotnik et al., 2011) defined by differences in the timing of when production begins, peaks, and ends (e.g., diminishing strength and speed with age affect careers in many sports fields). Passion and ability can emerge early in a few academic fields, such as mathematics, but serious study of other domains such as psychology is often postponed until early adulthood either by tradition (e.g., psychology is typically not offered until later in high school or in college) or because these fields require experience, maturity, insights into human behavior, or the development of significant foundational skills (Subotnik et al., 2011). Trajectories within domains can vary also. For example, in music, children can start violin instruction very young, while the study of wind instruments starts later when lungs and breathing mechanisms are more physically developed. These unique trajectories influence the optimal age at which identification and programming can occur in different domains but overall support the idea of a domain-specific approach to talent development starting no later than middle school.

An important difference between the traditional gifted child and talent development perspectives is a developmental focus on giftedness. In the traditional approach, exceptional ability and high intelligence are viewed as personal, genetically endowed, static traits (Delisle, 2012; Rinn & Bishop, 2015)—"you have it or you don't." In the talent development perspective, ability and talent are viewed as evolving (or not) over time, from potential for achievement in early childhood to growing competence and expertise if opportunities are provided and effort, practice, and study expended. The final stage of talent development, more likely achieved in adulthood by a small proportion of individuals, is creative productivity at an eminent level within one's field (Subotnik et al., 2011).

Children can vary in the timing or their progress through these stages as a result of opportunity or changes in motivation. Some children are ready for an advanced curriculum and accelerated placement in a subject at the start of school. Other children, as a result of poverty or other circumstances that have limited their opportunities, may have exceptional learning potential that is not obviously demonstrated through traditional achievement. These children likely need to start with challenging curriculum and instruction to ferret out and develop their potential.

Perspectives on Achievement

The traditional gifted child and talent development frameworks differ in how they view achievement and accomplishment in defining giftedness. In the traditional approach, a child can be gifted with or without demonstrating high achievement. The definition of gifted is based solely on a child's general intellectual ability, although in practice, many school programs emphasize both high ability and achievement in their selection and retention policies.

In the talent development perspective, a designation of *gifted* is always relative to an appropriate reference group (Subotnik et al., 2011). A child is deemed gifted by virtue of the fact that she is exceptional relative to children her age or grade. If a child is gifted in math at age 10, he can reason and think mathematically like someone much older and advanced in the subject.

An adult is considered gifted by virtue of the fact that his or her achievement is exceptional compared to others in the domain with similar levels of training and involvement. All of the golfers in the PGA tour are gifted compared to the general population, but only a select few earn the title of gifted by other golfers within the sport that compete at the same level. The expectations get higher as one progresses to higher stages of talent development and the peer group becomes more elite. The designation is earned by virtue of achievement or actualized ability—not the promise of future achievement as it is in childhood.

At the very highest level, achievement that is field-altering and exceptional even among other exceptional achievers earns one the title of eminent. Tiger Woods is eminent in golf by virtue of his enduring impact on the field. Jordan Speith, who has been ranked number one on occasion, is a gifted golfer, but not yet an eminent golfer.

Psychosocial Dimensions of Giftedness and Talent

In the gifted child approach, gifted individuals have distinctive social and emotional characteristics, such as overexcitabilities or asynchrony (Daniels & Piechowski, 2009), that are inherent in being gifted and result in a unique psychology of giftedness. Some in the field go so far as to suggest gifted children can be identified and giftedness defined based on these social and emotional characteristics (Delisle, 2012).

However, there is little empirical support for many of the distinct characteristics attributed to gifted students, nor evidence of a common psychological profile (Dai, 2010; Dai & Chen, 2014). Research does not support arguments that gifted children are more emotionally fragile or vulnerable as a result of being gifted (Erwin, 2015; Neihart, 1999), although this is a common view held by teachers and promoted to parents (Baudson & Preckel, 2013). Being gifted can certainly affect psychological outcomes, but whether these outcomes are positive or negative depends largely on the degree of support or match between a gifted child's needs and area of talent and supports within the environment, such as talent development services (Neihart, 1999).

For example, being gifted may pose special social and psychological challenges for children from low socioeconomic backgrounds whose parents are not highly educated or connected to out-of-school resources. These challenges are exacerbated if the children are attending schools primarily focused on meeting basic proficiency levels. Similarly, a STEM-talented and interested female may easily succumb to stereotyped feminine peer culture if she has a family that overtly values her for her social skills and further stresses typical gender roles.

If there is any consistency regarding a psychosocial profile, it is found for adult creative producers *within* domains of talent—scientists, artists, musicians—a finding that suggests that the experience of engaging in the study and practice of a talent domain helps to develop the psychosocial skills needed for success within that domain (Olszewski-Kubilius, Kulieke, & Krasney, 1989).

Research suggests that psychosocial skills, such as self-confidence, mindsets, and resilience, are important determiners of whether students can move to higher stages of talent development—and these can be taught and acquired through interactions with teachers and through gifted programming (Farrington et al., 2012; Subotnik et al., 2011; Subotnik, Pillmeier, & Jarvin, 2009). The particular psychosocial skills that individuals need will change as their talent develops; for example, growth mindsets and being open to instruction and feedback are needed when children are acquiring the foundational techniques and knowledge of a domain, yet independent thinking and the confidence to challenge instructors are needed when students are at more advanced levels (Olszewski-Kubilius, Subotnik, & Worrell, 2015; Subotnik & Jarvin, 2005).

Educational Programming

The traditional gifted child approach and the talent development approach share the perspective that exceptional ability and talent require specialized programming, including both enrichment options and opportunities for acceleration. For some fields, such as athletics, music, and dance, the majority of the talent development opportunities take place outside of school through special programs or schools and individual lessons. Although academic talents are largely developed within school, they also benefit from supplemental, outside-of-school programs (Wai, Lubinski, Benbow, & Steiger, 2010). An important difference is that, from the talent development perspective, the programming should be within domains rather than generic enrichment programs, which remain the most common model currently in schools.

Additionally, because the talent development framework emphasizes a developmental focus, programming needs to change in response to students' stages of developed talent. For example, enrichment is important for young children and at the beginning stages of talent development to bring out and develop potential and help identify areas of interest. A good example is Renzulli's Schoolwide Enrichment Model (Renzulli & Reis, 2014). Differentiated curriculum within cluster groups, fast-paced classes, curriculum compacting, telescoped classes, and all forms of acceleration can help children acquire important foundational skills and knowledge within their talent areas at an appropriately challenging pace. For high school aged and older students, internships, job shadowing, apprenticeships, and other types of programs that provide opportunities to do authentic work in the domain guided by adult professionals serve to bolster motivation, cement commitment, and engage individuals in the culture of the talent domain (Olszewski-Kubilius, 2015a). Examples might include working on real environmental or social issues within a community, working with journalists from a local paper or news station, or being a part of a research team of scientists from a local university.

Outcome of Gifted Education

A further difference between the gifted child and the talent development framework is the purported outcome of gifted programming. In both perspectives, the short-term goal is to provide educational programs that are a better match to students' learning pace and level of developed talent and knowledge. However, in the gifted child approach, the long-term goal is often vague or focuses on the personal development of the gifted individual (Dai, 2010).

In the talent development framework, at every level of schooling, the main outcome is to prepare students with the skills and knowledge they need to proceed to higher stages of talent development. The ultimate goal is to prepare more individuals to contribute "in a transcendent way to making societal life better and more beautiful" (Subotnik et al., 2011, p. 7) through their products and innovations. Moreover, by having the highest levels of achievement and domain-specific creative productivity as the long-term goal for gifted adults, many more gifted children will be put on paths toward reaching excellent levels of achievement in their areas of interest and talent, thereby potentially increasing the pool of individuals that motivation, ability, skill, and chance propel to eminent levels.

Implications for Practice of the Talent Development Perspective on Giftedness

Table 15.2 lists some implications for implementing features of the talent development perspective in terms of identification, the design of educational programs, and support services for gifted learners. In the section that follows, we highlight some implications for practice.

Implications for Identification

In talent domains such as music, languages, and mathematics, exceptional ability and interest can be obvious as early as in the preschool years (Olszewski-Kubilius, Limburg-Weber, & Pfeiffer, 2003), particularly among children who have had early exposure through enrichment opportunities or private lessons. For these children, formal talent development can begin right away, including accelerated placements in school via grade or subject acceleration or early school entrance. Identification in other domains such as writing or science will be affected by several factors: (a) when abilities and interests emerge and coalesce sufficiently to be displayed and assessed, (b) assessment instruments or methods that yield valid inferences of potential are available, and (c) appropriate opportunities exist to expose students to the domain and develop interest and potential. For example, interest and aptitude for science might not emerge until middle or secondary school and may be evident in behaviors such as engaging in scientific experiments at home, displaying advanced knowledge on class assignments, or questioning of the teacher that indicates higher level thinking.

IQ and other tests of general cognitive ability can be good initial indicators of potential and exceptional ability at the earliest stages of talent development, but by middle school valid and reliable assessments of more specific abilities, such as verbal and mathematical reasoning ability or spatial ability, are better in determining placement and guiding students toward appropriate accelerative options within domains, especially when measures of achievement use above-grade-level scoring (Olszewski-Kubilius, 2015b). For example, tests such as the ACT, which have subtests in reading, math, science, and English, can assess exceptional domain-specific abilities and achievement in multiple areas beyond grade-level expectations.

Table 15. 2
Implications for Practice of Talent Development Framework

	Implications for Practice
Domain specific abilities	• IQ test and general ability tests are useful, especially with young children and with students who have had limited opportunities to learn (e.g., low-income students) • Domain-specific assessments need to be used no later than middle school but a variety of assessments can be used, depending upon the domain (e.g., tests, auditions and judgments by professionals and experts, portfolios) • Critical to match assessment to the domain of talent
Domain specific developmental trajectories	• Students need different kinds of instruction/programming at different stages of talent development (e.g., exposure via enrichment to domains for younger children, development of skills and competency within domains for older children, opportunities to pursue special interests via independent projects for secondary students) • Articulated sequence of programs K–12 within major domains that enable students to move ahead at a faster pace and provide continuous skill development • Early exposure to domains for all students via enrichment in early grades, especially for low-income students • Earlier exposure to some fields, such as philosophy or engineering, typically not studied until college • More varied program models for secondary students are needed (e.g., mentorships, research opportunities, apprenticeships)—beyond AP and IB. • Ways to capture late bloomers via enrichment or multiple entry points to talent development paths must be in place • Focus on talent development needs to extend beyond grade 12 • All teachers need deeper content expertise; secondary teachers need multiple content area expertise
Ability is malleable	• Ongoing assessment so as to identify late bloomers and students whose talents emerge later due to poverty or lack of early opportunity • Creation of multiple opportunities and multiple paths for students to enter gifted programs (e.g., testing and portfolios) • Intense frontloading of opportunities in early years for students from poverty and underidentified gifted students • Preparatory programs to help students qualify for school gifted programs • Reverse the typical process of "identification, followed by programming" to offering opportunities for the development of abilities first, followed by assessment for placement—especially critical for students who have had fewer opportunities to learn due to poverty, etc.

Table 15.2, *Continued.*

	Implications for Practice
Psychosocial characteristics are essential and teachable	• Must be actively and deliberately cultivated via programming, counseling, and mentoring of students • Must involve parents in assisting with psychosocial skill development at home • Develop a plan for what skills to focus on at different stages of talent development (e.g., attitudes toward effort and ability, attitudes toward competition, resiliency, and coping skills, a scholar identity) • Understand what psychosocial skills are most important for particular domains of talent (e.g., performing arts vs. academic domains)
Opportunity must be available and taken	• Programming and educational opportunities should be available earlier for all children, especially low-income children • Multiple types of opportunities for students at different stages of developed talent need to be available at every level of schooling in major domains (e.g., enrichment for students with emergent talent and motivation, acceleration for students with well-developed ability and high motivation) • Include children in programs with high motivation and achievement even if ability is somewhat lower
Creative productivity in adulthood and eminence are the desired outcomes	• Opportunities to engage in creative production must be available to students earlier • Cultivation of attitudes and mindsets (e.g., openness, risk-taking) conducive to being a creative producer needs to be deliberate and a part of programming • Emotional support for students choosing a path of creative productivity needs to be continuous • Programming for students needs to go beyond high school and extend into the postsecondary years of education and development

Note. Adapted from "Talent Development as a Framework for Gifted Education," by P. Olszewski-Kubilius and D. Thomson, 2015, *Gifted Child Today, 38,* p. 55. Copyright 2015 by Sage Publications. Reprinted with permission.

Identification methods that closely mirror performance, such as auditions judged by experts and professionals, are used in theater, dance, or music, and product portfolios can be used in the visual arts (Subotnik et al., 2011). Even in some academic domains, such as writing or science, examples of creative writing pieces or lab reports can be used in identifying exceptional ability or talent, in lieu of or along with scores on standardized tests and grades (Johnsen, 2004). The ultimate goal is to find a strong match between the domain of ability and the assessment tools employed.

Under the talent development framework, as students get older and have had opportunities for instruction in the domain, there should be an increased emphasis on demonstrated achievement, interest, and motivation as evidence of giftedness. Although educators should always be watchful for late bloomers, by high school, demonstrated achievement and willingness to engage in study and practice within and outside of school should be given equal or even greater emphasis than test scores in selecting students for domain-oriented talent development programs.

Identifying potential among children who come from low-socioeconomic backgrounds and/or culturally and linguistically different backgrounds will require some special techniques. Best practice for these students under a talent development model include the following:

- *Assessment that is continuous, meaning educators are always looking for indications of exceptional potential, because ability is affected by opportunity.* These indicators can include test scores at every administration to identify students showing exceptional growth, logs of student behaviors that indicate advanced reasoning, or exceptional student products via portfolios. Identification systems that assess students at only one point in time with one set of instruments will miss many children whose talents become obvious later, often as a result of increased access to enrichment that sparks motivation and interest (e.g., children whose abilities are expressed in nontraditional ways such as creative oral storytelling). Treffinger, Young, Nassab, and Wittig (2004) proposed the Levels of Service model, which recognizes differences in students' readiness for types of gifted services by recommending acceleration and advanced classes as well as enrichment opportunities.
- *Procedures and policies that allow for different, multiple paths into gifted and advanced programs.* These paths might include qualifying for an advanced or accelerated program on the basis of test scores or, alternatively, via outstanding performance in a preparatory program, such as a pre-AP or pre-IB program (see the Nexus and Middle Years programs in Olszewski-Kubilius & Clarenbach, 2012), as well as the use of several, varied measures (e.g., test scores and/or portfolios of actual work; Olszewski-Kubilius & Clarenbach, 2012).

- *Selection procedures that take into consideration students' previous opportunities to learn.* This could involve using local, school, or district norms, which results in identifying students who demonstrate the highest levels of achievement compared to others with similar backgrounds and previous educational experiences (Lohman, 2005; Lohman & Lakin, 2008; Worrell & Erwin, 2011).
- *Reversing the typical order of "identify giftedness first, then provide opportunities" to "provide opportunities first, followed by assessment for placement and further service,"* especially for students from poverty (Olszewski-Kubilius & Clarenbach, 2012).

Implications for Programming

Because assessment of talent changes over time as students transition from potential to competency to expertise under the talent development framework, programming should change also. For younger children, enrichment in all domains that is challenging will define interests and develop motivation, thereby helping parents and educators to discern emerging abilities. Programming that focuses on acquiring foundational, domain-specific knowledge and techniques through all forms of acceleration and enrichment is optimal for elementary and middle school students. Early entrance to school, fast-paced classes, subject and grade acceleration, as well as enrichment seminars, afterschool clubs, and contests and competitions *within domains* are all viable options. Secondary students should be allowed to pursue programs of study that focus and specialize in their domains of interest and ability, via AP and IB courses and opportunities to pursue independent projects with adult professionals, including mentorships and apprenticeships that give them a taste of more realistic work in a domain. Enrichment at this stage could also consist of exposing students earlier to some domains of talent typically not studied until college, such as sociology, philosophy, or engineering. Clubs and competitions can also be integrated into talent development programming.

Research has documented the importance of a rich variety of school-based and outside-of-school, domain-specific educational opportunities for adult success and achievement (Wai et al., 2010). At all stages of talent development, in-school opportunities should be supplemented with outside-of-school programs. Schools can offer some of these but can also help by directing gifted students to other outside-of-school, supplemental opportunities at local community organizations such as Boys and Girls Clubs, museums, and universities. Educators can also work with other institutions to support and develop collaborative programming.

It is also important that the programming be at the appropriate level for students who are at different stages of talent development, regardless of age, and that programing be available at every level of schooling. Appropriate programming can include ongoing enrichment opportunities for "late bloomers" through afterschool clubs and enrichment and intense, challenging, content-rich preparatory programs that aim to enable students who have had fewer opportunities to learn to "catch up" and qualify for subsequent gifted programming (Olszewski-Kubilius & Clarenbach, 2012). Also, some learners will not discover their passions or interests until later or may have talent for domains in which formal instruction and training begins later (e.g., psychology, philosophy). These students still require access to advanced courses and outside-of school programs during their K–12 years.

Implications for Social, Emotional, and Psychological Development

Under the talent development framework, psychosocial skills are considered (a) essential to the fruition of ability into achievement, with particular skills being more important at particular stages of talent development and for particular domains of talent (e.g., performance areas such as sports or music versus academic domains; Olszewski-Kubilius et al., 2015); and (b) teachable and coachable.

Gifted education specialists can help children acquire these psychosocial skills by consciously building their development into the educational programs and counseling they provide. They can make sure they convey appropriate messages about the role of effort versus ability in their feedback to students (Dweck, 2008). Teachers can assure that challenging academic experiences are provided, coupled with support, particularly when children take intellectual risks or move to a more challenging and competitive academic environment. They can model resiliency and actively teach coping strategies for dealing with perceived failures, anxiety and fears, and temporary declines in academic self-concept.

Active discussion of biographies and films of gifted individuals in different domains can be used to both illustrate varied talent development paths and the responses of gifted individuals to obstacles such as feeling different, or even bullying (Hébert, 2009). School counselors, school psychologists, and social workers can be called on to work with gifted children who are being victimized or suffer from debilitating anxiety or perfectionism (e.g., Worrell & Young, 2011). Other often untapped resources include the expertise from sport psychologists, coaches, bandleaders, theater instructors, and others who work with students in performance domains to learn their techniques for dealing with performance anxiety and fear of competition. The development of psychosocial skills must be pursued as assiduously as cognitive skills because of their importance to gifted students' ultimate psychological health and success.

Conclusion

Talent development offers a framework for gifted education that puts greater focus on domain-specific abilities and achievement. It promotes the view that giftedness is a process or path that starts with potential and moves, with opportunities provided and effort expended, to higher level expression of talent. Because of these basic tenets, gifted education moves from being a single program to being a set of services designed to identify potential and nurture it to increasingly higher levels of achievement.

Big Ideas

1. The talent development framework puts a greater emphasis on domain-specific abilities than general intelligence, particularly at higher stages of talent development.

2. Within the talent development framework, abilities are seen as malleable.

3. The talent development framework views giftedness as developmental, which starts with potential, moves to competency and expertise, and at the highest stages, takes the form of eminent levels of creative productivity.

4. The two levers that enable gifted children to progress to higher stages of talent development are talent development opportunities and psychosocial skills training.

5. Under the talent development framework, programming should match the stage of talent development. Early enrichment is important for young children to ferret out talents and interests, followed by programming that builds foundational skills and knowledge. At higher stages of talent development, exposure to the culture of the talent domain through internships and authentic work is critical. Creativity should be fostered at all stages of talent development.

6. Psychosocial skills such as risk-taking, the ability to respond positively to challenge and competition, coping skills, persistence in the face of failure and setbacks, and growth mindsets are critical to talent development, especially at later stages.

7. The psychosocial skills that are important at each stage of talent development vary, and these can be developed and coached by teachers and parents.

8. Under the talent development framework, the designation of giftedness is always relative to others with whom an individual is being compared.

Discussion Questions

1. The talent development framework proposes that *preparation for* eminent levels of achievement and creative production should be the goal of gifted education. Do you agree? Why or why not?

2. The talent development framework emphasizes achievement and motivation rather than ability as hallmarks of giftedness, particularly as children progress to *higher* stages of development. What is your view on the role of demonstrated achievement in defining giftedness?

3. The talent development framework emphasizes the active development of psychosocial skills that support achievement rather than psychological traits inherent in giftedness. Where do you stand on this issue?

References

Baudson, T. J., & Preckel, F. (2013). Teachers' implicit theories about the gifted: An experimental approach. *School Psychology Quarterly, 28,* 37–46.

Dai, D. Y. (2010). *The nature and nurture of giftedness: A new framework for understanding gifted education.* New York, NY: Teachers College Press.

Dai, D. Y. (2011). Hopeless anarchy or saving pluralism? Reflections on our field in response to Ambrose, VanTassel-Baska, Coleman, and Cross. *Journal for the Education of the Gifted, 34,* 705–731.

Dai, D. Y., & Chen, F. (2014). *Paradigms of gifted education.* Waco, TX: Prufrock Press.

Daniels, S., & Piechowski, M. M. (2009). *Living with intensity.* Scottsdale, AZ: Great Potential Press.

Delisle, J. (2012). A defining moment. *Ohio Association for Gifted Children Review,* 13–14.

Dweck, C. S. (2008). *Mindset: The new psychology of success.* New York, NY: Ballantine.

Dweck, C. S. (2012). Mindsets and malleable minds: Implications for giftedness and talent. In R. F. Subotnik, A. Robinson, C. M. Callahan, & P. Johnson (Eds.), *Malleable minds: Translating insights from psychology and neuroscience to gifted education* (pp. 7–18). Storrs: University of Connecticut, The National Center for Research on Giftedness and Talent.

Ericsson, K. A., Nandagopal, K., & Roring, R. W. (2005). Giftedness viewed from the expert-performance perspective. *Journal for the Education of the Gifted, 28,* 287–311.

Erwin, J. O. (2015). Prevalence and impact of peer victimization among gifted children (Doctoral dissertation). Available from ProQuest Dissertations and Theses database. (UMI No. 3720478)

Farrington, C. A., Roderick, M., Allensworth, E., Nagaoka, J., Keyes, T. S., Johnson, D. W., & Beechum, N. O. (2012). *Teaching adolescents to become learners. The role of noncognitive factors in shaping school performance: A critical literature review.* Chicago, IL: University of Chicago Consortium on Chicago School Research.

Gavin, M. K., Casa, T. M., Firmender, J. M., & Carroll, S. R. (2013). The impact of advanced geometry and measurement curriculum units on the mathematics achievement of first-grade students. *Gifted Child Quarterly, 37,* 71–84.

Gottfredson, L. S. (1997). Mainstream science on intelligence: An editorial with 52 signatories, history, and bibliography. *Intelligence, 24,* 25–52. doi:10.1016/S0160-2896(97)90011-8

Hébert, P. (2009). Guiding gifted teenagers to self-understanding through biography. In J. L. VanTassel-Baska, T. L. Cross, & F. R. Olenchak (Eds.), *Social-emotional curriculum with gifted and talented students* (pp. 259–287). Waco, TX: Prufrock Press.

Horn, C. V. (2015). Young Scholars: A talent development model for finding and nurturing potential in underserved populations. *Gifted Child Today, 38,* 19–31.

Johnsen, S. K. (Ed.). (2004). *Identifying gifted students: A practical guide.* Waco, TX: Prufrock Press.

Lohman, D. F. (2005). The role of nonverbal ability tests in identifying academically gifted students: An aptitude perspective. *Gifted Child Quarterly, 49,* 111–138.

Lohman, D. F., & Lakin, J. (2008). Nonverbal test scores as one component of an identification system: Integrating ability, achievement, and teacher ratings. In J. VanTassel-Baska (Ed.), *Alternative assessments with gifted and talented students* (pp. 41–66). Waco, TX: Prufrock Press.

Matthews, D. J., & Foster, J. F. (2006). Mystery to mastery: Shifting paradigms in gifted education. *Roeper Review, 28,* 64–69.

Neihart, M. (1999). The impact of giftedness on psychological well-being: What does the empirical literature say? *Roeper Review, 22,* 10–17. doi:10.1080/02783199909553991

Nisbett, R. E., Aronson, J., Blair, C., Dickens, W., Flynn, J., Halpern, D. F., & Turkheimer, E. (2012). Intelligence: New findings and theoretical developments. *American Psychologist, 67,* 130–159. doi:10.1037/a0026699

Olszewski-Kubilius, P. (2015a). The role of out-of-school programs in talent development for secondary students. In F. A. Dixon & S. M. Moon (Eds.), *The handbook of secondary gifted education* (2nd ed., pp. 261–282). Waco, TX: Prufrock Press.

Olszewski-Kubilius, P. (2015b). Talent searches and accelerated programming for gifted students. In S. Assouline, N. Colangelo, J. VanTassel-Baska, & A. Lupkowski-Shoplik (Eds.), *A nation empowered: Evidence trumps the excuses holding back America's brightest students* (Vol. 2; pp. 111–122). Iowa City: The University of Iowa, The Connie Belin & Jacqueline N. Blank International Center for Gifted Education and Talent Development.

Olszewski-Kubilius, P., & Clarenbach, J. (2012). *Unlocking emergent talent: Supporting high achievement of low-income, high-ability students.* Washington, DC: National Association for Gifted Children.

Olszewski-Kubilius, P., Kulieke, M. J., & Krasney, N. (1989). Personality dimensions of gifted adolescents: A review of the empirical literature. *Gifted Child Quarterly, 32,* 347–352.

Olszewski-Kubilius, P., Limburg-Weber, L., & Pfeiffer, S. (Eds.). (2003). *Early gifts: Recognizing and nurturing children's talent.* Waco, TX: Prufrock Press.

Olszewski-Kubilius, P., Subotnik, R. F., & Worrell, F. C. (2015). Conceptualizations of giftedness and the development of talent: Implications for counselors. *Journal of Counseling and Development, 93,* 143–153. doi:10.1002/j.1556-6676.2015.00190.x

Olszewski-Kubilius, P., & Thomson, D. (2015). Talent development as a framework for gifted education. *Gifted Child Today, 38,* 49–59.

Park, G., Lubinski, D., & Benbow, C. P. (2007). Contrasting intellectual patterns predict creativity in the arts and sciences: Tracking intellectually precocious youth over 25 years. *Psychological Science, 18,* 948–952. doi:10.1111/j.1467-9280.2007.02007.x

Peters, S. J., Matthews, M., McBee, M., T., & McCoach, D. B. (2014). *Beyond gifted education: Designing and implementing advanced academic programs.* Waco, TX: Prufrock Press.

Plucker, J. A., Burroughs, N., & Song, R. (2010). *Mind the (other) gap! The growing excellence gap in K–12 education.* Bloomington: Indiana University, School of Education, Center for Evaluation and Education Policy.

Plucker, J. A., Hardesty, J., & Burroughs, N. (2014). *Talent on the sidelines: Excellence gaps and America's persistent talent underclass.* Storrs: University of Connecticut, Center for Education Policy Analysis.

Reis, S. M., McCoach, D. B., Little, C. A., Muller, L. M., & Kaniskan, R. B. (2011). The effects of differentiated instruction and enrichment pedagogy on reading achievement in five elementary schools. *American Educational Research Journal, 48,* 462–501.

Renzulli, J., & Reis, S. M. (2014). *The Schoolwide Enrichment Model: A how-to guide for talent development* (3rd ed.). Waco, TX: Prufrock Press.

Rinn, A. N., & Bishop, J. (2015). Gifted adults: A systematic review and analysis of the literature. *Gifted Child Quarterly, 59,* 213–235. doi:10.1177/0016 986215600795

Schroth, S. T., Collins, C. L., & Treffinger, D. J. (2012). Talent development: From theoretical conceptions to practical applications. In T. L. Cross & J. R. Cross (Eds.), *Handbook for counselors serving students with gifts and talents: Development, relationships, school issues, and counseling needs/interventions* (pp. 39–52). Waco, TX: Prufrock Press.

Subotnik, R. F., & Jarvin, L. (2005). Beyond expertise: Conceptions of giftedness as great performance. In R. J. Sternberg & J. E. Davidson (Eds.), *Conceptions of giftedness* (2nd ed., pp. 343–357). New York, NY: Cambridge University Press.

Subotnik, R. F., Olszewski-Kubilius, P., & Worrell, F. C. (2011). Rethinking giftedness and gifted education: A proposed direction forward based on psychological science. *Psychological Science in the Public Interest, 12,* 3–54. doi:10.1177/1529100611418056

Subotnik. R. F., Pillmeier, E., & Jarvin, L. (2009). The psychosocial dimensions of creativity in mathematics. In R. Leikin, A. Berman, & B. Koichu (Eds.), *Creativity in mathematics and the education of gifted students* (pp. 165–179). Rotterdam, Netherlands: Sense.

Tannenbaum, A. (2009). Defining, determining, discovering, and developing excellence. In J. S. Renzulli, E. J. Gubbins, K. S. McMillen, R. D. Eckert, & C. A. Little (Eds.) *Systems and models for developing programs for the gifted and talented* (2nd ed., pp. 503–570). Waco, TX: Prufrock Press.

Treffinger, D. J., Young, G. C., Nassab, C. A., & Wittig, C. V. (2004). *Enhancing and expanding gifted programs: The levels of service approach.* Waco, TX: Prufrock Press.

VanTassel-Baska, J., Bracken, B., Feng, A., & Brown, E. (2009). A longitudinal study of enhancing critical thinking and reading comprehension in Title 1 classrooms. *Journal of the Education of the Gifted, 33,* 7–37.

Wai, J., Lubinski, D., & Benbow, C. P. (2005). Creativity and occupational accomplishments among intellectually precocious youths: An age 13 to age 33 longitudinal study. *Journal of Educational Psychology, 97,* 484–492. doi:10. 1037/0022-0663.97.3.484

Wai, J., Lubinski, D., & Benbow, C. P. (2009). Spatial ability for STEM domains: Aligning over 50 years of cumulative psychological knowledge solidifies its importance. *Journal of Educational Psychology, 101,* 817–835.

Wai, J., Lubinski, D., Benbow, C. P., & Steiger, J. H. (2010). Accomplishment in science, technology, engineering, and mathematics (STEM) and its relation to STEM educational dose: A 25-year longitudinal study. *Journal of Educational Psychology, 102,* 860–871. doi:10.1037/a0019454

Worrell, F. C. (2014). Ethnically diverse students. In J. A. Plucker & C. M. Callahan (Eds.), *Critical issues and practices in gifted education: What the research says* (2nd ed., pp. 237–254). Waco, TX: Prufrock Press.

Worrell, F. C. (2015). Being gifted and adolescent: Issues and needs of diverse students. In F. A. Dixon & S M. Moon (Eds.), *The handbook of secondary gifted education* (2nd ed., pp. 121–153). Waco, TX: Prufrock Press.

Worrell, F. C., & Erwin, J. O. (2011). Best practices in identifying students for gifted and talented education (GATE) programs. *Journal of Applied School Psychology, 27,* 319–340. doi:10.1080/15377903.2011.615817

Worrell, F. C., & Young, A. E. (2011). Gifted children in urban settings. In T. L. Cross & J. R. Cross (Eds.), *Handbook for counselors serving students with gifts and talents: Development, relationships, school issues, and counseling needs/interventions* (pp. 137–151). Waco, TX: Prufrock Press.

CHAPTER 16

Creativity

*Definitions, Interventions,
and Assessments*

Jonathan A. Plucker and Jiajun Guo

Creativity is a wild mind and a disciplined eye.—Dorothy Parker

Essential Questions to Guide the Reader

1. How is creativity defined?

2. What are the primary models for understanding creativity and how it emerges?

3. How can long-term creative productivity be fostered?

4. What are the major strategies for assessing creativity in educational settings?

From creating works of art to finding medical cures, from restoring and improving urban infrastructure to generating new energy sources, the ability to produce and implement new, useful ideas is a critical skill for solving problems and increasing quality of life. Creativity is widely acknowledged to be an important 21st-century skill and is included in many countries' lists of desired college and career-ready outcomes for students. For example, creativity is included in the Partnership for 21st Century Skills' *Framework for 21st Century Learning* as a key Learning and Innovation Skill (Partnership for 21st Century Skills, 2015), and creativity is included in similar frameworks in several other countries such as New Zealand, the United Kingdom, and China.

Over the past half-century, many countries' economies have moved rapidly from being largely manufacturing-based to knowledge-based to innovation-based. This transition has been so profound and emphasizes innovation so strongly that several countries such as China have focused much of their economic planning and policies on education for creativity (e.g., Pang & Plucker, 2013). The innovation economy makes the ability to solve problems creatively a necessary skill for educational and workforce success. In an age when most of humanity's information can be quickly accessed on a smartphone, the ability to use that knowledge in creative ways to produce valuable outcomes and solve complex problems is a highly valued skill. The ability to innovate leads to positive outcomes in the workplace, the classroom, the playground, and the family room.

However, the conventional wisdom is that creativity cannot be defined, people do not know how to increase it, and it cannot be assessed. This conventional wisdom could not be more wrong: Creativity has been well-defined, researchers and educators have several promising interventions, and creative assessments are plentiful. The purpose of this chapter is to help educators and parents make sense of the available theory and research, reviewing conceptual, enhancement, and assessment issues in educational settings.

Conceptual Issues

Definitions

Although the term *creativity* has only been used for roughly 140 years, humans have been fascinated with the creative process at least as far back as the early Greeks. The large-scale, scientific study of creativity did not emerge until the decade after World War II, due in large part to an increased emphasis on creativity research within psychology and a surge in interest regarding scientific creativity in the post-Sputnik era. The centuries of popular interest in creativity combined with the relatively recent growth in the science of creativity have led to a preponderance of myths and legends about creativity, with one of the most enduring being that no common definition of the term exists.

However, creativity has been well-defined, both explicitly and implicitly, for decades. For example, Stein (1953) defined creativity as "a novel work that is accepted as tenable or useful or satisfying by a group in some point in time" (p. 311). Over time, nearly all definitions have included both novelty and usefulness in some form, with the stipulation that creativity involves *both* characteristics. In other words, "different" does not mean "creative."

Creative = novel and useful

But these definitions are not without their weaknesses. Perhaps the main drawback is that the classic definition does not acknowledge the tremendous amount of theoretical and empirical work on the contextual nature of creativity, learning, and the human experience more generally (e.g., Glăveanu, 2013; Plucker & Barab, 2005). A focus on context could help address the "eye of the beholder" phenomenon, in which many people believe creativity cannot be defined, let alone fostered or assessed, because it is such a relative construct.

In an effort to address these concerns, Plucker, Beghetto, and Dow (2004) proposed a new definition combining the unique-and-useful conceptualization with advances in learning theory and situated cognition: "Creativity is the interaction among aptitude, process, and environment by which an individual or group produces a perceptible product that is both novel and useful as defined within a social context" (p. 90).

This definition, which has been widely adopted in the literature, broadens yet contextualizes the traditional definition in several ways. For the purposes of this chapter, the social context aspect of the definition is most important: It emphasizes that judgments about creativity don't happen in a vacuum, and that the context in which the behaviors occur strongly influences evaluations of creativity. For example, the same product may be creative in a third-grade classroom but not creative in an engineering firm; conversely, the firm may have a product that is highly creative in their professional context but has no usefulness at all in the third-grade classroom.

Models/Types of Creativity

Several models have been developed to help us understand and enhance creativity.[1] (See Table 16.1). The first major model, which remains in widespread use, is Rhodes' (1961) Four-P model. Rhodes noticed that creativity could be conceptualized as four distinct yet overlapping components: *person, process, product,* and *press. Person* takes into account aspects of an individual that make her different from others, such as personality, ability, thinking style, attitude, and behavior. *Process* focuses on creative thinking, stages and phases of the creative process, and the causes of creative behaviors. *Product* is the end result of the creative process, which includes not only perceptible items such as buildings, paintings, and inventions, but also creative ideas that can be embodied into tangible forms. *Press,* or *Place,* refers to the ecological environment in which creative people find themselves.

The Four-P model's straightforward nature is almost certainly the reason for its enduring popularity, and it is a helpful framework for thinking about creativity. But in real life, the four components are often intertwined and difficult to disentangle. The Four-C model (Kaufman & Beghetto, 2009) in an effort to avoid this problem, proposes four different levels of creative accomplishment: *Big-C*: eminent creativity;

---

1   Readers interested in a more detailed review of models and theories are referred to comprehensive reviews such as Runco (2014) and Runco and Pritzker (2011).

Table 16.1
Model of Creativity

Model Name	Components	Primary Citation
Four-P Model	Person, Process, Product, and Press	(Rhodes, 1961)
Four-C Model	Big-C, Pro-c, little-c, and mini-c	(Kaufman & Beghetto, 2009)
Five-A Model	Actor, Action, Artifact, Audience, and Affordance	(Glăveanu, 2013)

Pro-c: creativity of professionals who have not yet attained eminent status; *little-c*: creativity dealing with daily activities and experiences; and *mini-c*: creativity involving the novel and personally meaningful insights and interpretations in learning and experience.

The Four-C model is popular, although some questions remain unanswered. For example, how do tools and materials (an element of press/environment in the Four-P model), such as the recent development of information technologies, play a role in shaping creativity? What is the influence of peers and colleagues on creativity achievement at different levels of the Four-Cs? Glăveanu (2013) approached this topic from a sociocultural perspective and proposed the Five-A framework, including *Actor*, *Action*, *Artifact*, *Audience*, and *Affordance*. Although this framework looks very different from the Four-P and Four-C models, three of the components in the Five-A and Four-P models have almost identical meanings (e.g., person ≈ actor, process ≈ action, product ≈ artifact). The primary differences come from the last two components—*Audience* and *Affordance*—which can be viewed as subcomponents of Press (or environment). Specifically, *Audience* refers to the social aspect of the environment, and *Affordance* refers to the material aspect of the environment. In educational settings, the former can be teachers' and peers' reviews and comments, and the latter can be resources such as books, computers, and online resources.

The neurological underpinnings of creativity are also widely researched and modeled. Unfortunately, a model has yet to emerge with enough evidence to gather a general consensus among neuroscientists and creativity researchers (Dietrich & Kanso, 2010). At the moment, the most well-accepted neurological model for creativity is Martindale's (1999) theory of cognitive disinhibition. According to Martindale, the frontal lobe of the brain is responsible for the inhibition of creative behavior, implying that humans are naturally creative, but our brains tone down our creativity so that we may function in day-to-day life. In experimental situations, those who are more creative show *less* activation in the frontal lobes—meaning their brains are doing less to "tone down" the natural creativity.

Enhancement

Educators seeking to foster their students' creativity are faced with a tricky paradox: We know of several effective strategies for enhancing student creativity in schools, yet few people attribute their creativity later in life to their school experiences—implying that we are not doing all we can to help students realize their creative potential.

Indeed, many researchers believe that school experiences suppress a child's creativity. For example, creative students, who can be nonconforming, compulsive, and emotional, are often not what a teacher thinks of as an ideal student (Westby & Dawson, 1995). Research also suggests that there is a significant drop in creative thinking that occurs in approximately half of the children in fourth grade—the so-called fourth grade slump (Torrance, 1967, 1968). However, not all children experience such a slump, especially gifted students, and the slump may occur at different points during childhood and adolescence in different cultures (Nash, 1974; Yi, Hu, Plucker, & McWilliams, 2013). What remains certain is that education and the experiences that children gain in school can impact students' creativity. This section summarizes recent work on research-based strategies and methods of creativity enhancement, ranging from relatively straightforward classroom-based strategies, such as attitude change and ideational training, to those requiring external resources, such as the use of technology and partnerships with creative practitioners.

Pedagogical Techniques

The first set of strategies can be classified as classroom-based or pedagogical techniques. These techniques require careful preparation and planning so that they can be integrated into the established curriculum. Two or more of these techniques can be combined to heighten the chance of success with students.

Fostering creative attitudes. Not all creativity is deliberate. However, the likelihood of fulfilling creative potentials greatly increases if they are intentionally targeted and enhanced (Runco, 2014). In fact, most creative achievements are the result of hard work and considerable time rather than a brief flash of insight (e.g., the "Aha!" moment). Unfortunately, many people, including both students and teachers, tend to hold some mystical views about creativity, contending that their unconscious, or Muse, is the source of inspiration while ignoring the role of intentionality and choice behind creative acts.

Similar myths have been identified by Plucker et al. (2004), who argued that creativity has long been subject to a number of inaccurate beliefs. Specifically, they described four prevalent myths. First, the myth that people are born creative or uncreative, which yields an inaccurate conclusion that creativity is an innate ability that cannot be taught. Second, the myth that creativity is intertwined with negative aspects of psychology, and society evokes the image of a mad genius with neurotic tendencies. Third, the myth that creativity is a fuzzy, soft construct, leading people to believe that creative behavior resides in the world of pop psychology and is not worthy of scientific scrutiny or empirically supported interventions. Fourth, the myth that creativity is always enhanced within a group, which leads to the belief that if more people work together, more ideas will be produced, and creativity will be enhanced.

These myths are detrimental to both personal (e.g., the development of one's unique talents; Silvia et at., 2014) and external (e.g., the enhancement of creativity in schools) creative processes. Given that attitudes toward creativity begin to develop in schools, educators can start to tackle these myths in educational settings. One way to tackle this problem is to provide students with the correct creativity "schema" as supported by scientific research (Plucker & Dow, 2010). Of course, teachers' attitudes toward creativity need to be changed as well, which in turn may influence students' attitudes and creative thinking (Grohman & Szmidt, 2013). In addition, other more general beliefs, such as beliefs about the nature of knowledge, may also impact teachers' creativity instruction. For example, teachers who perceive their instruction as enhancing student learning rather than merely presenting factual knowledge are more likely to infuse creativity into their teaching practice (Hong, Hartzell, & Greene, 2009).

Developing creative ideation. Ideation, or divergent thinking (DT), refers to the ability to generate multiple responses or solutions to a problem. It is regarded as an important indicator of creativity (Runco & Acar, 2012). Ideation has been scientifically investigated for more than six decades, especially in the area of assessment. Divergent thinking training is also a widely used intervention for enhancing the number and quality of students' ideas. The goal of DT training is to increase fluency (number of ideas), flexibility (the extent to which ideas are different from each other), originality (novelty of ideas), and elaboration (number of details generated).

Divergent thinking training can be used for different domains and has proven to be effective (Pyryt, 1999). For example, Baer (1996) used divergent thinking training in poetry, and creativity on a subsequent poetry writing task was significantly improved. As a result, he suggested that ideational training should focus on skills related to the task domain in order to improve creative performance. If a teacher wants to improve creative performance on different types of tasks, then the training should use a wide range of content in a variety of ideational exercises. Along the same line, Pang (2015) proposed several ideational tasks for different subjects that could promote creativity in classrooms. Students can be encouraged to interpret texts in different ways and to construct their own storylines in reading and writing class; math teachers could show students how to solve a problem using nontraditional methods so that risk-taking and creative thinking are encouraged; in science class, instructors could demonstrate the nature of constructing science knowledge by asking students to form and test their own hypotheses in an experiment; in art and music classes, students could design, compose, and create their own works with the help of a variety of tools (e.g., music and picture editing software).

Another way to encourage creative ideation, as proposed by Beghetto (2013), focuses on the role of teachers' responses to students' comments. Beghetto (2013) argued that teachers should recognize and respond to the opportunities provided by the unexpected and surprising ideas emerging in everyday practices and preplanned activities. These opportunities are called Micro-Moments (MM). Unlike the DT training method, the MM approach does not require that teachers make a detailed plan of how to encourage students to come up with as many "wild" ideas as possible. Rather, it asks teacher to expect the unexpected during planned lessons. Despite the fact that this would bring uncertainty to the established curricula, unexpected ideas can be task appropriate and perhaps more meaningful than, for instance, assigned brainstorming tasks. Although not yet supported empirically, the MM approach is reasonable and theoretically supported.

Play-based and game-based intervention. There is evidence that play-oriented or game-based approaches can support creativity development for people of different ages. This technique has received strong support because games are a common everyday activity that can be incorporated into almost any instructional practice. Russ (2014), for example, made a compelling case for pretend play and has suggested methods to conduct an intervention, suggesting that pretend play may provide important practice solving real-world problems and processing emotions, both of which foster creativity (Russ & Wallace, 2013). Other researchers have implemented interventions either based solely on pretend play (Garaigordobil, 2006) or that incorporate pretend play as part of a broader creativity intervention (Alfonso-Benlliure, Meléndez, & García-Ballesteros, 2013).

Although imaginative and pretend play have been shown to be particularly effective, other forms of play also boost creativity. For example, Cumming (2007) observed that, when endorsed and encouraged by teachers, students will interact eagerly with poetry and display their creativity through word play (see also Cremin, Burnard, & Craft, 2006; Kangas, 2010).

The game-based approach is not without its challenges. Teachers may find it difficult to adopt and switch between a variety of roles (e.g., facilitator, instructor, learner), and use of digital or video games may prove distracting (Davies et al., 2013; Groff, Howells, & Cranmer, 2012; Kangas, 2010). Educators need to consider several factors including game selection, how games align with their teaching goals, monitoring gaming to minimize distraction, and cost-effectiveness compared to other pedagogies.

Creative modeling. Many human behaviors, including creativity, are learned by observing an appropriate model. Evidence supporting the effects of creative modeling comes from a variety of sources, including classroom-based instruction (Yi,

[handwritten margin note: Students must also have time to develop creativity]

Plucker, & Guo, 2015). By demonstrating creativity themselves, teachers are actually establishing a creative environment that can inspire students and encourage them to come up with novel ideas, to take risks, and to show meaningful self-expression (Beghetto & Kaufman, 2014).

Teachers need not be the only models. Simply presenting examples of creative work produced by others (e.g., peers, former students, adults in the community) can inspire students. For example, Belcher (1975) found that the children who observed original models obtained higher creativity scores than children who observed unoriginal models. A convincing body of research supports the use of models to enhance the creativity of both children and adults (Amabile, 1983; Hooker, Nakamura, & Csikszentmihalyi, 2003).

Facilitating peer collaboration. Peers can serve as sources of creative inspiration and thus supplement many of the roles traditionally thought to belong to teachers alone (Hooker et al., 2003). Nonetheless, extensive literature on group creativity suggests peers may hinder the creative process while at the same time giving the illusion of productivity (Paulus, 2000). Take brainstorming as an example, with research finding that people may be more productive in solitary ideation rather than group brainstorming due to a variety of issues, such as lack of accountability, social pressure, awareness of evaluation from group members, and competition for speaking time (Paulus & Brown, 2003).

Successful collaboration requires far more than a group discussion or division of labor. In order for group members to learn and solve problems together, collaboration should emphasize continuous mutual effort from group members, including idea exchange, collective goal setting and achieving, negotiation, and consideration of other social dynamics. Costantino (2015) argued that timely feedback delivered by friends and classmates is a powerful tool for teachers to facilitate a creative environment where students are more likely to focus on creative tasks and thus achieve creative goals. An effective feedback process is characterized by clear goal setting, effective communication, actionable suggestions, and active monitoring.

Not all students, however, may participate effectively in collaboration, especially in groups where there is a large difference in abilities, goals, and social skills. One way to balance these differences is to provide a "script" for students to play specific roles (such as consultant and presenter) so that they can learn more from cooperation and collaboration (O'Donnell, 1999). Overall, the teacher's guidance—including setting up guidelines, motivating students, preventing disrupting behaviors, modeling appropriate conversations, and keeping students focused—is necessary and beneficial to the facilitation of group creativity.

External Resources

Our current educational accountability systems still put a strong emphasis on achievement tests, which often marginalizes creativity instruction (Beghetto & Plucker, 2006). Furthermore, even though many teachers value and teach creativity in the classroom, this may be a time-consuming, uncomfortable, and stressful task (Cremin, 2006; Plucker & Beghetto, 2003). One way to deal with this issue is to provide students and teachers with external resources. In this way, Glăveanu's (2013) Five-A's model may offer a more detailed picture of how creativity can be cultivated. In his model, two subcomponents of creative environment—Audience and Affordance—come into play when the teacher alone does not satisfy these needs. Specifically, Affordance refers to the material needs of a creative environment, such as technology, while Audience refers to the social participant aspect of environment, such as creative community outside of school.

Technology. Technology offers students and teachers additional opportunities to engage with information. There have been numerous studies on this topic using a variety of technologies, and these studies clearly show that technology holds great potential to enhance and assist creativity in the classroom (Guo & Woulfin, 2016). One such benefit of technology is its capability to provide immediate external representation of complex information, such as the visualization of creative processes. This representation can help enable creative actors to review and modify, improve, or enhance their creative action. For example, by using motion tracking and real-time animation techniques, teachers can help children enhance their ability to do creative storytelling as well as potentially provide an opportunity to increase their general creative self-efficacy (Yee, 2015). In the STEM disciplines, visual-spatial ability is especially important because it is a strong predictor of performance in disciplines such as engineering, science, and designing. However, in a traditional school context, students with exceptional visual-spatial ability usually cannot reach their full potential due to a lack of educational opportunities or means. However, computer visualization tools, such as geographic information systems, may provide for high spatial thinkers to develop their creative talents (Andersen, 2014).

Another benefit of using technology in the classroom is the enhancement of communication and collaboration in creative activities (Dilley, Fishlock, & Plucker, 2015; Plucker, Kennedy, & Dilley, 2015). For example, in a video-making project, Pignéguy (2004) found that creating a video as a group could enable disaffected students to learn both how to creatively use technologies and how to effectively interact with other people. This shows that, for disadvantaged students at least, technology can be especially useful in promoting creativity (Halsey, Jones, & Lord, 2006). With the proliferation of handheld devices, students can engage in interactive and collaborative problem solving situated in complex and authentic classroom practice, such as in a simulated problem context (Dunleavy, Dede, & Mitchell, 2009). Besides, a collaborative assignment or project that involves out-of-school literacy practices using digital technologies also offers an opportunity for schools to harness their creativity (Walsh, 2007). This requires that teachers recognize and take advantage of students' digital competences acquired outside school, so that curriculum can be more aligned with students' creative skills.

Creative communities of practice. Another way to relieve a teacher's burden is to connect students with a creative community outside of school. There is strong evidence that taking students out of school to work with others in a professional environment or inviting creative practitioners into the classroom can greatly enhance children's creativity. Indeed, this is a key component of many models of gifted education, including the Schoolwide Enrichment Model (Renzulli, 1999) educational program. The researchers found that using external spaces as sites (such as art galleries) for learning could enable students to reconceptualize the creative process. Connecting students with a creative community can also offer students the opportunity to learn more about the institutional context out of school.

Assessment

Creativity has long been treated as a part of giftedness, with creativity assessment being used as a part of giftedness identification processes (Hunsaker & Callahan, 1995; Torrance, 1984). The following section begins with a discussion of how creativity assessment was brought to the mainstream by gifted education, followed by an analysis of major assessment techniques with an emphasis on their strengths and weaknesses.

Divergent Thinking Tests

There are few areas in psychology and education where creativity assessment has been more frequently used than gifted education, and those assessments have primarily been divergent thinking (DT) measures (Kaufman, Plucker, & Baer, 2008). The usefulness of DT tests made them so popular in education that people, especially those who didn't know much about creativity, began to equate divergent thinking with creativity, rather than as one component of it. As Kaufman, Plucker, and Baer (2008) argued, one of the great ironies of the study of creativity is that there is not much divergence in the history of creativity assessment because so much energy and time have been focused on a single class of assessments—measures of divergent thinking.

New developments. Over the course of several decades, Torrance (1974) refined the administration and scoring of the Torrance Tests of Creative Thinking (TTCT), which may account for its enduring popularity. There also have been new developments in terms of scoring DT tasks, and scores are no longer limited to the traditional four components (fluency, originality, flexibility, and elaboration). Some studies have suggested using alternative, summative scores (adding up all four component scores), highly uncommon scores (top 5% in originality), weighted fluency scores, and percentage scores (dividing originality scores by fluency scores; see Benedek, Mühlmann, Jauk, & Neubauer, 2013; Plucker, Qian, & Wang, 2011).

In addition to the development of new objective scoring methods, subjective assessment has also been recommended by some researchers such as Silvia, Martin, and Nusbaum (2009), who proposed that a holistic rating can be provided by neutral raters, therefore providing a "snapshot" of creativity. A combination of both objective and subjective methods has also been recommended (Plucker, Qian, & Schmalensee, 2014).

Critiques of DT tests. Nonetheless, there is mixed evidence and conflicting opinion as to the psychometric quality and practical importance of DT tests. On one hand, the DT tests are associated with evidence of reliability and concurrent validity (e.g., Kaufman, Plucker, & Baer, 2008; Torrance, 1968). Plucker (1999), for example, reanalyzed data from Torrance's longitudinal study and found that divergent thinking was much more predictive for how people differed in creative achievement than was traditional IQ. On the other hand, many scholars have questioned DT tests' predictive validity (Baer, 1993, 1994; Gardner, 1993; Kogan & Pankove, 1974; Weisberg, 1993). This has led researchers and educators to avoid using DT tests and, broadly, leads to criticisms of the psychometric study of creativity (Plucker & Renzulli, 1999). Another controversial aspect of DT assessment is that people tend to overgeneralize DT test performance to all other aspects of creativity, such as problem identification (Runco & Okuda, 1988; Wakefield, 1985) and evaluative thinking (Okuda, Runco, & Berger, 1991; Runco, 1991; Runco & Chand, 1994), which are distinct cognitive processes and not commonly a focus of DT assessments.

Given these criticisms, it is not surprising that DT tests fell from favor over the previous generation. But as Kaufman, Plucker, and Baer (2008) noted, many of these criticisms have been overstated, and much of the research cited above has significantly improved the quality of DT test information, making divergent thinking assessments a reasonable choice for identification purposes.

Teacher Checklists

Some investigators have suggested that creative giftedness can be identified in terms of how other people, especially teachers in the context of a classroom, perceive a student's characteristics. One feasible way to extract information from what teachers know about a child's creativity is to give them a checklist and ask them to complete it according to their own observation. Well-designed checklists provide teachers with a reliable and efficient way to summarize their perception of a student based on a large number of classroom observations across a wide range of creative tasks. This method usually assumes that creativity is domain-general, thus providing a global impression of a student's creative traits and characteristics.

The Creativity Checklist designed by Proctor and Burnett (2004) serves as a good example of this approach. The instrument consists of nine items, with a three-point Likert scale, that illustrate nine different types of personal creativity traits, including (1) fluent thinker, (2) flexible thinker, (3) original thinker, (4) elaborative thinker, (5) intrinsically motivated student, (6) curious student who becomes immersed in the task, (7) risk taker, (8) imaginative or intuitive thinker, and (9) student who engages in complex tasks and enjoys a challenge. Another example is the Scales for Rating the Behavioral Characteristics of Superior Students (SRBCSS), devised by Renzulli and his colleagues (2010), which can help teachers select students who are eligible for gifted programs, with creativity being one of the 10 areas that are not measured by intelligence measures. Some illustrative items include "imaginative thinking ability," "a sense of humor," and "the ability to come up with unusual, unique, or clever responses." Test-retest and interrater reliability have been found to be excellent for the SRBCSS creativity scale (Jarosewich, Pfeiffer, & Morris, 2002; Renzulli et al., 2010).

Critiques of teacher's checklists. As Kaufman, Plucker, and Russell (2012) noted, the validity of creativity checklists depends largely on teachers' knowledge about the student's creativity, and the instruments are clearly subjective in nature. Therefore, the use of teacher rating scales as stand-alone assessments of creativity is generally discouraged, but creativity checklists can be used in concert with other types of creativity assessments to provide a comprehensive description of students' creativity.

Self-Assessments

One problem associated with teacher's checklists is that children's creativity does not always manifest itself in school environments. Another option is to ask students themselves about what they have done creatively. One of the first creativity self-assessments, the Creative Behavior Inventory (CBI), was developed by Hocevar (1979, 1981). Ninety items reflecting activities and achievements that were considered to be creative were listed to measure creativity in domains like literature, music, crafts, art, math and science, and performing art. A short, 28-item version of the CBI was created by Dollinger (2003) and covers the four domains of literacy, visual arts, performing arts, and crafts. What has been deleted are those infrequent and high-level achievements, such as publishing scientific work or founding literary magazines. As a result, the new version mainly reflects everyday creativity (Silvia, Wigert, Reiter-Palmon, & Kaufman, 2012), which makes the revised CBI a better fit for K–12 gifted education.

Another self-assessment scale, the Creative Achievement Questionnaire (CAQ), asks questions about creative activities and achievement in 10 domains (Carson, Peterson, & Higgins, 2005). However, the CAQ employs a more complex scoring method, with participants asked to place checkmarks next to items describing their creative accomplishments. Each domain has eight "ranked" items weighted with a score from 0 to 7 based on the degree to which they represent creative achievement. In addition, some items involve writing a number, such as the number of published works, instead of a checkmark, so that the number can be used to increase the points.

Critiques of self-assessment. One of the merits of these self-reports is their convenience. Students can complete the assessment very quickly, usually in 5 to 10 minutes. The scoring method is also straightforward and can be completed without any special training. However, one potential problem of achievement checklists is that students, especially young children, may not have sufficient opportunity to amass a large number of creative achievements. This explains why achievement checklists occasionally yield highly skewed results—few can produce Big-C achievement (Silvia et al., 2012). To address the problem, Runco designed a measure of ideational behavior—the Runco Ideational Behavior Scale (RIBS)—to help people capture the kind of general ability that could be independent of resources, experience, opportunities, and domain-specific skills. The RIBS can be regarded as a self-assessment of divergent thinking, which of course is easier and faster to administer and score than DT tests. The RIBS has proved to be a reliable creativity measure, with more work needed to increase its construct validity (Runco, Plucker, & Lim, 2000–2001).

Consensual Assessment Technique

Amabile (1983) approached creativity assessment in a very different way by using a domain-specific approach to measure creativity. She initially intended to develop a reliable, subjective method for assessing group creativity in different domains such as art, design, and poetry, and she asked judges (including both experts and nonexperts) to assess products created by children. The acceptable levels of reliability evidence demonstrated in Amabile's studies led to widespread interest in her approach, named the Consensual Assessment Technique (CAT). The CAT also shows strong face validity; typically, it measures exactly what it looks like it measures (Kaufman, Baer, Cole, & Sexton, 2008). As Runco (1989) argued, evaluating creative products may address measurement problems caused by the inconsistent psychometric quality of DT tests. Although there had been a few previous examples regarding the assessment of creative products before the development of the CAT, this technique is currently the most popular way of assessing the creativity of products (Kaufman, Baer et al., 2008).

More specifically, several steps should be taken to apply a consensual assessment technique. First, judges who have some experience with the domain are recruited; then they are asked to rate creative works independently and in a random order, and they do not need to be trained to agree with each other. This lack-of-training approach allows judges to use their implicit definitions of creativity as they rate each work; judges should rate each work relative to one another rather than against some absolute standards, such as those great works in the domain.

The CAT has been widely used to assess creativity in different domains. For example, Amabile (1983) applied the technique to collage making and poem writing, and she found it to be a reliable technique. The technique has also been applied to the creativity assessment of musical compositions to divide students into high and low creativity groups (Priest, 2006). In nonexperimental contexts where individuals may receive different instructions, the CAT can also be used to assess creativity. For example, Baer, Kaufman, and Gentile (2004) collected more than 300 writings, including poetry, fictional stories, and personal narratives, drawn from the 1998 National Assessment of Educational Progress (NAEP) and asked 13 judges to rate them for creativity. High interrater reliability was obtained, suggesting that the CAT could even be used for creative products that are made under open or uncontrolled conditions.

Critiques of CAT method. The CAT is not without its share of controversies. First, it was originally intended to estimate the creativity of groups in social psychology experiments, not individual students in educational contexts. Second, the use of expert versus nonexpert judges has been debated, with no consensus yet emerging. For example, Kaufman, Baer, et al.'s (2008) study showed that when both novices and experts were asked to rate poems for creativity, novices tend to have more disagreement not only within the group but also with the expert group. But in another study, when individuals with relatively more knowledge were asked to rate movies, their ratings were more correlated with expert ratings compared to novice ratings (Plucker, Kaufman, Temple, & Qian, 2009). This suggests that experience, knowledge, or expertise should be considered as a continuum in selecting judges. In real-world situations where people have time and budget restrictions, "amateurs" or "quasi-experts" may be an ideal alternative to an expert (Kaufman & Baer, 2012). Another important factor to consider is the amount of knowledge needed for rating a work, which somehow is determined by domains. For example, the arts may be in the lower end of expertise requirement whereas creative work in physics or engineering may require a large amount of background knowledge. In that sense, the relative position between the rater and task is a reasonable criteria for judge recruitment.

Third, and perhaps most importantly, advocates for the CAT have often been outspoken in their criticism of other forms of creativity assessment, especially DT tests, for what they perceive to be mixed evidence of predictive validity (e.g., Baer,

1993). Yet the predictive power of CAT scores has yet to be convincingly determined, suggesting that a great deal of additional research still needs to be conducted.

Conclusion

In this chapter, both theoretical and practical issues about creativity in gifted education have been discussed. Society's conceptual understanding of creativity has advanced significantly over the past generation, with the use of common definitions and well-supported theories now the rule rather than the exception. The 5-A framework (Glăveanu, 2013), in particular, reflects advances in sociocultural theory and research in fields such as psychology, educational psychology, and the learning sciences.

The conceptual advances have been matched with significant progress regarding interventions. This chapter provides an overview of several research-supported strategies that can be used with gifted students to foster and enhance their creativity regardless of content area or educational setting. Regarding assessment, there is no single best measure for creativity, and each type of assessment has its own strengths and limitations. When using creativity assessments with gifted students, at least two types of measures should be used to increase the reliability of the information and guard against some of the instruments' weaknesses.

The field of creativity has made substantial progress over the past quarter century, and the vibrant nature of the field suggests that this progress is continuing. The start of the 21st century will almost certainly be looked upon as an era during which our understanding of creativity and how to foster it in children advanced significantly.

Big Ideas

1. Contrary to conventional wisdom, creativity is a well-defined, well-understood construct.

2. Theories of creative development have progressed substantially over the past 20 years.

3. Promising interventions for improving student creativity exist but are in need of further development.

4. Numerous, high-quality assessments for creativity have been developed and used in educational settings; they have not, however, been "scaled up" for use with very large numbers of students.

Discussion Questions

1. How does your personal definition of creativity compare to the standard definitions of creativity?

2. Which model for thinking about creativity, such as the 4-C, 4-P, or 5-A, is most helpful as you think about creativity?

3. How can various interventions for enhancing creativity be used in your instructional role(s)?

4. What are the strengths and weaknesses of each type of creativity assessment?

References

Alfonso-Benlliure, V., Meléndez, J. C., & García-Ballesteros, M. (2013). Evaluation of a creativity intervention program for preschoolers. *Thinking Skills and Creativity, 10,* 112–120. doi:10.1016/j.tsc.2013.07.005

Amabile, T. M. (1983). *The social psychology of creativity.* New York, NY: Springer-Verlag. doi:10.1007/978-1-4612-5533-8

Andersen, L. (2014). Visual-spatial ability: Important in STEM, ignored in gifted education. *Roeper Review, 36,* 114–121. doi:10.1080/02783193.2014.884198

Baer, J. (1993). Why you shouldn't trust creativity tests. *Educational Leadership, 51,* 80–83.

Baer, J. (1994). Divergent thinking is not a general trait: A multi-domain training experiment. *Creativity Research Journal, 7,* 35–46. doi:10.1080/10400419409534507

Baer, J. (1996). The effects of task-specific divergent thinking training. *Journal of Creative Behavior, 30,* 183–187. doi:10.1002/j.2162-6057.1996.tb00767.x

Baer, J., Kaufman, J. C., & Gentile, C. A. (2004). Extension of the consensual assessment technique to nonparallel creative products. *Creativity Research Journal, 16,* 113–117.

Beghetto, R. A. (2013). Expect the unexpected: Teaching for creativity in the micromoment. In M. B. Gregerson, H. T. Snyder, & J. C. Kaufman (Eds.), *Teaching creatively and teaching creativity* (pp. 133–148). New York, NY: Springer. doi:10.1007/978-1-4614-5185-3_10

Beghetto, R. A., & Kaufman, J. C. (2014). Classroom contexts for creativity. *High Ability Studies, 25,* 53–69. doi:10.1080/13598139.2014.905247

Beghetto, R. A., & Plucker, J. A. (2006). The relationship among schooling, learning, and creativity: "All roads lead to creativity" or "You can't get there from here"? In J. C. Kaufman & J. Baer (Eds.), *Creativity and reason in cognitive development* (pp. 316–332). New York, NY: Cambridge University Press.

Belcher, T. L. (1975). Modeling original divergent responses: An initial investigation. *Journal of Educational Psychology, 67,* 351–358. doi:10.1037/h0076614

Benedek, M., Mühlmann, C., Jauk, E., & Neubauer, A. C. (2013). Assessment of divergent thinking by means of the subjective top-scoring method: Effects of the number of top-ideas and time-on-task on reliability and validity. *Psychology of Aesthetics, Creativity, and the Arts, 7,* 341–349. doi:10.1037/a0033644

Carson, S. H., Peterson, J. B., & Higgins, D. M. (2005). Reliability, validity, and factor structure of the creative achievement questionnaire. *Creativity Research Journal, 17,* 37–50. doi:10.1207/s15326934crj1701_4

Costantino, T. (2015). Lessons from art and design education: The role of in-process critique in the creative inquiry process. *Psychology of Aesthetics, Creativity, and the Arts, 9,* 118–121. doi:10.1037/aca0000013

Cremin, T. (2006). Creativity, uncertainty and discomfort: Teachers as writers. *Cambridge Journal of Education, 36,* 415–433. doi:10.1080/03057640600866023

Cremin, T., Burnard, P., & Craft, A. (2006). Pedagogy and possibility thinking in the early years. *Thinking Skills and Creativity, 1,* 108–119. doi:10.1016/j.tsc.2006.07.001

Cumming, R. (2007). Language play in the classroom: Encouraging children's intuitive creativity with words through poetry. *Literacy, 41,* 93–101. doi:10.1111/j.1467-9345.2007.00463.x

Davies, D., Jindal-Snape, D., Collier, C., Digby, R., Hay, P., & Howe, A. (2013). Creative learning environments in education—A systematic literature review. *Thinking Skills and Creativity, 8,* 80–91. doi:10.1016/j.tsc.2012.07.004

Dietrich, A., & Kanso, R. (2010). A review of EEG, ERP, and neuroimaging studies of creativity and insight. *Psychological Bulletin, 136,* 822–848. doi:10.1037/a0019749

Dilley, A., Fishlock, J., & Plucker, J. A. (2015). *What we know about communication* [P21 Research Series]. Washington, DC: Partnership for 21st Century Skills. Available at http://www.p21.org/our-work/4cs-research-series/communication

Dollinger, S. J. (2003). Need for uniqueness, need for cognition and creativity. *The Journal of Creative Behavior, 37,* 99–116. doi:10.1002/j.2162-6057.2003.tb00828.x

Dunleavy, M., Dede, C., & Mitchell, R. (2009). Affordances and limitations of immersive participatory augmented reality simulations for teaching and learning. *Journal of Science Education & Technology, 18,* 7–22. doi:10.1007/s10956-008-9119-1

Garaigordobil, M. (2006). Intervention in creativity with children aged 10 and 11 years: Impact of a play program on verbal and graphic–figural creativity. *Creativity Research Journal, 18,* 329–345. doi:10.1207/s15326934crj1803_8

Gardner, H. (1993). *Creating minds.* New York, NY: Basic Books.

Glăveanu, V. P. (2013). Rewriting the language of creativity: The Five A's framework. *Review of General Psychology, 17,* 69–81. doi:10.1037/a0029528

Groff, J., Howells, C., & Cranmer, S. (2012). Console game-based pedagogy: A study of primary and secondary classroom learning through console videogames. *International Journal of Game-Based Learning, 2,* 35–54. doi:10.4018/ijgbl.2012040103

Grohman, M. G., & Szmidt, K. J. (2013). Teaching for creativity: How to shape creative attitudes in teachers and in students. In M. B. Gregerson, H. T. Snyder, & J. C. Kaufman (Eds.), *Teaching creatively and teaching creativity* (pp. 15–35). New York, NY: Springer. doi:10.1007/978-1-4614-5185-3_2

Guo, J., & Woulfin, S. (2016). 21st century creativity: An investigation of how the P21 instructional frameworks reflect the principles of creativity. *Roeper Review, 38,* 153–161.

Halsey, K., Jones, M., & Lord, P. (2006). *What works in stimulating creativity amongst socially excluded young people.* Slough, Berkshire: National Foundation for Educational Research. Retrieved from http://nfernew.dudobi.com/nfer/publications/NES01/NES01.pdf

Hocevar, D. (1979, April). *The development of the Creative Behavior Inventory (CBI).* Paper presented at the Annual Meeting of the Rocky Mountain Psychological Association.

Hocevar, D. (1981). Measurement of creativity: Review and critique. *Journal of Personality Assessment, 45,* 450–464. doi:10.1207/s15327752jpa4505_1

Hong, E., Hartzell, S. A., & Greene, M. T. (2009). Fostering creativity in the classroom: Effects of teachers' epistemological beliefs, motivation, and goal orientation. *Journal of Creative Behavior, 43,* 192–208. doi:10.1002/j.2162-6057.2009.tb01314.x

Hooker, C., Nakamura, J., & Csikszentmihalyi, M. (2003). The group as mentor: Social capital and the systems model of creativity. In P. B. Paulus & B. A. Nijstad (Eds.), *Group creativity: Innovation through collaboration* (pp. 225–244). New York, NY: Oxford University Press.

Hunsaker, S. L., & Callahan, C. M. (1995). Creativity and giftedness: Published instrument uses and abuses. *Gifted Child Quarterly, 39,* 110–114. doi:10.1177/001698629503900207

Jarosewich, T., Pfeiffer, S. I., & Morris, J. (2002). Identifying gifted students using teacher rating scales: A review of existing instruments. *Journal of Psychoeducational Assessment, 20,* 322–336.

Kangas, M. (2010). Creative and playful learning: Learning through game co-creation and games in a playful learning environment. *Thinking Skills and Creativity, 5,* 1–15. doi:10.1016/j.tsc.2009.11.001

Kaufman, J. C., & Baer, J. (2012). Beyond new and appropriate: Who decides what is creative? *Creativity Research Journal, 24,* 83–91. doi:10.1080/10400419.2012.649237

Kaufman, J. C., Baer, J., Cole, J. C., & Sexton, J. D. (2008). A comparison of expert and nonexpert raters using the consensual assessment technique. *Creativity Research Journal, 20,* 171–178. doi:10.1080/10400410802059929

Kaufman, J. C., & Beghetto, R. A. (2009). Beyond big and little: The four c model of creativity. *Review of General Psychology, 13,* 1–12. doi:10.1037/a0013688

Kaufman, J. C., Plucker, J. A., & Baer, J. (2008). *Essentials of creativity assessment.* Hoboken, NJ: John Wiley.

Kaufman, J. C., Plucker, J. A., & Russell, C. M. (2012). Identifying and assessing creativity as a component of giftedness. *Journal of Psychoeducational Assessment, 30,* 60–73. doi:10.1177/0734282911428196

Kogan, N., & Pankove, E. (1974). Long-term predictive validity of divergent-thinking tests: Some negative evidence. *Journal of Educational Psychology, 66,* 802–810. doi:10.1037/h0021521

Martindale, C. (1999). Biological basis of creativity. In R. J. Sternberg (Ed.), *Handbook of creativity* (pp. 137–152). New York, NY: Cambridge University Press. doi:10.1017/CBO9780511807916.009

Nash, W. R. (1974). The effects of a school for the gifted in averting the fourth grade slump in creativity. *Gifted Child Quarterly, 18,* 168–170. doi:10.1177/001698627401800308

Okuda, S. M., Runco, M. A., & Berger, D. E. (1991). Creativity and the finding and solving of real-world problems. *Journal of Psychoeducational Assessment, 9,* 45–53. doi:10.1177/073428299100900104

O'Donnell, A. M. (1999). Structuring dyadic interaction through scripted cooperation. In A. M. O'Donnell & A. King (Eds.), *Cognitive perspectives on peer learning* (pp. 179–196). Mahwah, NJ: Lawrence Erlbaum.

Pang, W. (2015). Promoting creativity in the classroom: A generative view. *Psychology of Aesthetics, Creativity, and the Arts, 9,* 122–127. doi:10.1037/aca0000009

Pang, W., & Plucker, J. A. (2013). Recent transformations in China's economic, social, and education policies for promoting innovation and creativity. *The Journal of Creative Behavior, 46,* 247–273. doi:10.1002/jocb.17

Partnership for 21st Century Skills. (2015). *Framework for 21st century learning.* Retrieved from http://www.p21.org/our-work/p21-framework

Paulus, P. (2000). Groups, teams, and creativity: The creative potential of idea-generating groups. *Applied Psychology, 49,* 237–262.

Paulus, P. B., & Brown, V. R. (2003). Enhancing ideational creativity in groups: Lessons from research on brainstorming. In P. B. Paulus & B. A. Nijstad (Eds.), *Group creativity* (pp. 110–136). New York, NY: Oxford University Press. doi:10.1093/acprof:oso/9780195147308.003.0006

Pignéguy, S. (2004). Our Didcot: An inclusive arts project devised by a learning support unit. *Support for Learning, 19,* 77–80. doi:10.1111/j.0268-2141.2004.00324.x

Plucker, J. A. (1999). Is the proof in the pudding? Reanalyses of Torrance's (1958 to present) longitudinal study data. *Creativity Research Journal, 12,* 103–114. doi:10.1207/s15326934crj1202_3

Plucker, J. A., & Barab, S. A. (2005). The importance of contexts in theories of giftedness: Learning to embrace the messy joys of subjectivity. In R. J. Sternberg & J. A. Davidson (Eds.), *Conceptions of giftedness* (2nd ed., pp. 201–216). New York, NY: Cambridge University Press.

Plucker, J. A., & Beghetto, R. A. (2003). Why not be creative when we enhance creativity? In J. H. Borland (Ed.), *Rethinking gifted education* (pp. 215–226). New York, NY: Teachers College Press.

Plucker, J. A., Beghetto, R. A., & Dow, G. (2004). Why isn't creativity more important to educational psychologists? Potential, pitfalls, and future directions in creativity research. *Educational Psychologist, 39,* 83–96. doi:10.1207/s15326985ep3902_1

Plucker, J. A., & Dow, G. T. (2010). Attitude change as the precursor to creativity enhancement. In R. A. Beghetto & J. C. Kaufman (Eds.), *Nurturing creativity in the classroom* (pp. 362–379). New York, NY: Cambridge.

Plucker, J. A., Kaufman, J. C., Temple, J. S., & Qian, M. (2009). Do experts and novices evaluate movies the same way? *Psychology & Marketing, 26,* 470–478. doi:10.1002/mar.20283

Plucker, J. A., Kennedy, C., & Dilley, A. (2015). *What we know about collaboration* [P21 Research Series]. Washington, DC: Partnership for 21st Century Skills. Retrieved from http://www.p21.org/our-work/4cs-research-series/collaboration

Plucker, J. A., Qian, M., & Schmalensee, S. L. (2014). Is what you see what you really get? Comparison of scoring techniques in the assessment of real-world divergent thinking. *Creativity Research Journal, 26,* 135–143. doi:10.1080/10400419.2014.901023

Plucker, J. A., Qian, M., & Wang, S. (2011). Is originality in the eye of the beholder? Comparison of scoring techniques in the assessment of divergent thinking. *Journal of Creative Behavior, 45,* 1–22. doi:10.1002/j.2162-6057.2011.tb01081.x

Plucker, J. A., & Renzulli, J. S. (1999). Psychometric approaches to the study of human creativity. In R. J. Sternberg (Ed.), *Handbook of creativity* (pp. 35–60). New York, NY: Cambridge University Press. doi:10.1017/cbo9780511807916.005

Priest, T. (2006). Self-evaluation, creativity, and musical achievement. *Psychology of Music, 34,* 47–61. doi:10.1177/0305735606059104

Proctor, R. M., & Burnett, P. C. (2004). Measuring cognitive and dispositional characteristics of creativity in elementary students. *Creativity Research Journal, 16,* 421–429. doi:10.1207/s15326934crj1604_5

Pyryt, M. C. (1999). Effectiveness of training children's divergent thinking: A meta-analytic review. In A. S. Fishkin, B. Cramond, & P. Olszewski-Kubilius (Eds.), *Investigating creativity in youth: Research and methods* (pp. 351–365). Cresskill, NJ: Hampton.

Renzulli, J. S. (1999). What is this thing called giftedness, and how do we develop it? A twenty-five year perspective. *Journal for the Education of the Gifted, 23,* 3–54. doi:10.1177/016235329902300102

Renzulli, J. S., Smith, L. H., White, A. J., Callahan, C. M., Hartman, R. K., Westberg, K. L., . . . Systma Reed, R. E. (2010). *Scales for Rating the Behavioral Characteristics of Superior Students* (3rd ed.). Waco, TX: Prufrock Press.

Rhodes, M. (1961). An analysis of creativity. *Phi Delta Kappan, 42,* 305–310.

Runco, M. A. (1989). The creativity of children's art. *Child Study Journal, 19,* 177–189.

Runco, M. A. (1991). *Divergent thinking.* Norwood, NJ: Ablex.

Runco, M. A. (2014). *Creativity: Theories and themes: Research, development, and practice* (2nd ed.). San Diego, CA: Academic Press.

Runco, M. A., & Acar, S. (2012). Divergent thinking as an indicator of creative potential. *Creativity Research Journal, 24,* 66–75. doi:10.1080/10400419.2012.652929

Runco, M. A., & Chand, I. (1994). Problem finding, evaluative thinking, and creativity. In M. A. Runco (Ed.), *Problem finding, problem solving, and creativity* (pp. 40–76). Norwood, NJ: Ablex.

Runco, M. A., & Okuda, S. M. (1988). Problem discovery, divergent thinking, and the creative process. *Journal of Youth and Adolescence, 17,* 211–220.

Runco, M. A., Plucker, J. A., & Lim, W. (2000–2001). Development and psychometric integrity of a measure of ideational behavior. *Creativity Research Journal, 13,* 393–400. doi:10.1207/s15326934crj1334_16

Runco, M. A., & Pritzker, S. R. (Eds.). (2011). *Encyclopedia of creativity* (2nd ed.). Boston, MA: Academic Press.

Russ, S. W. (2014). *Pretend play in childhood: Foundation of adult creativity.* Washington, DC: American Psychological Association. doi:10.1037/14282-000

Russ, S. W., & Wallace, C. E. (2013). Pretend play and creative processes. *American Journal of Play, 6,* 136–148.

Silvia, P. J., Beaty, R. E., Nusbaum, E. C., Eddington, K. M., Levin-Aspenson, H., & Kwapil, T. R. (2014). Everyday creativity in daily life: An experience-sampling study of "little c" creativity. *Psychology of Aesthetics, Creativity, and the Arts, 8,* 183–188. doi:10.1037/a0035722

Silvia, P. J., Martin, C., & Nusbaum, E. C. (2009). A snapshot of creativity: Evaluating a quick and simple method for assessing divergent thinking. *Thinking Skills and Creativity, 4,* 79–85. doi:10.1016/j.tsc.2009.06.005

Silvia, P. J., Wigert, B., Reiter-Palmon, R., & Kaufman, J. C. (2012). Assessing creativity with self-report scales: A review and empirical evaluation. *Psychology of Aesthetics, Creativity, and the Arts, 6,* 19–34. doi:10.1037/a0024071

Stein, M. I. (1953). Creativity and culture. *The Journal of Psychology, 36,* 311–322. doi:10.1080/00223980.1953.9712897

Torrance, E. P. (1967). *Understanding the fourth grade slump in creative thinking* (No. BR-5-0508; CRP-994). Washington, DC: U.S. Office of Education.

Torrance, E. P. (1968). A longitudinal examination of the fourth grade slump in creativity. *Gifted Child Quarterly, 12,* 195–199. doi:10.1177/001698626801 200401

Torrance, E. P. (1974). *Torrance Tests of Creative Thinking: Norms-technical manual.* Bensenville, IL: Scholastic Testing Service.

Torrance, E. P. (1984). The role of creativity in identification of the gifted and talented. *Gifted Child Quarterly, 28,* 153–156. doi:10.1177/001698628402800403

Wakefield, J. F. (1985). Toward creativity: Problem finding in a divergent thinking exercise. *Child Study Journal, 15,* 265–270.

Walsh, C. S. (2007). Creativity as capital in the literacy classroom: Youth as multimodal designers. *Literacy, 41,* 79–85. doi:10.1111/j.1467-9345.2007.00461.x

Weisberg, R. W. (1993). *Creativity: Beyond the myth of genius.* New York, NY: W. H. Freeman.

Westby, E. L., & Dawson, V. L. (1995). Creativity: Asset or burden in the classroom? *Creativity Research Journal, 8,* 1–10. doi:10.1207/s15326934crj0801_1

Yee, S. L. C. Y. (2015). *Performative authoring: Nurturing children's creativity and creative self-efficacy through digitally-augmented enactment-based storytelling* (Unpublished doctoral dissertation). Texas A&M University, College Station, TX.

Yi, X., Hu, X., Plucker, J. A., & McWilliams, J. (2013). Is there a developmental slump in creativity in China? The relationship between organizational climate and creativity development in Chinese adolescents. *Journal of Creative Behavior, 47,* 22–40.

Yi, X., Plucker, J. A., & Guo, J. (2015). Modeling influences on divergent thinking and artistic creativity. *Thinking Skills and Creativity, 16,* 62–68. doi:10.1016/j.tsc.2015.02.002

SECTION V

Diversity of Learners

With the roof in place, the exterior and interior of the building can be finished. From windows installed to sidewalks poured, the exterior finishing work takes careful consideration. From style of light fixture to the color of the trim, the interior work is filled with myriad decisions. Each aspect has its own unique attributes and issues to consider. Should the windows be double paned? Should they be aluminum clad or wooden? If shuttered, which shutters are most cost efficient and long lasting? These decisions should be based on research and opinions of experts.

Likewise, the many issues facing diverse learners should be addressed through best practice and research. What can be done to reverse underachievement in gifted learners? How can more students from underrepresented populations be identified and served? What does research say about serving students who are from poverty or who have more than one exceptionality? Although the basics of advanced learning and programming for gifted learners provide an excellent structure to gifted education, consideration of diverse learners' needs adds the finishing touches to that structure.

This section has six chapters: "Understanding Underachievement"; "Underrepresented Culturally and Linguistically Diverse Gifted Students: Recommendations for Equitable Recruitment and Retention"; "Gifted Students From Low-Socioeconomic Backgrounds"; "The Interplay Between Geography and Giftedness"; "Educating Gifted Gay, Lesbian, Bisexual, Transgender, and Questioning Students"; and "Meeting the Needs of Students Who Are Twice-Exceptional."

Myths

» **Gifted learners are White, middle- and upper-class students.** Students with gifts and talents span all demographics. They come from all ethnicities, all economic backgrounds, all religions, and all areas of the country; they may not speak English as their first language and may be gay, lesbian, bisexual, transgender, or questioning.

» **Students with learning disabilities cannot be gifted.** Students are multifaceted, able to have gifts and talents accompanied by other exceptionalities, such as a learning disability, ADHD, or visual impairment. These students are twice-exceptional learners.

CHAPTER 17

Understanding Underachievement

Del Siegle

Student performance that falls noticeably short of potential, especially for young people with high ability, is bewildering and perhaps the most frustrating of all challenges both teachers and parents face.—Reis (1998, p. 12)

Essential Questions to Guide the Reader

1. Why is underachievement important to address?

2. What is underachievement?

3. What causes underachievement?

4. What are some possible solutions to underachievement?

Why Is Underachievement Important to Address?

Similar to many myths about gifted students, most people do not consider underachievement an issue associated with gifted students. However, as Colangelo, Kerr, Christensen, and Maxey (1993) noted, "most classroom teachers can quickly recall a student whose classroom performance seemed far below the evidence of high ability" (p. 155). Concern about gifted students' poor academic performance and low motivation extends to parents as well as teachers, and needs to be addressed.

Academic motivation is important for students' task persistence, academic performance, and career selection. Unfortunately, gifted students, like students of all ability levels, may not be academically motivated. Some have estimated that up to 50% of gifted students underachieve at some point (National Commission on Excellence in Education, 1983; Richert, 1991). Studies of high school dropouts suggest between 18% and 25% of the students who do not graduate are in the gifted range of abilities (Renzulli & Park, 2000; Solorzano, 1983).

More than a half century ago, Gowan (1955) described underachievement as "one of the greatest social wastes of our culture" (p. 247). Underachievement represents a loss to the student and to society (Rubenstein, Siegle, Reis, McCoach, & Burton, 2012). The student loses a sense of accomplishment, self-esteem, and confidence. Society loses the potential contributions of a bright and creative mind.

The history of underachievement is closely linked to the history of testing. The term *underachievement* became an educational issue "in the middle 1950s, when the measurement of ability and achievement were refined and accepted" (McCall, 1994, p. 15). It became possible to psychometrically compare potential performance with actual performance. Russia's launch of Sputnik in 1957 drew attention to the underachievement of gifted students, which resulted in a national effort to improve mathematics and science achievement (Davis, Rimm, & Siegle, 2011). More recently, lower-than-expected academic performance of students of color and students from lower income situations has gained the nation's attention (Plucker, Burroughs, & Song, 2010; Siegle et al., 2016).

Academic achievement is important because it is strongly linked to life achievement. Overall, students' life accomplishments 10 years after graduation are more closely related to their grades than their IQs. Students with high IQs and average grades achieve similarly to students with average IQs and average grades (McCall, Evahn, & Kratzer, 1992). Education level is directly related to earning income and employment opportunities. For example, in 2016 the U.S. unemployment rate for individuals with only a high school diploma was over three times higher than that of individuals with a college degree (Bui, 2016).

What Is Underachievement?

"Professionals have agreed for decades that the phenomenon of underachievement is complex, baffling, and challenging" (Baum, Renzulli, & Hébert, 1995, p. 224). However, they do not agree on a definition of gifted underachievers for two reasons. First, there is no universally accepted definition of giftedness. Second, disagreement surrounds what underachievement is. Informally, students whose grades have dropped, who are not doing their homework, or who put off completing projects could be considered candidates for underachievement (Siegle, 2013). Underachievement for gifted children may look different from underachievement for other students. For example, underachievement of a gifted student does not necessarily mean the student is failing the class—although many underachieving gifted students do fail classes. A gifted student who is underachieving may be doing average work when she is capable of performing at a much higher level. Also, a pattern of continuous decline in achievement test scores is a sure sign of underachievement (Rimm, 2008).

The National Association for Gifted Children (NAGC) released a 2010 position paper that provides some guidance for practitioners as they struggle with the concept of giftedness. It is also useful for framing underachievement. The NAGC definition suggests:

> Gifted individuals are those who demonstrate outstanding levels of aptitude (defined as an exceptional ability to reason and learn) or competence (documented performance or achievement in top 10% or rarer) in one or more domains. Domains include any structured area of activity with its own symbol system (e.g., mathematics, music, language) and/or set of sensorimotor skills (e.g., painting, dance, sports).
>
> The development of ability or talent is a lifelong process. It can be evident in young children as exceptional performance on tests and/or other measures of ability or as a rapid rate of learning, compared to other students of the same age, or in actual achievement in a domain. As individuals mature through childhood to adolescence, however, achievement and high levels of motivation in the domain become the primary characteristics of their giftedness. Various factors can either enhance or inhibit the development and expression of abilities. (para. 1–2)

Gifted students in the elementary years tend to do things a little earlier and at more advanced levels than other students of their same age. They also may be learning material more quickly. Some students could be doing things earlier or better if they had been given appropriate opportunities. Many students do not have appropriate educational opportunities for their giftedness to surface and flourish. They are sometimes referred to as *involuntary underachievers*. This is particularly true for students from underserved populations. These include students of color, students from poverty, students for whom English is a second language, and in some cases, students from rural and urban populations (Siegle et al., 2016).

As students grow older, their advanced abilities become more specialized, and potential is expected to manifest itself. Therefore, gifted underachievers are those who fail to further develop the advanced skills they initially demonstrated or those whose untapped potential failed to materialize. In both cases, it is a discrepancy between what is and what might be (Siegle, 2013). Most definitions of under-achievement include this discrepancy between potential or ability and performance or achievement (Reis & McCoach, 2000; Whitmore, 1980).

Emerick (1988) suggested this discrepancy might include any of the following combinations:

- high IQ score and low achievement test scores;
- high IQ score and low grades;
- high achievement test scores and low grades;
- high indicators of intellectual, creative potential, and low creative productivity; or
- high indicators of potential and limited presence of appropriate opportunity for intellectual and creative development.

The specific students identified by the various discrepancy definitions that Emerick proposed are likely to be quite different from one another. Therefore, lists describing characteristics of underachievers are often contradictory (McCoach & Siegle, 2003). Additionally, a high IQ score and low achievement test scores may indicate the presence of a learning disability, while high achievement test scores and low grades seldom indicate a learning disability. Moon and Hall (1998) suggested that gifted students who are underachieving should be screened for a learning disability. Educators and parents must be careful not to immediately assume a bright child who is having difficulty in school is underachieving; the student may have a learning disability.

Perhaps the most frustrating discrepancy on Emerick's list for teachers and parents is the student with high achievement scores and low grades. These students appear to be mastering their school material but are not doing well on factors that contribute to good grades, such as completing homework. Because these *nonproducers* (Delisle & Galbraith, 2002) know the content, should they be of concern? Many students reverse their underachievement when they encounter meaningful learning experiences. Some reverse their underachievement in college and in life (Peterson, 2001); however, others do not. *Selective consumers* are another group of underachievers that attract attention. Figg, Rogers, McCormick, and Low (2012) suggested that selective consumers, students who choose where they wish to achieve, are different from other types of underachievers in that they tend to have higher academic self-concept. Efforts should be made to understand and address the different types of underachievement.

Emerick's last category is an interesting one. With this definition, others have failed the child by not providing opportunities for the child's talents to manifest themselves. This concern has grown over the past decade as policymakers grapple with the expanding achievement gaps among different groups in the United States (Plucker et al., 2010).

McCoach and Siegle (2003) compared the characteristics of achievers and underachievers and documented the fact that, compared with achievers, underachievers differed in their attitude toward school and teachers, their motivation, and their valuing of school goals. Underachievers found neither intrinsic nor extrinsic value in their school experience. McCoach and Siegle also reported that the underachievers were not a homogeneous group but differed from each other; thus, they recommended that processes of reversing underachievement should also differ, depending on the unique profile of each underachiever. Although underachievers differ more from each other than achievers differ from each other, underachievers often exhibit some of the characteristics (see Table 17.1) described by Reis and McCoach (2000) in their review of the literature on gifted underachievers.

What Causes Underachievement?

Students underachieve for a variety of reasons. Some of these include underinvolved and nonencouraging parents and teachers, negative parental attitudes toward work, family conflict, lack of career direction, and family transitions (Peterson, 2001). Inflexible classroom environments with unrewarding curriculum, inability to function in competition, a fixed mindset, rebellion, perfectionism, excessive power as a young child, inconsistency and opposition between parents and between parents and teachers, and peer and cultural value conflict can be added to this list (Rimm, Siegle, & Davis, 2018).

For example, students may underachieve because they do not feel supported by their parents, teachers, or peers. Significant others who do not value work and achievement can influence students' attitudes toward school and achievement. Conflicts in their environment can distract students from school work. Gifted students who are not intellectually stimulated in their classrooms often become bored, discouraged, and underachieve. Students with fixed mindsets and perfection issues may fail to recognize that the path to success is not seamless and involves overcoming challenges and setbacks. Finally, students who do not differentiate when it is best to change the situation to fit their needs, adapt to the situation, or abandon the situation for better options are often caught in power struggles that reduce their chances for academic success.

Snyder and Linnenbrink-Garcia (2013) proposed a model to explain underachievement that included multiple developmental trajectories. Their model suggests that underachievement occurs when students have (a) particular fixed beliefs about giftedness and have maladaptive coping strategies or (b) declining value beliefs and increased perceptions of the cost associated with achievement.

social cost

Table 17.1
Common Characteristics of Underachievers

Personality Characteristics:
1. Low self-esteem, low self-concept, low self-efficacy.
2. Alienated or withdrawn; distrustful, or pessimistic.
3. Anxious, impulsive, inattentive, hyperactive, or distractible; may exhibit ADD or ADHD symptoms.
4. Aggressive, hostile, resentful, or touchy.
5. Depressed.
6. Passive-aggressive trait disturbance.
7. More socially than academically oriented. May be extroverted. May be easygoing, considerate, and/or unassuming.
8. Dependent, less resilient than high achievers.
9. Socially immature.

Internal Mediators:
10. Fear of failure; gifted underachievers may avoid competition or challenging situations to protect their self-image or their ability.
11. Fear of success.
12. Attribute successes or failures to outside forces; exhibit an external locus of control; attribute successes to luck and failures to lack of ability; externalize conflict and problems.
13. Negative attitude toward school.
14. Antisocial or rebellious.
15. Self-critical or perfectionistic; feeling guilty about not living up to the expectations of others.

Differential Thinking Skills/Styles:
16. Perform less well on tasks that require detail-oriented or convergent thinking skills than their achieving counterparts.
17. Score lower on sequential tasks such as repeating digits, repeating sentences, coding, computation, and spelling.
18. Lack insight and critical ability.

Maladaptive Strategies:
19. Lack goal-directed behavior; fail to set realistic goals for themselves.
20. Poor coping skills; develop coping mechanisms that successfully reduce short-term stress, but inhibit long-term success.
21. Possess poor self-regulation strategies; low tolerance for frustration; lack perseverance; lack self-control.
22. Use defense mechanisms.

Positive Attributes:
23. Intense outside interests, commitment to self-selected work.
24. Creative.
25. Demonstrate honesty and integrity in rejecting unchallenging coursework.

Note. Adapted from "The underachievement of gifted students: What do we know and where do we go?" (pp. 159–160) by S. M. Reis and D. B. McCoach, 2000, *Gifted Child Quarterly, 44.* Copyright 2000 National Association for Gifted Children. Adapted with permission of the authors.

Siegle and McCoach (2005) developed the Achievement Orientation Model (see Figure 17.1) as an explanation for understanding motivation and, subsequently, underachievement. According to the model, three key attitudes regulate whether students are willing to engage in an activity. Individuals must believe they have the required skills to perform the task at hand. Albert Bandura (1986) coined the term *self-efficacy* to describe this confidence in one's ability to perform a task. Within a school context, a student might be asking himself, "Am I smart enough to do this?" Although this is a major issue for traditional underachievers, it is less of an issue for gifted underachievers. Many gifted underachievers believe they could achieve if they desired. They simply do not wish to put forth the necessary effort for success. This leads to the second element in the model. In addition to having the confidence that one has the necessary skills, individuals must also value the task. It needs to be meaningful for them. If individuals do not value a task, they seldom engage in it. Wigfield and Eccles (2000) suggested individuals weight how much they value a task against the cost of performing it. When students believe the cost outweighs the benefit, achievement suffers. The question in the student's mind is "How important is this to me?" Many gifted underachievers do not find their school experiences meaningful (McCoach & Siegle, 2003). Assuming students believe they have the skill to perform a task and they value the task, they also need to believe they can be successful if they engage and put forth effort. Their perception of the support, or lack of support, in their environment influences their achievement. The question being addressed is "Can I be successful here?" Students need to believe their teachers, parents, and peers support their achievement efforts (Siegle, 2013).

→ support more than ability

Assuming students believe they have the skills to be successful at a task, find the task meaningful, and believe they are supported, they tend to self-regulate and become successful. Of course, self-regulating and being successful or not successful in the past influences perceptions about how successful they believe they will be in the future. Gifted students who have not been challenged or who have not found school meaningful in the past may refuse to engage even when those situations no longer exist. Students who have not learned the important role effort plays in success, possibly because school has been easy for them, may not wish to work hard or may question their ability if tasks suddenly are difficult. Gifted children are more likely to be achievers if they learn to put forth effort and set reasonably high but not unrealistically high expectations for themselves (Rimm, 2008). A fixed mindset (Dweck, 2006) can also lead underachievers to nonproductive avoidance behaviors both at school and at home (Rimm et al., 2018; Snyder & Linnenbrink-Garcia, 2013). For some gifted students with fixed mindsets, not submitting an assignment and receiving an "F" is preferable to submitting the assignment and receiving less than a perfect grade.

According to the Achievement Orientation Model, self-regulating behaviors interact with the three attitudes just described. Successful self-regulation that

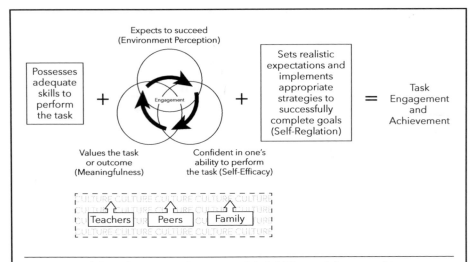

Figure 17.1. The Achievement Orientation Model. The model posits achievement results from the interaction of three beliefs (self-efficacy, meaningfulness, and environmental perceptions) and a behavior (self-regulation). Reprinted with permission from Dr. Del Siegle and Dr. Betsy McCoach.

results in achievement increases students' confidence, makes their learning experiences more meaningful, and builds trust in their learning situation. Unfortunately, simply teaching students study skills and how to self-regulate may not reverse their underachievement (Rubenstein et al., 2012). Before students will engage and attempt self-regulation, positive attitudes in the three areas just described need to be in place. Landis and Reschly (2013) posited that "student engagement may prove to be an essential construct in understanding, predicting, and preventing dropout behavior among gifted students" (p. 220) and also may be a key to addressing underachievement.

What Are Some Possible Solutions to Underachievement?

Effective teachers can encourage students' growth and satisfaction (building self-efficacy), as they make the content meaningful and challenging for their students (creating task valuation), and as they shape students' perception of support in their environment through building positive relationships and being knowledgeable about the content (fostering a positive environmental perception). Teachers with extensive depth and breadth of content knowledge are better able to foster gifted students' motivation and build students' confidence to learn (increase self-efficacy). These teachers have the background to be comfortable differentiating content, stray-

ing from the familiar textbook territory, and delving into a variety of instructional strategies, such as in-depth discussions, with their students. They are able to help students form interdisciplinary connections that make learning relevant (Siegle, Rubenstein, & Mitchell, 2014). Features of a classroom that fosters optimum motivation include "(a) tasks that are meaningful with reasonable challenge; (b) opportunity to participate in decision making and develop responsibility; and (c) an evaluation system that recognizes progress and mastery of content" (Alderman, 1999, p. 11). Matthews and McBee (2007) found that students who had previously underachieved in their traditional school environment did not underachieve in a summer program that met their educational needs with more appropriate and challenging enrichment experiences. Therefore, modifying the curriculum and learning environment to meet gifted students' unique learning needs may reduce underachievement. Hwang et al. (2014) found that university students who underachieved were able to turn their underachievement around by setting clear career goals, implementing effective learning strategies, putting forth more effort, and receiving external support. Therefore, counseling underachieving students is helpful. Most interventions to address underachievement involve curriculum modifications, counseling, or a combination of both.

There is no silver bullet for reversing underachievement. One model that has been successful across a variety of cases is Rimm's (2008) Trifocal Model. Rimm proposed an intervention for underachievement that involves collaboration among the student, school, and family in implementing six steps.

1. Assessment of Skills, Abilities, Reinforcement Contingencies, and Types of Underachievement
2. Communication
3. Changing Expectations of Important Others
4. Role Model Identification
5. Correcting Skill Deficiencies
6. Modifications of Reinforcements at Home and School

Rimm begins with a comprehensive assessment of the student's abilities, interests, and learning preferences. This eliminates the possibility of a learning disability and provides evidence of the student's ability to achieve and under what conditions the student best achieves. This evidence is communicated to the student, parents, and teacher. The communication includes reasons why a student might be underachieving and possible goals for the student to pursue. Everyone involved in the process must expect that the student can be successful, and everyone may need to adjust behaviors to make that success possible. The fourth step involves introducing an achieving role model into the student's life. Rimm et al. (2018) suggested, "All other treatments for underachievement dim in importance compared with strong identification with an achieving model" (pp. 255–256). Depending on how long the student has been underachieving, there may be skill deficiencies that need to be addressed. Fortunately, most gifted students can overcome these quickly with tutoring, Finally, "counselors, parents, and teachers can collaborate on making changes that support the student's achievement and discourage some of the behaviors that have fed the student's underachievement" (Siegle, 2013, p. 71).

Peterson (2001) found that "personality factors, achiever role models outside of the family, developmental task accomplishment, changes in location, and new academic courses may contribute to reversal of underachievement" (p. 236). Wigfield and Eccles (2000) reported that students are motivated when they enjoy an activity or a byproduct of that activity. Byproducts could include things such as praise, high grades, or the belief that learning the material will be useful to them. High, but not too high, expectations by parents and educators and respect between them matter as part of an achievement-friendly environment (Peterson, 2001; Rimm, 2008). Developing a work ethic, self-efficacy, and a growth mindset (Dweck, 2006) increase student engagement, and subsequently, their achievement. Finally, resilience, or the ability to cope with failure experiences without feeling like a failure, counts for motivation (Rimm et al., 2018).

> Gifted students' learning gains result from complex, advanced, and meaningful content provided by a knowledgeable teacher through high-quality curriculum and instruction at an appropriate pace with scaffolding and feedback. These elements exert influence that increases with dosage and within structures that facilitate student engagement in rigorous experiences, including interactions with one another. (Siegle et al., 2016, p. 103)

Conclusion

Students are engaged and motivated to do well in school when they believe they have the necessary skills to perform tasks (self-efficacy), they find tasks meaningful (goal/task valuation), and they see their environment as supportive (environmental perception). When these factors are present, students engage in the learning process and regulate themselves to complete the tasks (self-regulation; Siegle, 2013; Siegle & McCoach, 2005; Siegle, McCoach, & Roberts, 2017). As Whitmore (1980) noted more than three decades ago, ultimately the decision to achieve rests with the student.

Big Ideas

1. Gifted students, like other students, underachieve; however, their underachievement may look different.

2. Academic achievement is an important predictor of later life opportunities and success.

3. Underachievement is usually defined as a discrepancy between potential and performance.

4. Limited opportunities for some students result in their underachievement.

5. According to the Achievement Orientation Model, students self-regulate and achieve when they believe they have the skills to do well, find tasks meaningful, and believe they are in supportive environments.

6. Rimm proposed a six-step Trifocal Model that has been effectively used to reverse student underachievement.

7. Knowledgeable, caring teachers can make learning more meaningful and build students' confidence to learn.

8. Many gifted underachievers do not find school meaningful.

Discussion Questions

1. Why is it important to address gifted students' underachievement?

2. What home and school factors do you believe contribute to students becoming underachievers?

3. Given what you know about gifted students and their learning preferences, what can classroom teachers do to make learning more meaningful for gifted students?

4. Using the three attitudes described in the Achievement Orientation Model, how would efforts to reverse underachievement differ for a student who was low in one of them compared to a student who was low in a different one?

5. Do gifted students have a right "not to do their best" in areas of talent that do not interest them? If so, when?

6. What did you learn in the reading about educating this special population (and perhaps your prejudices) that you were unaware of before?

References

Alderman, M. K. (1999). *Motivation for achievement: Possibilities for teaching and learning.* Mahwah, NJ: Erlbaum.

Bandura, A. (1986). *Social foundations of thought and action: A social cognition theory.* Englewood Cliffs, NJ: Prentice-Hall.

Baum, S. M., Renzulli, J. S., & Hébert, T. P. (1995). Reversing underachievement: Creative productivity as a systematic intervention. *Gifted Child Quarterly, 39,* 224–235. doi:10.1177/001698629503900406

Bui, Q. (2016). The one question most Americans get wrong about college grades. *New York Times.* Retrieved from http://nyti.ms/1X1Ubkz

Colangelo, N., Kerr, B., Christensen, P., & Maxey, J. (1993). A comparison of gifted underachievers and gifted high achievers. *Gifted Child Quarterly, 37,* 155–160. doi:10.1177/001698629303700404

Davis, G. A., Rimm, S. B., & Siegle, D. (2011). *Education of the gifted and talented* (6th ed.). Boston, MA: Pearson.

Delisle, J., & Galbraith, J. (2002). *When gifted kids don't have all the answers: How to meet their social and emotional needs.* Minneapolis, MN: Free Spirit.

Dweck, C. S. (2006). *Mindset: The new psychology of success.* New York, NY: Random House.

Emerick, L. J. (1988). *Academic underachievement among the gifted: Students' perceptions of factors relating to the reversal of the academic underachievement pattern* (Unpublished doctoral dissertation). University of Connecticut, Storrs.

Figg, S. D., Rogers, K. B., McCormick, J., & Low, R. (2012). Differentiating low performance of the gifted learner: Achieving, underachieving, and selective consuming students. *Journal of Advanced Academics, 23,* 53–71. doi:10.1177/1932202X11430000

Gowan, J. C. (1955). The underachieving child: A problem for everyone. *Exceptional Children, 21,* 247–249, 270–271.

Hwang, M. H., Lee, D., Lim, H. J., Seon, H. Y., Hutchinson, B., & Pope, M. (2014). Academic underachievement and recovery: Student perspectives on effective career interventions. *The Career Development Quarterly, 62,* 81–94. doi:10.1002/j.2161-0045.2014.00072.x

Landis, R. N., & Reschly, A. L. (2013). Reexaming gifted underachievement and dropout through the lens of student engagement. *Journal for the Education of the Gifted, 36,* 220–249. doi:10.1177/0162353213480864

Matthews, M. S., & McBee, M. T. (2007). School factors and the underachievement of gifted students in a talent search summer program. *Gifted Child Quarterly, 51,* 167–181. doi:10.1177/0016986207299473

McCall, R. B. (1994). Academic underachievers. *Current Directions in Psychological Science, 3,* 15–19. doi:10.1111/1467-8721.ep10769838

McCall, R. B., Evahn, C., & Kratzer, L. (1992). *High school underachievers: What do they achieve as adults?* Newbury Park, CA: Sage.

McCoach, D. B., & Siegle, D. (2003). Factors that differentiate underachieving gifted students from high-achieving gifted students. *Gifted Child Quarterly, 47,* 144–154. doi:10.1177/001698620304700205

Moon, S. M., & Hall, A. S. (1998). Family therapy with intellectually and creatively gifted children. *Journal of Marital and Family Therapy, 24,* 59–80. doi:10.1111/j.1752-0606.1998.tb01063.x

National Association for Gifted Children. (2010). *Redefining giftedness for a new century: Shifting the paradigm.* Retrieved from https://www.nagc.org/sites/default/files/Position%20Statement/Redefining%20Giftedness%20for%20a%20New%20Century.pdf

National Commission on Excellence in Education. (1983). *A nation at risk: The imperative for educational reform.* Washington, DC: U.S. Government Printing Office.

Peterson, J. S. (2001). Successful adults who were once adolescent underachievers. *Gifted Child Quarterly, 45,* 236–250. doi:10.1177/001698620104500402

Plucker, J., Burroughs, N., & Song, R. (2010). *Mind the (other) gap!: The growing excellence gap in K–12 education.* Bloomington: Indiana University, School of Education, Center for Evaluation and Education Policy. Retrieved from http://www.jkcf.org/assets/1/7/ExcellenceGapBrief_-_Plucker.pdf

Reis, S. M. (1998). Underachievement for some, dropping out with dignity for others. *ITAG News, Iowa Talented and Gifted Association Newsletter, 23*(4), 12–15.

Reis, S. M., & McCoach, D. B. (2000). The underachievement of gifted students: What do we know and where do we go? *Gifted Child Quarterly, 44,* 158–170. doi:10.1177/001698520004400302

Renzulli, J. S., & Park, S. (2000). Gifted dropouts: The who and the why. *Gifted Child Quarterly, 44,* 261–271. doi:10.1177/001698620004400407

Richert, E. S. (1991). Patterns of underachievement among gifted students. In J. H. Borland (Series Ed.), M. Bireley & J. Genshaft (Vol. Eds.), *Understanding the gifted adolescent* (pp. 139–162). New York, NY: Teacher College Press.

Rimm, S. (2008). *Why bright kids get poor grades and what you can do about it: A six-step program for parents and teachers* (3rd ed.). Scottsdale, AZ: Great Potential Press.

Rimm, S. B., Siegle, D., & Davis, G. A. (2018). *Education of the gifted and talented* (7th ed.). New York, NY: Pearson.

Rubenstein, L. D., Siegle, D., Reis, S. M., McCoach, D. B., & Burton, M. G. (2012). A complex quest: The development and research of underachievement interventions for gifted students. *Psychology in the Schools, 49,* 678–694. doi:10.1002/pits.21620

Siegle, D. (2013). *The underachieving gifted child: Recognizing, understanding, and reversing underachievement.* Waco, TX: Prufrock Press.

Siegle, D., Gubbins, E. J., O'Rourke, P., Dulong Langley, S., Mun, R. U., Luria, S. R., . . . Plucker, J. A. (2016). Barriers to underserved students' participation in gifted programs and possible solutions. *Journal for the Education of the Gifted, 39,* 103–131. doi:10.1177/0162353216640930

Siegle, D., & McCoach D. B. (2005). *Motivating gifted students.* Waco, TX: Prufrock Press.

Siegle, D., McCoach, D. B., & Roberts, A. (2017). Why I achieve determines whether I achieve. *High Ability Studies, 28,* 59–72. doi:10.1080/13598139.2017.1302873

Siegle, D., Rubenstein, L. D., & Mitchell, M. S. (2014). Honors students' perceptions of their high school experiences: The influence of teachers. *Gifted Child Quarterly, 58,* 35–50. doi:10.1177/0016986213513496

Snyder, K. E., & Linnenbrink-Garcia, L. (2013). A developmental, person-centered approach to exploring multiple motivational pathways in gifted underachievement. *Educational Psychologist, 48,* 209–228. doi.10.1080/00461520.2013.835597

Solorzano, L. (1983, August). Now, gifted children get some breaks. *U.S. News & World Report, 8,* 32.

Whitmore, J. R. (1980). *Giftedness, conflict, and underachievement.* Boston, MA: Allyn & Bacon.

Wigfield, A., & Eccles, J. S. (2000). Expectancy-value theory of achievement motivation. *Contemporary Educational Psychology, 25,* 68–81. doi:10.1006/ceps

CHAPTER 18

Underrepresented Culturally and Linguistically Diverse Gifted Students

Recommendations for Equitable Recruitment and Retention

Donna Y. Ford and Jemimah L. Young

A mind is a terrible thing to waste.—United Negro College Fund
A mind is a terrible thing to erase.—Donna Y. Ford

Essential Questions to Guide the Reader

1. Why are Black and Hispanic[4] students[5] underidentified as gifted?

2. What are some of the primary barriers to these two culturally different groups of students being identified as gifted?

3. To what extent are these groups underidentified as gifted?

4. What are some equity-based policies, practices, and instruments that can be used to increase the identification of Black and Hispanic students?

5. At what point is underidentification inequitable, and what numerical goals can be set to achieve equity?

6. What supports do gifted educators need to be culturally competent, and what changes are needed to improve access to gifted education for underrepresented students?

---

4   The term *Hispanic* is used in this chapter, although the authors acknowledge that some prefer the term *Latino/a*.
5   Although there are other underrepresented populations in gifted education, the authors' work focuses on these two groups specifically because they comprise the largest population of underrepresented students in gifted education.

Across the nation and in most districts, culturally different students, including Black and Hispanic students, are underrepresented in gifted education, according to the Office for Civil Rights and various reports and studies (see http://ocrdata. ed.gov for more information; Ford, 2013; Grissom & Redding, 2016). In this chapter, recruitment and retention barriers are presented, along with recommendations for making gifted education more inclusive for all students, especially those who are underrepresented. Also shared is an equity formula to guide decision makers in setting representation goals that help decrease discrimination and increase access to gifted education.

The six essential questions listed on the previous page are shared to guide readers in their journey to being high-quality educators of all gifted students, which means being attentive to culture and seeking to be culturally responsive and competent. As the opening quotes indicate, when gifts and talents are not recognized and served, atrophy may be one negative outcome that has far-reaching consequences. Underidentified gifted students may act out in school, become underachievers, and/ or drop out, thus failing to reach their potential (Ford, 2010). As such, it is essential that beliefs, tests, policies, and procedures are based on inclusion, rather than exclusion, for underrepresented students. Legally, their right to an appropriate education must not be violated or denied. As noted in the Civil Rights Act of 1964:

> no person in the United States shall, on the basis of race, color, religion, sex, or national origin be excluded from participation in, be denied the benefits of, or be subjected to discrimination under any education program or activity receiving federal financial assistance. (Pub. L. 88–352, Title VI, § 601, July 2, 1964, 78 Stat. 252)

There is no place in educational settings for racial discrimination and segregation. *Brown v. Board of Education* (1954) declared segregation based on race illegal and unconstitutional. The Supreme Court mandated an end to separate and unequal education in America. Decades later, *Brown* and associated legal mandates have yet to be fulfilled, particularly in gifted education, Advanced Placement (AP) classes, and other courses for advanced learners (e.g., honors and International Baccalaureate [IB] classes), given ongoing underrepresentation of Black and Hispanic students in gifted education. In other words, Title VI (1964) stated, whether intentional or unintentional, the inequitable distribution of resources and opportunities to students based on race is unjust. Title VI was enacted as part of the landmark Civil Rights Act of 1964 to prohibit discrimination based on race, color, and national origin in programs and activities receiving federal financial assistance.

Another important case, *Griggs v. Duke Power Co.* (1971), focused on the utility of tests for employment purposes and found them to be discriminatory against Blacks. This court case set much of the groundwork for understanding disparate impact, which focuses on the outcomes of policies, procedures, and measures, regardless of intent. The court case also laid the foundation for questioning and challenging the fairness of tests and how they can—and do—decrease access to certain opportunities. This seminal 1971 court case has been applied to education in general and gifted education specifically when discrimination is alleged.

Inequitable opportunities promote and exacerbate educational disparities and create an unjust or inequitable system in which Black and Hispanic students are denied access to school programs that are important to students reaching their individual potential. Gifted education can promote and reinforce racial inequities (Ford, 2013; Grissom & Redding, 2016), which contribute to de facto and de jure segregation. A relatively recent court case in gifted education demonstrating both intentional and unintentional segregation is *McFadden v. Board of Education for Illinois School District U-46*, which was settled in 2013 (see Ford & Russo, 2015, for more information). The judge found that the district both intentionally and unintentionally discriminated against Hispanic students in its grade 4–6 gifted programs. They were operating two racially identifiable gifted programs: one for Whites and one for Hispanics. They also adopted instruments, policies, and procedures that discriminated against Hispanic students.

In the following sections, the authors provide an overview of gifted education using a cultural lens, along with a vignette of a gifted student. We share patterns in the representation of Black and Hispanic students in gifted education using the Office for Civil Rights' Civil Rights Data Collection[1] (CRDC) from 2009–2010 to 2011–2012, which is the most recent national data, and present an equity formula for districts and states to consider to reduce underrepresentation.

Gifted Education Definitions: Overview With Cultural Implications

In every school building and zip code, there are gifted students.
In every racial and ethnic group, there are gifted students.—(Ford, 2017, p. 185)

The U.S. Department of Education adopted six definitions of giftedness between 1970 and 2001. The only explicit mention of culture appears in 1993 (all others are colorblind):

Children and youth with outstanding talent perform, or show the potential for performing, at remarkably high levels of accom-

---

1   These Civil Rights Data Collection files are state and national estimations. The 2009–2010 estimations are based on a rolling stratified sample of approximately 7,000 districts and 72,000 schools, and on reported data from those districts that responded to the survey. See http://ocrdata.ed.gov for more information.

plishment when compared with others of their age, experience, or environment. These children and youth exhibit high performance capacity in intellectual, creative, and/or artistic areas, and unusual leadership capacity, or excel in specific academic fields. They require services or activities not ordinarily provided by the schools. Outstanding talents are present in children and youth from all cultural groups, across all economic strata, and in all areas of human endeavor. (U.S. Department of Education, 1993, p. 3)

The emphasis on potential and talent development is equitable. Talent development—the focus on early identification and potential, and ongoing supports—has the capacity to recruit and retain underrepresented gifted students. The culturally responsive U.S. Department of Education (1993) definition addressed two historically ignored or trivialized notions specific to culturally different students: (a) gifted students must be compared with others not just by age but also experience and environment and (b) outstanding talents are present in students from all cultural groups, across all economic strata, and in all areas of human endeavor. This definition calls for much-needed attention to local (and preferably building) norms. It is critically important to recognize that giftedness is relative, as noted in the 1993 definition (i.e., students should be compared with others of their age, experience, and environment). How fair is it to have a child who lives in poverty compete with a child whose parent(s) are high income and highly educated? It is most likely that children who have the most resources will outperform those facing more challenges and having fewer resources. Specifically, gifted students should be identified and served in every school building and compared to those within that building only. Within many school districts, there are well-resourced buildings and underresourced buildings, along with Title I buildings. Our collective experiences have found that the latter two tend to have few(er) students identified as gifted. In every building, even the lowest performing ones, there are students who need more challenge. These top students should be served as gifted.

Definitions and theories of giftedness are conceptualized, theorized, and normed on middle-class White students, not students of color and those who live in poverty (Ford, 2013; Sternberg, 2007a, 2007b). They have been operationalized heavily and almost exclusively by intelligence tests and achievement tests, respectively. In the majority of schools, students must obtain an IQ score of 130 or higher to be identified as intellectually gifted and/or they must score at or above the 93rd percentile on an achievement test (see http://www.nagc.org/resources-publications/gifted-state/2014-2015-state-states-gifted-education for more information). These reified criteria are based on the belief that giftedness is synonymous with intelligence and achievement and that both can be measured validly and reliably with standardized tests, regardless of culture and other demographic variables (e.g., income) and irrespective of exposure and opportunity. Both assumptions and criteria based on them trivialize and disregard the importance of culture, language, and experience on test performance, which were rightfully noted in the 1993 federal definition. Therefore, tests and other instruments (e.g., checklists, referral forms, nomination forms) must be selected and interpreted with the culture, income, and language of students in mind, along with equity (Ford, 2013; Sternberg, 2007a, 2007b).

In the following vignette, readers need to consider definitions and theories of giftedness, as well as assessment, for a student named Yessica. What accommodations should be made in order to advocate for students whose first language is not English? Yessica is one of the many thousands of students in U.S. schools whose first language is not English, and this population is growing drastically, particularly among Mexican students (Kena et al., 2016).

VIGNETTE: Meet Yessica

Yessica is a native Spanish-speaking middle school student. She came to the United States from Venezuela 4 years ago, where she attended elementary school. Her parents do not speak English. They came to the U.S. to provide a better life for their daughter. This includes a better education for her than what was offered in their native country. They are seeking the "American Dream."

After 2 months, Yessica's language arts teacher identifies her advanced academic performance and makes a referral for her to be screened for gifted education services. The district uses an achievement test for screening. No other measures are used, and students must score in the 93rd percentile or higher to receive additional consideration for gifted education identification and placement/services. The specific achievement test used to measure students' potential presents a variety of measures, including reading passages with a series of questions. One of the reading passages, which is followed by eight multiple-choice questions, is a personal narrative of a teenager's kayaking excursion. This is one of several culturally loaded passages that are biased against students of color yet favor White and more privileged students.

Given Yessica's lived experiences and language, as well as cultural activities customarily practiced in her country, she is not able to follow the narrative because she is unfamiliar with a kayak. As such, she struggles with the literacy components (such as imagery and plot development) presented within the assessment. The understanding of these language arts elements matters because they are heavily predicated upon the narrative and context used to assess achievement. This reading passage, while appropriate and relatable to some students, is not culturally responsive to Yessica. Although she does well on this assessment—scoring at the 90th percentile—cultural and language constraints prohibit her from scoring at the percentile necessary to receive gifted education services.

Given that gifted education is not federally mandated, states and districts have much discretion regarding identification and services. Yessica's district not only ignored cultural bias in its selection of assessments adopted and used, but it also ignored the commonsense fact that a person who has only spoken English for 4 years, yet who is advanced in language arts, can be gifted. Therefore, it is essential to consider definitions when recruiting and retaining culturally and linguistically different gifted students. All states and districts must adopt definitions, theories, instruments, and practices that include cultural dimensions, language considerations, income and associated inequities, talent development opportunities, and support for underachievers. This requires analyzing data and setting measurable equity goals, as described next.

Gifted Underrepresentation Formula and Equity Allowance Formula

Several statistics can be used to analyze disproportionality or representation discrepancies in gifted programs. The Relative Difference in Composition Index (RDCI) is used in this chapter (Ford, 2013). The RDCI for a racial group is the difference between its gifted education composition and general education composition, expressed as a discrepancy percentage. The basic question is "What is the difference between the composition (percentage) of Black or Hispanic students in general education compared to the composition of Black or Hispanic students in gifted education?" This formula permits educators to compare discrepancies. A discrepancy is significant when underrepresentation exceeds a threshold determined legally and/or by decision makers.

Racial quotas are illegal. It is important to note that equity thresholds or allowances are *not* racial quotas. With quotas, group representation in school enrollment and gifted education enrollment is proportional, meaning that if Black or Hispanic students comprise 50% of a school district (or even a school building), they must comprise 50% of the gifted education enrollment. Equity thresholds or allowances differ substantially. After sharing examples using the RDCI, an equity allowance formula is presented to help determine whether underrepresentation is beyond statistical chance—whether the imbalance is primarily influenced by human-made obstacles (e.g., subjectivity, deficit thinking, prejudice) and, thus, possibly discriminatory (see Ford, 2013; Ford & Grantham, 2003; Valencia, 2010). The RDCI for underrepresentation is computed as follows:

[100% – ((Composition (%) of Black/Hispanic students in gifted education)) / ((Composition (%) of Black/Hispanic students in general education))]

Each year, due to underrepresentation, an additional 500,000 Black and Hispanic students combined are not identified as gifted in the United States (Ford, 2010, 2013; Ford & Russo, 2015). Table 18.1 presents the national Civil Rights Data Collection by the Office for Civil Rights for 2006, 2009, and 2011. For Black students, underrepresentation has ranged from 43% to 47%; for Hispanic students, the range is from 31% to 37%. Underrepresentation exists in the majority of states and school districts for Black students (see Ford & King, 2014; Grissom & Redding, 2016).

After reviewing Table 18.1, we want educators to consider several important and valid questions:

- When is underrepresentation significant?
- How severe must underrepresentation be in order to require changes?
- How severe must underrepresentation be in order to be considered discriminatory or unjust?

When considering these questions, recall that when the percentage of underrepresentation *exceeds* the designated threshold in the Equity Allowance Formula, it is beyond statistical chance; therefore, whether intentional or not, human error is operating—attitudes, instruments, and policies and procedures may be discriminatory.

Intent matters when examining underrepresentation, depending on the legislation applied. For example, the doctrine of disparate impact holds that practices may be considered discriminatory and illegal if they have an "adverse impact" on students regarding a protected trait. Protected traits vary by statute, but most federal civil rights laws (e.g., Title VI) include race, color, religion, national origin, and gender as protected traits (Ford & Russo, 2015).

Under the disparate impact doctrine, a violation of Title VI of the 1964 Civil Rights Act may be proven by demonstrating that an instrument, practice, and/or policy has a disproportionately adverse effect on Black and Hispanic students. Therefore, the disparate impact doctrine (recall *Griggs v. Duke Power Co.*, 1971) prohibits school personnel from using a facially neutral practice that has an unjustified adverse impact on members of a protected class. Noteworthy is that a facially neutral employment practice is one that does not *appear* to be discriminatory on

Table 18.1

Black and Hispanic Students: Underrepresentation in Gifted Education Nationally (2006, 2009, 2011)

Year	Black Hispanic	National Enrollment	Gifted Enrollment	Percentage of Underrepresentation
2006	Black	17.13%	9.15%	47%
	Hispanic	20.4%	12.79%	37%
2009	Black	16.17%	9.9%	43%
	Hispanic	15.4%	11.3%	31%
2011	Black	19%	10%	47%
	Hispanic	25%	16%	36%

Note. Data from Office for Civil Rights (2006, 2009, 2011).

the surface; instead, it is discriminatory in its application and/or its effect (Ford & Russo, 2015; also see http://en.wikipedia.org/wiki/Disparate_impact).

Used in a decontextualized way, the RDCI is insufficient for determining inequitable and/or discriminatory underrepresentation. This is where the Equity Index (EI) is helpful. Calculating the EI is a two-step process. This formula can be used with any group of students, not just Black students. Black students are used as an example below.

- Step 1: ((Composition (%) of Black students in general education)) × Threshold of 20% = B. This is abbreviated as $C \times T = B$.
- Step 2: ((Composition (%) of Black students in general education)) − B = EI. This is abbreviated as $C - B = EI$.

Using the above to provide one example, if Black students were 19% of school enrollment in 2011, the EI using a 20% allowance would be B is 19% × 20% = 3.8% and EI is 19% − 3.8% = 15.2%. Thus, Black students should represent at *minimum* 15.2% of students in gifted education in the U.S. Nationally, the percentage for 2011 is 10%. The underrepresentation for Black students is not only significant, but also beyond statistical chance, suggesting that racial discrimination is operating. For some or many educators, it is difficult to talk about discrimination. However, discrimination does exist in education; to move forward, we must acknowledge this unfortunate reality and be part of the solution, which means advocating for *all* students rather than some students.

To achieve the minimal equity goal, educators must increase Black students' representation nationally from 10% to a minimum of 15.2%. This is presented in Table 18.2. The goals for Hispanic students also appear in Table 18.2, which means an increase from 16% to 20%. These data illustrate the troubling reality that our states' and nation's gifted programs are racially segregated. We, as an educational system, are far from fulfilling the mandates of *Brown* in gifted education.

Table 18.2

Black and Hispanic Students' Underrepresentation and Equity Allowance Goal Nationally (2006, 2009, 2011)

Year	Black Hispanic	National Enrollment	Gifted Enrollment	Percentage of Under-representation	Equity Allowance Goal
2006	Black	17.13%	9.15%	47%	13.7% (increase from 9.15% to 13.7%)
	Hispanic	20.4%	12.79%	37%	16.32% (increase from 12.79% to 16.32%)
2009	Black	16.17%	9.9%	43%	12.9% (increase from 9.9% to 12.9%)
	Hispanic	15.4%	11.3%	31%	12.32% (increase from 11.3% to 12.32%)
2011	Black	19%	10%	47%	15.2% (increase from 10% to 15.2%)
	Hispanic	25%	16%	36%	20% (increase from 16% to 20%)

Note. Data from Office for Civil Rights (2006, 2009, 2011).

Recommendations

Too many Black and Hispanic students fail to achieve their potential because they are denied access to gifted classes and services. Prejudice and stereotypes (e.g., deficit-oriented paradigms that focus on what educators think students cannot do as opposed to what they can do, meaning their resilience and grit) contribute to racially and economically segregated gifted programs (which violate the principles and mandates of *Brown*) that are sorely inadequate at recruitment and retention (Ford, 2013, 2014, 2015; Ford & Grantham, 2003; Valencia, 2010). Asset-based and strength-based paradigms must replace deficit-based paradigms. Recent court cases, specifically *McFadden v. Board of Education for Illinois School District U-46* (2013), remind and must compel us as educators to continue advocating for underrepresented groups; we must acknowledge that discrimination is not only unintentional, but also intentional; and we must not discount that discrimination in gifted education contributes to segregation. The professional will and accountability to eliminate human-made barriers, to take on the status quo, and to advocate for underrepresented gifted Black and Hispanic students and those who live in poverty, are crucial. The following recommendations are offered with this in mind.

Analyze and Disaggregate Underrepresentation Data

Attitudes (prejudice, deficit thinking, classism, and racism) and inequitable policies and practices must be acknowledged, examined, analyzed, challenged, and addressed to recruit and retain underrepresented students in gifted education. The following questions can be used to redress the aforementioned policies and practices:

- Are Black and Hispanic students being screened and referred by teachers in proportion to their representation in the district and state?
- How pervasive and severe is underrepresentation by race and income?
- Which factors contribute to underrepresentation (e.g., subjectivity in beliefs, attitudes, and values; subjective instruments, such as checklists and nomination forms; biased and unfair tests; and discriminatory policies and procedures)?
- Which policies and procedures contribute to and exacerbate underrepresentation (e.g., reliance on teacher referral or checklist vs. schoolwide grade-level screening; parent/caregiver referral or checklists; designated cutoff scores; grade at which gifted programs begin; ongoing screening; convenience and location of testing sites; modes of communicating in neighborhoods)?
- Which educators underrefer Black and Hispanic students, and how are they being assisted for accountability?
- How effective are family referrals for such students, and what is being done to increase such referrals and support families of color and those who live in poverty?

Determine Equity Allowance Goals

After studying the magnitude and causes for underrepresentation, equity goals must be set to desegregate gifted education using the 20% equity allowance (Ford, 2013). The equity allowance is a recognition that giftedness exists in *every* racial and economic group. Students' lived experiences, resources, and supports are not always equally and equitably distributed, as was illustrated with Yessica and so many like her. The equity allowance, which is measurable, takes such differences and injustices into account, thereby opening doors for many non-White students who might otherwise not be identified and served in gifted education. Figure 18.1 presents an equity reflection, with attention to teaching to the test.

Collect Data on the Experiences of Gifted Black and Hispanic Students

What are the experiences of former and current Black and Hispanic students in gifted education? Disaggregate data by gender and income: What are the experiences

The following example is drawn directly from the *Gifted Education Praxis Study Companion*, a guide that prepares teachers seeking formal certification to teach in gifted classrooms:

> Eight-year-old Sarah is working on advanced algebra, reading at a twelfth-grade level, and experimenting with a chemistry set at home. Her parents meet with her teacher and request testing for the program for gifted and talented students. Although the teacher agrees that Sarah is reading well above grade level, she is hesitant to refer Sarah for the program because she is often off task, rarely finishes class assignments, and has a tendency to cry when frustrated. The teacher would benefit from training to better recognize:
> (A) emotional dysfunction
> (B) self-efficacy
> (C) cognitive processes
> (D) asynchronous development

(Educational Testing Services, 2016, p. 15; see http://www.ets.org/praxis)

In considering exam questions such as the one presented above, it is important to understand the cultural dispositions and similarities and differences in the cognitive, affective, and behavioral outcomes of culturally and linguistically diverse students. For example, Black children often do not "cry when frustrated"; rather, they may begin to raise their voices as part of their off-task behavior, contrary to what the prompt suggests. Crying often evokes sympathy and compassion, whereas "being loud" provokes disciplinary actions by teachers who are not culturally adept.

Both of the aforementioned characteristics of off-task behavior require the teacher to recognize (D) asynchronous development as the correct answer; however, without providing cultural context, this point may not be universally understood. From something as simple as the name (Sarah) used in this prompt, to the specific student characteristics, it is apparent this question does not foster equitable preparation, policies, and practices.

Figure 18.1. Equity reflection: Teaching to the teaching test.

of males compared to females, and low-income students compared to high-income students? Surveys, interviews, focus groups, and case studies from such students and families regarding their experiences can be useful for both recruitment and retention. It is essential to study what encourages or motivates students to persist in gifted classes. Study relationships with classmates and with peers in the community.

- Do these students feel welcome in gifted classrooms?
- Do these gifted students feel valued and appreciated by their teachers, counselors, administrators, and other school personnel?
- How do gifted Black and Hispanic students find ways to fit in and be welcomed in gifted education?

- How supportive, involved, and informed are their families in order to serve as advocates and cultural brokers?

Evaluate and Promote Educators' Preparation in Gifted Education

Educators are seldom formally prepared in gifted education, despite their responsibility for referrals, nominations, and teaching gifted students. Gifted education preparation is essential and can take place via courses, degreed programs, and professional development (conferences and in-service workshops). Training must be continuous and substantive, which means targeting equitable identification and assessment instruments, policies and procedures, and development—affective, psychological, academic, social, and cultural (Ford, 2010, 2011). Culturally responsive educators are adept at motivating their gifted students and understand that Black and Hispanic students may face more challenges than their White classmates and peers, as already noted. They recognize that several goals must be addressed: motivate students cognitively, motivate students academically, motivate students socially-emotionally, and motivate students culturally.

Evaluate and Promote Cultural Competence Among Educators

Educators who lack cultural competence risk undermining the educational experiences of Black and Hispanic students and thus contribute to segregated gifted education programs. Formal, substantive, and comprehensive multicultural preparation helps ensure educational equity (Banks, 2010, 2015). Professional development on culture and cultural differences must be ongoing and deep, including defining and understanding culture and cultural differences without a deficit orientation, recognizing how culture impacts teaching and learning, testing and assessment, and classroom environment (e.g., relationships with teachers and classmates, classroom management). Sample opportunities consist of having field experiences, attending community events, and visiting families. Again, it is vital that educators connect with students culturally and that their work is culturally responsive and affirming.

Increase the Demographics of Black and Hispanic Educators in Gifted Education

White teachers comprise a significant proportion of the education profession (Kena et al., 2016). Specifically, at the national level, Whites comprise 85% of teachers, and Blacks represent 7% of teachers, as do Hispanics. Asians comprise 1% of teachers. Ford (2011) reported that Black teachers are virtually invisible in gifted education. Thus, students from every racial and cultural background continue to graduate without ever having a Black or Hispanic teacher, counselor, educational psychologist, and/or administrator; and this is the case in gifted education. Culturally different educators can and do serve as cultural brokers, role models, mentors, and strong advocates for Black and Hispanic students (Delpit, 2012; Ford, 2011; Gay, 2010; Grissom & Redding, 2016; Ladson-Billings, 2009).

Conclusion

In *Brown v. Board of Education* (1954), the Supreme Court ruled that segregating children on the basis of race was unconstitutional. It signaled the end of legalized racial segregation in the U.S. schools, overruling the "separate but equal" principle set forth in the 1896 *Plessy v. Ferguson* case. Yet, segregation persists in school settings and gifted education.

Discrimination in gifted education was found in the *McFadden* (2013) court case. Although other districts may not have been found guilty of *intentional* discrimination, it is clear that de facto and de jure segregation is operating—unintentionally and intentionally—in many school districts.

In principle and in practice, gifted education professionals must abide by the spirit and law of *Brown* (1954) regarding desegregating classrooms, programs, and services. Progress in gifted education underrepresentation has been insignificant and inequitable. Educators must be proactive, deliberate, and diligent about eliminating intentional *and* unintentional barriers to recruiting and retaining Black and Hispanic students in gifted education—to desegregating and integrating gifted education (see *Griggs v. Duke Power*, 1971).

Big Ideas

1. Denying access to gifted education, whether intentional or unintentional, has the same outcome: underrepresentation.

2. To improve access to gifted education for underrepresented Black and Hispanic students, educators must determine equity goals and how they will make changes to meet the goals.

3. Underrepresentation can be decreased when policies, procedures, instruments, and attitudes are culturally responsive and equity based.

4. Extensive training and preparation in gifted education must be complemented by extensive training and preparation in culturally competent education.

5. Families and communities must be supported in order to advocate for their culturally different gifted children. Home-school collaboration is essential.

Discussion Questions

1. What are the limitations of relying exclusively or extensively on tests to identify gifted students?

2. Calculate the percentage of underrepresentation in your district. Why does underrepresentation exist?

3. What is the equitable goal for underrepresented students in your district?

4. What are the shortcomings of teacher referrals for culturally and linguistically different students, and can such referrals be improved?

5. What are five or more strategies that should be implemented to improve access to gifted education for Black and Hispanic students overall and in your school district?

6. What are three to five topics concerning underrepresentation that should be discussed in professional development and coursework with gifted education teachers and other educators?

References

Banks, J. A. (2010). Approaches to multicultural curriculum reform. In J. A. Banks & C. A. M. Banks (Eds.), *Multicultural education: Issues and perspectives* (7th ed., pp. 233–258). Hoboken, NJ: John Wiley & Sons.

Banks, J. A. (2015). *Cultural diversity and education: Foundations, curriculum, and teaching* (6th ed.). Boston, MA: Pearson.

Brown v. Board of Education, 347 U.S. 483 (1954).

Civil Rights Act of 1964 § 7, 42 U.S.C. § 2000e et seq (1964).

Delpit, L. D. (2012). *Multiplication is for White people: Raising expectations for other people's children.* New York, NY: The New Press.

Educational Testing Services. (2016). *The Praxis study companion.* Washington, DC: Author.

Ford, D. Y. (2010). *Reversing underachievement among gifted Black students* (2nd ed.). Waco, TX: Prufrock Press.

Ford, D. Y. (2011). *Multicultural gifted education* (2nd ed.). Waco, TX: Prufrock Press.

Ford, D. Y. (2013). *Recruiting and retaining culturally different students in gifted education.* Waco, TX: Prufrock Press.

Ford, D. Y. (2014). Segregation and the underrepresentation of Blacks and Hispanics in gifted education: Social inequality and deficit paradigms. *Roeper Review, 36,* 143–154.

Ford, D. Y. (2015). Recruiting and retaining Black and Hispanic students in gifted education: Equality vs. equity schools. *Gifted Child Today, 38,* 187–191.

Ford, D. Y. (2017). Desegregating gifted education for culturally different students: Recommendations for equitable recruitment and retention. In J. T. DeCuir-Gunby & P. A. Schutz (Eds.), *Race and ethnicity in the study of motivation in education* (pp. 183–198). New York, NY: Routledge.

Ford, D. Y., & Grantham, T. C. (2003). Providing access for gifted culturally diverse students: From deficit thinking to dynamic thinking. *Theory Into Practice, 42,* 217–225.

Ford, D. Y., & King, R. A. (2014). No Blacks allowed: Segregated gifted education in the context of *Brown vs. Board of Education. Journal of Negro Education, 83,* 300–310.

Ford, D. Y., & Russo, C. J. (2015). No child left behind . . . unless a student is gifted and of color: Reflections on the need to meet the educational needs of the gifted. *Journal of Law in Society, 15,* 213–239.

Gay, J. (2010). *Culturally responsive teaching: Theory, research, and practice* (2nd ed.). New York, NY: Teachers College Press.

Griggs v. Duke Power Co., 401 U.S. 424 (1971).

Grissom, J. A., & Redding, C. (2016). Discretion and disproportionality: Explaining the underrepresentation of high-achieving students of color in gifted programs. *AERA Open, 2*(1), 1–25. doi:10.1177/2332858415622175

Kena, G., Hussar, W., McFarland, J., de Brey, C., Musu-Gillette, L., Wang, X., . . . Dunlop Velez, E. (2016). *The condition of education 2016.* Washington, DC: U.S. Department of Education, National Center for Education Statistics.

Ladson-Billings, G. (2009). *The dreamkeepers: Successful teachers of African American children* (2nd ed.). New York, NY: Jossey-Bass.

McFadden v. Bd. of Educ., 984 F. Supp. 2d 882, 2013 U.S. Dist. LEXIS 97179 (N.D. Ill. 2013). Retrieved from http://www.maldef.org/news/releases/maldef_u46_discrimination_case

Office for Civil Rights. (2006). *2006 national and state estimations.* Retrieved from http://ocrdata.ed.gov/StateNationalEstimations/Projections_2006

Office for Civil Rights. (2009). *2009–10 national and state estimations.* Retrieved from http://ocrdata.ed.gov/StateNationalEstimations/Projections_2009_10

Office for Civil Rights. (2011). *Civil rights data collection.* Retrieved from http://ocrdata.ed.gov

Plessy v. Ferguson, 163 U.S. 537 (1896).

Sternberg, R. J. (2007a). Who are the bright children? The cultural context of being and acting intelligent. *Educational Researcher, 36,* 148–155.

Sternberg, R. J. (2007b). Cultural concepts of giftedness. *Roeper Review, 29,* 160–166.

Title VI, 42 U.S.C. § 2000d et seq. (1964).

U.S. Department of Education, Office of Educational Research. (1993). *National excellence: A case for developing America's talent.* Washington, DC: U.S. Government Printing Office.

Valencia, R. R. (2010). *Dismantling contemporary deficit thinking: Educational thought and practice.* London, England: Routledge.

CHAPTER 19

Gifted Students From Low-Socioeconomic Backgrounds

Marcia Gentry and Kristen Seward

Hold fast to dreams
For if dreams die
Life is a broken-winged bird
That cannot fly.—Langston Hughes

Essential Questions to Guide the Reader

1. What biases might teachers, school leadership, or the community hold that may interfere with successfully identifying, teaching, and supporting high-ability students from low-income families?

2. What are the unique needs and characteristics of gifted students from low-socioeconomic backgrounds?

3. How can a talent development perspective support the identification and support of high-ability students from low-income families?

4. What curricular tools and supplemental services or programs in the school and in the community exist to consistently support high expectations and high achievement of high-ability students from low-income families throughout their Pre-K–16 education?

5. How can teacher education and professional development programs better prepare teachers for working with high-ability students from low-income families?

Gifted students from low-income families may be the most invisible group in education today. They perform well enough on standardized tests to rank positively in school improvement measures, but their scores are likely not high enough to qualify them for their school's gifted program (Callahan, 2005). Due to biases, teachers may believe these students are *over*achieving; thus, many disadvantaged students' abilities or achievement potentials go unrecognized, and teachers fail to nominate these students for gifted programming. In addition, teachers may not provide consistent academic challenge to or hold high expectations for students with high potential who come from lower income families. By the time they reach middle school, these students may appear to be only average in ability and achievement as a result of educators' failures to recognize and nurture their talents along the way (Wyner, Bridgeland, & DiIulio, 2009). By high school graduation, these students have been robbed of opportunities to take advanced coursework that would help them matriculate to top-tier universities. Finally, their dreams of a college degree are diminished as undermatching and underdeveloped support systems take their toll on persistence and college completion (Wyner et al., 2009). Like broken-winged birds, they are no longer capable of soaring above their circumstances.

by local norms

Prevalence of Gifted, Creative, and Talented Youth in Poverty

Living with poverty in the United States today means the ends never meet. Low-income families constantly struggle with food, housing, employment, and health insecurities. In fact, most of these families need income twice the federal poverty level in order to meet their basic needs (Wright, Chau, & Aratani, 2010). In 2014, more than 1 in 5 children under the age of 18 (21.1% or 15.5 million) lived in poverty (DeNavas-Walt & Proctor, 2015), and participation in the National School Lunch Program (NSLP) increased by 14.9 million students during the last decade (Food Research and Action Center, 2015). The actual number of gifted students from poor families is difficult to determine due to identification malpractice and the dearth of gifted programs in the schools that many of these students attend; a conservative estimate would suggest that of the approximately 15.5 million students who live in poverty, 775,000 should be identified and served if only 5% of these students were recognized. Embarrassingly, in actual practice fewer than half of this number are likely identified (Callahan, Moon, & Oh, 2014). If 10% or more of these students were identified, as is the case in higher income schools, then the numbers would more than double. However, excellence gaps, referring to the gaps between high-scoring subgroups on the National Assessment of Educational Progress (NAEP), show that students who qualify for the NSLP consistently score lower than their intellectual peers. The excellence gap between NSLP and non-

NSLP high-achieving students has widened since 2003 due to non-NSLP students making much larger score gains and/or NLSP students' scores remaining stagnant in grades 4 and 8 in both reading and math (Plucker, Burroughs, & Song, 2010; Plucker, Hardesty, & Burroughs, 2013).

Defying Definition

More than age, gender, race, ethnicity, or locale, poverty determines destiny (Ambrose, 2013; Burney & Beilke, 2008; Carman & Taylor, 2010; VanTassel-Baska, 2010; VanTassel-Baska & Stambaugh, 2007; Wyner et al., 2009). Gifted students from low-socioeconomic backgrounds represent every subgroup in our nation, including boys and girls from every ethnic group who play in urban parks, suburban streets, and rural woods. They begin school ill-prepared, and they continue to fall further behind academically in each subsequent year without appropriate intervention: "Starting-line disparities hamstring educational mobility" for gifted students from low-income families (Wyner et al., 2009, p. 5). Year after year, they fall further behind, are ill-prepared for college, and "are less likely to graduate from college than their higher-income peers. . . . even when they attend the least selective colleges (56 percent versus 83 percent)" (Wyner et al., 2009, p. 5). However, because "poverty manifests differently based on geography, ethnicity, and race . . . typical characteristics of gifted students may manifest differently in low-income, high-ability learners" (Olszewski-Kubilius & Clarenbach, 2012, p. 22). This complicates educational interventions that might work in one context but not others. For example, afterschool enrichment programs that successfully serve low-income, urban students who live in close proximity to the school will likely prove problematic for low-income, rural students whose parents' work schedules and/or lack of transportation prevent the students' participation. Still, many of these students overcome economic, social, and educational disadvantages to succeed in school and in life, inspiring us to reflect on our own beliefs about their abilities and positive life trajectories (Swanson, 2006). As educators, we must do our part to ensure that these students have access to school- and community-based resources and services that will support excellence throughout Pre-K–16.

Underidentified, Underrepresented, Underserved

Too often, educator bias toward students from low-income families and/or their reliance on traditional gifted identification procedures work against gifted students who live with poverty (Bernal, 2007; McBee, 2006; Swanson, 2006). Ford (2007) called for an end to "deficit thinking," which sees social and cultural differences as "deficits, disadvantages, or deviance," replacing it with the "difference paradigm [that emphasizes] how the environment affects opportunities, development, and outcomes" (p. 38). Teachers who practice the difference paradigm will provide enrichment and acceleration opportunities through well-developed Pre-K–12 gifted programming that promotes continual student talent development in order to overcome environmental barriers. In addition, Baldwin (2007) addressed six assumptions that must be made in order for educators to successfully identify and serve gifted students from low-income families:

1. Giftedness expressed in one dimension is just as important as giftedness expressed in another.
2. Giftedness can be expressed through a variety of behaviors.
3. Giftedness in any area can be a clue to the presence of potential giftedness in another area, or a catalyst for the development of giftedness in another area.
4. A total ability profile is crucial in the educational planning for the gifted child.
5. Carefully planned subjective assessment techniques can be used effectively in combination with objective assessment techniques.
6. All populations have gifted children who exhibit behaviors that are indicative of giftedness. (p. 24)

Traditional identification procedures and definitions of *gifted* are insufficient for discovering the potential of students who live with poverty (Borland, 2004; Borland, Schnur, & Wright, 2000; Borland & Wright, 1994, 2000; Olszewski-Kubilius, 2007; Worrell, 2007). A talent development perspective of giftedness (Dai & Chen, 2013) that also includes social intelligence and creativity (Bernal, 2007), task commitment (Renzulli, 1978), inter- and intrapersonal abilities (Callahan, 2005), spatial abilities (Callahan, 2007), and multiple intelligences (Gardner, 1983) would serve these students more justly than a cutoff score on any given test. Multiple, diverse, domain-specific assessments, both formal and informal, interpreted with local/school-level norms, have a much better chance of identifying the talents of these students (Olszewski-Kubilius, 2007; Peters, Matthews, McBee, & McCoach, 2014; Worrell, 2007). Once identified, these students deserve differentiated and individualized gifted programming and services that meet their educational, social, and emotional needs (Bernal, 2007; Callahan, 2007; Olszewski-Kubilius, 2007).

In addition to broadening the definition of gifted and implementing talent development programming, Callahan (2005) identified several other solutions to the inadequate services gifted students from low-income families receive in our schools:

- Provide exemplars of gifted performance and use the identification process to enhance understanding
- Identify early and often . . . [through] ongoing, persistent talent searches

- Use valid and reliable tools [for identification and diagnostic assessment]
- Use authentic, [performance-based] assessments
- Gather data over time and use portfolios. . . . As teachers in the talent-development process, we should be watching how children respond to the high-level challenge of tasks that go beyond the basics to require creativity, critical thinking and analysis, complex thinking, and in-depth inquiry
- Eliminate policies or practices that limit the number served in *the* gifted program. . . . First, it is critical to begin to consider a continuum of gifted services and to modify the curriculum according to student needs (Treffinger, Wittig, Young, & Nassab, 2003). Second, the number of gifted students is not a given and is not fixed in any community. (For a continuum of gifted services, see Figure 19.1 in the Promising Practices section.)
- Rewrite procedures for nomination, screening, and identifying to reflect an inclusive, expanded definition of giftedness
- Match curriculum and services to the identification procedure. . . . To engage in identification of underserved students for placement in programs that do not consider those students' needs is to engage in educational malpractice likely to lead to failure for both the student and the system. (pp. 101–103)

As more gifted students from low-socioeconomic backgrounds are identified, teachers must provide specialized instructional support and maintain high expectations (Hébert, 2002) to help these students succeed in the gifted program. Teachers who persist in deficit thinking (as mentioned above) will be ineffective, even harmful, to these students whose different needs require extra support to overcome the social, cultural, and socioeconomic barriers that have existed and likely continue to exist in their lives:

> Identifying underrepresented gifted students . . . requires examination of deeply held beliefs and longstanding practice, as well as a willingness to restructure thinking and behavior through not just one small alteration in process, but a fundamental restructuring of modes of thinking, beliefs, philosophy, and behaving. (Callahan, 2005, p. 104)

Closing the achievement gap has been the goal of national education policies for over a decade, including No Child Left Behind (NCLB) and Race to the Top (Abbott, 2013; Giroux & Schmidt, 2004). A concern for low-performing students is of national importance and should rightly be addressed and remedied, but do these policies go far enough in defining students who are considered low-performing? When educators consider low performance in relation to a test score, they focus

their attention on one particular set of students, but when they consider low performance in relation to ability, they focus on a different set of students entirely—students who are being left behind and who could accelerate our race to the top dramatically if educators did not completely ignore them. The education of high-ability
students from low-income families who have importance in national agendas should
be addressed. This oversight by government and educational institutions from the
local level to the national level is shameful, "robbing [these students] of opportunity
and our nation of a valuable resource" (Wyner et al., 2009, p. 5).

Promising Practices

Identification

Within the field of gifted education, several promising practices exist that can
help to counteract the trend of underidentification and underservice of children
from low-income families. An examination of a school corporation's identification
procedures for equitable practices is a good place to start. This means that districts
that have programs for gifted students (something all schools should implement)
should check demographic proportionality of those identified for gifted services
with the demographics of the school in which the program exists. If students from
lower income families are disproportionately underrepresented, and they likely will
be, then a plan must be put into place that will increase the numbers of students
from these families that are ultimately served in the gifted program. An all-too-
often occurrence is that schools with a large proportion of students from low-
income families have few students identified as gifted, and those who are identified
usually hail from higher income families.

YES!!

To reverse this trend, multiple criteria and multiple pathways can be implemented to include students from lower income families that otherwise might be
overlooked. Rather than using a matrix, which requires that students meet several
criteria, having students meet one of several criteria for inclusion will result in a
wider net being cast. All students should be screened, with the recognition that students from lower income families will score lower than those from higher income
families. Thus, a talent development approach with levels of services designed to
develop the potentials of high-scoring students from lower income families is essential. According to Wyner et al. (2009), a low-income student scoring in the top quar-
tile is equivalent to a high-income student scoring in the top percentages. If one
sets screening at the 90th percentile, students from low-income families with high
potential are omitted from further consideration. Worse, over time, they begin to
appear average as they lag behind their higher income peers, and potential talent is
lost forever.

The HOPE Scale (Gentry, Pereira, Peters, McIntosh, & Fugate, 2015) can help focus teachers' nominations based on gifted characteristics and behaviors that are not assessed on standardized tests, and this instrument has been shown to be invariant between low-income and non-low-income students. Using this instrument in conjunction with local group-specific norms can help increase the number of students from low-income families that are nominated for gifted services. Further, using group-specific norms, which allow comparison of like students, on any measure can also help to address disproportional representation. It is also very important to provide appropriate services that develop these students' talents once they have been identified. Due to the effects of poverty, these high-potential students may not be ready for the level of work required in the gifted program (Peters et al., 2014). Developing programs that address potential and prepare students for advanced work is essential to their success. As Gentry (2009) discussed, implementing a continuum of talent development services increases the chances of developing talents among more students. An overview of this continuum is reprinted with permission. As depicted in Figure 19.1, some services are good for all learners, but others target specific talents. With students from low-income families, providing opportunities and encouragement to develop strengths will help ensure that their potentials are not lost as they progress through school, and that they are not viewed as only average, despite having high potential that may not have been developed.

Programming Models

Some programs exist that have evidence of effectiveness with underserved gifted students. Expanded programming goes hand in hand with broadened identification procedures; together they can be used to ensure that students who grow up in poverty are afforded educational opportunities to develop their strengths and talents. Short descriptions of two such models follow. Many other services, as depicted in Figure 19.1, exist, and broader services lead to more inclusive practices serving more students.

Total School Cluster Grouping (Gentry, 2014) is an elementary programming model that has been shown to increase the number of students from underserved populations who are identified, over time, as high achieving, while decreasing the number of students identified as low achieving. Additionally, this model has resulted in higher achievement scores for all students and in improved teacher practices, as it uses gifted education pedagogy as the basis for instruction in all classrooms throughout the school with all teachers receiving training in using gifted education strategies. Features of this model include yearly identification of all students' achievement levels from low to high achieving to facilitate placement into classrooms with a reduced range of achievement levels to enable teachers to better target instruction. Groups of students who achieve at above-average levels are placed in all teachers'

A Comprehensive Continuum of Gifted Education and Talent Development Services[1,2]		
Elementary School	**Middle School**	**High School**
General Classroom Enrichment, Talents Unlimited, Junior Great Books	General Classroom Enrichment	General Classroom Enrichment
Discovery, Inquiry, Problem-Based Learning	Discovery, Inquiry, Problem-Based Learning	Discovery, Inquiry, Problem-Based Learning
Enrichment Clusters	Academies of Inquiry	Academies of Inquiry
Differentiation, Total School Cluster Grouping	Differentiation	Differentiation
Individual and Small Group Counseling	Individual and Small Group Counseling	Individual and Small Group Counseling
Social, Emotional, Physical Health	Social, Emotional, Physical Health	Social, Emotional, Physical Health
Career Awareness	Career Counseling	Career and Educational Counseling
Integrated Technology	Integrated Technology	Integrated Technology, Career and Technical Education Courses
Multicultural/Foreign Language Study	Multicultural/Foreign Language Study	Multicultural/Foreign Language Study
Independent Study in Interest Area	Independent Study in Interest Area	Independent Study in Interest Area
Arts Enrichment	Arts Enrichment	Arts Enrichment
Curriculum Compacting	Curriculum Compacting	Curriculum Compacting
Type III: Advanced Product/Service in Interest Area	Type III: Advanced Product/Service in Interest Area	Type III: Advanced Product/Service in Interest Area
Multi-age and Within-Class Grouping, Between Class Grouping by Skill Level	Within and Across Grade Level Advanced/Honors Classes	Honors Courses
Cluster Grouping, Small Group Flexible Grouping and Differentiation, Achievement Grouping	Small Group Flexible Grouping and Differentiation, Achievement Grouping	Advanced Placement Courses

Figure 19.1. A comprehensive continuum of gifted education and talent development services.

A Comprehensive Continuum of Gifted Education and Talent Development Services[1,2]		
Elementary School	**Middle School**	**High School**
Advanced Enrichment in Leadership, Music, Visual and Performing Arts	Advanced Options in Leadership, Music, Visual and Performing Arts	Advanced Options in Leadership, Music, Visual and Performing Arts
Within and Across Grade Pull-out by Targeted Ability, Subject and Interest Areas	Resource Room Send-out to Facilitate Advanced, Student-based Study	Self-designed Courses, Advanced Independent Study
Self-Contained Classes (Single or Multigrade)	Self-Contained Classes (Single or Multigrade)	International Baccalaureate, Advanced Academies
Magnet Schools	Magnet Schools	Magnet Schools, Special Schools
Individual Options: Internships, Apprenticeships, Mentorships, IEP, Dual Exceptionalities	*Individual Options:* Internships, Apprenticeships, Mentorships, IEP, Dual Exceptionalities	*Individual Options:* Internships, Apprenticeships, Mentorships, IEP, Dual Exceptionalities
Acceleration Options: Early Admission, Grade Skipping, Subject Acceleration, Dual Enrollment in Middle School Classes	*Acceleration Options:* Grade Skipping, Subject Acceleration, Telescoping, Dual Enrollment in High School Classes	*Acceleration Options:* Subject Acceleration, Telescoping, Dual Enrollment in College Classes, Credit by Exam, Early College Entry
Special Talent Programs: Young Writers, Saturday and Summer Programs, Future Problem Solving, Math Olympiad, Science Olympiad, Math Leagues, Science Fairs, Talent Searches, Odyssey of the Mind, History Day, Geography Bee, FIRST Robotics, Science Searches, Rube Goldberg Engineering, Lego League, Destination Imagination, Invention Convention, Youth in Government, Close up, Governors' Schools and Academies, etc.		

[1] Adapted, updated, and expanded from Renzulli (1994, p. 78). [2] Services for all young people are highlighted in grey, and these options do not constitute gifted services but do set the stage for discovery and development of talent in more youth and children. From "A comprehensive continuum of gifted education and talent development services: Discovering, developing, and enhancing young people's gifts and talents" (p. 264) by M. Gentry, 2009, *Gifted Child Quarterly, 53.* Copyright 2009 National Association for Gifted Children. Reprinted with permission of the author.

Figure 19.1. *Continued.*

classrooms, with the highest achievers grouped in one classroom and above-average achievers grouped in the other classrooms, giving them time to develop confidence and achievement. High expectations are maintained in all classrooms with enriched, inquiry-based learning for all children.

Enrichment clusters (Renzulli, Gentry, & Reis, 2014) bring gifted education to all students in a school during time when students work with facilitators in areas of strong interest. In the clusters, students use advanced content and authentic methods to create products and services for real-world audiences, much like Renzulli and Reis's (1985) Type III enrichment process, except that in the clusters, all students are involved in the program whether they are identified as gifted or not. Thus, the program offers gifted education programming for all students and gifted education experiences for all teachers, delivering authentic gifted education schoolwide. When working in their interest areas, students produce high-level products, are engaged in learning, and are focused on their strengths. This is optimal learning for all kids, many of whom would never qualify for the gifted program, but who benefit from the enriched teaching and learning.

Conclusion

It is important to include programs and services designed to reveal students' strengths and talents. Deliberate efforts are required to ensure equitable inclusion of students from low-income families, from identification procedures to programming practices. Developing understanding on the part of teachers about the potentials of students from poverty as well as the barriers they face is critical to reversing their underrepresentation in programs for gifted and talented youth.

Big Ideas

1. Low-socioeconomic status hinders a child's educational achievement more than any other demographic characteristic, including age, sex, race, and locale.

2. Gifted students from low-income families defy definition.

3. Gifted students from low-income families remain underidentified, underrepresented, and underserved in schools' gifted programs, if such programs even exist at their schools.

4. Identification and programming practices for talent discovery and development are crucial to realization of talent development for students from low-income families.

Discussion Questions

1. Respectfully confronting bias on personal, program, and institutional levels is vital to the success of any gifted program. All people have biases, and sometimes they are hidden from awareness. Complete the two-part Self-Awareness Assessment on the next page, reprinted with permission from J. A. Castellano and A. D. Frazier (2011), *Special Populations in Gifted Education: Understanding Our Most Able Students from Diverse Backgrounds* (p. 395–399), then discuss with a partner any challenges you may face while teaching high-ability students from low-income families.

2. Identify curricular tools and supplemental services, programs, and people both in the school and community that will support high-ability students from low-income families. Discuss how these can be incorporated into teaching and learning on a daily basis. Include an analysis of any potential barriers that might hinder a teacher's or a school's ability to do this (e.g., general district policies; gifted and talented program policies, including identification procedures; negative community or school-level attitudes and beliefs, including the negative beliefs of the low-income families and children themselves).

3. What did you learn in the reading about educating this special population (and perhaps your prejudices) that you were unaware of before?

Self-Awareness Assessment		
Self-Awareness (to do by yourself)	**Yes**	**No**
1. Have you thought about your own socioeconomic status, gender, racial, and ethnic identity and the various ways in which you are similar to, yet different from, the students and adults you work with?		
2. Have you thought about how your own socioeconomic status, gender, race, and ethnic identity have influenced how you learn and/or how you teach?		
3. Have you talked about how cultural background influences how you teach your students and/or your working relationships with adult colleagues who are of a different socioeconomic status, race, gender, and ethnicity?		
4. Have any people who are different from you with respect to your socioeconomic status, race, gender, and ethnicity shared with you how they think these same factors influence how they learn or teach?		
5. Have you thought about how your own teaching and learning styles, influenced by your own cultural background, are perceived by colleagues and peers who are of a different socioeconomic status, gender, racial, or ethnic group?		
6. Do you think that your school or district's most rigorous academic programs should reflect student demographics with respect to socioeconomic status, race, gender, and ethnicity?		
7. Are you willing to publicly advocate for the inclusion of students into your school or district's gifted education program who are poor, minority, and culturally and/or linguistically diverse?		

Self-Awareness Score:

Count one point for each "Yes" answer in this section.

6–7 Points: This score would put you in the cultural competence stage. That is, you see the difference, understand the difference that difference makes, and work with others to change it.

4–5 Points: You are on your way! Understanding and acknowledging your own biases and prejudices paves the way for greater cross-cultural communication and understanding. Share your insights with others.

0–3 Points: OK, we have some work to do. Personal reflection about your experiences with diversity may be a good starting point. It may be easier to first talk with an expert whose background is similar to yours.

Note. Adapted from Lindsey, Roberts, and Campbell-Jones (2009). Reprinted with permission from Castellano, J. A. (2011). Cultural competency: Implications for educational and instructional leaders in gifted education. In J. A. Castellano & A. D. Frazier (Eds.), *Special populations in gifted education* (pp. 395–399). Waco, TX: Prufrock Press.

References

Abbott, C. (2013). The "Race to the Top" and the inevitable fall to the bottom: How the principles of the "Campaign for Fiscal Equity" and economic integration can help close the achievement gap. *Brigham Young University Education and Law Journal.* Retrieved from http://digitalcommons.law.byu.edu/cgi/viewcontent.cgi?article=1325&context=elj

Ambrose, D. (2013). Socioeconomic inequality and giftedness: Suppression and distortion of high ability. *Roeper Review, 35,* 81–92. doi:10.1080/02783193.2013.766960

Baldwin, A. (2007). The untapped potential for excellence. In J. VanTassel-Baska & T. Stambaugh (Eds.), *Overlooked gems: A national perspective on low-income promising learners* (pp. 23–25). Washington, DC: National Association for Gifted Children.

Bernal, E. M. (2007). The plight of the culturally diverse student from poverty. In J. VanTassel-Baska & T. Stambaugh (Eds.), *Overlooked gems: A national perspective on low-income promising learners* (pp. 27–30). Washington, DC: National Association for Gifted Children.

Borland, J. H. (2004). *Issues and practices in the identification and education of gifted students from under-represented groups* (RM04186). Storrs: University of Connecticut, The National Research Center on the Gifted and Talented.

Borland, J. H., Schnur, R., & Wright, L. (2000). Economically disadvantaged students in a school for the academically gifted: A postpositivist inquiry into individual and family adjustment. *Gifted Child Quarterly, 44,* 13–32. doi:10.1177/001698620004400103

Borland, J. H., & Wright, L. (1994). Identifying young, potentially gifted, economically disadvantaged students. *Gifted Child Quarterly, 38,* 164–171. doi:10.1177/0016986294030042

Borland, J. H., & Wright, L. (2000). Identifying and educating poor and under-represented gifted students. In K. A. Heller, F. J. Mönks, R. J. Sternberg, & R. F. Subotnik (Eds.), *International handbook of giftedness and talent* (2nd ed., pp. 587–594). Oxford, England: Pergamon.

Burney, V. H., & Beilke, J. R. (2008). The constraints of poverty on high achievement. *Journal for the Education of the Gifted, 31,* 171–197.

Callahan, C. (2005). Identifying gifted students from underrepresented populations. *Theory Into Practice, 44,* 98–104. doi:10.1207/s15430421tip4402_4

Callahan, C. (2007). What can we learn from research about promising practices in developing the gifts and talents of low-income students? In J. VanTassel-Baska & T. Stambaugh (Eds.), *Overlooked gems: A national perspective on low-income promising learners* (pp. 53–56). Washington, DC: National Association for Gifted Children.

Callahan, C., Moon, T., & Oh, S. (2014). *National surveys of gifted programs: Executive summary*. Retrieved from http://www.nagc.org/sites/default/files/key%20reports/2014%20Survey%20of%20GT%20programs%20Exec%20Summ.pdf

Carman, C. A., & Taylor, D. K. (2010). Socioeconomic status effects on using the Naglieri Nonverbal Ability Test (NNAT) to identify the gifted/talented. *Gifted Child Quarterly, 54,* 75–84. doi:10.1177/0016986209355976

Castellano, J. A., & Frazier, A. D. (Eds.). (2011). *Special populations in gifted education: Understanding our most able students from diverse backgrounds.* Waco, TX: Prufrock Press.

Dai, D., & Chen, F. (2013). Three paradigms of gifted education: In search of conceptual clarity in research and practice. *Gifted Child Quarterly, 57,* 151–168. doi:10.1177/0016986213490020

DeNavas-Walt, C., & Proctor, B. (2015). *Income and poverty in the United States: 2014: Current population reports.* Retrieved from https://www.census.gov/content/dam/Census/library/publications/2015/demo/p60-252.pdf

Food Research and Action Center. (2015). *National school lunch program: Trends and factors affecting student participation.* Retrieved from http://frac.org/pdf/national_school_lunch_report_2015.pdf

Ford, D. (2007). Diamonds in the rough: Recognizing and meeting the needs of gifted children from low SES backgrounds. In J. VanTassel-Baska & T. Stambaugh (Eds.), *Overlooked gems: A national perspective on low-income promising learners* (pp. 37–41). Washington, DC: National Association for Gifted Children.

Gardner, H. (1983). *Frames of mind: The theory of multiple intelligences.* New York, NY: Basic Books.

Gentry, M. (2009). Myth 11: A comprehensive continuum of gifted education and talent development services: Discovering, developing, and enhancing young people's gifts and talents. *Gifted Child Quarterly, 53,* 262–265. doi:10.1177/0016986209346937

Gentry, M. (With K. A. Paul, J. McIntosh, C. M. Fugate, & E. Jen). (2014). *Total school cluster grouping: A comprehensive, research-based plan* for *raising student achievement and improving teacher practices* (2nd ed.). Waco, TX: Prufrock Press.

Gentry, M., Pereira, N., Peters, S., McIntosh, J., & Fugate, M. (2015). *The HOPE Teacher Rating Scale: Involving teachers in equitable identification of gifted and talented students in K–12.* Waco, TX: Prufrock Press.

Giroux, H. A., & Schmidt, M. (2004). Closing the achievement gap: A metaphor for children left behind. *Journal of Educational Change, 5,* 213–228. doi:10.1023/B:JEDU.0000041041.71525.67

Hébert, T. P. (2002). Educating gifted children from low socioeconomic backgrounds: Creating visions of a hopeful future. *Exceptionality: A Special Education Journal, 10,* 127–138. doi:10.1207/S15327035EX1002_6

Lindsey, R. B., Roberts, L. M., & Campbell-Jones, F. (2005). *The culturally proficient school: An implementation guide for school leaders.* Thousand Oaks, CA: Corwin Press.

McBee, M. T. (2006). A descriptive analysis of referral sources for gifted identification screening by race and socioeconomic status. *Journal of Secondary Gifted Education, 17,* 103–111. doi:10.4219/jsge-2006-686

Olszewski-Kubilius, P. (2007). Working with promising learners from poverty: Lessons learned. In J. VanTassel-Baska & T. Stambaugh (Eds.), *Overlooked gems: A national perspective on low-income promising learners* (pp. 43–46). Washington, DC: National Association for Gifted Children.

Olszewski-Kubilius, P., & Clarenbach, J. (2012). *Unlocking emergent talent: Supporting high achievement of low-income, high-ability students.* Washington, DC: National Association for Gifted Children.

Peters, S., Matthews, M., McBee, M., & McCoach, D. B. (2014). *Beyond gifted education: Designing and implementing advanced academic programs.* Waco, TX: Prufrock Press.

Plucker, J. A., Burroughs, N., & Song, R. (2010). *Mind the (other) gap! The growing excellence gap in K–12 education.* Bloomington: Indiana University, School of Education, Center for Evaluation and Education Policy.

Plucker, J., Hardesty, J., & Burroughs, N. (2013). *Talent on the sidelines: Excellence gaps and America's persistent talent underclass.* Retrieved from http://webdev.education.uconn.edu/static/sites/cepa/AG/excellence2013/Excellence-Gap-10-18-13_JP_LK.pdf

Renzulli, J. (1978). What makes giftedness? Reexamining a definition. *Phi Delta Kappan, 60,* 180–184, 261. doi:10.1177/003172171109200821

Renzulli, J. S. (1994). *Schools for talent development.* Mansfield Center, CT: Creative Learning Press.

Renzulli, J. S., Gentry, M., & Reis, S. M. (2014) *Enrichment clusters: A practical plan for real-world, student-driven learning.* Waco, TX: Prufrock Press.

Renzulli, J. S., & Reis, S. R. (1985). *The Schoolwide Enrichment Model: A comprehensive plan for educational excellence.* Mansfield Center, CT: Creative Leaning Press.

Swanson, J. D. (2006). Breaking through assumptions about low-income, minority gifted students. *Gifted Child Quarterly, 50,* 11–25. doi:10.1177/001698620605000103

Treffinger, D. J., Wittig, C. V., Young, G. C., & Nassab, C. A. (2003). *Enhancing and expanding gifted programs.* Waco, TX: Prufrock Press.

VanTassel-Baska, J. L. (Ed.). (2010). *Patterns and profiles of promising learners from poverty*. Waco, TX: Prufrock Press.

VanTassel-Baska, J., & Stambaugh, T. (Eds.). (2007). *Overlooked gems: A national perspective on low-income promising learners*. Washington, DC: National Association for Gifted Children.

Worrell, F. C. (2007). Identifying and including low-income learners in programs for the gifted and talented: Multiple complexities. In J. VanTassel-Baska & T. Stambaugh (Eds.), *Overlooked gems: A national perspective on low-income promising learners* (pp. 47–51). Washington, DC: National Association for Gifted Children.

Wright, V. R., Chau, M., & Aratani, Y. (2010). *Who are America's poor children? The official story*. Retrieved from http://www.nccp.org/publications/pub_912.html

Wyner, J. S., Bridgeland, J. M., & DiIulio, J. J., Jr. (2009). *Achievement trap: How America is failing millions of high-achieving students from lower-income families*. Lansdowne, VA: Jack Kent Cooke Foundation.

CHAPTER 20

The Interplay Between Geography and Giftedness

Tamra Stambaugh

Always design a thing by considering its next larger context—a chair in a room, a room in a house, a house in an environment, an environment in a city plan.—Eliel Saarinen, Finnish architect

Essential Questions to Guide the Reader

1. To what extent does geography impact gifted learners?

2. What should educators consider when identifying gifted learners?

3. What should educators consider when creating appropriate services and curriculum for gifted learners across a variety of educational regions?

Where one lives and how one perceives the world can dramatically impact her trajectory, goals, beliefs, educational attainment, and level to which she meets her potential. Geography is not the only factor that impacts gifted student achievement; however, it is a very important component that needs to be considered when providing services to gifted learners. Geography is not just a location but a reflection of the combination of one's social status, economic status, beliefs, values, and priorities. This chapter explores how giftedness is impacted by geography—which is defined here—and not simply a place in which one lives. It is the interaction of the individual with his local environment and the systems that connect the individual and the environment that are integral to talent development (Stambaugh & Wood, 2015).

A Systems Framework to Connect the Role of Geography and Giftedness: The Ecological Model of Human Development

Urie Bronfenbrenner (1974, 1979), theorist and cofounder of Head Start programs, proposed an ecological model of human development in the 1970s that posited two defining principles about individual development: (a) healthy development is a complex process of regularly effective interactions among many individuals and variables, and (b) environmental interactions that are close to and more distant from the student affect the outcome. He further asserted that the effects of the interactions between the individuals and their variables are more powerful than the environmental aspects, although each impacts the other (Bronfenbrenner, 1994). The process, person, context, and time all interact in ways that impact the individual.

Bronfenbrenner (1994) further compared the ecological environment of an individual to a set of "nesting dolls" (p. 39) in which the individual is the innermost center and interactions of other individuals and the environment extend outward to be encompassed by the passage of time. More specifically, he determined five different structures or systems that are impacted and interrelated within the context of the individual's life:

1. *Microsystems.* The microsystems that directly affect a student's development include his family, his school, and his friends—basically anyone in direct contact with the child will obviously impact his life.
2. *Mesosystems.* Mesosystems are described as a "system of microsystems" (p. 40) in which there are interactions among many different microsystems, such as the child and her family, the family and the school, or the family and the community.
3. *Exosystems.* The exosystem comprises the interaction between various systems for which the child may or may not have control, such as the parent and the parent's workplace that may directly affect home life or the relationship between the school and the community.
4. *Macrosystems.* Moving outward from the center, a macrosystem includes the beliefs, values, cultures, subcultures, lifestyles, opportunities, and barriers of the micro-, meso-, and exosystems.
5. *Chronosystems.* Finally, Bronfenbrenner defined the chronosystem as a third dimension that includes time. As the individual systems interact, they do so with the passage of time. The longer a student lives in poverty or in wealth or in a rural versus an urban environment, the more likely that stu-

dent will be impacted positively or negatively by the other systems at play within her particular context.

Bronfenbrenner's Ecological Model can serve as a framework for viewing giftedness and how it is (or is not) nurtured within a geographical context. A gifted child's needs must be viewed within the context of the larger environment, as opposed to an isolated bestowment of talent that will automatically manifest without support or outside interference. This includes the geographical impact on giftedness, such as the beliefs and values of a region and how a gifted student interacts within that environment.

Consider this scenario:

> Alex is a 6-year-old girl who is quite precocious for her age. She loves learning and completes her fourth-grade brother's homework just for fun (and with 100% accuracy). She lives in a remote rural area, and her school system administration argues that they don't have any "truly gifted" students in their school, although they do follow state guidelines for identifying gifted students after several reprimands from the state department. Alex scores well above average on her first-grade assessments in reading and math and is one of the only students who is able to read chapter books in her grade. She was recommended for additional testing by her teacher for possible entrance into the school's hour-per-week gifted program. After much deliberation, the family has agreed to testing as they recognize Alex's unique talents, but they worry that if she is identified she will grow up to be conceited or lose sight of what is important in life. The school district has one coordinator/teacher of the gifted who monitors and schedules Advanced Placement classes, oversees afterschool clubs including cheerleading and photography, and teaches pull-out classes for advanced students that consist of an hour per week, per grade level and building—the minimum number of minutes required by the state policy. The teacher of gifted is a strong advocate for gifted students but does not have formal training in gifted education. Most of the students in the district, including Alex, are low income. More than 80% of students in the district qualify for free lunch. Alex and her family have a strong social network, and they are actively involved in church and community leadership activities. Her family prioritizes church and family loyalty above all else. Alex's dad has been offered more lucrative paying jobs in the city but chooses to stay

in the area because he loves being "off the beaten path" and closer
to extended family.

In this case study, how might Bronfenbrenner's model be applied? Note that Alex's microsystems include her school, her family, and her friends. The interactions among the family and Alex or the family and the school are part of the mesosystem, while the school and family's beliefs about gifted encompass the exosystem. The macrosystem, then, includes the larger beliefs and lifestyle of the rural community at large as well as society's beliefs about rural and gifted, in general. The longer Alex remains in the same environment, the more likely she will be impacted by it (chronosystem). Therefore, the beliefs and values of Alex's family, the rural community, and the school system interact in ways that will impact Alex and the way she interacts with her environment.

Ponder what would happen if Alex moved to a different location, had a different family, or attended a different school. What if she lived in an urban instead of a rural area? How would the systems interact in different ways? What if Alex's family were wealthy? How would that change this scenario and the various meso-, exo-, and macrosystems for which she is a part? What would happen if Alex attended a private school designed for gifted students? How might her experiences and talent trajectory opportunities change within this new ecological system? What if she moved to the suburbs? Alex's geographic location plays an important part in the support structures available, her family beliefs, and her level of access to gifted services, for example. As such, one cannot examine giftedness or any other construct outside of the context of the individual and where she lives.

Throughout the chapter, consider how the interactions of Brofenbrenner's various contextual systems interact with geography and giftedness, and vice versa. It is also important to note that the content discussed here is based on generalities from the most available, but scant, research base. Urban and rural locales differ as much as they are alike. A rural Appalachia area is different from a rural area on the Northeastern Seaboard or an Indian reservation. Similarly, one's experiences in an urban area such as New York City will vary based on which borough he or she lives in, and even more so if compared to other urban areas in the Midwest, the West, or the South.

Geographical Influences: To What Extent Does Geography Affect Gifted Learners?

Opportunity Nation (2015), a bipartisan group that ranks states by the opportunities available for equitable education, prominently placed the following quote on the home page of its website: "We can't pick our ethnicity, the family we were born into, or our IQ. But if you work hard and play by the rules, your zip code shouldn't condemn you into an inescapable economic fate." Poverty plagues many geographical regions. More than 18% of those in rural areas are living in poverty compared to 15% in urban areas, moreover those living in rural areas report a higher percentage of high school dropouts, which ultimately leads to higher rates of poverty and more stagnant job growth as compared to urban areas (United States Department of Agriculture, Economic Research Service, 2016).

Lower academic achievement gains are also common in rural and urban areas. Graham and Provost (2012) found statistically significant lower math scores with both urban and rural students when compared to those living in suburban areas. Even after controlling for poverty and race, significant differences in scores were present by geographic locale, although poverty and race played significant roles in the scores. Additionally, students in rural areas showed the least amount of academic gain from Kindergarten to grade 8 when compared to those of other geographic regions. These issues are precipitated with other potential barriers. Percentages of federal funding and grant support are higher for urban than rural districts (Graham & Provost, 2012), although both locales struggle with the lack of a rigorous curriculum, fewer resources, ever-changing demographics, fewer choices of advanced course offerings (especially in low-income schools), accountability systems that do not take into account the needs of gifted learners, and less access to properly working technology and Internet access (Ford, 2015; Olszewski-Kubilius & Thomson, 2010; Stambaugh & Wood, 2015).

There are positives to living in different locales as well. For example, those in rural areas may enjoy smaller class sizes, opportunities for more one-to-one instruction and support, opportunities for increased participation in various school activities and extracurricular activities due to fewer students and a stronger sense of belonging (Stambaugh & Wood, 2015). Those attending urban schools may have more immediate access to a variety of learning opportunities in their areas of interest and more choices of course selections and extracurricular activities.

Designing Appropriate Identification Methods Across Varying Geographic Regions

Identification

The equitable identification of gifted students has recently received even more attention as gifted students who are Black, Hispanic, and low income are not as readily identified as their wealthier peers or those who are Asian or White (Ford, 2010; McBee, Shaunessy, & Matthews, 2012; Plucker, Hardesty, & Burroughs, 2013; VanTassel-Baska & Stambaugh, 2007). As previously discussed, one cannot consider the identification of gifted students outside of the context of their micro-, meso-, and exosystem influences. When school personnel are able to recognize and align the various systems at play and capitalize on those, they are able to approach gifted identification in ways that highlight the particular beliefs, strengths, and contextual elements of a community, district, or local school. The consequence is that more students are identified and supported. For example, when working with Native American students, Montgomery (2001) found that a portfolio-based, case study approach identified 87% more students than test scores alone and showcased their unique cultural strengths. Similarly, Spicker and Poling (1993) designed a characteristics checklist unique to rural Appalachian students and provided professional development to support teachers' knowledge of how these students may show their strengths in nontraditional ways. The questions on the checklist inquired about students' participation in 4-H or church groups, community events, and their knowledge of mechanics and environmental sciences. The researchers also emphasized that an individual subtest (i.e., verbal, nonverbal, or quantitative) be considered as part of an identification profile as opposed to requiring a full-battery ability score because most low-income Appalachian students showed uneven score profiles; consequently, promoting identification based on a full scale IQ score did not best represent students' strengths and minimized their true abilities. The researchers also found that many students may have been overlooked for programs because they did not speak in a traditional English dialect or show appropriate grammatical prowess even though their higher level thinking and analysis skills were well above the norm.

In both studies, more students were identified and supported because there were systems in place to help educators understand the unique needs of their particular gifted population using a tailored protocol. Moreover, educators were taught how to look for talent within the context of their school locale. Other researchers (see Lohman, 2005) suggested using local norms or varied cutoff scores based on the school's population or context (e.g., top 5% in a school) as a way to support talent in a particular region where students may not perform as highly on traditional assessments. This is also an ongoing recommendation for identifying students who are from low-income populations (Stambaugh, 2015a; VanTassel-Baska & Stambaugh, 2007).

In urban areas, programs such as the Young Scholars Talent Development Model (Horn, 2015), which is implemented in a diverse school district outside of Washington, DC, and has been replicated in many other regions across the United States, provide opportunities for talent development to all students early in their educational career as part of the general classroom model. Educators teach advanced-level lessons and then collect data on all students, looking specifically for those who learn at a faster pace or show understanding at a deeper level once they are exposed to specific higher level thinking strategies. Anecdotal case study evidence, behavioral checklists, ongoing professional development about unique characteristics of students in the district, and standardized test score subtests, such as nonverbal assessments or specific subject area achievement scores, are used to create a full portfolio of student performance. When using this "serve and then identify" approach coupled with a multifaceted data collection procedure, many students go on to be formally identified as gifted and to receive services based on their unique needs. These services run the gamut from in-classroom differentiation to specialized schools for gifted learners. Family and community support and afterschool and summer programs are also emphasized as important components.

Out-of-school programs such as Northwestern University's Center for Talent Development's Project LIVE and Project EXCITE (Olszewski-Kubilius & Thomson, 2010) target urban gifted low-income students in the Chicago area using a multifaceted identification approach that incorporates achievement tests, nonverbal ability tests (for STEM), parent nominations, essays (for ELA), and curriculum-based assessments (for ELA) to identify students for STEM or ELA afterschool enrichment programs, respectively. When students are identified through using multiple and varied assessments matched to their strengths and provided ongoing enrichment, they show significant gains in achievement and accelerated learning opportunities. Parental support and expectations also increase.

Successful projects such as those outlined here incorporated identification methods that were tailored to the region and needs of specific students within their geographic and personal context. Identification checklists and portfolio assessments accounted for the unique regional aspects. Teacher training was contextual and provided examples of how to find gifted students in their individual schools. Schools made use of multiple qualitative and quantitative assessments that took into consideration local population profiles and specific academic areas. Even though all of the projects used some type of qualitative and quantitative assessments, those assessments differed based on the regional needs and individual student case studies. Thus a robust identification system takes into account the unique characteristics and testing profiles of students of that school and the community assets and culture.

Providing Geography-Based Curriculum and Instruction for Gifted Learners

Regardless of where one lives, the need for high-quality curriculum and instruction does not change. The same strategies as discussed in other chapters apply here as well. However, the contextual considerations, content, application, and delivery should be adapted to the region. Additional strategies explored here can support gifted students from different regions as part of a comprehensive curriculum-based approach that considers geography in addition to giftedness. As such, this next section provides ideas for embedding geographical nuances into an already accelerated and enriched continuum of services for gifted learners. As previously mentioned, the literature regarding geography and gifted is scant, and, as such, some of these strategies are extrapolated from the general research and applied to gifted. Additional research on the impact of geography and giftedness—especially regarding specific instructional strategies—is needed.

Place-based education. Place-based education is typically purported by researchers as a strategy for rural education, but this strategy has recently been incorporated into urban settings as well (Gruenewald, 2008). Sobel (2005) described place-based education as "the process of using the local community and environment as a starting point to teach concepts in language arts, mathematics, social studies, science and other subjects across the curriculum" (p. 6).

Successful examples of place-based education projects are numerous and include activities such as the creation of urban community gardens, community revitalization projects, local government and public service campaigns, local newspaper publishing, and environmental science projects within a region's river and park areas. Surveys from students, teachers, and administrators suggest that place-based education increases student motivation, motivates teachers to collaborate, encourages the use of authentic resources for planning, increases school-community connections, changes school culture, and promotes student learning as students are more likely to engage with the text and learn more when they can see the benefits of their work or study in their backyard (Place-Based Education Evaluation Collaborative, 2010). Students who engage in place-based environmental integration programs also show increased achievement and critical thinking test gains when compared to similar schools that used more traditional approaches to learning (Chawla & Escalante, 2007).

Although many proponents of rural gifted education support the use of place-based education, there is no quantitative research at this time regarding the impact of such practices on gifted student achievement or perceptions. However, given the research base on effective strategies in gifted education, it is logical to hypothesize that place-based education can be a good fit for gifted students as well. Evidence-supported strategies typically purported in gifted education, such as problem-based learning, mentorships, acceleration, service learning, access to content experts, practice applying processes of the discipline, and the creation of authentic products to solve real-world problems, can easily be incorporated within a place-based model and promote community connections and pride.

Mirrors and windows. Bishop (1990) outlined the need for mirrors and windows as part of the literacy curriculum. This concept has since been translated to other academic areas and real-life situations. Students need exposure to both mirrors (reflections of characters, writers, individuals, and settings similar to theirs) and windows (access to the outside world that reflects different points of view, cultures, and perspectives) reflected in their lives and their curriculum. In gifted education, this insinuates reading advanced-level books with gifted protagonists, biography studies of famous individuals, discussions of affective real-world issues that are conceptually covered in books (i.e., dealing with failure, perfectionism, achieving success, work ethic, overcoming obstacles), and connecting gifted students with real-life academic and social mentors. When considering the added component of geography, a gifted child's mirrors would also reflect someone from a geographic region similar to theirs, and windows would showcase those from other areas who view a situation from a different perspective or geographic lens.

Gifted students from rural areas are more likely to struggle with whether to leave or stay and sometimes feel disconnected when returning home after college. They may be accused of "getting above their raising" or "acting too good for others" because they have acquired a different dialect and vocabulary and may not be comfortable code switching to the community vernacular. From an early age, they may feel isolated because they process information differently, learn at a faster pace, or have different interests than their same-age peers. In rural communities there may not be a critical mass of other gifted students like them. Books, content and social mentors, and biography studies of others who have dealt with similar concerns may serve as mirrors and windows for them to cope with their shared sense of place on one level, but their differences in other areas. The same would be applied to urban areas, too, and could focus on different ethnic or cultural considerations of a particular urban population.

Service delivery models. A national survey focused on gifted programming (Callahan, Moon, & Oh, 2013) in elementary schools found that the top modes of service delivery for urban, rural, and suburban schools included part-time pull-out services followed by cluster grouping. Suburban schools were more likely to offer special classes and afterschool programs than urban and rural schools. Although only a very small percentage of schools (regardless of locale) offered grade and subject area accelerative opportunities, when grade or subject acceleration was reported as being used, it was in suburban and rural districts. The amount of time per week students are provided services in gifted education also differed by locale. A slightly higher percentage of rural elementary school districts (7%) reported their gifted students receive less than an hour per week of services as compared to suburban (4%) and urban schools (3%) where more hours per week of services are provided, including full-time opportunities offered in 20% of urban, 21% of suburban, and only 13% of rural schools.

When looking specifically at urban schools, VanTassel-Baska (2010) suggested that throughout history urban centers have shown innovation in gifted programming and services, although more recently these services have been at risk for programming cessation. As recently as the past 5 years, 16% of urban elementary schools reported their program was discontinued or cut (Callahan et al., 2013). Hallmarks of strong urban gifted programs include the use of community-wide resources to support and extend student learning (i.e., universities, libraries, museums), programs that focus on content-based curriculum, a comprehensive alignment of services from Kindergarten through grade 12 (including full-time services and schools for gifted learners), a focus on students' social-emotional needs, and a focus on and recognition of a variety of gifted learners' individual academic needs (VanTassel-Baska, 2010). However, urban schools have undergone many changes that have diminished the full-time nature and attention to gifted learners and even engaged in practices that are not viable for meeting the needs of gifted learners. In a review of the top urban districts throughout history, VanTassel-Baska suggested that urban schools revitalize their programs, building upon past success, instead of "destroying its footprint":

> Many current students of gifted education think that our contemporary models are all equal in their capacity to meet the needs of diverse gifted learners in diverse areas of learning. Yet our history suggests that this is not true—that some organizational models like special classes and schools have proven their viability as contexts where differentiated curriculum is best delivered; that using a differentiation model within subject areas allows for the most effective reorganization of curriculum for the gifted, using differentiated materials as the tool; and that multiple program offerings are essential to adequately address the needs of a diverse group of learners. These conclusions have been well documented in the literature of the field (Little, Feng, VanTassel-Baska, Rogers, & Avery, 2007; Neihart, 2007; Sternberg, Torff, & Grigorenko, 1998). (p. 26)

She also called for a more focused approach to working with students of color and of poverty through accessible programs on Saturdays and summers and the need for early intervention.

In rural schools, a critical mass of gifted students is difficult to obtain due to population size. Budget and program cuts are also a problem as, in a recent survey, 13% of rural districts reported their programs had been cut over the past 5 years (Callahan et al., 2013). In addition, rural districts are less likely than their urban and suburban counterparts to employ a full-time administrator in charge of gifted education, to require specialized training for teachers of gifted beyond state mandates, or to have a specified framework for serving gifted students (Callahan et al., 2013). Gifted students in rural settings also reported feeling less academically challenged than their urban and suburban counterparts, although they were happier with school in general (Gentry, Rizza, & Gable, 2001). Seward and Gentry (2015) suggested that rural schools consider Total School Cluster Grouping. In this model, all students in the school—gifted or not—are deliberately placed or clustered in a classroom that best meets their needs and readiness levels. This type of grouping allows for heterogeneous classrooms but narrows the range of instructional levels in each classroom so that teachers can ensure that every student has a chance to be appropriately challenged and engaged at his or her particular level. Although there can be reluctance on the part of some teachers and administrators to provide this type of grouping in rural schools—many times due to belief systems—empirical evidence supports the effectiveness of this model as it increases the number of students identified as gifted, increases student achievement across the school, and improves teacher practice through ongoing, schoolwide professional development (Gentry & Owen, 1999).

Collaborative partnerships and opportunities for distance learning are also effective ways to support rural gifted learners. Given the smaller size of rural schools, these schools can be more flexible in supporting acceleration for gifted learners. Besides the traditional methods of acceleration (which includes more than just grade skipping or subject acceleration), there has been documented success with rural school students enrolling in advanced courses not offered by their school through carefully developed online collaborative partnership programs between a consortium of rural schools and a university. Rural students are able to gain access to STEM courses not typically offered in their school as well as other accelerated courses for which there may not be a critical mass. Data from the Iowa Online AP Academy, one example of this type of learning, show that the number of students who score above a 3 on exams has increased over time, as has student participation and interest (Assouline, Flanary, & Foley Nicpon, 2015).

The role of extracurricular programs. Many positive effects are noted when extracurricular and accelerated opportunities are provided. Programs beyond the school allow additional opportunities for students to extend their learning, access more advanced curriculum, and be exposed to content experts earlier in their school career, which increases their desire to take more advanced courses in their high school and consider more challenging careers. In particular, students who participate in university-based accelerated programs are more likely to show higher career aspirations and to matriculate to more selective universities and colleges (Olszewski-Kubilius, Lee, & Peternel, 2009). When gifted students compared their participation in extracurricular accelerated opportunities to services in their local schools, statistically significant differences were noted in students' perceptions of their experience. Students reported that when participating in accelerated, extracurricular programs, they had more academically minded friends, more enjoyable classes, a higher level of challenge, a stronger desire to attend class, an excitement to learn, and less boredom. They also felt the instructors had higher expectations, yet they felt more comfortable expressing their thoughts and working with like-minded peers (Stambaugh, n.d.). Wai, Lubinski, Benbow, and Steiger (2010) also found that students who had a "higher STEM dose" (p. 860; with "dose" defined as supplemental programs, including competitions, clubs, advanced courses, and summer programs) were more likely to show exceptional productivity in creative STEM accomplishments later in life, including publications in prestigious journals, patents, and selection to prestigious doctoral programs in their field. Thus, the impact of providing ongoing supplemental accelerated opportunities earlier in a child's school career can have a lasting effect over the lifespan.

Although extracurricular programming is a powerful model for many gifted students regardless of location, there is added value to students in urban and rural settings. Students of poverty—of which the majority live in rural and urban settings—benefit even more from accelerated activities and bridging programs offered beyond the school day (Olszewski-Kubilius & Clarenbach, 2012; Olszewski-Kubilius & Thomson, 2010; VanTassel-Baska & Stambaugh, 2007). Moreover, when students are away from their home school and interacting with others of like academic ability, they are less likely to feel pressure to hide their abilities due to the unique culture of their school, which may not promote a culture of learning (Olszewski-Kubilius & Thomson, 2010; Stambaugh & Wood, 2015). Summer programs, especially those designed by talent search organizations and affiliates, typically enroll students from all over the world and allow for rural and urban students to find a critical mass of others who are like them as well as those with diverse perspectives and experiences. Thus, their uniqueness can be normalized. Although supplemental programs can be costly, many programs offer financial aid to support students of need.

Other considerations. Professional development, carefully crafted state and district policies, and the cultivation of relationships between the home, family, and the larger community also matter when working with students from diverse geographic areas. Collaborative partnerships with neighborhood schools or counties provide ongoing support and maximize resources. Similarly, college, career, and guidance counseling opportunities serve as a "window" for students to view opportunities beyond their local neighborhood or county and learn about themselves as a gifted student. Each consideration warrants further examination.

- *Professional development needs to take into account the local area and unique student and regional characteristics.* Professional development and accountability are important for positive change. Professional development workshops need to be nested within the context of where a child lives and the unique characteristics of students within that region. All teachers new to a district should be required to attend special sessions that help them understand the students within the particular school or district and also include how giftedness is manifested within that particular population.
- *Policymakers need to ensure that the policies set forth for schools do not have any unintended negative consequences or advantages for students in certain regions.* For example, funding formulas that are based on numbers instead of percentages may negatively impact those in rural communities. Likewise,

What obstacles might become apparent (i.e., vernacular, dialectal, or accent, vary)?

policies that require unfunded mandates are likely to hurt schools that are low income and already struggling.

- *Collaboration with families and the community matters.* Schools in rural and urban areas need to forge strong relationships with families and community members. Schools need to focus on cultivating family relationships and educating the family on what giftedness means or how the identification process works so all have equal access. Families are a valuable resource to support gifted student achievement. They play an impactful role in the development of talent (Csikszentmihalyi, Rathunde, & Whalen, 1997). Moreover, community members can add value to school-based services and provide unique services to schools that teachers may not have the time or resources to carry out. Among these are mentorships, internships, specialized accelerated tutoring, and exposure to and interaction with positive role models that serve as mirrors and windows to the community and beyond. In rural communities, this may extend beyond a neighborhood to collaborative partnerships among neighboring counties as a way to share resources and create a critical mass.

- *Provide targeted career and guidance counseling.* Students in rural and urban schools, especially those that are low income, need to know more about themselves as gifted students as well as the availability of college and career opportunities. As previously noted, gifted students may struggle with whether to leave or stay in their community or how to switch between different family and school or class systems. They may also feel isolated if they are one of the only students identified as gifted in their school. Counselors need to be aware of these issues and how to support gifted students within their context. Families need to be involved in the conversation so students can be nurtured at home and school. Family involvement is also important in career counseling. In a review of individual perceptions about working and learning in rural schools, one guidance counselor, new to living and working in a rural community, noted the following:

> I learned quickly that in order to fully engage the students and help them work through their career, academic, or personal concerns, I had to connect with more than just the student; I had to include the entire family. My students considered their college and career decisions by the impact it would have on their family. Almost all of my students either chose career paths that kept them closer to home or chose colleges that were within a couple of hours of their homes. (Stambaugh, 2015b, p. 366)

Other participants said that they really didn't know much about college, as their teachers or guidance counselors did not discuss it. They were often left to figure things out on their own or emulate parents or others they knew in their neighborhood or community. Awareness and access are essential.

Conclusion

Schools mimic their larger community. If educators are not from the area where they teach, they need to learn and understand how the larger geographic area serves as an extension of their students and a large part of what shapes who their students are as community members and gifted individuals. It is also important to know the unique community assets as well as how the community feels about giftedness. In rural areas, this means understanding the culture, beliefs, and strengths of the community and how to best forge relationships within the community context. This also means not being surprised if the educator is stopped in the middle of the grocery store aisle to talk about a child. In urban areas, this means understanding the melting pot of students in the classroom and the unique flavor of the neighborhoods where students reside. This also means figuring out how to develop trust and respect from the students and their families.

Big Ideas

1. Giftedness must be recognized within the context of one's location and the interactions of systems in which one is involved.

2. Zip code should not matter with regard to access to accelerated curriculum and high-quality gifted services and qualified professionals.

3. Identification methods for gifted learners should allow flexibility for students to show their giftedness in ways that are unique to their own culture, region, and experience. "Serve first and then identify" approaches allow for opportunity and access prior to identification.

4. Services for gifted students must be evidence-supported and tailored to the context of local schools including place-based opportunities that highlight community assets, accelerated experiences during and beyond the school day, curriculum opportunities that provide "mirrors and windows," and ongoing work with like-ability peers and specialized programs.

Big Ideas, *Continued.*

5. Collaborative partnerships with families and community members must be developed as ways to support gifted students within their local area. This includes college and career counseling, mentorships and internships, and other opportunities for students to have access to mirrors and windows. In rural areas, collaborative partnerships may involve resource sharing with other counties for professional development or student extracurricular programs.

6. Community norms and characteristics must be embedded in professional development workshops so that strategies effective for gifted learners can be tailored to particular schools or regions.

7. Opportunities beyond the school day must be supported as part of a talent development model.

Discussion Questions

1. Consider a gifted student you know. How does Bronfenbrenner's model apply to his or her giftedness? If you were to provide changes to one part of that student's system, how would the other systems interact and what impact might that make? Which part of the system do you think most impacts this student and why?

2. How did where you live impact who you are today? To what extent did giftedness (either being identified or not being identified) matter within that context? How does this apply to Bronfenbrenner's model?

3. To what extent does geography matter in the identification of gifted students? What recommendations do you have for your school district to ensure that the unique characteristics of the region and students are considered as part of an identification system?

4. How might the concept of mirrors and windows be applied to giftedness in your area?

5. What would place-based education for gifted students look like in your school or community?

6. What did you learn in the reading about educating this special population that you were unaware of before?

References

Assouline, S. G., Flanary, K., & Foley Nicpon, M. (2015). Challenges and solutions for serving rural gifted students: Accelerative strategies. In T. Stambaugh & S. Wood (Eds.), *Serving gifted students in rural settings* (pp. 135–153). Waco, TX: Prufrock Press.

Bishop, R. S. (1990). Mirrors, windows, and sliding glass doors. *Perspectives: Choosing and Using Books for the Classroom, 6,* ix–xi.

Bronfenbrenner, U. (1974). Developmental research, public policy and the ecology of childhood. *Child Development, 45,* 1–5.

Bronfenbrenner, U. (1979). *The ecology of human development: Experiments by nature and design.* Cambridge, MA: Harvard University Press.

Bronfenbrenner, U. (1994). Ecological models of human development. In *International Encyclopedia of Education* (Vol. 3, 2nd ed., pp. 1643–1647). Oxford, England: Elsevier Sciences.

Callahan, C. M., Moon, T. R., & Oh, S. (2013). *Status of elementary gifted programs 2013.* Charlottesville: University of Virginia, The National Research Center on the Gifted and Talented. Retrieved from http://www.nagc.org/sites/default/files/key%20reports/ELEM%20school%20GT%20Survey%20Report.pdf

Chawla, L., & Escalante M. (2007). *Student gains from place-based education— Fact sheet number 2.* Denver: University of Colorado at Denver and Health Sciences Center, Children, Youth and Environments Center for Research and Design. Retrieved from http://www.peecworks.org/PEEC/PEEC_Research/0179ABB8-001D0211.0/student%20gains%20fr%20PBE%20fact%20sheet%202%20Nov%202007%20web.pdf

Csikszentmihalyi, M., Rathunde, K., & Whalen, S. (1997). *Talented teenagers: The roots of success and failure.* New York, NY: Cambridge University Press.

Ford, D. Y. (2010). *Reversing underachievement among gifted Black students: Theory, research, and practice* (2nd ed.). Waco, TX: Prufrock Press.

Ford, D. Y. (2015). Like finding a needle in a haystack: Gifted Black and Hispanic students in rural settings. In T. Stambaugh & S. Wood (Eds.), *Serving gifted students in rural settings* (pp. 71–90). Waco, TX: Prufrock Press.

Gentry, M., & Owen, S. V. (1999). An investigation of the effects of total school flexible cluster grouping on identification, achievement, and classroom practices. *Gifted Child Quarterly, 43,* 224–243.

Gentry, M., Rizza, M. G., & Gable, R. K. (2001). Gifted students' perceptions of their class activities: Differences among rural, urban, and suburban student attitudes. *Gifted Child Quarterly, 45,* 115–129.

Graham, S. E., & Provost, L. E. (2012). *Mathematics achievement gaps between suburban students and their rural and urban peers increase over time.* Retrieved from http://scholars.unh.edu/cgi/viewcontent.cgi?article=1171&context=carsey

Gruenewald, D. A. (2008). The best of both worlds: A critical pedagogy of place. *Environmental Education Research, 14,* 308–324. Retrieved from http://www.geos.ed.ac.uk/~sallen/hamish/Gruenewald%20%282008%29.%20The%20best%20of%20both%20worlds%20-%20a%20critical%20pedagogy%20of%20place.pdf

Horn, C. (2015). Young scholars: A talent development model for finding and nurturing potential in underserved populations. *Gifted Child Today, 38,* 19–31.

Lohman, D. F. (2005). An aptitude perspective on talent: Implications for identification of academically gifted minority students. *Journal for the Education of the Gifted, 28,* 333–359.

McBee, M. T., Shaunessy, E., & Matthews, M. S. (2012). Policy matters: An analysis of district-level efforts to increase the identification of underrepresented learners. *Journal of Advanced Academics, 23,* 326–344.

Montgomery, D. (2001). Increasing Native American Indian involvement in gifted programs in rural schools. *Psychology in the Schools, 38,* 467–475.

Olszewski-Kubilius, P., & Clarenbach, J. (2012). *Unlocking emergent talent: Supporting high achievement of low-income, high-ability students.* Washington, DC: National Association for Gifted Students. Retrieved from http://www.nagc.org/sites/default/files/key%20reports/Unlocking%20Emergent%20Talent%20(final).pdf

Olszewski-Kubilius, P., Lee, S.-Y., & Peternel, G. (2009). Follow-up with students after six years of participation in Project EXCITE. *Gifted Child Quarterly, 53,* 137–156.

Olszewski-Kubilius, P., & Thomson, D. L. (2010). Gifted programming for poor or minority urban students: Issues and lessons learned. *Gifted Child Today, 33,* 58–64.

Opportunity Nation. (2015). *Opportunity index.* Retrieved from http://opportunityindex.org/about

Place-Based Education Evaluation Collaborative. (2010). *The benefits of place-based education: A report from the Place-Based Education Evaluation Collaborative* (2nd ed.). Retrieved from http://tinyurl.com/PEECBrochure

Plucker, J. A., Hardesty, J., & Burroughs, N. (2013). *Talent on the sidelines: Excellence gaps and America's persistent talent underclass.* Storrs: University of Connecticut, Center for Education Policy Analysis.

Seward, K., & Gentry, M. (2015). Grouping and instructional management strategies. In T. Stambaugh & S. Wood (Eds.), *Serving gifted students in rural settings* (pp. 111–134). Waco, TX: Prufrock Press.

Sobel, D. (2005). *Place-based education: Connecting classrooms and communities.* Great Barrington, MA: The Orion Society.

Spicker, H., & Poling, S. N. (1993). *Identifying rural disadvantaged gifted students. Project Spring: Special Populations Resources Information Network for the Gifted.*

Bloomington: Indiana University. (ERIC Document Reproduction Service No. ED365065)

Stambaugh, T. (2015a). Celebrating talent: Identification of rural gifted students. In T. Stambaugh & S. Wood (Eds.), *Serving gifted students in rural settings* (pp. 97–110). Waco, TX: Prufrock Press.

Stambaugh, T. (2015b). Concluding thoughts and voice from gifted individuals in rural areas. In T. Stambaugh & S. Wood (Eds.), *Serving gifted students in rural settings* (pp. 363–379). Waco, TX: Prufrock Press.

Stambaugh, T. (n.d.). *Benefits of programs.* Nashville, TN: Programs for Talented Youth. Retrieved from https://pty.vanderbilt.edu/research/question3

Stambaugh, T., & Wood, S. (Eds.). (2015). *Serving gifted students in rural settings.* Waco, TX: Prufrock Press.

United States Department of Agriculture, Economic Research Service. (2016). *Poverty overview.* Retrieved from http://www.ers.usda.gov/topics/rural-economy-population/rural-poverty-well-being/poverty-overview.aspx

VanTassel-Baska, J. (2010). The history of urban gifted education. *Gifted Child Today, 33*(4), 18–27.

VanTassel-Baska, J., & Stambaugh, T. (2007). (Eds.). *Overlooked gems: A national perspective on promising students of poverty.* Washington, DC: National Association of Gifted Children.

Wai, J., Lubinski, D., Benbow, C. P., & Steiger, J. H. (2010). Accomplishment in science, technology, engineering, and mathematics (STEM) and its relation to STEM educational dose: A 25-year longitudinal study. *Journal of Educational Psychology, 102,* 860–871.

CHAPTER 21

Educating Gifted Gay, Lesbian, Bisexual, Transgender, and Questioning Students

Terry Friedrichs

We are everywhere . . . —Harvey Milk

Essential Questions to Guide the Reader

1. Why is it important for educators to consider in their daily instruction gifted GLBTQ students' sexual orientations and gender identities as well as these youths' distinctive needs?

2. What are the specific, educationally related needs of gifted GLBTQ students?

3. How can educators address the distinctive needs of gifted GLBTQ students in classrooms and schools?

Overview: The Importance of Understanding

Educators need to know about gifted gay, lesbian, bisexual, transgender, and questioning (GLBTQ) students' sexual orientations (their attractions to males, females, and other genders) and their gender identities (their identifications with those genders). (See Table 21.1 for definitions.) First, up to approximately 2.2% of the student population across the U.S. is gifted GLBTQ; thus, most secondary

Table 21.1
Definitions

Term	Definition
Gay	Males oriented mostly toward other males in their sexual attractions, behaviors, and/or self-acknowledged identities.
Lesbian	Females oriented mostly toward other females in their sexual attractions, behaviors, and/or self-acknowledged identities.
Bisexual	Males and females oriented substantially toward both genders.
Transgender	Transgender girls are born with male anatomy and identify as female, and transgender males are born with female anatomy and identify as male. Transgender youth may be attracted to, or may be sexually active with, either gender.
Questioning	Individuals who are exploring or unsure about their genders, sexual identities, or sexual orientations.

schools will have at least one gifted GLBTQ youth (Friedrichs, 2012). Second, educators in many states and many educational disciplines now have legal and professional responsibilities to demonstrate sensitivity to these youth (Friedrichs, 2014). Many states have laws or educational statutes that call for safety and equity for GLBTQ youth, and various professional educational organizations call for that same protective and equitable treatment. All educators have the ethical responsibility to provide such treatment. Third, when educators act in a GLBTQ-supportive fashion, many of their students benefit from this support for the rest of their lives, as has been seen in gifted GLBTQ biographical accounts from the last two generations. These accounts speak of the importance of professional modeling and of inspiration in these youths' educational experiences (Feinberg, 1996; Miller & Fodo, 2013).

Historically, many educators, parents, and peers, as well as gifted GLBTQ students themselves, were negatively impacted by mistaken societal views. Too often, youth were discouraged and provided negative information because teachers, counselors, and administrators had been socialized to believe that these students had moral deficits (Socarides, 1968), psychological illnesses (American Psychological Association, 1975), or social challenges (Money, 1975). In addition, as gifted young people, they were already dealing with intensity and the other characteristics that often set them apart from the mainstream of society; in some cases, an open GLBTQ identification multiplied the negative effects. In fact, the stigma of being sexual or gender minorities—an umbrella term sometimes used as a synonym for GLBTQ people, according to the Human Rights Campaign (2016)—often overshadowed high-potential GLBTQ youths' gifts, not only in society's minds but also in the minds of some of the youth themselves (McNaught, 1977). As intellectually gifted students, the brighter these sexual-minority pupils were, the more sensitive they were to anti-GLBTQ social structures—and the more uncertain these youth, therefore, felt about their futures within American society (Reid, 1975; Sedillo, 2017). As creative youth, the more divergent they were, the more they had to hide their differences between the lines of their art (Haring, 1995). As adept leaders, the stronger they were, the more that society seemed to stifle them (Shilts, 1982).

However, with society's increasing openness to people who are GLBTQ and to GLBTQ-related knowledge, there has been much progress for sexual and gender minorities in the United States since the millennium. Today, almost all adults, including educators, know someone who is a sexual or a gender minority (Swan, 2015). As predicted four decades ago by San Francisco City Council Member Harvey Milk (Shilts, 1982), who fought for sexual-minority teachers' rights to be themselves and to "come out of the closet," the movement of people coming out to families, friends, and coworkers has had profoundly positive effects on society's GLBTQ-related acceptance (National LGBTQ Task Force, 2015). This acceptance includes GLBTQ youth who are gifted and talented.

Educators must understand the deeper need for change-supportive school personnel to consider the overall historical progress that GLBTQ youth and adults have made—and that they still need to make (Friedrichs, 2012). Legal rulings have spurred more widespread sexual-minority acceptance, as has greater understanding of GLBTQ persons within U.S. families and coworker groups. Specific legal factors include many states' requirements for equal employment opportunities as well as the federal government's requirements for equal marriage and military service rights for GLB people (National LGBTQ Task Force, 2015). Unfortunately, despite recent progress, there still are fewer such opportunities and fewer rights for transgender than for GLB people (National Center for Transgender Equality, 2017a).

Professional education organizations have started to advocate for equality for GLBTQ youth, beginning with large and influential general education groups, such as the American Federation of Teachers (1972) and the National Education Association (1973). Official educator support has spread to special education and gifted education groups, starting with the Council for Exceptional Children (CEC, 1995) and the National Association for Gifted Children (NAGC, 1998). CEC offered relatively early support of gay-lesbian-bisexual educators and students through its inauguration of CEC's Gay-Lesbian-Bisexual Caucus. NAGC added a position statement in 2001 (updated in 2015), which touted gifted GLBTQ youth's distinctive educational needs and charged educators to address those needs. Supporting the Emotional Needs of the Gifted (SENG) held strands at its 2012 and 2013 annual conferences on how educators and parents could support this population. Some recent publications, both within professional gifted education and sexual- and gender-minority organizations, have focused on meeting the critical needs of gifted GLBTQ youth (Cross & Cross, 2012; Friedrichs, Manzella, & Seney, 2017). These books and chapters describe characteristics and best educational practices stemming from empirical studies, practitioner accounts, and first-person stories.

In spite of the advances in GLBTQ acceptance, problems still exist. Prejudicial communities, filled with anti-GLBTQ hate and verbal and physical harassment, negatively impact these students. And there is still silence, in some areas of the country, among some sexual- and gender-minority youth and educators themselves regarding their public attitudes toward GLBTQ rights. Approximately half of the states do not have equal employment rights for sexual-minority and GLBTQ-supportive educators (National LGBTQ Task Force, 2015). Within many prejudicial communities, silence about inequalities on basic human rights, such as equal employment, housing, credit, and education, remain more pronounced toward transgender than toward other GLBTQ people (National Center for Transgender Equality, 2017b). However, it is clear, based on the rapid progress of the last 40 years, that serving gifted sexual- and gender-minority students specifically and sensitively will probably be a wave of the future.

Needs of Gifted GLBTQ Students

The needs of high-potential sexual and gender minorities have become increasingly evident in recent years. They share cognitive, social, and emotional needs of gifted youth as well as the needs of nongifted GLBTQ students. Gifted GLBTQ youth's dual sets of needs often complicate the ways in which their needs can be addressed by educators.

The research on gifted GLBTQ, especially that of the late 20th century, consists primarily of biographies and autobiographies. These works mentioned traits shown by multiple historical sexual- and gender-minority figures (Friedrichs & Etheridge, 1995). The literature also contains questionnaire responses from multiple teens (Friedrichs, 2012), interviews from college youth (Peterson & Rischar, 2000), and surveys from hundreds of adults reflecting on their teen years (Treat, 2008). These studies revealed pressing but evolving challenges to these GLBTQ youths' intellectual, academic, social, and emotional growth and well-being.

Role Models in Media and Literature

Some of the most highly gifted GLBTQ students, such as early women's studies scholar Charlotte Bunch (1987), had to strain to break through their oppressive social circumstances so that they could even consider a gay life as a possibility, much less an openly gay life of a prominent intellectual. Few examples of that life existed with real people or in media depictions. It was to these eminent persons' tribute that they created a compelling vision of a better life—a vision that many gifted students had already developed but that many GLBTQ youth may have lacked due to social oppression. Many high-potential GLBTQ students today are still stymied by the relatively few books or movies dealing well with GLBTQ life, although many books on that topic are no longer locked up outside of youths' view (Friedrichs, 2013). Youth currently have more access to GLBTQ-themed movies—films that formerly had such highly restrictive ratings that teens couldn't see them (Friedrichs, 2006). Although GLBTQ television and movie actors and themes are no longer necessarily taboo, few authentic, positive, and instructive examples of these actors and themes are available. Thus, GLBTQ students continue to need strong role models.

Freedom to Study GLBTQ Topics

In spite of increased social acceptance as well as more available literature with GLBTQ characters or themes, students cannot always engage safely in the study of sexual- and gender-minority topics within their schools or cannot read books containing GLBTQ characters. In many areas of the country, the prohibition on learning about these topics still holds (Hutcheson & Tieso, 2014). Such study can get interested students suspended and can get their teachers fired (Friedrichs, 2014). Some states' and localities' guidelines, which prohibit planned mention of sexual- and gender-minority people, make it difficult for teachers to offer academic lessons about GLBTQ people (Friedrichs, 2014). Teachers may not have appropriate materials and, even when they have them, may not feel empowered to utilize them (Letts, 1999). Few students realize the possibility of studying GLBTQ curricula, on or off campus, and they strongly wish for sexual- and gender-minority mentors (Gay, Lesbian & Straight Education Network [GLSEN], 2013, 2015).

Peer Groups

Many gifted students often have two peer groups: age-mates and idea-mates (Roberts & Boggess, 2011). GLBTQ students may have three: age-mates, idea-mates, and mates within the GLBTQ community. Gifted GLBTQ students often struggle to find an accepting community and can find it even harder to discover a community of kindred spirits. Countless gifted sexual- and gender-minority students, such as famed sociologist Edgar Z. Friedenberg (1970), assumed a study mode and excelled academically to build their fragile self-esteems. Some of these youth tried to be good at all subjects, simply so that they could feel "average" (Peterson & Rischar, 2000). When there is a large enough youth community, gifted GLBTQ students, similar to other gifted students who want a peer group, have met together, focusing their attention on building knowledge and rapport. This sharing can be both thought provoking and comforting (Millett, 1974). Many students, however, lack access to Gay-Straight Alliances (school-based groups of GLBTQ and supportive straight teens) and to community-based GLBTQ-youth groups (GLSEN, 2015). Historically, such students have often been discouraged from meeting together.

Safe Learning and Living Environments

In spite of the growth in understanding, some in society still consider sexual and gender minorities' orientations as more of a deviance than a difference. Saddled with sometimes-damning terms such as "fags" or "dykes," gifted GLBTQ students often learn to worry and to avoid, never truly feeling secure in school settings (Duberman, 1992). Some gifted GLBTQ students have begun to take risks to congregate, share information, and fight still-prevailing misconceptions and prejudice. In order to ensure a safe learning and living environment, it is important to remember Maslow's (1943) hierarchy of needs, in which assurance of safety is extremely beneficial before other needs, such as intellectual ones, can begin to be addressed.

Addressing the Needs

In the era of greater GLBTQ approval, educational improvements have tended to follow legal advancements (Friedrichs, 2014). Various areas of student excellence have also followed GLBTQ-rights advances (Sears, 2005; Swan, 2015). In order to create a safe learning environment and to remove the learning ceiling, educators are encouraged to incorporate some of the following strategies into their schools and classrooms.

Incorporating GLBTQ Themes and Topics

Considering the almost complete absence of information about gifted GLBTQ youth before 1995, there has been a significant increase in the number of books, professional articles, and films that provide insights into what it is to be simultaneously gifted and gay, lesbian, bisexual, or transgender (Friedrichs, 2012; Sedillo, 2017). Young men and women today (whether they are open about their sexual and gender identifications or not) can benefit from increasingly available information, especially with the encouragement of educators. With more information, youth can better understand themselves and current GLBTQ-related events and trends, and they can imagine future possibilities (Savin-Williams, 2005). Educators, both informally and through planned lessons, can effectively bring up GLBTQ cultural topics with a range of student ages.

Issues include anti-bullying, sexual-minority families, and current books and court rulings related to GLBTQ awareness (Letts, 1999). Secondary educators can lead classroom discussions with their students, covering a wide variety of sexual-minority issues. Packaged curricula do exist, such as sociological simulations from Lipkin (2000) and history units from Hogan (1996). With increasingly organized teacher curricula (Villanueva, 2016), students should have opportunities to explore examples of GLBTQ life from society, as well as from art (Whittenburg,

2014). Curricular inclusion should afford a sense of belonging and/or toler-ance. Academically, gifted sexual and gender minorities need more opportunities, through expanded curricular and instructional options, to learn about and demon-strate understanding of GLBTQ individuals within general and gifted education (Friedrichs, 2014). NAGC (2015) recommended that schools offer GLBTQ stud-ies for school credit. Such studies may create interest in accessing opportunities in college for advanced sexual- and gender-minority studies (Windmeyer, Humphrey, & Baker, 2013). With educators' increased interest in GLBTQ issues and with more opportunities to learn, gifted sexual and gender minorities may need to take fewer risks, both in learning who they are and in balancing their intrapersonal quests with their academic excellence.

Create Safe Learning Environments

Educators need to take action against any anti-GLBTQ behavior that occurs in school halls, locker rooms, and parking lots, in addition to intellectual and aca-demic settings (GLSEN, 2013). Another way for students to receive support is by participating in GLBTQ-Straight Alliances, in which they and other students meet regularly to discuss strategies for successful school interactions and learn about GLBTQ issues. Some gifted GLBTQ from more conservative areas are beginning to experience more comfortable conditions in school; some high potential sexual- and gender-minorities in other locations may experience progress more quickly, in terms of both curricular specifics and instructor and peer openness on GLBTQ issues (Swan, 2015). Sexual and gender minorities may increasingly find niches in many diverse student groups who accept being GLBTQ as "just another difference." Ideally, educators will understand the stresses of being sexual and gender minorities, and counselors and psychologists will see those stresses as the faults of society rather than of GLBTQ individuals (Ryan, 2012).

Encourage and Facilitate the Finding of Peers

Optimally, future gifted GLBTQ students will feel less socially isolated, due to many new school-based curricular and extracurricular connections established with the help of educators (Outfront Minnesota, 2015). With teacher and parent encour-agement, they may seek out fellow energizing sexual- and gender-minority youth in social activities, specialty arts, and leadership groups in the community (Friedrichs, 2007). Some GLBTQ youth may find themselves welcome within school environ-ments that prize diversity. High-potential sexual- and gender-minority students may join with other diverse school youth to achieve important legislative advocacy objec-tives. Many students from gay-straight alliances have worked together successfully in the past for GLBTQ rights, in both speakers' bureaus and political advocacy groups; that experience could transfer to other advocacy initiatives. In addition, students can participate in school service projects done specifically on behalf of GLBTQ people (Silverman, 2011). Thus, with educators' help, gifted GLBTQ students can now congregate, share feelings, and function more fully as individuals. In safe environments, they may actively volunteer in those activities in which they previously just wished to be involved.

Another way for gifted sexual and gender minorities to grow is through community mentorships (although some schools still do not have such alliances, and many students live too far away from large cities to access GLBTQ mentorships). Through community organizations' leadership initiatives, gifted GLBTQ youth may start to attain leadership positions for which they previously didn't even apply. Sexual- and gender-minority youth may have a range of opportunities in which to distinguish themselves (Villanueva, 2016). Once students form a community with other like-minded individuals, the growth may be rapid.

Conclusion

Given the arc of recent decades' trends, there may well be more future opportunities than challenges for educators who wish to assist sexual- and gender-minority students (NAGC, 2015). Educators may present GLBTQ students and parents with ideas for youths' viability of being open sexual or gender minorities. Academically, increasing numbers of educators at the university and the K–12 levels may speak openly to youth on GLBTQ and many other issues. In addition, professors in university GLBTQ-studies departments may develop a significant focus on K–12 sexual- and gender-minority curricula (American Educational Research Association GLBTQ SIG, 2015), just as African American and women's studies professors previously have contributed to the growth of culturally relevant high school units. Through the work of caring educators, gifted GLBTQ students have a much better opportunity than ever before for a quality education.

Big Ideas

1. Gifted GLBTQ students have the unique needs of both gifted young people and GLBTQ students.

2. Educators address the needs of this special population by incorporating GLBTQ themes and topics into the curriculum, creating a safe learning environment, and encouraging and facilitating the finding of peers.

Discussion Questions

1. In your school building(s), how might gifted GLBTQ students' sexual orientations and gender identities affect their gifted education needs?

2. What are two or three goals you could set for addressing the needs of GLBTQ students in your school and in gifted programming within it?

3. What did you learn that you were unaware of before, in reading about educating this special population and in examining your personal attitudes about GLBTQ people?

References

American Educational Research Association GLBTQ SIG. (2015). *Annual LGBTQ studies awards*. Retrieved from http://www.aera.net

American Federation of Teachers. (1972). *Policy statement on discrimination and gay and lesbian faculty and students*. Washington, DC: Author.

American Psychological Association. (1975). *Policy statement on discrimination against homosexuals*. Washington, DC: Author.

Bunch, C. (1987). *Passionate politics*. New York, NY: St. Martin's Press.

Council for Exceptional Children. (1995). CEC Gay-Lesbian-Bisexual Caucus begins. *Exceptional Pride, 1*(1), 1–2.

Cross, T. L., & Cross, J. R. (Eds.). (2012). *Handbook for counselors serving students with gifts and talents: Development, relationships, school issues, and counseling needs/interventions* Waco, TX: Prufrock Press.

Duberman, M. (1992). *Cures: A gay man's odyssey*. New York, NY: Plume.

Feinberg, L. (1996). *Transgender warriors: Making history from Joan of Arc to Dennis Rodman*. Boston, MA: Beacon Press.

Friedenberg, E. Z. (1970). *The vanishing adolescent*. New York, NY: Penguin.

Friedrichs, T. P. (2006). Whoa is me: Personal and professional barriers to progress for gifted GLBTQ students. *Quest, 12*–20.

Friedrichs, T. P. (2007, Spring). Social and emotional needs, and preferred educational approaches, for gifted gay and bisexual males. *Significance, 3*–4.

Friedrichs T. P. (2012). Counseling gifted GLBT students along paths to freedom. In T. L. Cross & J. R. Cross (Eds.), *Handbook for counselors serving students with gifts and talents: Development, relationships, school issues, and counseling needs/interventions* (pp. 153–177). Waco, TX: Prufrock Press.

Friedrichs, T. P. (2013). The fighter. In H. Endo & P. C. Miller (Eds.), *Queer voices in the classroom* (pp. 195–202). Charlotte, NC: Information Age.

Friedrichs, T. P. (2014). Appropriately serving an emerging group: Educational practices and legal implementation for gifted GLBTQ students. *Excellence and Diversity in Gifted Education, 1,* 8–13.

Friedrichs, T. P., & Etheridge, R. L (1995). Gifted and gay—reasons to help. *The Association for the Gifted Newsletter, 17*(1), 4–5.

Friedrichs, T. P., Manzella, T. R., & Seney, R. W. (2017). *Gifted gay, lesbian, bisexual, and transgender youth: Needs and approaches.* Washington, DC: National Association for Gifted Children.

Gay, Lesbian & Straight Education Network. (2013). *The 2013 national school climate survey: The experiences of lesbian, gay, bisexual, and transgender students in our nation's schools.* Retrieved from https://www.glsen.org/sites/default/files/2013%20National%20School%20Climate%20Survey%20Full%20Report_0.pdf

Gay, Lesbian & Straight Education Network. (2015). *The 2015 national school climate survey: The experiences of lesbian, gay, bisexual, and transgender students in our nation's schools.* Retrieved from https://www.glsen.org/article/2015-national-school-climate-survey

Haring, K. (1995). *In a different light: Visual culture, sexual identity, and queer practice.* San Francisco, CA: City Lights Books.

Hogan, K. (1996). *History units.* San Francisco, CA: San Francisco Unified School District.

Human Rights Campaign. (2016, October). *NIH designates sexual and gender minority populations as a health disparity population for research.* Retrieved from http://www.hrc.org/blog/nih-designates-sexual-and-gender-minority-populations-as-a-health-disparity

Hutcheson, V., & Tieso, C. (2014). Social coping of gifted and LGBTQ adolescents. *Journal for the Education of the Gifted, 37,* 355–377.

Letts, W. J. (1999). How to make "boys" and "girls" in the classroom: The heteronormative nature of elementary school science. In W. J. Letts & J. T. Sears (Eds.), *Queering elementary education: Advancing dialogue about sexualities and schooling* (pp. 97–110). Lanham, MD: Rowman & Littlefield.

Lipkin, A. (2000). *Understanding homosexuality, changing schools.* Boulder, CO: Westview Press.

Maslow, A. (1943). A theory of human motivation. *Psychological Review, 50,* 370–396.

McNaught, B. (1977). *A disturbed peace: Selected writings of an Irish Catholic homosexual.* Washington, DC: Dignity.

Miller, P. C., & Fodo, H. (2013). *Queer voices from the classroom.* New York, NY: Information Age.

Millett, K. (1974). *Flying.* New York, NY: Knopf.

Money, J. (1975). *Sexual signatures: On being a man or woman.* Oxford, England: Little, Brown.

National Association for Gifted Children. (1998). *Non-discrimination policy on gay, lesbian, and bisexual persons.* Washington, DC: Author.

National Association for Gifted Children. (2001). *Position paper on gifted gay, lesbian, bisexual, and transgendered students.* Washington, DC: Author.

National Association for Gifted Children. (2015). *Position statement on the evaluation of gifted GLBTQ students.* Washington, DC: Author.

National Center for Transgender Equality. (2017a). *Issues.* Retrieved from http://www.transequality.org/issues

National Center for Transgender Equality. (2017b). *Know your rights.* Retrieved from http://www.transequality.org/know-your-rights

National Education Association. (1973). *Statement of non-discrimination toward gay and lesbians.* Washington, DC: Author.

National LGBTQ Task Force. (2015). *Maps: States with GLBTQ rights.* Retrieved from http://www.thetaskforce.org/nondiscrimination-laws-map

Outfront Minnesota. (2015). *Youth.* Retrieved from http://www.outfront.org/youth

Peterson, J. S., & Rischar, S. (2000). Gifted and gay: The adolescent experience. *Gifted Child Quarterly, 43,* 430–444.

Reid, J. (1975). *The best little boy in the world.* New York, NY: Ballantine.

Roberts, J. L., & Boggess, J. R. (2011). *Teacher's survival guide: Gifted education.* Waco, TX: Prufrock Press.

Ryan, C. (2012). *Supportive families, healthy children.* San Francisco, CA: San Francisco State University Family Acceptance Project.

Savin-Williams, R. (2005). *The new gay teenager.* Cambridge, MA: Harvard University Press.

Sears, J. T. (2005). Introduction. In J. T. Sears (Ed.), *Youth, education, and sexualities: An international encyclopedia* (pp. xvii–xxxviii). Westport, CT: Greenwood.

Sedillo, P. J. (2017). *The "T" is missing for "GLBT": Gifted transgender individuals.* Manuscript submitted for publication.

Shilts, R. (1982). *The major of Castro Street: The life and times of Harvey Milk.* New York, NY: St. Martin's Press.

Silverman, L. (2011). *Unique inner lives of gifted children.* Retrieved from http://www.heliosns.org/article-the-unique-inner-lives-of-gifted-children

Socarides, C. W. (1968). *The overt homosexual.* New York, NY: Grune & Stratton.

Swan, W. (2015). *Gay, lesbian, bisexual, and transgender civil rights: A public policy agenda for uniting a divided America.* New York, NY: CRC Press.

Treat, A. R. (2008). *Beyond analysis by gender: Overexcitability dimensions of sexually diverse persons.* Ann Arbor, MI: UMI.

Villanueva, M. (2016, Fall). We are artists, out and proud: My experiences attending a visual and performing arts school supportive of LGBTQ culture (Part II). *NAGC GLBTQ Network Newsletter,* 17–27.

Whittenburg, B. (2014). Pas de deaux: Gifted dancers. *NAGC GLBTQ Network Newsletter,* 7–9.

Windmeyer, S., Humphrey, K., & Baker, D. (2013). *Institutional responsibility: Tracking retention and academic success of out LGBT students.* Retrieved from http://www.myacpa.org/article/institutional-responsibility-tracking-retention-academic-success-out-lgbt-students

CHAPTER 22

Meeting the Needs of Students Who Are Twice-Exceptional

Daphne Pereles, Mary Ruth Coleman, and Lois Baldwin

A bad year, without bad people really, no one exactly to blame, just
a sequence of events
a class that didn't belong to me, and I not belonging to it
the round peg in the square whole [*sic*] . . .
as words sprang and papers vanished, I became more and more
confused
and most of all sad
and so the round peg, found a round whole
and so the story ends, at least it was without villains—
Shane Wilder (2E Student), 2004; first appeared in Kirk, Gallagher,
and Coleman (2015, p. 126)

Essential Questions to Guide the Reader

1. Who are twice-exceptional (2e) learners, what are some of their characteristics, and how can we identify these students?

2. What kinds of programming responses should be in place to address 2e students' strengths and needs?

3. In what ways can Universal Design for Learning (UDL) help us provide strategies for students who are 2e?

4. What social and emotional supports should be available to address the overall well-being of students who are 2e?

5. What special considerations should be given to family life and transition needs of students who are 2e?

Meet the Students: Jose and Brittany

Jose is an eighth-grade student with autism spectrum disorder. He is mainstreamed into classes that are cotaught for the four basic subjects in the general education setting. In addition, he has a one-on-one aide to help with organizational skills, negotiating the hallways between classes, and for his special classes. Jose likes school, and his attendance is excellent. However, he is frequently bored and will spend a great deal of time in class doodling. Because he gets his homework done at school, frequently before he even leaves class, he will put his head down in study hall and sleep, a behavior that has distressed the staff. His grades in all classes are mediocre. Several of the teachers complain that he rushes through the work, doesn't understand it, or that he does not answer the question. He will frequently read much more into the assignment than is required, so his answers do not fit the basic question, thus making them wrong. Last year's English language arts teacher appreciated his wit and the critiques that he would write beside a question. However, this year's teachers find this behavior annoying and disrespectful and mark him down when he does this on the paper.

Jose has a curious mind, a sharp wit, and numerous interests. His parents state that he has his own company that allows him to repair and rebuild computers for his clients. His basement is full of computer pieces that are organized and classified. He is also a master at Minecraft, a game about placing blocks to build anything you can imagine, and has been asked to judge competitions that have included adult participants. Although this has been communicated with the school, this information has not been incorporated into consideration of his schedule or academic program. In addition, he scored above grade level on his math pretest at the beginning of the year, but he is still enrolled in the basic math curriculum.

Brittany, a quiet, verbally precocious third grader was identified for a gifted program when she was in first grade. She loves stories and enjoys reading, hearing, and creating them. She has a very active imagination, a great sense of humor, and a vast knowledge base beyond her years. Her vocabulary is extensive and adults, including her parents, wonder where she learns many of the words that she uses correctly in speaking. She has a flare for acting out her stories and is frequently trying to incorporate other girls into her imaginative play at recess.

Although Brittany has always been a quiet and reserved child, she has become even more withdrawn and anxious in third grade, to the concern of her teacher and parents. Even though she has great ideas, she either writes a limited amount or refuses to put her thoughts on paper during English language arts, stating that she will do it for homework instead. Her answers to questions are limited to short sentences, basic vocabulary, and misspellings even when the word might have been in the previous sentence. For a student who used to look forward to school and was ready 10 minutes before the bus was to arrive, her resistance to go has gradually increased and is more noticeable.

Overview of New Twice-Exceptional Definition and Pathways to Identification

As these case studies illustrate, there are students who have characteristics of giftedness while at the same time have academic and/or social-emotional challenges indicative of a disability. Because they often do not fit the stereotypical characteristics of students with giftedness or a disability (Baum & Owen, 2004), this population of students is known as twice-exceptional. This unique group of students is frequently an enigma to educators. To address these challenges, in 2014 and 2015, a group of representatives from multiple professional organizations, including the Council for Exceptional Children, National Association for Gifted Children, and National Center for Learning Disabilities, to name a few, collaborated through a Community of Practice approach to create an agreed-upon, consistent definition for twice-exceptional individuals that could be used nationally. The definition is as follows:

> Twice exceptional (2e) individuals evidence exceptional ability and disability, which results in a unique set of circumstances. Their exceptional ability may dominate, hiding their disability; their disability may dominate, hiding their exceptional ability; each may mask the other so that neither is recognized or addressed.
>
> 2e students, who may perform below, at, or above grade level, require the following:
> - Specialized methods of identification that consider the possible interaction of the exceptionalities
> - Enriched/advanced educational opportunities that develop the child's interests, gifts, and talents while also meeting the child's learning needs
> - Simultaneous supports that ensure the child's academic success and social-emotional well-being, such as accommodations, therapeutic interventions, and specialized instruction.

Working successfully with this unique population requires specialized academic training and ongoing professional development. (Baldwin, Baum, Pereles, & Hughes, 2015, pp. 216–225)

This definition brings together the perspectives from disability organizations as well as gifted organizations and provides an opportunity to examine all elements of twice-exceptionality. It represents a more cohesive, meaningful understanding of twice-exceptionality than any definitions of the past and honors current research and knowledge regarding this unique population of learners.

Identification of twice-exceptional students can be difficult for many school systems. This definition guides the identification process, focusing on the early recognition of learning behaviors related to the student's areas of giftedness and areas of disability. This approach assists the process of building a body of evidence over time to support, if necessary, formal identification of the student.

Recognizing Characteristics of Twice-Exceptional Students

In the case of twice-exceptional students, their educational needs—whether advanced or remedial—may not be observed for a variety of reasons. Baum and Owen (2004) identified three types of conditions that make it difficult for educators to recognize these special students. In the first condition, the disability is recognized but not the strengths. The second condition is the reverse: giftedness is recognized but not the disability. For the last condition, neither strengths nor disabilities are recognized. The first two conditions are illustrated in the case studies presented in this chapter. In Jose's case, his disability was addressed through special education, but his advanced abilities evidenced through computers, math, and Minecraft were ignored. On the other hand, Brittany's giftedness was acknowledged early and nurtured in school, but students like Brittany often "hit the wall" when they are not able to compensate with their ability to memorize material or to verbalize responses (McEachern & Bornot, 2001). It is not unusual to hear adults mistakenly say that a student is "lazy" or "not trying hard enough" when there is a mismatch between skills and performance (Baldwin, Omdal, & Pereles, 2015). Twice-exceptional learners combine the characteristics of giftedness (e.g., ability to learn easily, strong verbal skills, critical thinking abilities, curiosity, creativity, and problem solving) with areas of challenge reflecting their disability (e.g., struggling with basic skills, impulsivity, difficulty with organization, problems with focus, challenges with social skills). Each individual 2e student will have her own unique combination of strengths and challenges, and so educators' educational responses must be tailored for each student.

K–12 Programming for Strengths, Needs, and Solutions

Building an appropriate support system that responds to the complex and unique combinations of strengths and needs of each 2e student requires going beyond traditional educational structures: It takes a team! The provision of multidimensional, flexible, customized supports that honor and extend the student's strengths while remediating and supporting his areas of challenge requires the combined educational expertise of special, gifted, and general educators (Coleman & Gallagher, 2015). The team, however, also may need the expertise of related service providers (e.g., occupational therapists, speech language pathologists, physical therapists, and mental health providers) to support the 2e student's success (Trail, 2011). Counselors also may be needed to support social-emotional development and/or educational/career planning needs (Trail, 2011). Finally, the student and her family are key members of the team, guiding the planning and partnering in the implementation of the plan. Although this may sound like a daunting prospect, a team approach has extended benefits that may go well beyond the success of students who are 2e (Kirk et al., 2015).

Bringing together multiple sources of information, the teams use a problem-solving process to make decisions. The problem-solving process involves (a) defining area of need, (b) collecting and analyzing data, (c) implementing a plan, and (d) evaluating the progress (Pereles, Omdal, & Baldwin, 2009). Twice-exceptional students require a dual-emphasis approach—one that focuses on strengths and talents while supporting and addressing the disability (Assouline & Whiteman, 2011; Baum, Cooper, & Neu, 2001). When planning for instruction of twice-exceptional students, the first critical consideration is identification of the student's academic and intellectual strengths, talents, and interests in and outside of school and other personal factors such as creativity, intrinsic motivation, and sustained attention (King, 2005; Olenchak, 2009; Reis, Baum, & Burk, 2014). In addition to identifying the student's areas of strength, the team must also determine area of challenge and social or emotional adjustment needs. Once the problem-solving team has this important information as part of a comprehensive data set, they can begin to determine a plan for the student. Plans will be tailored to the student's particular strengths, learning needs, and personality. Figure 22.1 offers a sampling of questions that can guide the collection of information on the student's strengths, areas of challenge, and social or emotional needs.

Effective educational teaming cannot happen without a supportive infrastructure that provides personnel preparation, policies that facilitate cooperation, and time for coordinated planning and interventions (Coleman & Gallagher, 2015; Coleman, Gallagher, & Job, 2012; Roberts, Pereira, & Knotts, 2015). One approach

- What are the subjects where the student excels, shows evidence of high-level thinking, or expresses a strong interest?
- What is the student's favored mode of learning and expressing himself?
- In what subject(s) does the student have difficulty, and what is the nature of the difficulty?
- What tasks, learning activities, or situations does the student avoid?
- Does the student demonstrate negative or unexpected behaviors during certain learning tasks or activities?
- What learning/academic incongruities are present (e.g., advanced comprehension of material presented visually and/or aurally, but low comprehension if read)?
- To what degree does the challenge/disability impact the ability of the student to pursue strengths and interests?
- What triggers or contexts, if any, set the student off?
- What behaviors does the student exhibit that interfere with learning?
- To what degree does the student exhibit heightened empathy and sensitivity?
- Does the student make derogatory comments, such as "I'm dumb," about herself?
- What, if any, uneven development exists physically, emotionally, and/or socially?
- How does the student hide his strengths and/or his disabilities to fit in with peers? (Baldwin et al., 2015)

Figure 22.1. Sample questions to help determine a student's strengths, areas of challenge, and social or emotional needs.

that seems to hold promise for teaming is the Multi-Tiered System of Supports (MTSS; Pereles, Baldwin, & Omdal, 2011). MTSS is a term that has been integrated into the reauthorization of the Elementary and Secondary Education Act, called the Every Student Succeeds Act (ESSA) which was passed in December of 2015 (U.S. Department of Education, 2015). It encourages states and districts to utilize a tiered approach for support offered to all students, especially those with diverse educational needs. Students identified as having an educational need are provided with interventions at increasing levels of duration and intensity. The problem-solving process utilized in MTSS allows for a discussion of the whole child, starting with strengths. This multitiered system allows for an ongoing discussion about each student's needs without a push to get the child tested for special education. Interventions can occur without a label (Pereles et al., 2011).

Because the MTSS approach is a comprehensive systems approach to providing supports for all student needs (both remedial and advanced), it is possible to create student plans that consider both. This MTSS approach, when implemented well, provides for more opportunities to team across disciplines and provide more flexible supports for students. With the new legislation of ESSA in place, the educational system is closer than ever before to providing success of the personalized supports and integrated methods to support these students. The flexible, multidimensional, and customized educational programming that supports the success of students who are 2e will ultimately help all students thrive. And, when our educational structures can support the success of students with the most complex needs, these structures are likely to optimize the success of *all* students!

Curriculum Intervention Strategies With Universal Design for Learning

Many students who are 2e experience challenges with processing information (Kirk et al., 2015). These challenges can include taking information in (e.g., visual, auditory, kinesthetic processing), the actual processing of information (e.g., forming categories, thinking about and storing information in memory), and output of information (e.g., writing, speaking, drawing, expressing emotions). In addition to the input, processing, and output functions, information processing also includes executive function or decision making, where there can also be difficulties; all of this takes place within an emotional context. Effective processing of information is key to learning, so when students experience difficulties with any aspect of information processing, learning is harder for them (Coleman, 2015a). Universal Design for Learning (UDL) can help guide us in selecting support strategies for 2e students across each area of information processing difficulty.

UDL is a framework for interventions. It entails (a) multiple ways to represent information, (b) multiple ways to engage the learner with information, and (c) multiple ways to allow the learner to express or show what she has learned (Coleman, 2015b). Table 22.1 shows how the principles of UDL can be linked with the challenge areas within information processing that many 2e students face to identify appropriate strategies to support the student's academic and social-emotional success.

The educational provisions educators make are critical for the student's academic, social, and emotional success, yet these will be much more effective if they are done in partnership with the child's family.

Partnering With Families

Family involvement is important for every student; however, it is essential for the twice-exceptional student. Families engaged in a positive relationship with schools can have a direct impact on the achievement of students (Henderson & Mapp, 2002). In fact, twice-exceptional students are at increased risk for failure and underachievement without a partnership with families (Reis, Neu, & McGuire, 1995). Many times the child at home seems to be very different from the child seen within a school environment, where she may be experiencing less support and success. True family partnerships involve an openness to having the family at the table from the very beginning so that they can participate and contribute to planning the

Table 22.1

Information Processing and Universal Design for Learning Strategies

	UDL Representation	UDL Engagement	UDL Assessment
IP Input	Books on tape Manipulatives Videos/Pictures Graphics/Charts Story boards Timelines Matrixes Highlighting Color coding Large/Bold font Audio files Tactile graphics Use of all senses		
IP Processing		Kinesthetic activities Discussions Debates Plays/Drama/Dance Music/Song Building models Writing activities (Journals, poetry, stories, reports, plays, essays, etc.) Role playing Simulation games Critical thinking Creative thinking Research skills Data collection Data analysis	
IP Output			Discussions Debates Product-based assessments of plays, models, written work, etc. Drawing/Sculpting Music/Song Experimentation Charts/Graphs Pictures/Photos

Table 22.1, *Continued.*

	UDL Representation, *Continued.*	**UDL Engagement,** *Continued.*	**UDL Assessment,** *Continued.*
Executive Function	Graphic organizers Thinking maps Concept maps Learning frames Outlines Chapter headings Advance organizers Syllabi Study guides Highlighting Prompts (verbal, visual)	Thematic lessons Big ideas Concept-based learning Metacognitive strategies Learning strategies Study skills	Rubrics (with open areas of student choice) Self-assessments Student-selected products
Emotional Context	Safe environment Structured rules Encouragement Rewards vs. punishment	Choice of activities Interest-based assignments Support available Study buddy Breaks for movement	Use of non-punitive assessments that reward student growth Environment supportive of risk-taking Provision of separate grades Effort for content and form

Note. Reprinted from "Meeting the needs of students who are twice exceptional: Information processing model and universal design for learning," (p.4) by M. R. Coleman, 2015, *North Carolina Association for the Gifted and Talented Newsletter, 34.* Copyright 2015 by the North Carolina Association for the Gifted and Talented. Reprinted with permission.

support for their child. This type of collaboration may be new to families and educators, so the ongoing roles required for this teaming process will need to be defined and guided (Miller & Kraft, 2008).

Collaborating as partners in examining data, developing and implementing interventions, monitoring progress, and evaluating effectiveness are often new skills for all. The most important elements to achieve success are clear communication, common language, and identified role expectations (Lines, Miller, & Arthur-Stanley, 2011). With this type of partnership, twice-exceptional students can feel more consistently supported in school and at home. Family and school personnel share ownership when they work closely together to create and modify a successful plan for a child.

Educational Transition Beyond K–12

The more effective K–12 programming is for 2e students, the more planning is needed for college and career transitions. Under the Americans with Disabilities Act (ADA, 1990), colleges and universities that receive any federal support (this is basically all institutions of higher education) must provide academic accommodations for students with disabilities (Fahr, 2015). Most colleges provide tutoring, academic coaching (e.g., writing and math labs), and counseling for any students who request these services. In addition, many colleges have extended programs for students with disabilities. Accessing the disability supports and services at the college level builds on the student's K–12 accommodations, so the student's K–12 records must be up to date. Additional assessments may also be required to help with academic placement decisions. Some campuses offer special programming options for language classes, peer-group support, and/or career planning for students with disabilities (Fahr, 2015). At the college level, however, students with disabilities do not automatically receive these services—*students must self-activate all supports that they feel would help them succeed.* Self-advocacy is critical for success at the college level (Reis, McGuire, & Neu, 2000), and being able to effectively advocate for oneself, as noted earlier, requires self-knowledge, self-confidence, and a lot of practice. College students can advocate for a range of accommodations, including extended drop-add periods, modified schedules, note-takers for classes or access to the professor's notes, extended time on tests, testing in a quiet location, modified testing format, audiotaped lectures, books on tape, sign language or an interpreter, modified labs to support students with physical limitations, private or quiet dorm accommodations, medical support for health needs, and counseling support for emotional well-being. Essentially, students may self-advocate for any support or service that they feel would help them succeed. Self-advocacy does not guarantee that a support or service will be provided, but, with some creative problem solving, often a pathway can be found to overcome most obstacles to the student's success.

Conclusion

The aim of all supports and services for 2e students is to enhance students' autonomy, build their confidence, and safeguard their opportunity for success. Each 2e student has a unique set of strengths and challenges, and educational responses must be tailored for each student. Effective programming for 2e students includes team problem solving to address academic as well social and emotional needs, and families are key partners in ensuring student success. The structures and supports that help twice-exceptional students meet with success will help *all* students thrive. Although educators understand how to support 2e students' success, the remaining challenge is how to bring these practices to scale. To do this, educators will need appropriate policies, professional development, and sustained commitment to the teaming approaches that facilitate collaboration. Most of all, educators need the collective will to implement educational practices that focus on every student's success.

Big Ideas

1. Each 2e student has a unique combination of strengths and challenges, so educational responses must be tailored to address these needs.

2. Supports and services must address academic, social, and emotional needs, focused on the well-being of the whole student.

3. A team approach using problem solving is critical to developing and implementing a plan for student success.

4. Parents and families are essential partners in supporting the twice-exceptional student's success in K–12 and beyond.

5. The educational structures that support the success for 2e students will help all students thrive.

Discussion Questions

1. How does the 2e students' combination of strengths and needs make programing for their success more challenging?

2. What are obstacles to the kind of collaborative teaming described in this chapter, and what are ways to overcome these obstacles?

3. In what ways would all students benefit if teachers used Universal Design for Learning approaches in their classrooms?

4. Why are partnerships with parents and families essential for planning educational services and strategies for 2e children, and what can be done to strengthen these partnerships?

5. What did you learn in the reading about educating this special population (and perhaps your prejudices) that you were unaware of before?

References

Americans with Disabilities Act, 42 U.S.C. §§ 12102 et seq. (1990).

Assouline, S. G., & Whiteman, C. S. (2011). Twice-exceptionality: Implications for school psychologists in the post–IDEA 2004 era. *Journal of Applied School Psychology, 27,* 380–402.

Baldwin, L., Baum, S., Pereles, D., & Hughes, C. (2015). Twice-exceptional learners: The journey toward a shared vision. *Gifted Child Today, 38,* 206–214.

Baldwin, L., Omdal, S. N., & Pereles, D. (2015). Beyond stereotypes: Understanding, recognizing, and working with twice-exceptional learners. *Teaching Exceptional Children, 47,* 216–225.

Baum, S., Cooper, C., & Neu, T. (2001). Dual differentiation: An approach for meeting the curricular needs of gifted students with learning disabilities. *Psychology in the Schools, 38,* 477–490.

Baum, S., & Owen, S. (2004). *To be gifted and learning disabled: Strategies for helping bright students with LD, ADHD, and more.* Waco, TX: Prufrock Press.

Coleman, M. R. (2015a). Meeting the needs of students who are twice exceptional: Information processing model and universal design for learning (Part 1). *North Carolina Association for the Gifted & Talented, 34*(2), 1–5.

Coleman, M. R. (2015b). Meeting the needs of students who are twice exceptional: Information processing model and universal design for learning (Part 2). *North Carolina Association for the Gifted & Talented, 34*(3), 1–4.

Coleman, M. R., & Gallagher, S. (2015). Meeting the needs of students with 2e: It takes a team. *Gifted Child Today, 38,* 252–254.

Coleman, M. R., Gallagher, J. J., & Job, J. (2012). Developing and sustaining professionalism within gifted education. *Gifted Child Today, 35,* 27–36.

Fahr, L. (2015). *A postsecondary model for students with learning disabilities.* Retrieved from http://exclusive.multibriefs.com/content/a-postsecondary-tutoring-and-coaching-model-for-students-with-learning-disa/education

Henderson, A. T., & Mapp, K. L. (2002). *A new wave of evidence: The impact of school, family and community connections on student achievement.* Austin, TX: Southwest Educational Development Lab.

King, E. W. (2005). Addressing the social and emotional needs of twice-exceptional students. *Teaching Exceptional Children, 38*(1), 16–20.

Kirk, S., Gallagher, J., & Coleman, M.R., (2015). *Educating exceptional children* (14th ed.). Belmont, CA: Cengage.

Lines, C., Miller, G., & Arthur-Stanley, A. (2011). *The power of family-school partnering (fsp).* New York, NY: Routledge.

McEachern, A. G., & Bornot, J. (2001). Gifted students with learning disabilities: Implications and strategies for school counselors. *Professional School Counseling, 5,* 34–41.

Miller, D., & Kraft, N. (2008). Best practices in communicating with and involving parents. In A. Thomas & J. Grimes (Eds.), *Best practices in school psychology V* (pp. 937–951). Bethesda, MD: National Association of School Psychologists.

Olenchak, F. R. (2009). Effects of talents unlimited counseling on gifted/learning disabled students. *Gifted Education International, 25,* 144–164.

Pereles, D., Baldwin, L., & Omdal, S. (2011). Addressing the needs of students who are twice-exceptional. In M. R. Coleman & S. K. Johnsen (Eds.), *RtI for gifted students* (pp. 65–88). Waco, TX: Prufrock Press.

Pereles, D. A., Omdal, S. N., & Baldwin, L. (2009). Response to intervention and twice-exceptional learners: A promising fit. *Gifted Child Today, 32*(3), 40–51.

Reis, S. M., Baum, S. M., & Burk, E. (2014). An operational definition of twice-exceptional learners: Implications and applications. *Gifted Child Quarterly, 58,* 217–230.

Reis, S. M., McGuire, J. M., & Neu, T. W. (2000). Compensation strategies used by high ability students with learning disabilities who succeed in college. *Gifted Child Quarterly, 44,* 123–134.

Reis, S. M., Neu, T. W., & McGuire, J. M. (1995). *Talents in two places: Case studies of high ability students with learning disabilities who have achieved.* Storrs: University of Connecticut, The National Research Center on the Gifted and Talented.

Roberts, J. L., Pereira, N., & Knotts, J. D. (2015). State law and policy related to twice-exceptional learners: Implications for practitioners and policymakers. *Gifted Child Today, 38,* 215–219.

Trail, B. A. (2011). *Twice-exceptional gifted children: Understanding, teaching, and counseling students.* Waco, TX: Prufrock Press.

U.S. Department of Education. (2015). *Every Student Succeeds Act.* Retrieved from https://www.gpo.gov/fdsys/pkg/BILLS-114s1177enr/pdf/BILLS-114s1177enr.pdf

SECTION VI

Improving Services for Gifted Learners

Moving Forward

From the onlooker's perspective, the home is complete. A welcome mat graces the front stoop, and a wreath decorates the door. The family is settling in, unloading boxes and setting them out for recycling. To the insider, however, not everything is complete. There's a punch list, an agenda of final steps, that needs attention. Perhaps a switch plate is crooked, the drywall needs patching on the top floor, or a stretch of quarter round needs a second coat of paint. Regardless of the task, special attention is needed.

Likewise, a punch list exists for gifted education. In order to improve identification of and services for learners with gifts and talents, more is needed. Educators need professional learning; policies need to be created or tweaked to best serve gifted students; and messages need to be sent to decision-makers at the local, state, and national levels.

This section contains three chapters: "Professional Development," "Policy in Gifted Education," and "Advocacy."

Professional Development, Policy, and Advocacy combine to educate educators, parents, and decision-makers in order for them to support educational practices, establish policies, and advocate for gifted learners to learn with appropriate challenge in K–12 settings. In short, the goal is to abolish the myths (presented in each section) that are so prevalent and that get in the way of continuous progress for gifted learners.

Myth

» **Gifted education is elitist.** When appropriate identification measures are used, gifted learners come from all demographics. These learners are exceptional students in that they learn differently from the typical learner. Strategies should address their unique needs.

413

CHAPTER 23

Professional Development

Mary Evans

Who dares to teach must never cease to learn.—John Cotton Dana

Essential Questions to Guide the Reader

1. What are the skills and abilities needed for working with gifted students?

2. How do we establish the need for ongoing professional development in gifted education?

3. What is effective professional development for gifted education?

4. What are appropriate techniques for monitoring and evaluating professional development in gifted education?

Two weeks after Margie Elliot began her new principalship at Hollingsworth Elementary School, a small group of parents came to visit. After welcoming her, they expressed some concerns about their children's learning at the school. One parent said she frequently volunteered in her children's classes and saw that all the students were given the same spelling words, same math problems, and same social studies reports with the very same expectations. She saw some children struggling because the work was very difficult for them, while her child and a few others in the classroom finished the assignments very quickly and then drew pictures, read books from the library, were asked to help other students, or were disruptive. Another parent

415

described the math assignments his child brought home as being very simple and repetitive, and his child who used to love math began to say that math was not fun anymore because he was not learning anything new. The third parent said her son had begun to dislike school, saying he was tired of waiting for other students to finish their work. Plus students took turns reading out loud from their textbooks, and it was so boring. One of the parents asked if it would be possible to have some enriching extracurricular activities at the school, such as an academic team, science club, and art club.

After the parents left, the new principal pondered the discussion and knew she wanted what the parents wanted: Hollingsworth Elementary School should have a vibrant, rich learning environment that supported each student and each teacher so that each was challenged to be the best that he could be. She decided that a first step was to form a committee of teachers and parents to discuss professional development needs for the school. The committee would collect and analyze data from students, staff, parents, and community members; plan professional learning opportunities aligned to school and district goals as well as professional development standards; implement professional learning opportunities; provide support and follow up; and monitor and assess progress along the way. The journey of continuous improvement began—the journey to become a school that addressed the needs of all students, including the needs of gifted students.

Skills and Abilities Needed for Working With Gifted Students

Many factors contribute to how a student learns in the classroom, such as socioeconomic status, physical and mental health, home and community influences, and peer relationships. Most of these factors occur beyond the school walls, but the role of the teacher has a highly significant impact. Teachers must be prepared to meet the wide range of learner needs in their classrooms so that all students learn at a level and a pace that are appropriate for them.

Characteristics of Effective Teachers of Gifted Students

Numerous studies have been undertaken to determine the characteristics and prerequisites necessary for successful teachers of gifted children. Effective teachers of the gifted possess traits like maturity, experience, self-confidence, high intelligence and achievement, sense of humor, flexibility, enthusiasm, appreciation of giftedness, broadly cultured background, subject matter expertise, ability to foster higher level thinking, high expectations, a passion for teaching, and capacity to meet personal and social needs of gifted students (Bishop, 1980; Feldhusen, 1985;

Gentry, Steenbergen-Hu, & Choi, 2011; Hansen & Feldhusen, 1994; Hultgren & Seeley, 1982; Robinson, 2008; Whitlock & DuCette, 1989).

Ford and Frazier Trotman (2001) described desired characteristics needed when teachers work with gifted students who are culturally, ethnically, or linguistically diverse. They recommend that teachers of the gifted demonstrate respect for the student's primary language, embrace a holistic teaching philosophy, and represent teacher diversity. In addition, teachers should implement culturally sensitive assessments, culturally congruent instructional practices, culturally relevant pedagogy, and equity pedagogy.

Mills (2003) conducted a study to explore the characteristics of exceptional teachers of gifted students. She found that it is important to select teachers with a strong background in the academic discipline being taught and with a passion for the subject matter. Mills also reported that gifted students might benefit from greater contact with teachers who are more similar to them in personality and cognitive style.

Vialle and Tischler (2009) classified key characteristics associated with teachers of the gifted into three areas: personal-social characteristics, teaching strategies and approaches, and intellectual characteristics. Personal-social characteristics include a sense of humor; having insights into the cognitive, social, and emotional needs of gifted students; willingness to make mistakes; enthusiasm; and being culturally responsive. Examples of teaching strategies and approaches are skills in differentiating the curriculum for gifted students, encouraging higher level thinking, encouraging students to be independent learners, providing student-centered learning opportunities, being well-organized, acting as a facilitator, and creating a nonthreatening learning environment. Intellectual-cognitive characteristics include possessing in-depth knowledge of subject matter, having broad interests, having above-average intelligence, being a lifelong learner, thinking creatively, and possessing excellent communication skills. Vialle and Tischler found that gifted students appreciated teachers who combined favorable personal characteristics with positive intellectual qualities and varied, active pedagogical approaches.

Robinson (2014) encouraged school leaders who are hiring teachers to work with gifted students to consider both cognitive and affective factors in candidates being interviewed. Effective teachers of gifted students need strong subject area expertise and an understanding of and appreciation for the special needs of gifted students.

What Effective Teachers Need to Know

All teachers need to be able to recognize high-ability students who need opportunities to work at levels and paces matched to their abilities. They need to know how to provide advanced curriculum for these students and be able to determine when further assessment and services beyond the regular classroom are needed. The field has developed several sets of standards, including the NAGC Pre-K–Grade 12 Gifted Education Standards (NAGC, 2010; see Chapter 3). These standards represent professional consensus on what teachers need to know and be able to do as they work with all gifted students. The standards should be used to guide the planning of professional development in schools.

The Need for a Comprehensive Professional Development Program

Hansen and Feldhusen (1994) studied the classroom competencies and performance of trained and untrained teachers of the gifted. Their research showed highly significant differences in the performance of the two groups. Trained teachers showed more major proficiencies in these areas than their untrained counterparts: fast pacing of instruction, emphasis on creativity and thinking skills, teacher-student interactions, appropriate motivational techniques, student-directed activities, and the use of media and models in teaching.

Cramer (1991) conducted a Delphi study of gifted education involving 29 experts. The experts concluded that all teachers should receive some basic education of the needs and characteristics of gifted and talented children and that certification of teachers who work with groups of gifted children should be mandatory. They confirmed that gifted children require a differentiated curriculum and that teachers should be trained to develop and use such differentiated curriculum in their classrooms.

Farkas and Duffett (2008) conducted a National Teacher Survey and found that most teachers feel pressure to focus primarily on their lowest achieving students and neglect the high achievers, even though this offends their sense of fairness. These teachers reported receiving little training on how to work with academically advanced students, citing that their preparation programs, as well as the professional development received, did not emphasize this kind of training. Nearly two thirds (65%) said that their teacher preparation classes offered very little, if any, information on how to best teach academically advanced students. Fifty-eight percent of the teachers reported they have had no professional development over the past few years that specifically focused on teaching academically advanced students.

New Teacher Center's TELL Survey (2017; Teaching, Empowering, Leading and Learning) gathers educator perceptions of teaching and learning conditions in their schools. The information from this online anonymous survey can be used to plan professional development. Statewide data are available from Delaware, Kentucky, Maryland, North Carolina, and Oregon. An average of 55% of the teachers from those five states responded that they needed more professional development in differentiation, and an average of 49% said they needed more training in working with gifted and talented students. Fewer than 10% replied that they had participated in 10 or more clock hours of professional development on working with gifted and talented students in the past 2 years.

One of the most important ways that schools can help students learn is to provide high-quality professional development for their teachers. Increasing the effectiveness of professional development has the greatest potential for improving the performance of educators. Gubbins (2014) emphasized that developing effective professional development plans requires educators to work together toward common goals. She also noted the issues teachers of gifted students face as they seek to provide access to challenging curricula in schools pressured by accountability and high-stakes test scores.

A formal definition of professional development was prepared by Learning Forward, the professional learning association, for use in the reauthorized version of The Elementary and Secondary Education Act of 1965 (ESEA), known as the Every Student Succeeds Act (ESSA, 2015). This definition describes professional development as a comprehensive, sustained, and intensive approach to improving teachers' and principals' effectiveness in raising student achievement. Other key points are that professional development should foster collective responsibility for improved performance, must be aligned with state student academic standards as well as local school improvement goals, and be job embedded, data driven, and classroom focused so that teams of educators engage in a continuous cycle of improvement.

Learning Forward (2011) has developed seven Standards for Professional Learning (see Table 23.1). The decision to call these Standards for Professional Learning rather than Standards for Professional Development emphasizes that educators must take active roles in their own growth, keeping the focus on learning. Learning for educators must lead to learning for students. The greatest impact occurs when educators collaborate with a systemwide plan for learning tied to a set of goals connecting all classrooms and schools in the district. Having a systemwide plan for learning about gifted education is extremely important. Gifted students are found in most classrooms, making it very important for all educators to address their needs and facilitate continuous progress.

Guskey (2014) noted that the first consideration in planning professional development should be determining specific student learning outcomes. Educators must examine the learning progress of gifted students, paying careful attention to students from different socioeconomic backgrounds, language experiences, races, and ethnicities. Too often gifted students are making minimal progress because they are sitting in classrooms where the pace and level of instruction are not matched to their ability levels.

Professional development is vital for all educators working with gifted students. Because students with gifts and talents spend the majority of their time in regular

Table 23.1

Learning Forward's (2011) Seven Standards for Professional Learning

Learning Communities: Professional learning that increases educator effectiveness and results for all students occurs within learning communities committed to continuous improvement, collective responsibility, and goal alignment.
Leadership: Professional learning that increases educator effectiveness and results for all students requires skillful leaders who develop capacity, advocate, and create support systems for professional learning.
Resources: Professional learning that increases educator effectiveness and results for all students requires prioritizing, monitoring, and coordinating resources for educator learning.
Data: Professional learning that increases educator effectiveness and results for all students uses a variety of sources and types of student, educator, and system data to plan, assess, and evaluate professional learning.
Learning Designs: Professional learning that increases educator effectiveness and results for all students integrates theories, research, and models of human learning to achieve its intended outcomes.
Implementation: Professional learning that increases educator effectiveness and results for all students applies research on change and sustains support for implementation of professional learning for long-term change.
Outcomes: Professional learning that increases educator effectiveness and results for all students aligns its outcomes with educator performance and student curriculum standards.

education classrooms (Borland, 2013), general education teachers need to receive professional development that prepares them to recognize the characteristics of giftedness in students so that they can assist in the referral and identification process for their local school and district. They also need professional development, so they have a repertoire of differentiation, enrichment, and acceleration strategies. Administrators, coordinators, curriculum specialists, regular education teachers, special education teachers, gifted education teachers, and guidance counselors all need to develop understanding and expertise in gifted education, so they can be the talent scouts who find these students and then develop/implement the services they need to reach their potential. The Pre-K–Grade 12 Gifted Programming Standards (NAGC, 2010) can serve as the foundation.

Every Student Succeeds Act (ESSA)

The Every Student Succeeds Act (ESSA) is legislation passed in 2015 that revised and reauthorized ESEA. ESSA requires that Title II plans address how the state will prepare teachers and other school leaders to identify gifted and talented students and provide instruction matched to their needs. Districts receiving Title II funds are required to address the learning needs of gifted and talented students. Districts may use their Title II professional development funds to provide training for administrators and teachers on how to identify gifted students and on how to serve them using gifted education instructional practices, such as acceleration, curriculum compacting, and differentiation.

ESSA provides funding for professional development in gifted education that had not been available in the past. This allows state, district, and school leaders to plan professional learning that will benefit all students with high potential, especially those from previously underrepresented groups (English language learners, minority students, low-income students, and twice-exceptional students).

Needs Assessment and Self-Reflection

It is important to determine teachers' attitudes and concerns about gifted education before professional development planning begins. Dettmer, Landrum, and Miller's (2006) needs sensing, a way to determine the wants and needs of participants, should occur before a needs assessment to look for sensitivity and readiness toward staff development themes. Techniques used in needs sensing include informal interviews, observations in classes, analysis of requests for materials and other resources, discussions with individuals and small groups, and watching reactions when gifted topics or gifted students are mentioned.

The informal information gained from needs sensing can then be used to design more formal needs assessment instruments, such as surveys, checklists, and questionnaires, that are conducted online for quick and easy analyzing. Many aspects of gifted education need to be addressed in order for teachers to have the background knowledge and latest information and research in order to teach gifted students well. A school can utilize an online form with a list of possible topics, such as characteristics and needs of students with gifts and talents in diverse populations, twice-exceptional gifted students, assessment, curriculum planning, underachievement, perfectionism, mentorships, designing independent studies, and differentiation. Teachers select their areas of interest, and many online platforms (such as Google Docs) will instantly compile the information. From there, differentiated professional development is planned. Teachers will recognize that their ideas have been taken into consideration and feel they have some ownership in professional development activities. It is important to have teacher input regarding the topics to be explored, and they also need a voice in when, where, and how they will learn. Very few teachers like the "sit and get" format of an hour-long slide presentation after a full day of teaching. They might prefer to meet with a small group of teachers for a book study at a local coffee shop on a Saturday morning or take an online course in their pajamas while sitting on their couch at home. Just as a choice in learning activities is important for students, teachers appreciate having a choice.

Job-Embedded Professional Development

The value of job-embedded professional development has been increasingly recognized in recent years. Darling-Hammond and McLaughlin (1995) and Hirsh (2009) describe job-embedded professional development as teacher learning that is grounded in day-to-day teaching practice and designed to enhance teachers' instructional practices with the intent of improving student learning. Closely connected to the classroom, it involves teachers finding solutions for immediate problems they face on a daily basis in their classrooms. Too frequently, teachers walk away from a day of in-service at a conference center with an expert nationally known in the field of gifted education unable to make the connection to the cluster group of gifted students in their classroom. The next day, when they are back in their classroom, they are too overwhelmed by the needs of the students with behavior problems or the complications of the new student data system to try any of the new strategies that were shared.

Job-embedded professional development takes place in the classroom or in the school, in real time, with current students, or shortly before or after instruction away from the students. It is always centered on issues of actual practice. Although job-embedded professional development can be undertaken by a teacher alone, if implemented and supported effectively, it can contribute to the development of all teachers on a team by stimulating conversations about teaching and learning. Two examples are shared below.

Example 1. During a formal observation, the principal noticed that a fourth-grade teacher was especially skilled at asking higher level questions. He arranged to cover the classes of two teachers who set using more high-level questions as their professional growth goal so they could observe this teacher. The teachers took notes describing and analyzing what they saw. During small-group work, the teachers talked with students about what they were learning. Just after the students left, the teachers discussed how these higher level questions facilitated learning, and how the teacher was able to assess students' understanding through questioning.

Example 2. During her planning period, a teacher posted a question to an online learning community about how to monitor students working on independent study projects. Several teachers from across the state offered strategies and resources. The teacher tried to implement their suggestions, posted her experience to the online community later that week, and received additional feedback.

Professional Learning Formats

Professional learning comes in many different formats, including professional learning communities, conferences and workshops, outside experts, book studies, lunch and learn, faculty meeting: quick share, and online learning. These are shared below.

Professional Learning Community

A Professional Learning Community (PLC) is a goal-driven, student-focused, collaborative effort among teachers to improve student learning. Teachers are organized into either grade-level or content-area teams to meet regularly to review student data, collaborate on teaching strategies, solve problems, and set common instructional goals. They identify what's working and what's not and set goals for future teaching and learning success. PLCs often provide the support that teachers need to find and serve the high-ability students in their classes.

Working collaboratively, the teachers in a PLC focus their work on four critical questions:

> What knowledge and skills should every student acquire as a result of this unit of instruction? How will we know when each student has acquired the essential knowledge and skills? How will we respond when some students do not learn? How will we respond when some students clearly achieved the intended outcomes? (DuFour, DuFour, Eaker, & Many, 2006, p. 21)

The needs of gifted students should be addressed in PLCs just as much as the needs of students who are struggling with grade-level content. Members of PLCs work together to find ways to extend and enrich the learning for students who have demonstrated proficiency.

Example. After sitting through hours of monthly and quarterly Data Team Meetings reviewing information from computerized tests, teacher-made assessments, and student work samples for students who were working below grade level, a principal and teacher team wondered why they were not doing this for their students who were above grade level. Substitute teachers were hired to provide release time, and meetings were scheduled so that grade-level teams of teachers could analyze the assessment data of their high-ability students with the same amount of scrutiny they had been using with the data of their struggling students. They found that many students identified as gifted and talented were making very little academic progress. Teams of teachers went to work setting short- and long-term goals for these students to show progress that was commensurate with their ability. Specific, measurable goals were developed jointly with the students and documented in their Gifted Student Service Plans. Students tracked their progress toward reaching their goals in their Data Notebooks.

Working in small groups, teachers began to ask, "What strategies do I need to be using to help my high-ability students reach their goals?" The building-level gifted resource teacher was a good source of ideas for effective strategies. The teacher teams discussed how they would utilize the new strategies in their teaching. The teachers practiced the strategies with their students, brought work samples back to the team meetings, received reactions and advice from their colleagues, and refined their teaching further as they built confidence with using the strategies. Teachers were analyzing and interpreting the student work rather than evaluating each other's teaching skills. Taking ownership of their professional learning, teachers decided when and how they would apply new strategies, what they would bring to the team for review, and how they would interact in team meetings. School leadership, including the principal and curriculum specialist, encouraged the teachers to own their learning by listening to them and using their feedback to make decisions about use of school resources, such as time and money.

Conferences and Workshops

State and national conferences offer a variety of sessions with experienced and knowledgeable keynote speakers and presenters. These usually span 2–4 days and are great places to network and learn about available resources. One- and 2-week summer institutes at universities provide a way for teachers to deepen their understanding about gifted education. Daylong workshops and seminars also provide helpful information. Presenters are frequently practitioners who leave their own schools and districts for a day of sharing with other teachers. Effective workshops focus on the use of research-based instructional practices, involve active learning experiences for participants, and provide teachers with opportunities to adapt the practices to their individual classroom situations.

Outside Experts

Although there is much emphasis on professional learning being school based and utilizing the combined expertise of teachers in the school to explore common problems and seek solutions, the use of outside experts should not be discounted. A research synthesis conducted by Guskey and Yoon (2009) found that professional development efforts that brought improvements in student learning focused primarily on ideas gained through the involvement of outside experts, such as program authors or researchers who presented ideas directly to teachers and then helped facilitate implementation.

Book Studies

Book studies provide another format to increase teachers' understanding of gifted students. The principal and gifted and talented resource teacher could introduce books on a variety of topics in gifted education at a faculty meeting. Teachers then sign up for the book study group that interests them based on the needs of their current students. Topics such as acceleration, differentiation using centers, or problem-based learning could be the focus for book studies. There could be an orchestrated discussion of the book, teachers could implement strategies shared in the book and then discuss the results, or an individual could develop a project that stemmed from reading the book and then model a strategy—the possibilities for a book study are numerous.

Lunch and Learn

Teachers select a relevant topic to discuss during lunch. The National Association for Gifted Children (NAGC) YouTube channel (https://www.youtube.com/user/nagcgifted) has instructional videos that can be used to start the discussion. Participants can bring their lunch, or pizza can be ordered for those participating. The informal setting is conducive to honest discussion and sharing of ideas.

Faculty Meeting: Quick Share

Whitaker and Breaux (2013) wrote about the 10-minute in-service, and the importance of keeping the training simple, engaging, and ultra clear. Presenters need to model, coach, explain, and show rather than just tell. A quick way to bring gifted education information to teachers is by sharing a brief article during a faculty meeting. Assign sections of the article to small groups of teachers. Each group reads and becomes "experts" on its section. The groups then share what they learned in their section of the article with the rest of the teachers. State gifted association newsletters are a good source of practical articles that are not too lengthy.

Online Learning

Online learning allows teachers to choose topics of interest and learn from experts and practitioners in the field. Little and Housand (2011) described online activities as effective ways to connect gifted education professionals across several schools and districts. Online professional development courses allow teachers to pursue areas of immediate need. For example, NAGC offers online professional learning opportunities for its members, covering topics such as classroom practice, differentiation, curriculum, identification, programs and services, social-emotional needs, STEM, and underserved populations. Teachers can read, watch, and listen to other teachers demonstrate best practices, then implement them. The teacher has the opportunity for ongoing discourse with other teachers about ideas and their implementation.

Webinars. Webinars are web-based events conducted using video conferencing software. Educators can participate live and pose questions to or share their experiences with presenters and other attendees. Programs are archived for later viewing. A wide variety of topics are offered, such as acceleration, underachievement, best practices, and social-emotional issues. SENG, an organization supporting the social-emotional needs of gifted individuals, offers SENGinars, webinars featuring knowledgeable experts discussing issues such as perfectionism, underachievement, and motivation.

Discussion forums. A discussion forum is an online bulletin board where people can leave messages and expect to see responses to those messages. One example comes from the Davidson Institute for Talent Development, a national nonprofit group dedicated to supporting profoundly gifted students. The free Gifted Issues Discussion Forum (http://www.davidsongifted.org/Search-Database/entry/R15069) provides a place for people to discuss advocacy, research, and other gifted issues.

Social media. Many resources are available through social media. Teachers can create Personal Learning Networks (PLNs) that support individual learning goals aligned to school and district improvement goals. PLNs are typically online, open, and informal and encourage a free flow of ideas. Teachers build their PLNs by finding and connecting with people who share their areas of interest and passions. A PLN can be a blend of face-to-face and digital interactions with colleagues, mentors, and experts in the field. A PLN includes organizations, communities, and individuals who can help them grow in their profession. A good way to find professionals in the field of gifted education is to connect with the state and national gifted associations. Once teachers join these organizations, they can get on their e-mail lists and follow them on social media. They can connect with authors, researchers, and speakers from conferences.

Many connected educators know the benefits of Twitter as a form of professional development. Educators from near and far can take part in conversations on Twitter. Twitter chats are a way for educators to connect on relevant topics as well as share resources and best practices. Moderators pose questions on a predetermined topic, and participants use a consistent hashtag (#), such as #edchat, to link the tweets together in a virtual conversation. Teachers interested in gifted education can follow @HoagiesGifted on Twitter, which hosts a weekly chat using the hashtag #gtchat. Visser, Calvert Evering, and Barrett (2014) investigated K–12 teachers' access, usage, and perceptions of Twitter. They found that the "culture of Twitter" fosters collaboration and participation. Carpenter and Krutka (2014) found that educators value Twitter's personalized, immediate nature and that its use helps combat feelings of teacher isolation and fosters a positive collaborative community of learners.

Blogging is another form of social media that can be used as a professional development tool for gifted education. Educators can use this form of informal, open communication to share ideas, reflect on their educational practices, and collaborate with one another. A teacher could blog about her experiences with various grouping strategies and get feedback from others who are also trying different grouping arrangements in their classrooms.

Support for School Personnel

District- and building-level leaders must facilitate the talent development of teachers just as teachers must facilitate the development of talent in their students. This begins with the development of a building-wide philosophy that the business of schools is about finding and nurturing talent. The adults in the school must see themselves as "talent scouts" looking for evidence of high potential in areas ranging from academics, such as math, science, and writing, to music, dance, creativity, and leadership.

It is important for the principal to emphasize continuous learning for all faculty in how to identify and address the wide range of student needs. The principal establishes a school culture among teachers where continued learning is considered an essential aspect of professional practice. The principal models a commitment to her own ongoing professional learning and emphasizes this when hiring new teachers and during formal and informal meetings with teachers.

The principal must identify teacher leaders who understand gifted learners and who are comfortable sharing their understandings and teaching practices with colleagues. These teacher leaders should be provided with additional training in gifted education, print and technology resources, and release time so they can facilitate effective professional learning with the teachers on the team and in their school.

Monitoring and Evaluating Professional Learning

Planners of professional learning in gifted education must include evaluation as a key part of the professional development process. It is important to collect, analyze, and share evidence of the value of professional learning experiences. Guskey (2000, 2002) has written about five crucial levels of evidence to consider when evaluating professional development: (a) participants' reactions, (b) participants' learning of new knowledge and skills, (c) organizational support and change, (d) participants' use of new knowledge and skills, and (e) student learning outcomes. The levels are ordered from simple to more complex, and Guskey emphasized that success at one level is necessary for success at the next level; the ultimate goal of the professional development is to improve student learning.

The following questions could be asked to evaluate professional development in gifted education at each of these five levels:

1. *Participants' reactions*: Do the participants feel more confident in their ability to design effective learning experiences for gifted learners?
2. *Participants' new knowledge and skills*: Do the participants know more about the nature and needs of gifted students?
3. *Organizational support and change*: Do the participants have the support and resources they need to provide appropriate learning opportunities for gifted students? Do new understandings about gifted students and how they learn lead to policy changes in the school/district, such as new or revised policies related to grouping or acceleration?
4. *Participants' use of new knowledge and skills*: Are the participants utilizing new teaching strategies that are designed to take the ceiling off of learning?
5. *Student learning outcomes*: Are gifted students showing learning gains that are commensurate with their ability?

Hunzicker (2011) reviewed research on effective professional development and identified the following five characteristics of effective professional development: supportive, job-embedded, instructionally focused, collaborative, and ongoing. She prepared a checklist (see Table 23.2) for school leaders to use when designing learning opportunities for teachers based on these characteristics (Hunzicker, 2011). This checklist could also be used to review professional development experiences to see how well they met the characteristics.

A workgroup (Cotabish et al., 2015) for NAGC designed a self-study guide for teachers and gifted coordinators to reflect on and improve their teaching practices and gifted education programs to support the student outcomes in the six programming standards. The self-study guide is arranged in a six-step process:

1. Review the programming standards.
2. Identify data sources to measure student outcomes.
3. Complete the self-study checklist.
4. Conduct a gap analysis.
5. Develop an action plan.
6. Monitor progress.

The authors of the self-study guide developed questions to guide school leaders in using the Pre-K–Grade 12 Standards and suggested that the questions can serve as a form of self-assessment. For example, the following questions were given for Standard 6, Professional Development:

Table 23.2

Characteristics of Effective Professional Development: A Checklist

Supportive	Yes	Partly	No
• Does it combine the needs of individuals with school/district goals?			
• Does it engage teachers, paraprofessionals, and administrators?			
• Does it address the learning needs of specific schools, classrooms, grade levels, and/or teachers?			
• Does it accommodate varying teaching assignments, career stages, and teacher responses to educational innovation?			
• Does it accommodate individual learning styles and preferences?			
• Does it integrate teacher input and allow teachers to make choices?			
Job-embedded			
• Does it connect to teachers' daily responsibilities?			
• Does it include follow up activities that require teachers to apply their learning?			
• Does it require teachers to reflect in writing?			
Instructional-focus			
• Does it emphasize improving student learning outcomes?			
• Does it address subject content *and* how to teach it?			
• Does it help teachers to anticipate student misconceptions?			
• Does it equip teachers with a wide range of instructional strategies?			
Collaborative			
• Does it engage teachers physically, cognitively, and emotionally?			
• Does it engage teachers socially in working together toward common goals?			
• Does it require teachers to give and receive peer feedback?			
Ongoing			
• Does it require a high number of contact hours over several months' time?			
• Does it provide teachers with many opportunities over time to interact with ideas and procedures or practice new skills?			
• Does it "build" on or relate to other professional development experiences in which teachers are required to engage?			

Note. Reprinted from "Characteristics of Effective Professional Development: A Checklist," (pp. 177–179) by J. Hunzicker, 2011, *Professional Development in Education, 37*(2). Copyright 2011 by Taylor & Francis, http://www.informaworld.com. Reprinted with permission.

- Are all teachers, counselors, and instructional support staff given sufficient time and funds to regularly participate in a variety of research-supported professional development options in order to increase their expertise in the pedagogy and practice of gifted and talented education and to familiarize themselves with the resources available to meet the academic and socio-emotional needs of their students?
- Is the professional development utilized aligned to the NAGC-CEC Teacher Preparation Standards in Gifted Education and in compliance with the rules, policies, and standards of ethical practice? (NAGC, n. d., para. 8)

Evaluation is a key component in the cycle of continuous improvement. The primary reasons to evaluate professional development are to determine the impact of the professional learning, to make evidence-based decisions about how to improve the activities being implemented, and to share effective practices. Educators examine data to understand what student and adult learners need, set professional learning goals, determine learning strategies, apply new learning, and assess the impact of what they have applied in their classes and schools. Successes must be shared and celebrated and the cycle continued.

Conclusion

Professional learning is vital for all educators working with gifted students. Teachers need to be able to recognize high-ability students in their classrooms and know how to provide advanced learning opportunities to address their gifts and talents. District- and building-level leaders must conduct a needs assessment and then facilitate a comprehensive professional development program that is sustained, job embedded, data driven, and focused on continuous learning for all students, including gifted students. Ongoing monitoring and evaluation are necessary to track progress toward meeting professional development goals.

Big Ideas

1. School personnel need special skills and abilities in order to recognize exceptional potential and talent in students and to facilitate the development of these gifts and talents.

2. A comprehensive professional learning program must be provided for all school personnel working with gifted students.

Big Ideas, *Continued.*

3. Professional development should be based on a needs assessment and self-reflection.

4. Professional development must be differentiated to meet the wide range of needs of school personnel who work with gifted students.

5. School personnel require support for their specific efforts related to the education of gifted children.

Discussion Questions

1. You are a member of the professional development committee at your school. How would you convince other members of the committee of the need to include professional development in gifted education in the school improvement plan?

2. Every teacher in a school is required to design an individualized personal development plan. What should a regular classroom teacher take into consideration in the creation of his or her plan?

3. Who needs professional development in gifted education, and how does what is needed differ by role group?

4. What are some ways that the goals of professional development in gifted education can be integrated with the goals of professional development in general education?

References

Bishop, W. E. (1980). Successful teachers of the gifted. In J. S. Renzulli & E. P. Stoddard (Eds.), *Under one cover: Gifted and talented education in perspective* (pp. 152–160). Reston, VA: Council for Exceptional Children.

Borland, J. H. (2013). Problematizing gifted education. In C. M. Callahan & H. L. Hertberg-Davis (Eds.), *Fundamentals of gifted education: Considering multiple perspectives* (pp. 69–80). New York, NY: Routledge.

Carpenter, J., & Krutka, D. (2014). How and why educators use Twitter: A survey of the field. *Journal of Research on Technology in Education, 46,* 414–434.

Cotabish, A., Shaunessy-Dedrick, E., Dailey, D., Keilty, B., Pratt, D., & Adams, C. (2015). *Self-assess your P–12 practice or program using the NAGC gifted programming standards.* Washington, DC: National Association for Gifted Children.

Cramer, R. (1991). The education of gifted children in the United States: A Delphi study. *Gifted Child Quarterly, 35,* 84–91.

Darling-Hammond, L., & McLaughlin, M.W. (1995). Policies that support professional development in an era of reform. *Phi Delta Kappan, 76,* 597–604.

Dettmer, P., Landrum, M., & Miller, T. (2006). Professional development for the education of secondary gifted students. In F. A. Dixon & S. M. Moon (Eds.), *The handbook of secondary gifted education* (pp. 611–648). Waco, TX: Prufrock Press.

DuFour, R., DuFour, R., Eaker, R., & Many, T. (2006). *Learning by doing: A handbook for professional learning communities at work.* Bloomington, IN: Solution Tree.

Every Student Succeeds Act, 20 U.S.C. 6301 (2015).

Farkas, S., & Duffett, A. (2008). *High-achieving students in the era of NCLB: Results from a national teacher survey.* Washington, DC: Thomas B. Fordham Institute.

Feldhusen, J. F. (1985). The teacher of gifted students. *Gifted Education International, 3,* 87–93.

Ford, D. Y., & Frazier Trotman, M. (2001). Teachers of gifted students: Suggested multicultural characteristics and competencies. *Roeper Review, 23,* 235–239.

Gentry, M., Steenbergen-Hu, S., & Choi, B. (2011). Student-identified exemplary teachers: Insights from talented teachers. *Gifted Child Quarterly, 55,* 111–125.

Gubbins, E. J. (2014). Professional development for novice and experienced teachers. In J. A. Plucker & C. M. Callahan (Eds.), *Critical issues and practices in gifted education* (2nd ed., pp. 505–517). Waco, TX: Prufrock Press.

Guskey, T. (2000). *Evaluating professional development.* Thousand Oaks, CA: Corwin.

Guskey, T. (2002). Does it make a difference? Evaluating professional development. *Educational Leadership, 59*(6), 45–51.

Guskey, T. (2014). Planning professional learning. *Educational Leadership, 71*(8), 10–16.

Guskey, T., & Yoon, S. (2009). What works in professional development? *Phi Delta Kappan, 90,* 495–500.

Hansen, J. B., & Feldhusen, J. F. (1994). Comparison of trained and untrained teachers of gifted students. *Gifted Child Quarterly, 39,* 115–123.

Hirsh, S. (2009). A new definition. *Journal of Staff Development, 30*(4), 10–16.

Hultgren, H. W., & Seeley, K. R. (1982). *Training teachers of the gifted: A research monograph on teacher competencies.* Denver, CO: University of Denver.

Hunzicker, J. (2011). Effective professional development: A checklist. *Professional Development in Education, 37,* 177–179.

Learning Forward. (2011). *Standards for professional learning.* Retrieved from http://www.learningforward.org/standards-for-professional-learning

Little, C. A., & Housand, B. C. (2011). Avenues to professional learning online: Technology tips and tools for professional development in gifted education. *Gifted Child Today, 34,* 19–27.

Mills, C. J. (2003). Characteristics of effective teachers of gifted students: Teacher background and personality styles of students. *Gifted Child Quarterly, 47,* 272–281.

National Association for Gifted Children. (n.d.). *Guiding questions to apply the Pre–K to Grade 12 Gifted Programming Standards.* Retrieved from https://www.nagc.org/resources-publications/resources/national-standards-gifted-and-talented-education/pre-k-grade-12-7

National Association for Gifted Children. (2010). *NAGC Pre-K–Grade 12 Gifted Programming Standards: A blueprint for quality gifted education programs.* Washington, DC: Author.

New Teacher Center. (2017). *TELL survey initiative.* Retrieved from https://newteachercenter.org/approach/teaching-empowering-leading-and-learning-tell

Robinson, A. (2008). Teacher characteristics. In J. A. Plucker, & C. M. Callahan (Eds.), *Critical issues and practices in gifted education* (pp. 669–680). Waco, TX: Prufrock Press.

Robinson, A. (2014). Teacher characteristics and high-ability learners. In J. A. Plucker & C. M. Callahan (Eds.), *Critical issues and practices in gifted education* (2nd ed., pp. 645–658). Waco, TX: Prufrock Press.

Vialle, W., & Tischler, K. (2009). Gifted students' perceptions of the characteristics of effective teachers. In D. Wood (Eds.), *The gifted challenge: Challenging the gifted* (pp. 115–124). Merrylands, Australia: NSWAGTC.

Visser, R., Calvert Evering, L., & Barrett, D. (2014). #Twitter for teachers: The implications of Twitter as a self-directed professional development tool for K–12 teachers. *Journal of Research on Technology in Education, 46,* 396–413.

Whitaker, T., & Breaux, A. (2013). *The ten-minute inservice: 40 quick training sessions that build teacher effectiveness.* San Francisco, CA: Jossey-Bass.

Whitlock, M. S., & DuCette, J. P. (1989). Outstanding and average teachers of the gifted: A comparative study. *Gifted Child Quarterly, 33,* 15–21.

CHAPTER 24

Policy in Gifted Education

Jonathan A. Plucker

Governments will always play a huge part in solving big problems. They set public policy and are uniquely able to provide the resources to make sure solutions reach everyone who needs them.—Bill Gates

Essential Questions to Guide the Reader

1. What is education policy, and how does it differ from other aspects of education?

2. Who should be concerned about the creation and implementation of education policies?

3. How do education policies impact gifted education and the lives of gifted students?

4. How can educators and advocates for gifted students influence education policy?

Why Policy?

Public policy determines how education is organized, how it is funded, how its effects are evaluated, and how it can be changed. Policy serves as the foundation and framework of our education system. It is the foundation because all goals and aspirations of our schools are built upon policies, and it is the framework because all aspects of school organization and operations are created and implemented within the rules and guidelines created by policy. Anyone seeking to work within or change education would be well served to understand the many complexities of how policy is created, implemented, and evaluated.

There is a general understanding in the field of gifted education that we have not paid enough attention to policy, and this matches my personal observations. This is not to say that the field does not have committed advocates. To the contrary, the field not only has these individuals, who spend countless hours interacting with policymakers to improve the lives of gifted students, but it has also focused attention on how we can become better advocates (e.g., Davis, 2010; Roberts, 2009; Robinson & Moon, 2003; Walker, 2002).

But we can improve our advocacy efforts, and one way to accomplish this is to gain a better understanding of how policy works. In other words, hiking the Appalachian Trail is not easy, but it is much easier with the right equipment and a thorough understanding of the terrain. The purpose of this chapter is to provide readers with that equipment and understanding.

In addition to how policy can help create positive change for gifted education, it can help us understand why certain interventions do *not* work well. Why do some programs appear to have a long-term influence, yet others tend to create little lasting, positive impact? Plucker and Callahan (2014), in a review of research within gifted education, noted several areas well-supported by research (e.g., lack of challenge and differentiation in the regular classroom, the benefits of acceleration, positive outcomes associated with the use of prescriptive curriculum) and several that are not (e.g., interventions to address social and emotional issues, interventions to address racial and ethnic underrepresentation). A knowledge of the relevant policies can help us understand why these interventions are or are not working, serving as a guide to the design of future programs.

Of course, policy is not the only lens through which to focus on education issues. When I attend meetings of educational psychologists, the discussion rarely touches on policy, focusing instead on how we can create optimal learning environments for advanced students; how we can create rigorous, differentiated curriculum to ensure gifted students are appropriately challenged; how we can develop students' creativity more effectively and efficiently. But when attending meetings of education policy experts, the conversation rarely includes discussions of how students learn and create, focusing instead on how accountability systems can be modified to encourage schools to focus more attention on high-ability learners, how school choice can provide options to underserved gifted students, and how homeschooling regulations should be crafted to provide gifted students with improved educational experiences. Clearly, both policy and nonpolicy topics matter *a lot*, and an integrated approach will be the main theme in this chapter.[1] Again, thinking of policy as the foundation and framework leaves a lot of other necessary material (e.g., curriculum, instruction, students, families, leadership) to build the house of gifted education.

Terms, Processes, and Levels of Education Policy

The basic terms and organization of policymaking are fairly straightforward. It may not feel that way to someone who has little experience working within policy, but that would be true for someone looking in on any big, complex system.[2] The basic terms and processes are very similar for most policymaking systems.

Defining Policy

First and foremost, we need to define *policy*. Gallagher (2002) offered the following definition: "Social policy creates the rules and standards by which scarce resources are allocated to meet almost unlimited social needs" (p. 1). This definition encapsulates many important facets of policy, but in this chapter we will use a modified version: Education policy creates the rules and standards by which limited resources are allocated to meet perceived needs. These changes are important because (a) sometimes resources aren't scarce, such as in states with large inflows of oil and gas money, but those resources are never unlimited; and (b) defining needs as essentially unlimited feels too broad—there are always perceived needs, but policymakers (and communities at large) make value judgments all the time about whether a perceived need does or does not need to be addressed. Saying those needs are unlimited can imply that they are universally accepted as critical needs, when often they are not.

The Gallagher definition also implies that someone is making the policy (policymaker/s), and that it applies to one or more groups.[3] With this in mind, it may be helpful to think of a policy as a set of guidelines that describe how members of a group interact with other groups or individuals. From this perspective, a policy can be some guidelines on how educators in a particular school (the group) imple-

---

1   That said, within the field of gifted education, I have been in far more meetings where policy is never discussed than situations where people overfocused on policy. As with The Force, we need balance.

2   For example, how world religions are organized (and interact with one another) looks almost unfathomable from the outside, but once you are immersed in your local church, your local piece of that complex system feels straightforward and comfortable.

3   A policy governing one person is very uncommon and generally ill-advised. For example, I may declare a personal policy of "no yard work on the weekend," but that is really a preference and not a rule that will be observed, in large part because the larger group that is my family won't accept it.

ment acceleration strategies with a specific student (an individual) or set of students (another group). Or consider a policy that sets forth a dress code for teachers or students (how an individual teacher or student interacts with others in their group).

Other Policy Terms

With respect to government policy, especially at the federal and state level, a handful of common policy terms describe various types of policies (see Table 24.1). In basic terms, a bill is a proposed law, an approved bill is a law, and a regulation is a binding rule put in place to help people follow the law. All three are policy vehicles.

A good recent example is the reauthorization of the Elementary and Secondary Education Act (ESEA) by the U.S. Congress. Although scheduled for reauthorization in 2007, the controversial nature of the latest iteration of the law, the No Child Left Behind Act, prevented any progress toward that goal. Various bills for reauthorizing the law were introduced over the years, and although some received committee hearings, none came to the floor of the House of Representatives or Senate for a vote. Yet beginning in late 2014, a bipartisan group of senators introduced a new reauthorization bill, the Every Student Succeeds Act, which was eventually approved by both houses of Congress and signed into law by President Obama in late 2015.

Processes of Policy

The life cycle of a government policy is depicted in Figure 24.1. These steps apply to the creation of policy at the state level, but they also describe the federal process in general terms. In the first step, the idea for the bill is formed. This can happen in many ways: A summer study committee of the legislature may create it, an advocacy group may work with a legislator or group of legislators to craft the bill, or a legislator may produce the idea on her own, among many other possible pathways. But the end result is a draft bill that one or more legislators introduces as a formal bill in their house of the legislature.

The next few steps involve legislative deliberation and votes on the bill. In most states (and the U.S. Congress), the house of origin (i.e., the legislative chamber where the bill originated) considers the bill in an assigned committee—for most education bills, the chamber's education committee—and, after a public hearing and discussion, the committee votes on whether to pass the bill to the floor of their particular chamber. If the vote fails, the bill is usually (but not always) finished. If it passes, it is generally scheduled for a full vote by the entire chamber. If it passes there, it is sent over to the other house, where the process repeats itself. Should the bill eventually pass the second chamber, usually with some modifications, a conference committee of members from both houses is formed to consider the bill and negotiate any differences. The resulting negotiated bill is then voted on in both houses of the state or

Table 24.1

Common Education Policy Terms

Term	Definition	Example
Policy	Rules and standards by which limited resources are allocated to meet perceived needs. Includes bills, laws, and regulations, among many others.	Everything from how peace treaties are negotiated and approved to how school cafeteria staff organize how students receive lunch each day.
Bill	Proposed law under consideration by a legislature.	A state senator proposes a bill to expand state-funded AP test participation.
Law	A bill that has been approved by the legislative and executive branches. Also referred to as acts or statutes.	A bill to expand state-funded AP test participation is approved by the legislature and governor, becoming a law.
Regulation	Binding rule or guideline that describes how specific laws are implemented.	The state department of education issues regulations to guide how the AP test participation law will be implemented and monitored.

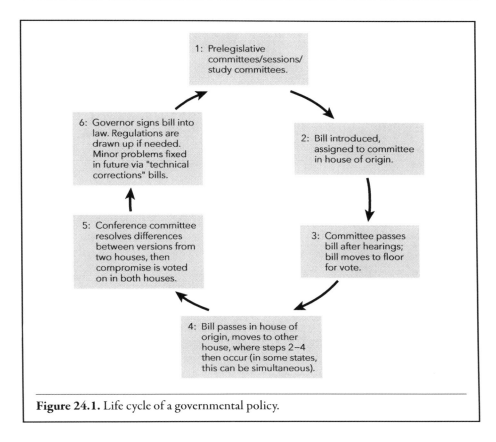

Figure 24.1. Life cycle of a governmental policy.

federal legislature and, if approved, is sent to the executive branch (a governor or the president) for approval. If the executive signs the bill, it becomes law.

That, however, is hardly the end of the process, as regulations often need to be created to help people interpret how the law will be implemented. After the regulations are drawn up and the law becomes effective, laws are often monitored for effectiveness. This monitoring process frequently uncovers minor issues and complexities regarding the law's effects. Sometimes it takes years for these effects to be noticed, sometimes only a few weeks. If the issues are minor, they can be addressed in subsequent legislative sessions in technical corrections bills, which can often read like a menu of minor tweaks to a series of laws.

All phases of the policy creation process are important for gifted education. For example, consider the issue of whether Title I funds can be used to provide programming for gifted students. Some states interpreted the current ESEA language as allowing the funds to be spent this way, but most did not. Being able to use these important resources for advanced education could be an important step in closing excellence gaps. During the creation and revision of the bill in Congress, advocates asked for the language on this issue to be clarified, and the law now contains that language. But the regulations need to reinforce that Title I funds can be used for this purpose; otherwise states may not be comfortable doing so (as of the writing of this chapter, the regulations appear favorable in this regard).

Key points are that (a) there is a formal process; (b) there are carefully designed rules that govern the process; (c) paradoxically, the process in this figure does not describe any one real-life situation perfectly but does describe most processes generally; (d) there are many ways in which a bill can fail, as the process is designed to be both highly deliberative and difficult for new laws to be created; and (e) the process does not have a "finish line" in the sense that after a certain point the policy does not need to have attention paid to it.

Levels of Policy

Gallagher (2013) proposed three *levels* of policy—national, state, and local—with various sublevels within each. For example, at the national level, Gallagher noted the importance of Congress, courts, the U.S. Department of Education, and national professional organizations (e.g., NAGC, CEC, SENG); to these players we can add political interest groups, such as the U.S. Chamber of Commerce, national professional organizations that do not specifically focus on gifted education, such as the Council of Chief State School Officers, Chiefs for Change, the National School Board Association, and the National Governor's Association; national think tanks (which can be quite partisan, such as the American Enterprise Institute, Fordham Institute, Brookings Institution, and The Education Trust); and foundations that are national in scope, such as the Jack Kent Cooke Foundation, Davidson Institute for Talent Development, and Overdeck Family Foundation.

At the state level, Gallagher (2013) mentioned legislatures, governors, state departments of public instruction, state associations for gifted education for educators and parents, and the governing boards of residential and governors' schools. Add to the list state courts, state boards of education, state professional organizations (state superintendents association, teachers unions, state and regional think tanks [again, often quite partisan]), state businesses and business associations (a state's largest employer, the state manufacturers association, the state public employees union), and state and regional foundations.

And at the local level, Gallagher (2013) mentioned schools boards, superintendents, teachers, parent advocates, parent groups (PTO/PTA), and local gifted education advocacy groups. Local business groups, such as the town chamber of commerce, the major employers in a district, and local civic groups (e.g., the local chapter of the League of Women Voters) can all play important roles in education policy.

Although talking about policy *levels* is useful and technically correct, it may be more helpful to think of different levels of *systems* of policy. Each individual and group at a specific level interacts with the others, sometimes subtly. These interactions are important because forgetting about a specific player at, say, the state level does not mean they aren't important on a given issue—it just means they were forgotten. For example, if a state is considering a change to its school funding law that may reduce resources for gifted students, it is tempting to focus advocacy efforts on the legislative leaders overseeing the school funding legislation. But those legislators are also influenced by other individuals and groups—perhaps they turn to the state chamber of commerce or state manufacturers' association for advice, or maybe the state superintendents' association has their ear. Taking a broad systems view of education policy allows people to identify a range of allies that may not otherwise come to mind, helping them reach their advocacy goals more effectively.

Gifted Education Policy

Policy research on gifted education is rather thin, with few studies published over the past 30 years. Gallagher's (2002, 2004, 2013) policy work is well-respected, and Passow and Rudnitski (1993) wrote a monograph for The National Research Center on the Gifted and Talented in which they conducted a wide-ranging survey of state policies related to gifted education (perhaps the first such comprehensive survey). They found evidence that all 50 states had "formulated policies in the form of legislation, regulations, rules, or guidelines that support education of the gifted and talented," a finding they rightly labeled "a very significant achievement" (Passow & Rudnitski, 1993, p. 69). However, they did not find a consistent pattern of policies that could serve as a model for a state seeking an improved policy environment for gifted education. This seminal policy study inspired and has been succeeded by other similar efforts, such as the State of the States policy report conducted by the National Association for Gifted Children and Council of State Directors of Programs for the Gifted (e.g., NAGC & CSDPG, 2015) and a state policy report focused on income-based excellence gaps from the Jack Kent Cooke Foundation and its collaborators (Plucker, Giancola, Healey, Arndt, & Wang, 2015), both of which are produced biennially.

Other areas of concentrated research include the relationship between gifted education and school funding and related state policies (e.g., Baker & Friedman-Nimz, 2003; Baker & McIntire, 2003), school choice and gifted students (Baker & Richards, 1998; Decker, Eckes, & Plucker, 2010; Eckes & Plucker, 2005; Plucker, Makel, Hansen, & Muller, 2008; Plucker, Makel, & Rapp, 2008), and case law regarding the rights of gifted students to an appropriate education (e.g., Klupinski, Rothenberg, & Uzl, 2014; Plucker, 2008). This knowledge base, although more extensive than many people assume, is becoming dated and needs to be refreshed to see if trends from the late 1990s and early 2000s are still relevant today.

A good example of gifted education policy research conducted within the state and local policy systems is Purcell's (1992, 1993, 1995) work on the status of gifted education programs. Through the use of interviews, surveys, and policy analysis, she found evidence that, in an era of decreasing public education budgets, gifted programs were quickly eliminated or scaled back in a state without a mandate (Purcell, 1992) and that the divisive nature of many program eliminations may force parents to consider nonpublic options for educating their gifted child (Purcell, 1993). Furthermore, in a larger scale study of all 50 states, she found that programs tended to expand in states with mandates and a positive state fiscal context, but that states without a mandate or in a negative fiscal context were in decline. Baker (2001) and colleagues extended this work, noting that even in a state perceived to have a strong mandate and growing economy such as Texas, considerable discrepancies exist in the availability of and funding for programs for low-income and minority students (see also Baker & Friedman-Nimz, 2002).

Excellence Gap

As a case in point of the potential impact of gifted education policy research, this section will describe my team's recent work on the concept of excellence gaps, those achievement gaps at the highest levels of performance. Frustrated by the limited attention given to advanced learning within the national and state policy systems, we examined the political context and noted that the idea of achievement gaps, thanks in large part to NCLB, had firmly taken hold in the minds of many policymakers and educators around the country.

In other words, policymakers and educators did not seem to care deeply about high-ability students, but they cared about achievement gaps. Then why not, we wondered aloud, try to focus attention on achievement gaps at the top end of student performance?

Our work in this area was originally published in two reports, *Mind the (Other) Gap! The Growing Excellence Gap in K–12 Education* (Plucker, Burroughs, & Song, 2010) and *Talent on the Sidelines: Excellence Gaps and America's Persistent Talent Underclass* (Plucker, Hardesty, & Burroughs, 2013). The purposes of the first report were to establish—in clear, audience-friendly language—that excellence gaps exist and that the conventional wisdom that "a rising tide lifts all ships" was empirically incorrect. Incorporating feedback from *Mind the (Other) Gap!*, the second report sought to show that excellence gaps are longstanding and somewhat permanent in the absence of interventions to close them, and that excellence gaps serve to depress overall rates of academic excellence among our K–12 students. We chose self-published reports rather than journal articles because, to be frank, policymakers tend not to read journal articles.

That said, we also published in traditional academic journals to help establish the scientific credibility of the excellence gap concept. Papers have included studies of excellence gaps in other countries (Plucker, 2015; Rutkowski, Rutkowski, & Plucker, 2012) and a series of applied pieces on how educational technology (Hardesty, McWilliams, & Plucker, 2014) and school psychologists and counselors (Harris & Plucker, 2014) can address excellence gaps. In addition, our team wrote several blog posts, participated in Twitter chats and podcasts, and made presentations for teachers, administrators, and policymakers at a variety of venues.

Throughout this entire process, we sought partnerships from both within and outside of the field. NAGC and the Council for Exceptional Children were early and strong champions for this work, which helped us get access to state and federal policymakers. These initial experiences were invaluable opportunities to fine tune our message and determine which data points had the greatest impact on educators and policymakers. More recently, the Jack Kent Cooke Foundation and Fordham Institute have worked the concept of excellence gaps into their scholarship and advocacy, expanding the reach and impact of our research (e.g., Plucker et al., 2015). And several state associations, such as the Colorado Association for the Gifted and Talented and Kentucky Association for Gifted Education, have helped disseminate information on excellence gaps to their members.

Finally, Plucker and Peters (2016) recently wrote a book summarizing the research on excellence gaps in order to provide a platform for the next wave of research and intervention efforts. This next stage of excellence gap research will include more complex studies of how excellence gaps grow over the course of K–12 education and targeted interventions that may shrink and eventually eliminate excellence gaps.

The Law of Unintended Consequences

The Law of Unintended Consequences is the only scientific law that applies to education policy. It reflects the fact that any piece of policy will always have effects that were neither intended nor anticipated by policymakers. Unintended consequences are an especially big problem for gifted education, because the effects of a particular piece of legislation on gifted students are often an afterthought, if they cross the minds of policymakers at all. Sometimes the unintended consequences can be positive or benign, but they can often be quite negative.

This is probably due, at least in part, to the fact that much of education legislation focuses on improving the educational experiences of low-achieving students. That is obviously a laudable and necessary goal, but policies that improve the learning context for low-achieving students can be assumed to not necessarily address the needs of high-achieving students.

A good example is that of high school graduation requirements, which hold a number of unintended consequences for accelerated learners. Roughly a decade ago, many states focused renewed energy on boosting the number of students receiving high school diplomas. One clever policy initiative was to tie state aid for higher education to a high school diploma, thereby providing additional incentive for students to graduate and helping facilitate higher education at the same time. But "graduation" in many states is operationally defined as achieving a certain number of high school credits, making early graduation impossible for students who seek to enter college early. Most states did not take early college entrance into account when crafting their high school graduation policies, and they unintentionally added a large barrier for students interested in pursuing this form of academic acceleration.

For this reason, the policymaker truism that "These kids can take care of themselves" becomes ironic. Even if they could take care of themselves, and the available data strongly suggest that they do not, this statement would be odd because the law of unintended consequences suggests that policymakers often put up barriers and roadblocks, however unintentional, for advanced students. In other words, if they can take care of themselves, why are you bothering them with anti-excellence policies?

One way that our team has worked on addressing unintended consequences is to work with policymakers to ask two questions whenever they are dealing with an education-related piece of policy (*especially* when it does not directly appear to impact gifted students):

1. How will the proposed policy impact our highest achieving students?
2. How will the proposed policy help more students achieve at the highest levels?

As implied above, the law of unintended consequences cannot be avoided—life is simply too complex to allow us to predict exactly what a policy will and will not do. But working with policymakers to ask these two questions when they are considering the creation or implementation of any policy is one way to minimize the frequency and impact of unintended, negative consequences for gifted students. If nothing else, asking these questions can sensitize policymakers to the needs of advanced learners.

Commonsense Policy Strategies for Gifted Education

Education policy can be used to improve the opportunities offered to gifted students and at a scale that is hard to achieve with other interventions. The following observations are meant to suggest practical strategies that educators and other advocates can use to help influence the policymaking process.

Remember that policymaking is a long-term process marked by short-term wins and losses. Successfully advocating for a new district acceleration policy is important and worth celebrating, but the implementation of the new policy and evaluation of its (intended and unintended) effects is an ongoing process. And if the program is subsequently improved, the implementation and evaluation process starts anew. There is no end zone or finish line in the sport of policymaking.

Focus on the level of policy systems that can make the change you desire. If you want your local district to change its dual enrollment policy, speaking to your U.S. congressperson's staff will not be fruitful. If you want to modify your state K–12 accountability system to include indicators related to academic excellence, your local principal probably cannot help very much, but the head of your state House or Senate education committee probably can.

In a similar vein, be sensitive to that fact that policymakers focus on what they can change, which may be a tightly focused slice of the bigger picture. Because policymakers have finite time, energy, and resources, yet almost unlimited demands, they often focus like a laser on the level of policy systems—and often subsystems—upon which they have influence. I once prepared some briefing documents for a national-level elected official on a specific issue, and his education aide later let me know how much he appreciated the material, and how he had read it carefully and shared it with some of his peers across party lines. As I began to (inwardly) bask in my pride, the aide said, "Of course, he could never vote for this, but he still really appreciated the information." I was initially shocked, and then realized that of course he could not vote for it, as his party was strongly opposed to the issue, and it just was not important enough for the policymaker to go out on a limb on this particular issue. That does not mean our work on that issue was unimportant, just that it did not pay immediate dividends. Perhaps the political context would change, making it possible for the senator to support our position publicly; perhaps the goodwill we earned would pay off on a later, more important issue; or perhaps we should be satisfied that the policymaker shared our work with his peers. Policy change is a long-term game, and one must try to focus on the end result and not intermediary victories and losses.

Big Ideas

1. Everyone concerned about education and children has a stake in education policy.

2. Anyone involved with education or children is impacted by education policy.

3. Education policy has numerous levels, actors, and pressure points, and understanding this policy landscape is the key to understanding, creating, and influencing policy.

4. Policy related to gifted education is similar to many other areas of education policy, but it does have unique characteristics.

5. Evidence suggests that traditional approaches to advocacy and policy involvement are not highly effective, but new approaches are being developed and show promise.

Discussion Questions

1. What are some policies in your context that impact high-achieving students? Which are explicit? Implicit? How would your strategies for addressing these issues differ based on whether they are explicit or implicit?

2. Who are the key players in your local education policy system? How can you most effectively interact with each individual or group?

References

Baker, B. D. (2001). Measuring the outcomes of state policies for gifted education: An equity analysis of Texas school districts. *Gifted Child Quarterly, 45*(1), 4-15.

Baker, B. D., & Friedman-Nimz, R. (2002). Determinants of the availability of opportunities for gifted children: Evidence from NELS '88. *Leadership and Policy in Schools, 1*(1), 52–71.

Baker, B. D., & Friedman-Nimz, R. (2003). Gifted children, vertical equity, and state school finance policies and practices. *Journal of Education Finance, 28,* 523–555.

Baker, B. D., & McIntire, J. (2003). Evaluating state funding for gifted education programs. *Roeper Review, 25,* 173–179.

Baker, B. D., & Richards, C. E. (1998). Equity through vouchers: The special case of gifted children. *Educational Policy, 12,* 363–379.

Davis, J. L. (2010). *Bright, talented, and Black: A guide for families of African American gifted learners.* Tucson, AZ: Great Potential Press.

Decker, J. R., Eckes, S. E., & Plucker, J. A. (2010). Charter schools designed for gifted and talented students: Legal and policy issues and considerations. *Education Law Reporter, 259*(1), 1–18.

Eckes, S. E., & Plucker, J. A. (2005). Charter schools and gifted education: Legal obligations. *Journal of Law and Education, 34,* 421–436.

Gallagher, J. J. (2002). *Society's role in educating gifted students: The role of public policy* (RM02162). Storrs: University of Connecticut, The National Research Center on the Gifted and Talented.

Gallagher, J. J. (2004). No Child Left Behind and gifted education. *Roeper Review, 26,* 121–123.

Gallagher, J. J. (2013). Political issues in gifted education. In C. M. Callahan & H. L. Hertberg-Davis (Eds.), *Fundamentals of gifted education: Considering multiple perspectives* (pp. 458–469). New York, NY: Routledge.

Hardesty, J., McWilliams, J., & Plucker, J. A. (2014). Excellence gaps: What they are, why they are bad, and how smart contexts can address them . . . or make them worse. *High Ability Studies, 25,* 71–80. Retrieved from http://www.tandfonline.com/eprint/CxEN4szD3IFXscJ6xbNj/full

Harris, B., & Plucker, J. A. (2014). Achieving equity and excellence: The role of school mental health providers in shrinking excellence gaps. *Gifted Child Today, 37,* 110–116.

Klupinski, S., Rothenberg, B., & Uzl, N. (2014). Legal issues in gifted education. In J. A. Plucker & C. M. Callahan (Eds.), *Critical issues and practices in gifted education: What the research says* (2nd ed., pp. 363–375). Waco, TX: Prufrock Press.

National Association for Gifted Children, & Council of State Directors of Programs for the Gifted. (2015). *2014–2015 state of the states in gifted education: Policy and practice data.* Washington, DC: Author. Retrieved from http://www.nagc.org/sites/default/files/key%20reports/2014-2015%20State%20of%20the%20States%20%28final%29.pdf

Passow, A. H., & Rudnitski, R. A. (1993). *State policies regarding education of the gifted as reflected in legislation and regulation* (CRS93302). Storrs: University of Connecticut, The National Research Center on the Gifted and Talented.

Plucker, J. A. (2008). Gifted education. In C. J. Russo (Ed.), *Encyclopedia of education law* (pp. 380–382). Thousand Oaks, CA: Sage.

Plucker, J. A. (2015, August). *Advanced academic performance: Exploring country-level differences in the pursuit of educational excellence* [Policy Brief 7]. Amsterdam, The Netherlands: International Association for the Evaluation of Educational Achievement. Retrieved from http://www.iea.nl/fileadmin/user_upload/Policy_Briefs/IEA_policy_brief_Aug2015.pdf

Plucker, J. A., Burroughs, N., & Song, R. (2010). *Mind the (other) gap! The growing excellence gap in K–12 education.* Bloomington: Indiana University, School of Education, Center for Evaluation and Education Policy. Retrieved from http://ceep.indiana.edu/pdf/The_Growing_Excellence_Gap_K12_Education.pdf

Plucker, J. A., & Callahan, C. M. (2014). Research on giftedness and gifted education status of the field and considerations for the future. *Exceptional Children, 80,* 390–406.

Plucker, J. A., Giancola, J., Healey, G., Arndt, D., & Wang, C. (2015). *Equal talents, unequal opportunities: A report card on state support for academically talented low-income students.* Lansdowne, VA: Jack Kent Cooke Foundation. Retrieved from http://www.jkcf.org/assets/1/7/JKCF_ETUO_Report_with_State_Cards_rv.pdf

Plucker, J. A., Hardesty, J., & Burroughs, N. (2013). *Talent on the sidelines: Excellence gaps and America's persistent talent underclass.* Storrs: University of Connecticut, Center for Education Policy Analysis. Retrieved from http://cepa.uconn.edu/mindthegap

Plucker, J. A., Makel, M. C., Hansen, J. A., & Muller, P. A. (2008). Achievement effects of the Cleveland voucher program on high ability elementary school students. *Journal of School Choice, 1*(4), 77–88.

Plucker, J. A., Makel, M. C., & Rapp, K. E. (2008). The impact of charter schools on promoting high levels of mathematics achievement. *Journal of School Choice, 1*(4), 63–76.

Plucker, J. A., & Peters, S. J. (2016). *Excellence gaps: What they are and what to do about them.* Cambridge, MA: Harvard Education Press.

Purcell, J. (1992). State of the states: Programs for the gifted in a state without a mandate: An "endangered species?" *Roeper Review, 15,* 93–95.

Purcell, J. H. (1993). The effects of the elimination of gifted and talented programs on participating students and their parents. *Gifted Child Quarterly, 37,* 177–187.

Purcell, J. H. (1995). Gifted education at a crossroads: The program status study. *Gifted Child Quarterly, 39*(2), 57–65.

Roberts, J. L. (2009). Lessons learned: Advocating for a specialized school of mathematics and science. *Roeper Review, 32,* 42–47.

Robinson, A., & Moon, S. M. (2003). A national study of local and state advocacy in gifted education. *Gifted Child Quarterly, 47,* 8–25.

Rutkowski, D., Rutkowski, L., & Plucker, J. A. (2012). Trends in education excellence gaps: A 12-year international perspective via the multilevel model for change. *High Ability Studies, 23,* 143–166. Retrieved from http://www.tandfonline.com/eprint/xmmMecjnEYiF4sk5hTQR/full

Walker, S. Y. (2002). *The survival guide for parents of gifted kids: How to understand, live with, and stick up for your gifted child.* Minneapolis, MN: Free Spirit.

CHAPTER 25

Advocacy

Julia Link Roberts

A gifted child has the right to learn something new every day.
—Del Siegle (2007)

Essential Questions to Guide the Reader

1. Why advocate for gifted children?

2. What steps are likely to lead to effective advocacy?

3. When and where is advocacy for gifted children important?

4. What are the benefits of belonging to an advocacy organization, and how do advocacy organizations help gifted children?

Advocacy: What Is It?

Advocacy is speaking out on behalf of something: "an idea, cause, or policy" (National Association for Gifted Children [NAGC], n.d.). In gifted education, advocates speak out on behalf of practices or services that will allow gifted children to make continuous progress and/or support their cognitive or socioemotional needs. They may advocate for a policy that will put in place a practice or service that will make it possible for many young people to benefit rather than making decisions on a case-by-case basis (e.g., acceleration policy). They may advocate for legislation that will mandate services for gifted children or establish recognition for a group of gifted children (e.g., twice-exceptional children).

Teachers advocate on an ongoing basis as they discuss gifted children with colleagues, including grade-level teachers or content specialists. They plan with other educators and parents on behalf of a service, policy, or legislation that they believe would benefit a child or children with gifts and talents. They join others in organizations that provide professional development and advocacy for gifted learners.

History of Advocacy for Exceptional Children

Advocacy for exceptional children resulted in federal legislation. The Individuals with Disabilities Education Act (IDEA, 1990) set the requirements for states to provide services for children and young people with special education needs. Parents sharing their stories sent powerful and influential messages to legislators that provided the impetus that led to IDEA. It is important to note that gifted children were not included in IDEA.

Advocacy for gifted children at the federal level has been fueled by crises and national reports. The launch of Sputnik led to a spike of interest in providing high-level learning opportunities, especially in mathematics and science. Examples of advocacy that resulted in legislation for gifted education include the passage of the Jacob K. Javits Gifted and Talented Students Education Act (1988) and the reauthorization of the Elementary and Secondary Education Act (2015), known by the moniker Every Student Succeeds Act (ESSA; U.S. Department of Education, 2015; see Chapter 2).

The history of advocacy at the state level varies from state to state. Advocacy in some states has produced mandates to identify and/or provide services for gifted children, while other states have no legislation in regard to gifted children. Likewise, there are states that provide funding for gifted education and others with no funding (NAGC & Council of State Directors of Programs for the Gifted [CSDPG], 2015).

Effective Advocacy

Rationale

Why is it important to advocate for gifted children? Many individuals, including outstanding educators, do not recognize the needs of gifted children. Gifted children may not look needy as their needs are created by strengths rather than by deficits or areas that need to be supported, Many parents are satisfied with good grades even if the children are not learning at an appropriately challenging level. Some parents are hesitant to speak out on behalf of their children, thinking that it would be as unpopular as saying, "I've been trying to gain weight and just can't do it." In other words, there are many myths and misunderstandings about gifted children.

The overarching reason to advocate is to ensure that gifted children are learning on a daily basis in classrooms and schools that respect difference. The need to learn on an ongoing basis provides ample incentive to advocate for appropriate educational opportunities for children with gifts and talents. After all, the purpose for school is to engage students in learning. The bottom line is that students cannot learn what they already know, so advocacy must focus on policies and practices that must be in place for all children to make continuous progress, including offering appropriately challenging learning experiences for those with gifts and talents as well as all students who are ready for them.

Advocacy in one's classroom and school can be ongoing. It may be directing the conversation in a team meeting to data on an underachieving student or a cluster of students needing challenge in math or reading. It may be regularly asking the questions: "How will this (decision) affect our brightest student? How will this (decision) help other students begin to achieve at high levels?" (Plucker, 2011).

The well-being of children with gifts and talents depends on adults speaking out on their behalf. As the title of an article on advocacy highlights, the challenge is "If not you—who?" In other words, who will advocate for children in your classroom, school, school district, state, or country (Roberts & Siegle, 2012).

Goals for Advocacy

In gifted education, advocacy goals may be to increase information about and understanding of children who are gifted and talented and their educational and social-emotional needs. At the school level, the advocacy goal may be to get a *practice* or *service* implemented. At the school district level, the goal may be to establish *policy* that will open doors to learners and eliminate barriers to high-level learning. The goal may be to establish a *special school* at the district or state level. At the state level, the advocacy goal may be to secure *legislation* that will create opportunities for gifted children. Likewise, at the national level, *legislation*, *policy*, and *regulations* provide goals for advocacy.

There are important considerations or steps to take that maximize opportunities to advocate effectively. Each supports the others, and they combine to enhance advocacy for a practice, service, policy, legislation, or regulations.

Steps in Effective Advocacy

The opportunity for advocacy to be effective becomes more likely to occur when thought and planning precede action. The following steps are important to note.

1. *A clear, focused message is known and shared.* The message must be articulated and shared among advocates. Everyone who is advocating must communicate the same message to the decision-maker(s). What is it that you want to have in place in a classroom, school, school district, state, or nation? Taking time to sharpen the request is time well spent. This step in the process provides focus for the remainder of the advocacy work, and it certainly is not necessarily an easy task. A key element of the message must be that it presents a positive solution to a need you believe must be addressed. After all, that is what sparked your advocacy.

2. *Others who share your interests or concerns are located.* It may be that Steps 1 and 2 flip-flop in their order as advocates may identify others who share their interests and then work together to clarify the message. Either way, advocates will be far more effective with others than if they strike out on their advocacy journey alone. Numbers count in advocacy, so combining energy and effort works to everyone's advantage. You may find others who share concerns at other organizations, so stay open to collaborating.

3. *A well-developed plan must be put in place and followed.* Making a plan involves analyzing the situation to determine points along the way to reach the advocacy goal. Who are the key people who will make the decision related to the advocacy message? Is it the jurisdiction of the principal to make the decision, or is it a school decision-making council's or the school board's responsibility? Who in the school district will make the decision: the superintendent or the school board? If it is a decision to be made by a legislative body, what committee must introduce the bill, who are influential individuals on that committee, and what is the timeline for decision making? It is so important to think about such questions and how the message can be conveyed to those who will be in the room when the decision is made. A wise move would be to poll members of the advocacy group to see who knows whom and their involvement in the decision-making process.

4. *Advocates must persevere.* Advocates cannot be easily discouraged, as often success does not come on the first try. They must be ready to carry out the advocacy plan and add to it in order to get the message translated into practice in a school, policy within a school or school district, or into regulation or legislation at the state or national level. Expecting immediate action often leads to discouragement. Advocates must persevere.

Tips for Making Advocacy Messages Effective

1. *Use research to support advocacy.* Advocates need to be familiar with research that supports the advocacy goal. If they do not know the research, they know where to locate that information.

2. *Use messages that resonate.* For example, grade-level learning should be the starting point, but it should not limit learning for children who are ready to learn at more advanced levels. Often athletic examples help to convey the importance of learning at the appropriate level, as young athletes are given opportunities to play up with other children who are performing at the same level of skill.

3. *Tell stories about young people that make your advocacy point.* Dr. James Gallagher suggested, "What [decision-makers] do seems to be influenced by personal, direct testimony from those with direct experience who have little reason to shade their answers for personal gain (including professors who have grants and promotions on the line)" (personal communication, January 5, 2013).

4. *Write personal notes or letters to decision-makers.* It is too easy to delete e-mails, and form letters can readily be recognized as such.

The Empowering Results of Advocacy

Advocacy can lead to valuable changes that impact the learning of gifted children. Policy protects services that are in place in classrooms and schools. Policy guides decisions, including how resources are allocated. Gallagher (1994) stated:

> Social policy creates the rules and standards by which scarce resources are allocated to meet almost unlimited social needs. An effective social policy should answer the following questions:
> 1. Who shall receive the resources?
> 2. Who shall deliver the resources?
> 3. What are the resources to be delivered?
> 4. What are the conditions under which the resources are delivered? (p. 337)

Policies protect services, eliminating the need to advocate on an ongoing basis for the same or similar services.

Advocacy Organizations

Educators and parents may join local, state, or national organizations. They offer the opportunity for members to stay up-to-date through reading newsletters and journals, participate in professional learning, and join with others in speaking out for gifted children. Three national advocacy organizations provide multiple resources for their members.

- National Association for Gifted Children (http://www.nagc.org),
- Supporting the Emotional Needs of the Gifted (http://www.sengifted.org), and
- The Association for the Gifted, a division of the Council for Exceptional Children (http://www.cectag.com).

Most states have state advocacy organizations. There are various reasons to join a state advocacy organization, including the following:

1. You will learn about opportunities for your children who are gifted and talented.
2. You will receive newsletters, e-mails, and mailings to keep you up-to-date about what is happening that relates to the education of children who are gifted and talented.
3. You will be in a network with others who are working to ensure appropriate educational opportunities for children who are gifted and talented in your state and across the country.
4. In combining your voice with others who advocate for children who are gifted and talented, you can make a difference. (Roberts & Inman, 2009, p. 10)

Conclusion

Advocacy in gifted education can be focused at the classroom, school, school district, state, or national levels. When advocacy results in policy or legislation, it makes the greatest changes. Policy or legislation often removes the need to advocate for services for one child or a few children as policy and legislation put in place services for many children throughout a school, school district, state, or nation. That being said, it is important to "think big" when embarking on an advocacy journey. And, no matter the level of advocacy, there are some important lessons to guide advocates when speaking out on behalf of gifted children and their social-emotional and cognitive needs.

Remember that the gifted children and young people constitute a small number of the total school population, making it imperative that parents, educators, and other citizens who support every child learning every day they are in school speak out on behalf of appropriately challenging learning opportunities for them. If not you, then who?

Big Ideas

1. Advocacy for gifted children is speaking out for a service—often an opportunity for enrichment, acceleration, and differentiation.

2. Advocacy occurs at the classroom, school, district, state, and national levels.

3. Putting policy in place sets the stage for offering appropriately challenging learning opportunities.

4. Effective advocacy is well planned with a message that resonates.

5. A solitary voice may effect change, but the possibilities increase when collaboration occurs.

Discussion Questions

1. What is something you would like to have in place in your school? How would you begin to advocate for that service, strategy, or policy?

2. Teachers advocate in numerous ways. What is an example of advocating for a gifted child or gifted children in your school or school district?

3. Does your school district have an acceleration policy? If not, investigate what would be the value of having such a policy in place. If yes, how does the acceleration policy open opportunities for gifted students? How could you advocate to implement, change, or improve this policy?

4. How can you use standards to support your advocacy for gifted children?

References

Gallagher, J. J. (1994). Policy designed for diversity: New initiatives for children with disabilities. In D. Bryant & M. Graham (Eds.), *Implementing early interventions* (pp. 336–350). New York, NY: Guilford.

Individuals with Disabilities Education Act, 20 U.S.C. §1401 et seq. (1990).

National Association for Gifted Children (n.d.). *Advocate for high-ability learners*. Retrieved from http://www.nagc.org/get-involved/advocate-high-ability-learners

National Association for Gifted Children, & Council of State Directors of Programs for the Gifted. (2015). *2014–2015 State of the states in gifted education: Policy and practice data*. Washington, DC: Author.

Plucker, J. A., (2011, September). *Mind the excellence gap!* Session presented at Western Kentucky University's Victoria Fellows Program, Bowling Green, KY.

Roberts, J. L., & Inman, T. F. (2009, December). Advocacy: The importance of joining your state gifted association. *Parenting for High Potential*, 9–10.

Roberts, J. L., & Siegle, D. (2012). If not you—who? Teachers as advocates. *Gifted Child Today, 35,* 58–61.

Siegle, D. (2007). *Gifted children's bill of rights*. Retrieved from http://www.nagc.org/resources-publications/resources-parents/gifted-childrens-bill-rights

Title V, Part D. [Jacob K. Javits Gifted and Talented Students Education Act of 1988], Elementary and Secondary Education Act of 1988 (2002), 20 U.S.C. sec. 7253 et seq.

U.S. Department of Education. (2015). *Every Student Succeeds Act*. Retrieved from https://www.gpo.gov/fdsys/pkg/BILLS-114s1177enr/pdf/BILLS-114s1177enr.pdf

About the Editors

Julia Link Roberts, Ed.D., is the Mahurin Professor of Gifted Studies and the Executive Director of The Center for Gifted Studies at Western Kentucky University and The Carol Martin Gatton Academy of Mathematics and Science in Kentucky. Dr. Roberts is active in state, national, and international organizations. She has served as one of seven elected members of the Executive Committee and is the current president of the World Council for Gifted and Talented Children. She is the past-president of The Association for the Gifted (a division of the Council for Exceptional Children; CEC-TAG), a member of the advisory board for the National Research Center on Gifted Education, a board member of the Kentucky Association for Gifted Education, and chair of the Kentucky Advisory Board on Gifted Education. Her writing focuses on differentiation, curriculum, assessment, advocacy, and STEM schools. She was recognized with the first National Association for Gifted Children (NAGC) David W. Belin Award (2001), the Acorn Award as the outstanding professor at a Kentucky 4-year college or university (2011), the William Nallia Award for Innovative Leadership in Kentucky (2011), the NAGC Distinguished Service Award (2012), the Palmarium Award at the University of Denver Institute for the Development of Gifted Education, and as one of the 55 outstanding gifted educators in the U.S. (2003). Dr. Roberts directs year-round programming for children and young people and travels internationally with high school students.

Tracy Ford Inman, Ed.D., is associate director of The Center for Gifted Studies at Western Kentucky University and active on the state, national, and international levels in gifted education. She has taught English at the high school and collegiate levels, as well as in summer programs for gifted and talented youth. In addition to writing and cowriting several articles and chapters, Tracy has coauthored three books with Julia Roberts through Prufrock Press: *Teacher's Survival Guide: Differentiating Instruction in the Elementary Classroom*; *Strategies for Differentiating Instruction: Best Practices for the Classroom* (3rd ed.); and *Assessing Differentiated Student Products: A Protocol for Development and Evaluation* (2nd ed.). Tracy and Julia received the Legacy Book Award from the Texas Association for the Gifted and Talented for *Strategies for Differentiating Instruction*. Tracy was coeditor of *Parenting Gifted Children: The Authoritative Guide from the National Association for Gifted Children*, a compilation of the best articles in *Parenting for High Potential*, which won the Legacy Award in 2011. Her latest book is *Parenting Gifted Children 101: An Introduction to Gifted Kids and Their Needs,* coauthored by Dr. Jana Kirchner.

Jennifer H. Robins, Ph.D., is the Director of Publications and Professional Development at the Center for Gifted Education at William & Mary and a clinical assistant professor. She received her doctorate in educational psychology with an emphasis in gifted education from Baylor University. Prior to receiving her doctorate, she taught elementary gifted and talented students in Waco, TX. She also worked as senior editor at Prufrock Press, focusing on the development of scholarly materials, including gifted education textbooks and professional development books, as well as classroom materials for teachers of gifted and advanced students. Currently she is managing editor of the *Journal for the Education of the Gifted* and treasurer of The Association for the Gifted, Council for Exceptional Children. She recently coedited (with Dr. Rebecca Eckert) *Designing Services and Programs for High-Ability Learners: A Guidebook for Gifted Education*, published by Corwin Press. Her areas of interest include the history of gifted education and underrepresented populations.

About the Authors

Lori Andersen, Ph.D., is the science research lead for the Dynamic Learning Maps project at the University of Kansas. Previously she served as an assistant professor at Kansas State University and as a teacher of advanced high school science. Her current research involves building a cognitive learning map model for K–12 science. She has published many articles and book chapters in the fields of science education and gifted education. She has received several National Association for Gifted Children (NAGC) awards, including Doctoral Student Award (2013), Dissertation Award (2nd place, 2014), and Doctoral-Level Research Award (2012).

Susan G. Assouline, Ph.D., directs the Belin-Blank Center at the University of Iowa, holds the Myron and Jacqueline N. Blank Endowed Chair in Gifted Education, and is a professor of school psychology. She is especially interested in identification of academic talent in elementary students and coauthored (with Ann Lupkowski-Shoplik) both editions of *Developing Math Talent: A Comprehensive Guide to Math Education for Gifted Students in Elementary and Middle School*. She also is codeveloper of the Iowa Acceleration Scale, a tool designed to guide educators and parents through decisions about grade skipping students. In 2015, she coedited *A Nation Empowered: Evidence Trumps the Excuses Holding Back America's Brightest Students*. She is the 2016 recipient of the NAGC Distinguished Scholar Award and the 2017 University of Iowa Faculty Excellence Award.

Lois Baldwin, Ed.D., an educational consultant specializing in the areas of twice-exceptional and Multi-Tiered System of Supports (MTSS), has been both a teacher of twice-exceptional students and the administrator of one of the first programs in the country serving students who were gifted with learning and emotional needs. She cofounded the Association for the Education of Gifted Underachieving

Students where she serves as the president. Dr. Baldwin has taught courses on gift-edness and twice-exceptionality at Manhattanville College, Pace University, The College of New Rochelle, and Regis University and has been a consultant and speaker at numerous national conferences and symposiums. An author of numerous professional articles on the subjects of twice-exceptional individuals, Response to Intervention, and MTSS, Dr. Baldwin has chaired NAGC Twice-Exceptional Special Interest Group and cofacilitated the 2e Community of Practice action group.

Camelia Birlean, Ph.D., completed her undergraduate education and teacher preparation in Romania where she also worked as a teacher of Latin and Language Arts. At McGill University, she earned a master's degree in educational psychology and a Ph.D. in educational psychology, specializing in cognition and instruction. Currently a lecturer in the Department of Educational and Counseling Psychology at McGill University, she teaches gifted education and educational psychology classes for preservice teachers. She also supervises numerous M.Ed. research and professional development projects. Dr. Birlean serves as Educational Consultant of Teacher Education and Services for Gifted Students and Students with Special Needs at ECS School in Montreal. Her research interests focus on differences between teachers' pedagogical expertise and subject-matter expertise.

Lynette Breedlove, Ph.D., is the director of The Gatton Academy of Mathematics and Science at Western Kentucky University, a statewide public residential STEM school for gifted and talented students. Previously, she served the needs of gifted and talented students in public schools as teacher, gifted and talented facilitator, and central office coordinator/director where she led the establishment of a school for highly gifted students. Active in local, state, and national advocacy organizations, she has served as board president of the Texas Association for the Gifted and Talented (TAGT), within NAGC in various leadership roles, and on The Association for the Gifted, Council for Exceptional Children (CEC-TAG) board. She earned a master's degree in gifted and talented education at the University of St. Thomas and a doctorate in educational psychology at Texas A&M University.

Mary Ruth Coleman, Ph.D., is Senior Scientist, Emeritus, at the Frank Porter Graham Child Development Institute at the University of North Carolina at Chapel Hill. She directs Project U-STARS~PLUS (Using Science, Talents and Abilities to Recognize Students ~ Promoting Learning in Underrepresented Students). Previous projects include ACCESS (Achievement in Content and Curriculum for Every Student's Success), funded by OSEP, and Recognition & Response Project, sponsored by the Emily Hall Tremaine Foundation. Dr. Coleman has numerous publications, including the 14th edition of the seminal textbook, *Educating Exceptional Children* (coauthored by Samuel Kirk and James Gallagher). She has served three terms on the CEC-TAG Board, for one of which she was president; three terms on the NAGC Board; and two terms (one as president) on CEC's Board of Directors.

Jennifer Riedl Cross, Ph.D., Director of Research at the William & Mary Center for Gifted Education, earned a doctorate in educational psychology specializing in cognitive and social processes from Ball State University. Coeditor of *Handbook for Counselors Serving Students With Gifts and Talents,* she is a leadership team member of the W&M Institute for Research on the Suicide of Gifted Students. She coauthored a chapter on suicide for the *American Psychological Association Handbook of Giftedness and Talent* and an article on clinical and mental health issues for a special issue of the *Journal for Counseling and Development.* A social psychologist, Dr. Cross studies peer relationships, with a focus on adolescents; her gifted education research emphasizes social aspects, from individuals coping with the stigma of giftedness to attitudes toward giftedness and gifted education.

Tracy L. Cross, Ph.D., holds an endowed chair as the Jody and Layton Smith Professor of Psychology and Gifted Education and is the executive director of the Center for Gifted Education and the Institute for Research on the Suicide of Gifted Students at William & Mary. Previously he served Ball State University as George and Frances Ball Distinguished Professor of Psychology and Gifted Studies and executive director of the Center for Gifted Studies and Talent Development. Dr. Cross was also executive director of the Indiana Academy for Science, Mathematics, and Humanities. A prolific writer and editor, he has published more than 210 articles, chapters, columns, and books and edited seven journals. A recent Fulbright Scholar, his awards include NAGC and TAG's Distinguished Service Award; NAGC's Early Leader, Early Scholar, and Distinguished Scholar Awards; and MENSA's Lifetime Achievement Award.

Mary Evans, Ed.D., is program developer at The Center for Gifted Studies at Western Kentucky University working with the Javits Reaching Academic Potential (RAP) Project. She assists with the implementation of the Young Scholars model at five very diverse, high-poverty elementary schools by providing professional development for teachers and administrators. She is also working with statewide dissemination of information and strategies for reducing the excellence gap. Under her leadership as principal of an elementary school, the school was named a School of Distinction for scoring in the top 2% of elementary schools in Kentucky on the state assessment; she was named a National Distinguished Principal in 2013. She received a doctorate in Educational Leadership from The University of Louisville.

Donna Y. Ford, Ph.D., is the Cornelius Vanderbilt Endowed Chair and professor of Education and Human Development at Vanderbilt University and the former

2013 Harvie Branscomb Distinguished Professor and Betts Chair of Education & Human Development. Primarily conducting research in gifted education and multicultural/urban education, her work focuses on the achievement gap; recruiting and retaining culturally different students in gifted education; multicultural curriculum and instruction; culturally competent teacher training and development; African American identity; and African American family involvement. A prolific writer, she has published hundreds of articles, chapters, and books as well as serving on numerous editorial boards. Her many awards include Research Award from the Shannon Center for Advanced Studies; American Educational Research Association's Early Career and Career Awards; NAGC's Early and Senior Scholars Award; the National Association of Black Psychologist's Esteemed Scholarship Award; and CEC-TAG's Outstanding Service Award. As Vanderbilt University SEC Faculty Award recipient, she is humbled by her numerous awards from student organizations.

Terry Friedrichs, Ph.D., Ed.D., is an ardent advocate for gifted elders, high-potential students with disabilities, and gifted GLBTQ persons. He has worked for gifted GLBTQ youth and adults for 40 years, as student, teacher, researcher, youth group liaison, legislative advocate, and professional leader. He directs Friedrichs Education, an assessment, instructional, and school consulting center. Dr. Friedrichs focuses his writing on research on the educational and affective needs of gifted GLBTQ students, having published 15 articles and one book (with Teresa Manzella and Bob Seney), *Gifted GLBTQ Students: Needs and Approaches*. He currently serves as inaugural chair of the NAGC GLBTQ Network (2015–2017), which he worked to establish for 25 years.

Marcia Gentry, Ph.D., professor of educational studies, directs the Gifted Education Resource Institute at Purdue University where she has received multiple grants worth several million dollars in support of her work with programming practices and underrepresented populations in gifted education. Dr. Gentry's research interests include student attitudes toward school and their connection to learning and motivation; use of cluster-grouping and differentiation to meet the needs of all students; use of nontraditional settings for talent development; and development and recognition of talent among underserved populations (e.g., Native American youth and children from poverty). An active participant in NAGC and AERA, she frequently contributes to the gifted education literature and regularly serves as a speaker and consultant. In 2014, Dr. Gentry received NAGC's prestigious Distinguished Scholar Award (at the same time two of her students received the Early Scholar Award and the Doctoral Student Award).

Jiajun Guo, Ph.D., received a doctorate in educational psychology at the University of Connecticut. Before that, he received his B.A. and M.Ed. in psychology and special education from East China Normal University. His research interests include developing creativity measurement instruments and assessment tools, gifted and talented education, development of creative potentials, teaching creativity in the classroom, and use of technology in creativity enhancement. His work has been published in *Roeper Review*, *Thinking Skills and Creativity*, and *Creativity: Theories–Research–Applications*.

Thomas P. Hébert, Ph.D., professor of gifted and talented education in the College of Education at the University of South Carolina, has more than a decade of K–12 classroom experience working with gifted students and 20 years in higher education training graduate students and educators in gifted education. Having conducted research for the National Research Center on the Gifted and Talented (NRC/GT), his interests include social and emotional development of gifted students, gifted culturally diverse students, and problems faced by gifted young men. He has published widely, including more than 100 refereed journal articles, book chapters, and scholarly reports. He is the author of the award-winning text *Understanding the Social and Emotional Lives of Gifted Students*. A former CEC-TAG and NAGC Board Member, Dr. Hébert has received numerous awards including NAGC's 2000 Early Scholar Award and 2012 Distinguished Alumni Award from the Neag School of Education at the University of Connecticut.

Gail Fischer Hubbard served as a gifted resource high school teacher for a decade and as Supervisor of Gifted Education for Prince William County Public Schools for 26 years. She also taught in Washington, DC, and New York. An alumna from Bryn Mawr College and Harvard University, she has presented on the state and national levels. Once a rural student herself, she coauthored a chapter on serving gifted students in rural settings. Mrs. Hubbard had a leadership role in the development of Virginia's Regulations Governing Educational Services for Gifted Students. She has served as president of the Virginia Association for the Gifted, chairperson of the Virginia Consortium of Administrators of Gifted Programs, and chairperson of the Virginia Advisory Committee for the Education of the Gifted.

Susan K. Johnsen, Ph.D., is a professor in the Department of Educational Psychology at Baylor University, where she directs programs related to gifted and talented education. She is editor-in-chief of *Gifted Child Today* and editor or coauthor of *Identifying Gifted Students: A Practical Guide*, *Using the NAGC Pre-K–Grade 12 Gifted Programming Standards*, and more than 250 articles, monographs, technical reports, chapters, and other books related to gifted education. She has written three tests used in identifying gifted students. Dr. Johnsen audits programs in gifted education for the Council for the Accreditation of Educator Preparation and is past chair of the Knowledge and Skills Subcommittee of CEC and past chair of NAGC's

Professional Standards Committee. A past president of CEC-TAG and TAGT, she has received awards for her work, including NAGC's President's Award, CEC's Leadership Award, TAG's Leadership Award, TAGT's President's Award, TAGT's Advocacy Award, and Baylor University's Investigator Award, Teaching Award, and Contributions to the Academic Community Award.

Jennifer L. Jolly, Ph.D., is a senior lecturer in gifted education at the University of New South Wales. Her research interests include the history of gifted education, motivation and gifted children, and parents of gifted children. Jennifer has written and edited several books, including *A Century of Contributions to Gifted Education: Illuminating Lives* (Routledge) with Ann Robinson. She is the current Association Editor for NAGC. For her work in gifted education, she received the NAGC Early Leader Award, the Award for Excellence in Research from the Mensa Foundation, and the Michael Pyryt Collaboration Award, AERA/Research Creativity, Giftedness and Talent.

Todd Kettler, Ph.D., is an assistant professor of educational psychology at the University of North Texas where he teaches courses in gifted and talented curriculum and creativity. His *Modern Curriculum for Gifted and Advanced Academic Students* (Prufrock, 2016) won the 2016 Legacy Award for the Best Scholarly Work in Gifted Education, and he coauthored *A Teacher's Guide to Using the Common Core State Standards With Gifted and Advanced Learners in the English/Language Arts* (Prufrock Press, 2014). Dr. Kettler's research has appeared in *Gifted Child Quarterly*, *Journal for the Education of the Gifted*, *Journal of Advanced Academics*, *Psychology of Aesthetics, Creativity and the Arts*, and *Thinking Skills and Creativity*. He earned his Ph.D. in educational psychology at Baylor University, and he is a former middle school and high school teacher.

Ann Lupkowski-Shoplik, Ph.D., is the administrator for the Acceleration Institute and Research at the Belin-Blank Center for Gifted Education and Talent Development and an adjunct professor at the University of Iowa. After earning a doctorate from Texas A&M University, she completed a postdoctoral fellowship with Johns Hopkins' Study of Mathematically Precocious Youth, then went on to found and direct the Carnegie Mellon Institute for Talented Elementary Students. A recipient of the Pennsylvania Association for Gifted Education Neuber-Pregler award, she focuses her research on acceleration of gifted students and identifying young mathematically talented students and studying their characteristics and academic needs. In addition to many articles, she cowrote *Developing Math Talent: A Comprehensive Guide to Math Education for Gifted Students in Elementary and Middle School* (2nd ed.). She is also coauthor of the Iowa Acceleration Scale and coeditor of *A Nation Empowered*.

Sakhavat Mammadov, Ph.D., is a postdoctoral researcher at the University of Washington Nancy and Halbert Robinson Center for Young Scholars. Dr. Mammadov received his doctorate in educational policy, planning, and leadership with an emphasis in gifted education and a cognate in psychology from William & Mary. He has worked with gifted children and their families for many years in a variety of contexts. His research interests focus on the social-emotional lives of gifted children, personality, motivation, and administrative and policy issues in gifted education. Dr. Mammadov is the recipient of NAGC's 2015 Doctoral Student Award and the Armand J. & Mary Faust Galfo Education Research Fellowship.

Michael S. Matthews, Ph.D., Professor and Director of the Academically & Intellectually Gifted graduate programs at the University of North Carolina at Charlotte, is coeditor of *Gifted Child Quarterly* and *Journal of Advanced Academics*, as well as an NAGC board member. He chairs AERA's Special Interest Group, Research on Giftedness, Creativity, and Talent. A former board member for a charter school, North Carolina Association for the Gifted & Talented, and the Florida Association for the Gifted, Dr. Matthews has authored or edited five books, more than 30 peer-reviewed journal articles, and numerous book chapters. His professional interests include research methods, education policy, science learning, motivation and underachievement, parenting, and advanced learners from diverse backgrounds, especially English learners. He has received NAGC's Early Scholar Award, AERA's Michael Pyryt Collaboration Award, and TAGT's Legacy Book Award.

Paula Olszewski-Kubilius, Ph.D., is the director of the Center for Talent Development at Northwestern University and a professor in the School of Education and Social Policy. Over the past 32 years, she has created programs for all kinds of gifted learners and written extensively about talent development. She has served as the editor of *Gifted Child Quarterly*, coeditor of *Journal of Secondary Gifted Education*, and on the editorial boards of *Gifted and Talented International*, *Roeper Review*, and *Gifted Child Today*. She currently is on the board of trustees of the Illinois Mathematics and Science Academy and the Illinois Association for the Gifted. She also serves on advisory boards for William & Mary's Center for Gifted Education and the University of Washington's Robinson Center for Young Scholars. She is past president of NAGC and received NAGC's Distinguished Scholar Award in 2009.

Daphne Pereles, M.S., is an educational consultant specializing in twice-exceptional and MTSS. Her 30-plus-year career has included positions as a teacher (general, special, and gifted education), district level special education/gifted coordinator, and as the Executive Director for Learning Supports at the Colorado Department of Education. Her career has centered on students with disabilities and gifts and the development of more effective educational systems to support learning needs of all students. An author of multiple articles on twice-exceptional students as well as response to intervention and MTSS, Ms. Pereles is a member of the National 2e Community of Practice, a group founded to create a consistent message regarding the support of 2e individuals. She is a lifetime member of the Colorado Academy of Educators for the Gifted, Talented, and Creative; a member of CEC; and a board member of the Association for the Education of Gifted Underachieving Students.

Jonathan Plucker, Ph.D., is the Julian C. Stanley Endowed Professor of Talent Development at Johns Hopkins University, where he works in the Center for Talented Youth and School of Education. He graduated with degrees in chemistry education and educational psychology from the University of Connecticut. After teaching elementary school science, he received his Ph.D. in educational psychology from the University of Virginia. His research examines education policy and talent development, with more than 200 publications to his credit. His books include *Excellence Gaps in Education* with Scott Peters, *Critical Issues and Practices in Gifted Education* (2nd ed.) with Carolyn Callahan, *Intelligence 101* with Amber Esping, and *Creativity and Innovation.* Dr. Plucker has worked on projects involving educators, schools, and students in all 50 states and several countries. He is a Fellow of American Psychological Association (APA), AERA, Association for Psychological Science, and American Association for the Advancement of Science and recipient of APA's Arnheim Award for Outstanding Achievement and NAGC's Distinguished Scholar Award.

Ann Robinson, Ph.D., professor of educational psychology and founding director of the Jodie Mahony Center for Gifted Education, coordinates graduate programs in gifted education at the University of Arkansas–Little Rock. She is past president of NAGC, former editor of *Gifted Child Quarterly,* and associate editor of *Gifted and Talented International.* Dr. Robinson has been honored by NAGC as Early Scholar, Early Leader, Distinguished Scholar, and for Distinguished Service, and by Purdue University with the Alumni Award of Distinction for the College of Education. She has authored, coauthored, or edited six books, numerous chapters, and journal publications, and is the lead author on the best-selling *Best Practices in Gifted Education: An Evidence-Based Guide.* Dr. Robinson's research interests include biographical methods, school intervention studies of evidence-based practices, and teacher professional development.

Kristen Seward, Ph.D., Clinical Assistant Professor, Certification Advisor, and Associate Director of the Gifted Education Resource Institute at Purdue University, has more than 17 years in K–12 public schools as a teacher, at-risk counselor, and guidance director. She enjoys teaching undergraduate and graduate-level classes and coordinating GERI youth programs for students in grades Pre-K–12. Kristen has spoken to many parent groups, students, and K–12 educators regarding various topics related to the education of gifted students, including meeting their needs in the classroom, in the counseling office, and at home. Her research interests include the affective needs of gifted students (including career development), gifted education in rural contexts and in impoverished areas, gifted education teaching and learning for all students, and professional development.

Bruce M. Shore, Ph.D., a licensed teacher and psychologist in Quebec, is Professor Emeritus of Educational Psychology at McGill University. A former mathematics teacher, Prof. Shore has devoted decades to teaching, supervision, and research of undergraduate and graduate students. His research addresses exceptionally able students' cognitive and social thinking, the special qualities of inquiry-driven teaching and learning as an optimal learning environment, and outcomes of inquiry-based instruction. He has received numerous awards: NAGC's Distinguished Scholar Award, six American Mensa Education and Research Foundation and Mensa International Awards for Excellence for Research in Human Intelligence and Intellectual Giftedness for studies coauthored with students, Faculty of Education Distinguished Teaching Award, McGill University David Thomson Award for Excellence in Graduate Supervision and Teaching, and Canadian Committee for Graduate Students in Education Mentorship Award. Prof. Shore was listed among the "53 most influential people in gifted education" and elected AERA Fellow.

Del Siegle, Ph.D., is Associate Dean for Research and Faculty Development in the Neag School of Education at the University of Connecticut, where he also serves as Director of the National Center for Research on Gifted Education. He is a past president of the NAGC, past president of the Montana Association of Gifted and Talented Education, and past chair of the Research on Giftedness, Creativity, and Talent SIG of AERA. Along with D. Betsy McCoach, he coedited *Gifted Child Quarterly*. He writes a technology column for *Gifted Child Today*. Dr. Siegle is coauthor with Gary Davis and Sylvia Rimm of *Education of the Gifted and Talented*. He is also author of *The Underachieving Gifted Child: Recognizing, Understanding, & Reversing Underachievement*. Prior to becoming a professor, Del worked with gifted and talented students in Montana.

Tamra Stambaugh, Ph.D., is an assistant research professor in special education and executive director of Programs for Talented Youth at Vanderbilt University. She conducts research in gifted education with a focus on curriculum and instruction, students living in rural settings, and students of poverty. She is the coauthor/editor of several books including Comprehensive Curriculum for Gifted Learners (with Joyce VanTassel-Baska) and Serving Gifted Students in Rural Settings (with

Susannah Wood) which received the Legacy Award for scholarly work in gifted education. She also writes articles, book chapters, and curriculum units for gifted learners including the Vanderbilt Programs for Talented Youth award-winning curriculum, as recognized by the National Association for Gifted Children. She provides keynotes, consultation, and professional development workshops nationally and internationally and serves on various NAGC committees. Dr. Stambaugh is the recipient of the Margaret The Lady Thatcher Medallion from the William & Mary School of Education and NAGC's Doctoral Student Award, Early Leader Award and multiple curriculum awards. She has also been recognized for her work by state affiliate organizations in Ohio and Tennessee.

Kristen R. Stephens, Ph.D., is an associate professor of the practice in the Program in Education at Duke University where she directs the Academically/Intellectually Gifted Licensure Program for teachers. Prior to this appointment, Dr. Stephens served as the gifted education research specialist for the Duke University Talent Identification Program. She is the coauthor of numerous books and coeditor of the *Practical Strategies Series in Gifted Education* (Prufrock Press), a series comprising 30 books on issues pertinent to gifted child education. Dr. Stephens has served on the board of directors for NAGC and is past-president of the North Carolina Association for Gifted and Talented.

Rena F. Subotnik, Ph.D., is director of APA's Center for Psychology in Schools and Education. She is coauthor of the following recent publications (with Paula Olszewski-Kubilius and Frank Worrell): "The Talent Gap: The U.S. Is Neglecting Its Most Promising Science Students" (*Scientific American*); "Nurturing the Young Genius: Renewing our Commitment to Gifted Education Is Key to a More Innovative, Productive and Culturally Rich Society" (*Scientific American Mind*); "Rethinking Giftedness and Gifted Education: A Proposed Direction Forward Based on Psychological Science" (in *Psychological Science in the Public Interest*); and (with Ann Robinson, Carolyn Callahan, and Patricia Johnson) *Malleable Minds: Translating Insights from Psychology and Neuroscience to Gifted Education* (NRC/GT).

Dana Thomson, Ph.D., is a professor and research associate in the Applied Developmental and Educational Psychology Department at Boston College's Lynch School of Education, where she focuses on the role of family environment and engagement in early child developmental and educational outcomes. Most recently, her research has examined the role of cumulative contextual stress in the association between poverty in early childhood and long-term child academic and social-emotional outcomes, as well as the role of family processes in moderating these associations and helping children thrive in the face of disadvantage. Previously, she served as Director of Research at the Center for Talent Development at Northwestern

University's School of Education and Social Policy. She received a B.A. in philosophy from Carleton College and an M.Ed. from Northwestern University.

Joyce VanTassel-Baska, Ed.D., is the Jody and Layton Smith Professor Emerita of Education and founding director of the Center for Gifted Education at William & Mary. She also initiated and directed the Center for Talent Development at Northwestern University. A past president of CEC-TAG, NAGC, and the Northwestern University Chapter of Phi Delta Kappa, Dr. VanTassel-Baska has published widely, including 30 books and more than 550 refereed journal articles, book chapters, and scholarly reports. She also served as the editor of *Gifted and Talented International,* a research journal of the World Council for Gifted and Talented Children (WCGTC). She has received numerous awards for her work, including several from NAGC, Mensa, and WCGTC. She was selected as a Fulbright Scholar to New Zealand and a visiting scholar to Cambridge University in England.

Frank C. Worrell, Ph.D., is a professor in the Graduate School of Education at the University of California, Berkeley, where he serves as faculty director of the School Psychology Program, the Academic Talent Development Program, and the California College Preparatory Academy. He holds an affiliate appointment in UC Berkeley's Psychology Department and a Visiting Professor Appointment at the University of Auckland. His areas of expertise include talent development/gifted education, at-risk youth, cultural identities, scale development and validation, teacher effectiveness, and the translation of psychological research findings into school-based practice. A current APA board member, Dr. Worrell is a Fellow in APA, AERA, and five divisions of APA as well as an elected member in the Society for the Study of School Psychology. He was a recipient of NAGC's Distinguished Scholar Award and the Distinguished Contributions to Research Award from the Society for the Psychological Study of Culture, Ethnicity, and Race.

Jemimah L. Young, Ph.D., is assistant professor in teacher education and administration at the University of North Texas. Her areas of expertise include multicultural education, urban education, and the sociology of education, while her research interests center on the academic achievement of students of color, intersectional research of Black girls, educational outcomes for marginalized populations, as well as culturally responsive pedagogy. In addition to her faculty role, Dr. Young currently serves as the president of the Texas Chapter of the National Association for Multicultural Education, advisor to a chapter of the Texas Alliance of Black School Educators, and founder of a departmental Diversity and Equity committee. Dr. Young is the coeditor of the book *Cultivating Achievement, Respect, and Empowerment (CARE) for African American Girls in Pre-K–12 Settings: Implications for Access, Equity, and Achievement* (2017) and serves as associate editor of the *Journal for Multicultural Affairs.*

Index